New Ways in Teaching Vocabulary
Paul Nation, Editor

New Ways in TESOL Series
Innovative Classroom Techniques
Jack C. Richards, Series Editor
Teachers of English to Speakers of Other Languages, Inc.

Typeset in Garamond Book and Tiffany Demi
by Automated Graphic Systems, White Plains, Maryland
and printed by
Pantagraph Printing, Bloomington, Illinois USA

Teachers of English to Speakers of Other Languages, Inc.
1600 Cameron Street, Suite 300
Alexandria, Virginia 22314 USA
Tel 703-836-0774 • Fax 703-836-7864

Director of Communications and Marketing: Helen Kornblum
Senior Editor: Marilyn Kupetz
Cover Design and Spot Art: Ann Kammerer
Part Title Illustrations: David Connell

ISBN 0-939791-51-X
Library of Congress Catalogue No. 93-061731

Contents

Introduction

There are several strong reasons for which the vocabulary component of a language course needs to be carefully planned. Several of the points raised here are dealt with in more detail in the introductions to the various sections of the book.

Firstly, because different vocabulary gives greatly different returns for learning, it is important to make sure that the learners have good control of the high frequency words of the language before moving on to the less frequent vocabulary. In addition, the focus of teaching for high frequency vocabulary is different from the focus of teaching for low frequency vocabulary. A good vocabulary learning program should therefore focus on the appropriate level of vocabulary for the learners and should do this in the appropriate way.

Secondly, most language teaching courses make vocabulary learning more difficult than it should be as a result of the way vocabulary in the course is sequenced. Grouping opposites, synonyms, and items in a lexical set together causes interference that results in confusion for the learners. It is a simple matter to avoid this problem.

Thirdly, vocabulary learning opportunities and the quality of vocabulary learning can be greatly increased through the careful design of both vocabulary and other skill activities. Let us look at an example of this.

In a detailed study of negotiation and vocabulary learning from communication activities, Newton (1993) found that all of the negotiated vocabulary in the activity occurred in the written input to the activity and that the negotiation of the meaning of words contributed significantly to their learning. This vocabulary learning occurred even though the learners' attention was focused on the communication activity and its solution. Newton's findings have several implications for teachers.

1. The written input (the sheets given to the learners) in a communication activity such as ranking or problem solving are the means of

determining what vocabulary will receive special attention from the learners during the activity. These sheets should be carefully designed and their effects monitored to provide the best opportunity for the learners to make use of the new vocabulary they contain.

2. Teachers should not be overly concerned if some learners are not participating a lot in the communication activities. Newton (1993) found that learners who observed the negotiation learned as well as those who actually performed the negotiation.

3. Communication activities can be a major source of planned, indirect vocabulary learning.

Table 1 is an overview, based on Nation (1990), that can be the basis for teachers to evaluate and develop the vocabulary component of their language teaching program. Most of the points in the table are covered in the following parts of this introduction and in the introductions to the various sections of this book.

This book has been divided into the following sections to reflect the major components of a language learning course:

1. Meeting new vocabulary for the first time
2. Establishing previously met vocabulary
3. Enriching previously met vocabulary
4. Developing vocabulary strategies
5. Developing fluency with known vocabulary

Meeting New Vocabulary for the First Time

There are no generally accepted figures for the rate at which learners should meet new vocabulary in a language course. This is most likely the result of the widely differing conditions under which English is learned throughout the world. But meeting new words through formal presentation in a language course is only one of the ways to meet new vocabulary. Another very important way is through extensive reading and extensive listening. During extensive reading, including reading of simplified texts or graded readers, new words should not be met at a rate greater than one or two new words per hundred known running words if learners are

Table 1. Evaluating the Vocabulary Component of an ESL Program

What to Look For	How to Look for It	How to Include It
Does the teacher know what the learners' vocabulary level and needs are?	Ask the teacher	Use the levels test (Nation, 1990) Interview the learners
Is the program focusing appropriately on the appropriate level of vocabulary?	Look at what vocabulary or strategies are being taught	Decide whether the focus is high, academic, or low frequency vocabulary
Is the vocabulary helpfully sequenced?	Check that opposites, near synonyms, lexical sets are not being presented in the same lesson	Use texts and normal use to sequence the vocabulary
Are the skill activities designed to help vocabulary learning?	Look at the written input to the activities Ask the teacher	Include and monitor wanted vocabulary in the written input
Is there a suitable proportion of opportunities to develop fluency with known vocabulary?	Look at the amount of graded reading, listening to stories, free writing and message-based speaking	Use techniques that develop well-beaten paths and rich maps
Does the presentation of vocabulary help learning?	Look for deliberate repetition and spacing Rate the activities for depth of processing	Develop teaching and revision cycles Choose a few deep processing techniques to use often
Are the learners excited about their progress?	Watch the learners doing tasks Ask the learners	Set goals Give feedback on progress Keep records

to gain pleasure from reading. At this rate in a typical middle-level graded reader, a learner could expect to meet roughly 50–70 new words (Wodinsky & Nation, 1988). Elley's (1989) research on learning vocabulary through listening to stories shows that this enjoyable activity can be a useful means of vocabulary learning, particularly if the person reading aloud or telling the story gives the new words a little attention such as briefly explaining them or noting them on the board without interrupting the story too much.

We have seen that new vocabulary can be met in communicative activities and that the written input for these activities can be an effective source of new vocabulary.

Finally, in the classroom, new vocabulary can be met in activities where the learners work individually, or in pairs or small groups to reach the outcome of a self-motivating task.

Establishing Previously Met Vocabulary

There is an important distinction between communicating the meaning of unknown vocabulary and learning new vocabulary. Although some words may be learned after one meeting, this is exceptional. Although a teacher may clearly communicate the meaning of a word, that does not ensure the word will be learned. To assist learning, further meetings will be necessary.

Very few coursebooks build spaced repetition of the target vocabulary into the course. It is left to the teacher to make sure that the target vocabulary is established and that the time and effort that went into initially presenting the vocabulary is not wasted through the absence of later attention.

This repetition of vocabulary can be added to a course in several complementary ways:

- by setting aside class time for revision, for example reviewing learners' vocabulary notebooks
- by periodically and systematically testing previously met vocabulary and following up on the results and

- by planning the recycling of previously met vocabulary through pair and group activities.

Enriching Previously Met Vocabulary

One reason for which it is difficult to learn a word from one encounter is that there are many things to know about a word: As what part of speech can it function? What range of meanings can it have? What is its core meaning? What prefixes and suffixes can it take? With what other words does it collocate? What grammatical patterns does it fit into? What particular positive and negative associations does it have? Is it a frequently used word or an infrequently used word?

The answers to these questions come from meeting and having to use the word in a variety of new contexts.

Developing Vocabulary Strategies

In addition to learning new vocabulary, learners need to be able to use strategies to cope with unknown vocabulary met in listening or reading texts, to make up for gaps in productive vocabulary in speaking and writing, to gain fluency in using known vocabulary, and to learn new words in isolation. Most of these strategies can begin to be developed in the earliest English classes. The time spent on them is well repaid by the amount of use the learners will find for them.

Developing Fluency With Known Vocabulary

Vocabulary learning is not an end in itself. A rich vocabulary makes the skills of listening, speaking, reading, and writing easier to perform. Learners' growth in vocabulary must be accompanied by opportunities to become fluent with that vocabulary. This fluency can be partly achieved through activities that lead to the establishment and enrichment of vocabulary knowledge, but the essential element in developing fluency lies in the opportunity for the meaningful use of vocabulary in tasks with a low cognitive load.

References

Elley, W. B. (1989). Vocabulary acquisition from listening to stories. *Reading Research Quarterly, 24*(2), 174–187.

Nation, I. S. P. (1990). *Teaching and learning vocabulary.* New York: Heinle & Heinle.

Newton, J. (1993). *Task-based interaction among adult learners of English and its role in second language development.* Unpublished doctoral dissertation. Victoria University of Wellington, New Zealand.

Wodinsky, M., & Nation, P. (1988). Learning from graded readers. *Reading in a Foreign Language, 5*(1), 155–161.

Users' Guide to Activities

Words in Texts

Part II: Establishing Vocabulary

Revising Words

Working With Definitions

Words and Actions

Giving Learners Control

Part V: Developing Fluency With Known Vocabulary

Part I: Meeting New Vocabulary for the First Time

Editor's Note

The activities in this section focus mainly on the initial presentation of new vocabulary. Many of them draw on the use of reading texts, advertisements, news broadcasts and tape recordings to bring the outside world into the classroom.

There are two important cautions that need to be considered when presenting new vocabulary. The first relates to which words are given attention in the classroom. This is a caution regarding *selection*. The second relates to the order in which items are dealt with. This is a caution regarding *sequencing*.

Selecting Vocabulary to Teach

On the basis of frequency studies of vocabulary, a distinction is usually drawn between high frequency and low frequency vocabulary. High frequency vocabulary consists of words that are used very often in normal language use in all four skills and across the full range of situations of use. It consists of most of the function words of English (e.g., *the, because, could, to*) and the most common content words (e.g., *agree, time, slow, sometimes*). Although the distinction between high and low frequency words is arbitrary, recent research confirms that the most sensible place to make the distinction is around the 2,000-word level (Hwang & Nation, forthcoming). This means that we regard the high frequency vocabulary as consisting of about 2,000 word families. These 2,000 words are used so often that they make up about 87% of the running words in formal written texts and more than 95% of the words in informal spoken texts.

The low frequency words on the other hand are a very large group. Estimates based on *Webster's Third International Dictionary* indicate that this group includes well over 100,000 word families. They cover only a small proportion of the running words of a continuous text.

Clearly the return to the learner from teaching high frequency words is much greater than the return from teaching low frequency words. It is thus very important that teachers are aware of the words that make up the high frequency words of English (Michael West's (1953) *General Service List* is still a reliable source), and that teachers give classroom time to high frequency words.

When the high frequency words are well known, then teachers may wish to spend time on low frequency words. Generally it is wiser to use the time to train learners in strategies that allow them to cope with and learn this vocabulary independent of a teacher. These strategies include guessing from context, using word parts, using word cards along with mnemonic techniques like the keyword technique.

Teachers should look carefully at any vocabulary learning activity they use and see if they are spending time on the high frequency vocabulary. If most of the vocabulary in the activity is low frequency vocabulary, their time and their learners' time might be better spent on other items.

Grouping New Vocabulary in Lessons

Research by Higa (1963) shows that learning near synonyms, opposites, and free associates in the same lesson makes learning more difficult. Thus teaching a pair of words like *hot* and *cold*, *open* and *shut*, *prevent* and *protect*, *table* and *chair* makes learning more difficult. This difficulty is caused by the similarity between the two items strengthening their association, and the differences interfering with each other. This means that as a result of teaching *prevent* and *protect* together, learners get confused and some may think *protect* means "prevent," and *prevent* means "protect" and are uncertain whether you should say *protect someone from bad weather* or **prevent someone from bad weather*. This possibility for interference and confusion occurs when both of the words are new for the learners. In order to avoid such interference such items should be separated from each other so that one of them is taught first (*prevent* is the most frequent) and then some time later, perhaps several weeks, the other is taught.

There is also direct evidence to show the negative effect of teaching words in a "lexical set" like the names of fruit, days of the week, parts of the kitchen, adjectives of emotion (Tinkham, 1993) through encouraging interference between the words in a set. Such interference is largely avoided if words are taught according to their frequency of occurrence, with high frequency words taught before lower frequency words, or if words are taught as they occur in normal written and spoken discourse.

Presenting New Vocabulary

The "levels of processing" theory of learning (Craik & Lockhart, 1972; Craik & Tulving, 1975) suggests that a very important factor in learning is the quality of mental activity in the brain of the learner at the moment the learning occurs. If this activity is at a deep and thoughtful level, the learning will remain for a long time. If the activity is shallow and mechanical, little learning will occur.

It is thus useful for a teacher to consider the possible depth of processing that a particular vocabulary activity could give rise to. If the activity does not give rise to deep and thoughtful processing, it is worthwhile replacing the activity with one that does, or adapting it in some way. Deep and thoughtful processing can result from:

- relating the new word to previous knowledge
- having to create a context for the word
- drawing on a range of clues to recall the word
- having to appropriately relate the word to a variety of aspects
- using the word in a goal directed activity like solving problems.

References

Craik, F. I. M., & Lockhart, R. S. (1972). Levels of processing: A framework for memory research. *Journal of Verbal Learning and Verbal Behavior, 11,* 671–684.

Craik, F. I. M., & Tulving, E. (1975). Depth of processing and the retention of words in episodic memory. *Journal of Experimental Psychology, 104,* 268–284.

Higa, M. (1963). Interference effects of intralist word relationships in verbal learning. *Journal of Verbal Learning and Verbal Behavior, 2,* 170–175.

Hwang, K., & Nation, P. (forthcoming). *Where does general service vocabulary stop and special purposes vocabulary begin?*

Tinkham, T. (1993). The effect of semantic clustering on the learning of second language vocabulary. *System, 21,* 371–380.

West, M. (1953). *A general service list of English words.* London: Longman.

◆ Receptive Use
Learning Vocabulary Through Ranking Tasks

Levels
Any

Aims
Use new vocabulary in
interaction
Develop reasoning skills
Speak with greater
fluency

Class Time
30–40 minutes

Preparation Time
15–30 minutes

Resources
A list of items, people,
events, activities to be
ranked

Ranking tasks are a popular way of encouraging interaction between language learners. Although many published ranking tasks are available, it is not difficult to design new tasks to include vocabulary that is relevant to the needs of particular learners and that covers part of a given syllabus. Ranking tasks integrated into classwork in this way have a more obvious learning rationale. In the discussion which follows, the caveats and options provide the important ideas.

Procedure

1. In groups, get the learners to read through the list of items that are to be ranked and discuss comprehension problems that may arise.
2. During a short silent period, have students begin their own ranking and consider the criteria that are most important to them.
3. Ask learners to work toward consensus on a single ranking through group discussion.
4. Under teacher direction, have groups share their final ranking with the class. These rankings may be placed on a grid on a black/white board for comparison between groups. No one right answer is required.

Caveats and Options

1. Research shows that learners will make an effort to clarify unfamiliar words in a ranking task because the process of ranking requires both knowledge of, and deep thinking about, the items in question. Research also shows that as a result of clarifying unfamiliar words and then using them repeatedly and meaningfully to complete the task, these words are likely to be learned. A ranking task therefore

provides effective opportunities for learners to gain control over new words. For these reasons, the content of the task should contain important and useful vocabulary.

2. Items should not be numbered or labeled to encourage learners to refer to items directly rather than simply referring to a number or label.

3. Because each learner in a group of four will bring knowledge of different vocabulary to the task, they should be encouraged to help each other clarify the meaning of words (in Step 1 above) before calling on the teacher's assistance.

4. The list of items to be ranked can be divided among group members to encourage them to practice saying the items and listening to each other.

5. Ranking tasks involve reasoning and expressing opinions and disagreement. With learners of lower proficiency, it may be useful to preteach some key vocabulary and structures that perform these language functions (e.g., *If . . . then . . .; I think . . . because . . .; That's a good point, but what about . . .*).

6. A learning focus can be integrated into a ranking task by asking learners to rank various study and learning techniques according to how effective each is.

7. A linguistic focus can be integrated into a ranking task by asking learners to rank a list of phrases according to the degree of politeness or appropriateness.

Contributor

Jonathan Newton has taught in China and at the English Language Institute, Victoria University of Wellington, in New Zealand, where he has been for the past 6 years. He recently completed his PhD.

Arranging Students Into Groups Using Vocabulary

Levels
Any

Aims
Study unfamiliar or
unusual vocabulary
activities
Use unfamiliar or
unusual vocabulary to
create small-group
activities

Class Time
5 minutes

Preparation Time
5–10 minutes

Resources
Thesaurus
(teacher's resource)
Dictionaries
(learners' resource)

As language teachers, we often control the vocabulary used in a lesson, especially with low-level students. However, students are frequently intrigued to learn some new words that are not part of the lesson, and often the more bizarre the vocabulary, the more interested the students become.

When preparing students to begin group work, the standard procedure is usually one of the following:

- students are given a number 1,2,3,4; 1,2,3,4 . . .
- the students are arranged into a group by the teacher, "Leo, Ahmed and Pong in one group" (there is usually a reason behind this type of arrangement);
- the students organize themselves into groups

The following is a way of organizing group work (a feature of most English language teaching these days) by using unusual or unfamiliar vocabulary.

Procedure

1. Look at the lesson and try to find a topic or theme. There may be more than one topic in a lesson, and there may be more than one group activity. Then, look up the topic in a thesaurus and find four or five words associated with it. For instance, the topic may be Family, and we may want to introduce some synonyms, so we could choose *brood, folk, kin, clan, tribe*.
2. When it is time for group work tell the students that you are going to give each person an unusual word and that they should try to remember it.

3. Then go around the class saying each of the words in sequence out loud.
4. After each student has been given a word tell them you want them to organize themselves into groups according to which word they received and say "All the people with *brood* make a group," etc. The students rarely forget the word they have been given as they hear it several times, and the organization into groups is done immediately after hearing the words.
5. After the groups have been formed, quickly write the words on the board and group them together under the topic:

Family
Brood Folk
Kin Clan
Tribe

6. Once the students have had a look at the words and perhaps pronounced them again once or twice, clean the board and begin the group work.

Caveats and Options

1. Ask the students to copy down the unusual words in a special section of their notebooks and do occasional revision practice.
2. This technique of introducing unusual or unfamiliar vocabulary does seem to be going against the grain of popular language teaching in that students are saying words they do not understand. However, I have found that students I have used this technique with look forward to the unusual group of words thrown into the lesson. The words do not have to be very unusual, it depends on the level of the students.
   The following are some possible word groups:

- Hyponyms
  e.g., Family: mother, father, brother, sister.
- Synonyms
  e.g., Holiday: break, leave, recess, time off.
- Collocates
  e.g., Exam: pass, fail, sit, mock.

- Sound and spelling
  e.g., -ough: rough, dough, bough, cough.

Contributor

Lindsay Miller is a lecturer in the English Department at City Polytechnic of Hong Kong. He has taught English in Europe, the Middle East, and Southeast Asia for the past 14 years. Arthur McNeill commented on and added to this idea.

Learning Vocabulary With Cards

Levels
Any

Aims
Create personal
dictionaries

Class Time
10–20 minutes

Preparation
10–20 minutes

Resources
Assigned textbooks,
newspapers, magazines,
radio, television, library
books

Procedure

1. Get the students to read. a story or article from a textbook or a newspaper.
2. Dictate words from the story to be highlighted for vocabulary study.
3. Get the students to listen to the radio or television.
4. Dictate words from the radio or TV program for vocabulary study.
5. Show the students how to write each new word on an index card (one word per card), with the word divided into syllables, with the part of speech, the meaning, and a sentence containing the word.
6. The students work in pairs or groups with their individual stack of cards. One group or person asks, "What is the word form for . . .?" "What is the meaning of . . .?" Monitor the activity.

Caveats and Options

1. Have a card exchange day.
2. Have a competition based on questioning about the words.

Contributor

Devi Spencer teaches in the Language and Culture Center of the University of Houston. She has taught ESL/EFL in the United States, Canada, and Japan during the past 10 years.

Real Words From the Real World

Levels
Any

Aims
Work interactively
Expand vocabulary and
vocabulary awareness

Class Time
15 minutes

Preparation Time
None

Resources
None

This activity gets students more involved in the learning process, and provides new vocabulary that is more interesting, varied, and useful than is provided by most textbooks. The method is adaptable for all levels and ages as well as different group sizes and time schedules. The student-taught lessons are sometimes serious and sometimes hilarious. The teacher must have a thick skin because sometimes students bring in words that are rude or related to sexual or bathroom activities. These are words they have encountered in real life, and they need to know how to use them (or avoid them). The lessons can lead to broader discussions of current word problems. A lesson on the word *condom* has led to discussions of abortion and AIDS. Such discussions can be vehicles for learning more vocabulary and developing cross-cultural understanding.

Procedure

1. Give the students a weekly assignment for which each brings in one new word or phrase that they have encountered during the week. These words may be from any nonacademic source: conversations, television, films, songs, signs, books, magazines or newspapers. Students must teach their new words or phrases to their classmates. They must include the pronunciation, correct spelling, and meaning(s), as well as the sentence or context in which they found the word or phrase. Any teaching method, except translation, is allowable. This might include (but is not limited to) bringing in an object, drawing a picture, acting out a movement or story, playing a tape, or simply explaining.

2. Classmates may ask questions or provide additional information or examples to add to the understanding of the word or phrase. A lesson on *come on* might lead to the various meanings of this two-word

combination, other combinations of *come* + preposition(s), and the great variety of such idiomatic expressions in English. Monitor the discussion and also add further information concerning cognates, word histories, or related expressions, depending on the level of the students.

Caveats and Options

Train the learners to use a set procedure to present their words to make sure that all important aspects are covered. The questioners can also draw on set questions.

Contributor

Janan M. Malinowski is Lecturer in ESL at Hawaii Community College and the University of Hawaii at Hilo. She has been teaching ESL for more than 20 years in Micronesia and the mainland United States.

Listening to the News Headlines

Levels
Intermediate +

Aims
Become fluent listeners
of the news by repeated
listening to
international news
headlines

Class Time
20 minutes

Preparation Time
2–3 minutes

Resources
A good quality
recording of the
international news (e.g.,
BBC World News)—
headlines only

Procedure

1. Record the BBC World News headlines (usually three–five items), making sure that you can spell the names mentioned.
2. Play the headlines to the class once straight through, then headline by headline.
3. On the second playing, pause after each headline and ask the class to work together to build up each news headline on the board. Either you or a student can write what the class suggests. Different students will have heard different things.
4. Once all headlines have been built up in this way, play the headlines again. Discuss frequently occurring phrases and interesting collocations with your students. The technique needs to be repeated over time to get the benefits of repeated listening and processing of vocabulary items.

Contributor

David Pepperle teaches at the Seafield School of English in Christchurch, New Zealand.

Guess the Meaning

Levels
Beginning

Aims
Focus repeated
attention to new
vocabulary

Class Time
10 minutes

Preparation Time
None

Resources
Objects or pictures

The aim of this activity is to get learners to listen to a lot of repetitions of new vocabulary while they are interested and attentive.

Procedure

1. Put 10–12 objects or pictures where all the class can see them.
2. Call a learner to come to the front.
3. Repeatedly say the name of one of the objects while the learner guesses which object has that name by pointing at each object in turn. If the learner points to the wrong object, keep repeating the word. When the learner points to the correct object, say "Yes!" and repeat the name of the object.
4. Say the name of another of the objects, while the learner points. When the learner eventually points to the correct item, quickly revise the previous items by saying their name and getting the learner to point.
5. Continue until all the objects have been named.

Caveats and Options

Instead of objects or pictures, L1 translations can be written on the blackboard for the learner to point to.

Contributor

Paul Nation teaches at the English Language Institute, Victoria University of Wellington, New Zealand. H. V. George introduced him to this idea.

Matching Exercises

Levels
Intermediate +

Aims
Learn new words
quickly
Use resources

Class Time
20 minutes

Preparation Time
20 minutes

Resources
Words and definitions

When working from a textbook, it is necessary to understand the new words that appear in each unit. Otherwise, the exercises become little more than meaningless repetition of patterns. The density of new vocabulary often makes it impractical to deal with new words as they arise—to do so would disrupt the flow of the lesson. The following activity enables learners to approach text exercises with greater confidence and virtually eliminates the "dictionary panic" that can make text lessons such an ordeal.

Procedure

1. Divide the learners into groups.
2. Give them a list of words from the textbook and a list of definitions that need to be matched.
3. The learners use group discussion, dictionaries, and the textbook to match the words and the definitions. In the process, they encounter many additional L2 words and form associations that may help them to remember the meaning; moreover, once they have worked out the meaning through the L2, they usually add a corresponding L1 equivalent that serves as further reinforcement. Thus, the benefits of both methods—L1 definitions and L2 translations—are captured in a single exercise that can be easily finished in one class period.

Caveats and Options

An amusing variation on the above that is useful for review is an activity I call the *omikuji* vocabulary game. The same definitions that appeared in the above activity are printed on small slips of paper resembling the *omikuji*, or fortunes, that are sold at shrines and temples in Japan. The teacher becomes a vendor of "fortunes," and learners take turns "buying" *omikuji*. As the fortunes (definitions) are read, learners try to guess the word before anyone else can.

Contributor

Richard Dean teaches in Japan.

Words and the World

Levels
Advanced

Aims
Develop awareness of etymology

Class Time
15 minutes

Preparation Time
10 minutes

Resources
A wall-size world map
A list of words that have traveled around the world
A copy (enlarged for easier reading) of the entry for each word from a dictionary with detailed etymologies
A copy of the dictionary's list of country abbreviations

This technique lets students learn new vocabulary or review old vocabulary while learning names of countries and languages by looking at the word's etymology. Students will also get experience reading dictionary entries and using maps.

Procedure

1. Organize the class into small groups of students and let each group choose a word.
2. Give them a few minutes to study their entries, consulting the wall map if necessary.
3. A representative from each group then explains to the class their word's etymology using the map.

Caveats and Options

1. Students can place stars or tacks on their countries. The emerging pattern after several words would instruct the class about English's global development.
2. To make this activity, easier the teacher can (a) rewrite the dictionary entries or (b) let the students write their findings on a prepared worksheet.
3. To make this activity more challenging the teacher can (a) provide entries from several dictionaries or (b) let the students make their report into a short speech using specific target structures (e.g., "Rice was grown in China, then it was brought to Japan. . .").

Contributor

Van Le is a language instructor at the Japan Intercultural Academy of Municipalities. She is also Editor of Hands on Team Teaching *(Hokkaido AJET), a collection of simple activities in Japanese. Her interests include intercultural education, English as an International Language and Computer Assisted Instruction.*

◆ Receptive Use: Individualized Work
One More Sentence

Procedure

Levels
Any

Aims
Individualize the learning of new vocabulary

Class Time
15 minutes

Preparation Time
25 minutes

Resources
Prepared activity

1. Prepare an activity dealing with 10 words, similar to the following example (the example deals with 5 words). Several similar exercises are kept together in a "vocabulary box," so that learners can work on them in their own time and at their own speed.
   - A *restaurant* is a building. A person sells food in a restaurant. People can buy many kinds of food and drink there.
   - A *bee* can fly. A bee is yellow and black. A bee makes honey.
   - *Petrol* burns very easily. People use petrol in cars, trucks, and buses. Without petrol a car cannot move.
   - A *tent* is made of cloth. People sometimes carry a tent when they walk far from home. A tent is like a small room.
   - A *map* is very useful. A map is a picture of streets, roads, towns and cities. A map also shows us hills, mountains, and rivers.

   Use these sentences to add to the groups above.

   1. Soldiers sometimes live in it.
   2. We use it when we want to know the way.
   3. It can hurt people.
   4. People go there to eat.
   5. We buy it at a garage.

2. The learners choose a sheet, read each set of sentences and choose the sentence to complete each set. They write the word and the number of the missing sentence, for example, *tent* 1.
3. The learners mark their answers themselves with an answer key.

Caveats and Options

Arrange the sentences in each group so that the first sentences do not contain a lot of information. This makes it necessary for the learners to read all the sentences in a group.

Contributor

Paul Nation teaches at the English Language Institute, Victoria University of Wellington, New Zealand.

Enrichment Packets

Levels
Any

Aims
Quickly expand
vocabulary learning

Class Time
20 minutes

Preparation Time
30–40 minutes

Resources
Sears and Roebuck
catalogue (or similar
commercial product)

Each learner's foreign vocabulary is different from all others'. This is only one of several reasons that make it difficult to address the teaching of vocabulary during class time. Any immigrant or visitor faces the daunting task of learning a massive amount of vocabulary for the purposes of daily living, the largest class of words being nouns. There are various classes of nouns that concern each aspect of our lives. What better source is there for these nouns, and their attendant window on the culture, than a major mail order catalogue? For the purposes of enriching my students' knowledge of U.S. culture and enlarging their lexicons, I have used a Sears and Roebuck catalogue.

Procedure

1. Cut up the catalogue into hundreds of pieces, arranging the pictures into topic sets and placing them in clear plastic sandwich bags. On the back of each mounted picture, write the English word for the object in question. Along with the set of mounted pictures, place a set of cards with the English words on them. These packets (there are dozens) are neatly packaged lessons on a wide variety of subjects, activities, all aspects of our lives. Everything from fashions, sports, household matters, leisure activities, and baby care, to music, travel, and jewelry are covered.
2. Encourage the students to make use of these packets when they have completed their in-class work. They may work alone or in pairs.
3. The development of collocation relationships can easily be integrated into the use of these packets by having the students, in groups, create adjectival phrases, verb phrases and the like. In fact, four or five sentences could be written on the back of each mounted picture card illustrating typical sentence patterns and collocations. In a similar

vein, the actual caption or legend could be pasted on the back. Further work may be done with the packets by asking students to physically arrange the items into some sort of semantic web, or form of hyponymy.

There are a number of advantages to this activity: Vocabulary study and learning can be individualized, class time is maximized, packets cover a wide range of human interest and endeavor, visual as well as verbal input maximizes retention, and concepts of both syntagmatic and paradigmatic relationships can be introduced and reinforced.

Contributor

Mark James is Director of the TESOL program at Brigham Young University, Hawaii, in the United States. He is also Editor of the TESL Reporter.

Peer Teaching

Levels
Beginning

Aims
Encourage native speakers to help nonnative speakers with their vocabulary

Class Time
25 minutes

Preparation Time
15 minutes

Resources
A sheet of pictures
A sheet of names for the pictures

Contributor

Procedure

1. Give the native speakers a sheet containing 20 words that need to be taught to the nonnative speaker. Give the nonnative speaker a sheet of 20 pictures that match the words but which are not in the same order as the native speaker's list of words.
2. Get the learners to sit in pairs facing each other so they cannot see each other's words or pictures.
3. Tell the native speaker to say a word from the sheet and explain the meaning to the nonnative speaker. The nonnative speaker has to try to understand the explanation and find the matching picture. When it is found, the native speaker spells the word for the native speaker to write next to the picture. The nonnative speaker tells the native speaker the number of the picture.
4. Ask the native speaker to continue describing all the words until every picture and word has been matched.
5. Put the two sheets together to see if the matching is correct.

Paul Nation is the author of Teaching and Learning Vocabulary *(Heinle & Heinle, 1990).*

Words in Code

Levels
Intermediate

Aims
Develop close attention
to the form of words

Class Time
20 minutes

Preparation Time
50 minutes

Resources
Code activity sheets

Because learners have varied vocabularies, it is useful to have activities that they can do individually.

Procedure

1. Prepare sheets like the example. It is possible to fit about 50 items on a sheet.

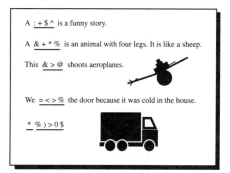

A : + $ ^ is a funny story.

A & + * % is an animal with four legs. It is like a sheep.

This & > @ shoots aeroplanes.

We = < > % the door because it was cold in the house.

* %) > 0 $

2. The learners work on the sheets in their own time. They do not need to be marked.

Caveats and Options

1. The words in code on the sheet are chosen so that they are all made up of no more than 12–15 different letters of the alphabet.
2. Some of the words on the sheet that are already known to the learners must use all of these letters so that the learners can successfully decode the unknown words.

Contributor

Paul Nation has taught at the English Language Institute, Victoria University of Wellington, New Zealand, for more than 25 years.

25

Individualized Picture Matching

Levels
Intermediate

Aims
Learn new words
through context and
pictures

Class Time
15 minutes

Preparation Time
50 minutes

Resources
Activity sheet

Procedure

1. Prepare a sheet containing about 20 small pictures and 20 sentences. The sentences should consist of the word to be learned in a simple context that will allow the learners to match it with the appropriate picture. Highlight the word in the sentence to be matched with the picture. Here is part of a sheet.

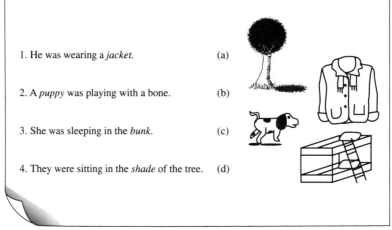

1. He was wearing a *jacket*.   (a)

2. A *puppy* was playing with a bone.   (b)

3. She was sleeping in the *bunk*.   (c)

4. They were sitting in the *shade* of the tree. (d)

2. Have each learner work individually to match the sentences with the pictures. When they are finished, they mark their work from an answer sheet.

Contributor

Paul Nation is the author of Teaching and Learning Vocabulary *(Heinle & Heinle, 1990).*

♦ Productive Use
State It, Say It, and Erase It

Levels
Intermediate +

Aims
Develop observation
skills to help learning

Class Time
20 minutes

Preparation Time
5 minutes

Resources
Words in a closed set

This teaching technique is especially effective for the learning of closed set vocabulary such as the months of the year, the days of the week, the four seasons, the four cardinal directions, cardinal and ordinal numbers up to one hundred, and the like. It also works well with synonyms, antonyms, and hyponyms when they are introduced as a closed set.

Procedure

1. Practice the pronunciation of the words in natural sequence, then at random.
2. When the learners are sufficiently familiar with the words, say, after about 3 minutes, start erasing the words one by one in the middle of the choral practice, sequentially or at random, until all the words have been erased.
3. Invite the whole class to practice saying the words for the last time, as if they were still visible on the board. Students will be surprised to discover that they can remember the words without much difficulty.
4. Present the words a few days later in exactly the same positions on the board, asking the students to provide as many of the set as they can remember.

Caveats and Options

While writing the words on the board, take care to put them in a particular order or sequence. For example, the months of the year should be in four columns, roughly correlating with the four seasons. This is important because the relative position of individual words on the board provides an extra visual stimulus for learners to retrieve the words in question.

Contributor

David Li Chor-shing teaches in the English Department of the City Polytechnic of Hong Kong.

Occupations

Procedure

1. Introduce and practice names of different occupations.
2. Introduce a sentence pattern to practice this vocabulary, such as *When I was a child, I wanted to be a pianist* or *If I graduate from college, I would like to be a lawyer.*
3. Make a grid with occupations lined up horizontally on top and names of the teachers/students lined up vertically on the left.
4. Make sentences or question-and-answer dialogues about the teachers/students themselves and their occupations.

	Baseball player	Florist	Doctor	Pilot	Farmer
Mr. Tanaka					
Mrs. Ortiz					
Mr. Van Els					
Ms. Freich					
Miss Kobayashi					

Examples:

Teacher: When Mr. Tanaka was a child, he wanted to be a baseball player.

(The student marks a circle in the corresponding grid box).

or

Teacher: When Miss Kobayashi was a child, did she want to be a florist?

Student: No, she didn't.

(The student marks a cross (x) in the corresponding grid box.)

5. Thus, students listen and mark with a tick or cross in the relevant box.

Contributor

Elizabeth Lange currently teaches at Temple University Japan. She has also taught ESL and EFL in New Zealand, Australia, Singapore, and South Korea.

Let's Go Shopping

Levels
Beginning–low
intermediate

Aims
Become familiar with
numbers in prices
Improve vocabulary for
shopping
Practice verbal skills in
a real-life setting

Class Time
40 minutes

Preparation Time
15 minutes

Resources
Local daily newspapers
with sales
advertisements
(in color)
Coupon books
Advertisements

Procedures

1. Cut out pictures with prices of food items, clothes, and other items for sale.
2. Organize pictures into different folders.
3. Distribute the pictures to the students.
4. Point to, read and pronounce a few unfamiliar items at the beginning of class from one advertisement, for example, *zucchini, eggplant, Lean Cuisine, bike shorts, discount coupons.*
5. Ask students to write the new vocabulary in their books and then read, pronounce, and study the new vocabulary and numbers.
6. Have the students work in pairs or groups. One group or person asks "What is this?" "How much is this?" Others answer.
7. Suggest that students go on shopping trips in the classroom. Divide the class into shoppers, cashier, sales person and store manager. Have imaginary products and get students to use their pictures of products and their coupons.
8. Give a dictation on numbers and essential shopping vocabulary.

Caveats and Options

1. Add further pictures for specialty shops.
2. Have a sale day.
3. Discuss cost comparisons of products in the United States and the students' home countries.

Contributors

Devi Spencer teaches in the Language and Culture Center of the University of Houston. She has taught ESL/EFL in the United States, Canada, and Japan during the past 10 years.

Wynell Biles teaches in the Texas A&M University English Language Institute in College Station, Texas. She has taught ESL/EFL for 16 years in the United States and Japan.

Vocabulary Keys for Interaction

Levels
Intermediate +

Aims
Practice using
conversational
vocabulary items

Class Time
25–40 minutes

Preparation Time
Homework assignment
plus 10 minutes by
students in class

Resources
None

When students of ESL/EFL communicate in English, they often do not know how to respond verbally to show surprise, dismay, consent, disagreement, or other emotions; instead, they often remain silent, which may lead to communication breakdown. Such backchanneling, however, is vital in English. The following is a way in which to get students to focus on the backchanneling vocabulary that facilitates communication.

Procedure

1. Provide examples of when the following kinds of responses are used.

   Oh, yes.
   Oh, yeah?
   Oh, were/have/are we?
   Yes, I am/do; he/she/it is/does; we/they are/do.
   No, I don't; he/she/it isn't/doesn't; we/they aren't/don't.
   Sounds (It/That sounds)/They sound good/great!
   It/That/They sound(s) nice.
   Oh, it/that's/they're great!
   Oh, really?
   I see.
   Sure.
   Oh, why?
   Oh, that's nice.
   Gee, I have no idea.

   Great!   No, I'm not.   Oh, sorry.   All right.   A ha!   Oh, did we?   Uh-huh.   Yes, I think so.

2. Give each student a different response to work on and ask him/her to prepare three situations and associated dialogues by listening to the radio, watching TV, or asking other native speakers. One may be from a conversation textbook.

3. Have each student choose one dialogue and in pairs they practice the dialogues so they can then present them to the whole class. (Each pair presents two short dialogues to the class.)
4. After the demonstrations, tell the students to hand in a written version of the situations they have prepared including the one they have demonstrated. Jumble them up and give a different one to each student. Let each student say the first part of the dialogue and with the other students giving a proper response.
5. Finally, orally test the students with some of the other dialogues submitted by the students by citing the first part and waiting for their response.

Contributors

Elizabeth Lange currently teaches at Temple University Japan. She has also taught ESL/EFL in New Zealand, Australia, Singapore, and South Korea.

Jong-Oe Park teaches English in Japan. He has also taught English in South Korea at the secondary and tertiary levels.

Co-occurrences in English

Levels
Intermediate

Aims
Learn lexicalized
collocations

Class Time
25 minutes

Preparation Time
15 minutes

Resources
Cards with one word of
a co-occurrence on
each

English contains a number of expressions that are made up of two or three words that often occur together in a fixed order. These expressions, or co-occurrences, are joined together with the connectives *and* or *or*. Learning co-occurrences involves the learning of semantically related words as well as the learning of conventional word order.

This activity can be carried out by students working in groups or pairs. To make it more competitive and challenging, it helps to set a limit on the amount of time the class has to complete the task. The amount of time may vary depending on the level of the class.

Procedure

1. Compile a list of the co-occurrences you wish to teach. (An extensive list follows.)
2. Write the words from each co-occurrence on a card or piece of paper (omitting the connective).
3. Give each group or pair of students a set of cards, tell them the connective to use, and set the clock.
4. Students must work together in groups or with a partner to match words correctly using the connective given. Additional attention must be paid to word order.
5. Give groups or pairs points for (a) the order in which they complete the task (e.g., most points being given to those who finish first) and (b) completing the task in the time allowed.
6. Subtract points for any errors made and declare a final winner.

Caveats and Options

1. This activity can be carried out in rounds by first assembling co-occurrences joined by *and*, then those joined by *or*, and finally those made up of three items.

35

2. This activity encourages students to associate semantically similar vocabulary items and develop their awareness of word order. Teachers should be aware that some co-occurrences in English do not exist in or vary in word order from those in the students' L1, and special help with these expressions may be needed.

3. Many co-occurrences sound trite when used inappropriately or too often. Care must be taken when selecting expressions for this activity and some explanation may be required to caution students on how to use them.

Appendix: Sample List of Co-occurrences

1.	Mom and Dad	25.	hit and run
2.	brothers and sisters	26.	forgive and forget
3.	sons and daughters	27.	ask and answer
4.	nephews and nieces	28.	top and bottom
5.	husband and wife	29.	left and right
6.	bride and groom	30.	up and down
7.	aunts and uncles	31.	in and out
8.	mother and father	32.	straight and narrow
9.	prince and princess	33.	far and wide
10.	ladies and gentlemen	34.	off and on
11.	boys and girls	35.	before and after
12.	shoes and socks	36.	thunder and lightning
13.	hat and coat	37.	bows and arrows
14.	tables and chairs	38.	supply and demand
15.	lock and key	39.	pros and cons
16.	needle and thread	40.	do's and don'ts
17.	pins and needles	41.	black and white/blue
18.	tooth and nail	42.	thick and thin
19.	arms and legs	43.	pure and simple
20.	aches and pains	44.	safe and sound
21.	heel and toe	45.	flora and fauna
22.	heart and soul	46.	cards and letters
23.	stop and go	47.	cats and dogs
24.	buy and sell	48.	this or that

Contributor

Kathleen S. Foley received her MA in Applied Linguistics from Indiana University. She has taught in the United States and the People's Republic of China. She currently teaches at Aoyama Gakuin Women's Junior College in Tokyo, Japan.

A to Z Vocabulary

Levels
Intermediate +

Aims
Take responsibility for
own learning

Class Time
20 minutes

Preparation Time
None

Resources
None

Many problems present themselves when teaching vocabulary. Do we teach straight from vocabulary lists, having the students memorize the lists and, then, test that memorization? This seems to be a common teaching method, although it is far from clear as to whether this is an effective way to teach vocabulary. The new words are soon lost because the students have not learned them in a real environment. Vocabulary needs to be taught from "natural" environments and exposure must occur in various ways (such as speaking and writing), before the student will be able to retain the words. The following exercise illustrates this point.

Procedure

1. Once a week (or more often, if desired), assign each student a letter from the alphabet. Start with *A* and work your way through. In smaller classes this will mean that the entire alphabet will not be covered that week. This is perfectly acceptable, as this exercise can be used throughout the semester.
2. Tell the students to find two words which begin with their assigned letter. These words must be in a natural environment (books, newspapers, etc.). Emphasize that the students should look for words that relate to their field of study. For example, if a student in the biological sciences were given the letter *A*, they might find the words *agriculture* and *arboretum*. The engineering student who has *B* might find *brick* and *building*.
3. They must then copy the sentences in which the words occur and write two original sentences, using the words in their correct context.
4. When the students return to class, divide them into heterogeneous groups of four, where they exchange words and definitions. Each

student's goal is to use at least four of the words from their group in a paragraph.

Caveats and Options

1. Give some type of prize for the student who is able to use all eight words in their proper context in the paragraph.
2. Move into a peer-editing session, during which each member in the group is given the opportunity to comment on the other members' writing.
3. Having the students choose their own words, and by ensuring that the words relate to their field, accomplishes a number of tasks related to improving retention. First, the students have chosen words that directly relate to their future learning. Second, the students have used the words communicatively in group discussion and in writing. Finally, the students have been given the opportunity to guide their learning. Because retention is the most important variable in vocabulary building, it becomes imperative that the words the students are to learn have relevance and importance for them. The students learn vocabulary they have chosen to learn.

Contributor

Thomas Nixon teaches in the American English Institute at California State University, Fresno, in the United States, and is a candidate for the MA in Linguistics (ESL Option).

Ghost Story

Levels
Intermediate +

Aims
Learn the vocabulary
needed to tell a ghost
story

Class Time
15 minutes per person

Preparation Time
10 minutes

Resources
None

Caveats and Options

Procedure

1. Give the students 1 week to prepare a ghost story to tell the class. Although this will typically be a traditional tale, some students may share personal experiences of the paranormal.
2. Divide the class into groups that contain students from different cultural backgrounds.
3. Students tell their stories to their groups. Generally, a story requires 10–15 minutes as students are frequently interrupted by questions from other group members. If the class is divided into groups of four, the activity lasts about an hour.
4. The teacher monitors group work, supplying vocabulary as needed and writing new words on the blackboard. In low intermediate classes, it may be necessary for the teacher to restate parts of some students' stories for a group.

1. Use the vocabulary written on the blackboard during the activity as material for future lessons.
2. Lead a class discussion examining ghost stories from different countries for common elements.
3. Tell a traditional ghost story to the class.
4. Supply the students with the text of a short ghost story. The students read silently as the teacher reads the story aloud.
5. This activity presents new vocabulary in a striking context. In addition to searching for new vocabulary while preparing a story, students are exposed to more new vocabulary when each of their peers relates a story. The teacher supplies vocabulary as needed during the activity. For example, while explaining the difference between a Chinese

vampire and the American version, one student demonstrated the Chinese vampire's form of travel (hopping) which led to discussion of a series of words describing movement. Students work in groups of three to six in order to eliminate the fear of speaking to a large audience.

Contributor

Michele Kilgore is an ESL instructor at Georgia State University in the United States. She has an MS in Applied Linguistics and is working on her doctorate.

Stars and Signs

Levels
Advanced

Aims
Consolidate and expand
abstract adjectives in a
vivid and meaningful
context

Class Time
25 minutes

Preparation Time
None

Resources
List of horoscope signs
Overhead projector
(OHP)

Stars and Signs will generate a set of synonyms and act as a class-created thesaurus. The teacher's comments on the student-produced lexis after each group's mimes will help students towards an understanding of different shades of meaning among synonym clusters. There is a game element in the search for the correct word that motivates the students to activate and search their own vocabulary resources. Informed guessing as a strategy is built into the game.

Procedure

1. Ask the students to get into groups according to either their astrological sign, for example, Aries, Taurus, Libra, or to their Chinese Horoscope sign, for example, Ox, Monkey, Dragon. Information about which months correspond with which astrological sign and which years correspond with which Chinese signs, should be made available to students who are unclear about which group they belong to.

41

2. Ask the groups to discuss the salient characteristics of the sign they were born under, and to come up with two positive and two negative attributes of that sign. For example, Libras are said to be fair and peace loving, lazy, and indecisive. The Ox, on the other hand, is industrious and determined, stubborn and slow. The students then have to think of mimed improvisations that will illustrate these characteristics.

3. Have the groups perform their mimes as the other groups watch and call out the adjectives they think the miming group is trying to convey. A group stops miming when the correct adjective has been guessed and the next one assumes the stage.

4. Have each group participate until all the groups have mimed the attributes of their sign.

5. Write down all the adjectives called out by the observing students on an OHP. And at the end of each miming session, review all the vocabulary. This vocabulary will normally consist of a set of synonyms clustered around the original core concept of the students' chosen attribute; for example, for the Ox, the words called out for one of the mimed attributes may have been, *hard-working, busy, energetic, energetic, industrious.*

Contributor

Dino Mahoney is Senior Lecturer in the English Department of the City Polytechnic of Hong Kong. He teaches on BA and MA TESL programs including the teaching of modules on drama in ESL. He has also lived and taught in England, Greece, and the United Arab Emirates.

Whattya Hear?

Levels
Advanced

Aims
Extend vocabulary in
context

Class Time
20–25 minutes

Preparation Time
10–15 minutes

Resources
Audiotape of sounds

The following activity combines listening, speaking, and writing skills in contextualized, interactive, purposeful, and interesting ways that enable students to learn new vocabulary items. This task is meaningful, involves semantic processing, and provides a basis for organization and retention in the student's memory. It can be extended to many other sounds and situations.

Procedure

1. Play an audiotape of the following sounds: applause, whispering, sneezing, whistling, screaming, coughing, laughing, yawning, sighing, kissing, and chewing. The students will recognize these everyday sounds and will be given the vocabulary (in this case, verbs) in English.
2. Use each word in a sentence to give it a meaningful context. Amusing visuals can be made up by the teacher to be used in this introductory segment of the exercise. These should vary according to the age of the students.
3. Ask the students to think of other sentences in which the new words can be used. Correct pronunciation should be emphasized as the words are introduced if the new items are to be used effectively and understood without difficulty by native speakers.
4. Ask the class to write a short story incorporating as many of the new words as possible. This can be done as a class exercise, with the teacher or a volunteer student writing on the board. This exercise allows the teacher to verify if students have understood the new words and can use them in appropriate contexts. (See sample text in Appendix.)

Caveats and Options

1. As a follow-up or homework exercise, ask the students to make up a different version of the story incorporating the new words.
2. Ask the students to use the new words in different tenses as they are all verbs. Through manipulation and use of the new forms, they will be made aware of the many contexts in which these words can be used and can more readily fix them in memory.

Appendix: Sample Text

Randy is whistling because he is happy. He is watching a comedy show on TV. He laughs and applauds each time he hears a good joke. His little sister appears and Randy notices that she is coughing and sneezing. When she sees that her mother is not in the room, she starts to cry and then scream. Randy tries to get her to stop. He gives her some medicine. He kisses her and whispers comforting words, but she continues. He sighs deeply. He is very happy when she stops and begins to yawn. He puts her to sleep in her room and returns to the kitchen as he is hungry. He prepares an enormous sandwich for himself and begins to chew noisily. He then returns to watching TV.

Contributor

Celia Davidson-Maxwell is at the University of Florida in the United States.

◆ Words in Texts
Read and Retell

Levels
Any

Aims
Meet new vocabulary
through supportive,
interactive reading
Increase control over
vocabulary through
repeated use in
speaking
Speak with greater
fluency

Class Time
30–50 minutes

Preparation Time
30 minutes or less if
texts are available

Resources
Two short stories or
newspaper articles with
narrative structure
(250–500 words)

This is an active and enjoyable task in which use of new vocabulary is integrated with reading, speaking, listening, and cooperative group work. The steps in the activity provide learners with the resources and the practice to extend their productive vocabulary use and to speak more fluently and for longer than they would otherwise be able to.

Procedure

1. Give one half of the class copies of one story and give the other half the second story.
2. Tell the learners with the same story to read their story in groups of three or four so they can help each other with comprehension problems.
3. Ask the learners to practice telling the story to each other in the first person, referring to the text to help them with details. Each group member should have a turn at adding a further step in the narrative.
4. Tell each learner to pair up with someone from the other half of the class. They should tell their stories to each other (in the first person) with a 4-minute time limit. (They may also change partners and tell the story again, this time with a 3-minute time limit.)
5. Ask the groups to reassemble and reconstruct the story they listened to. One group member takes notes covering the main points of Who? When? Where? and What?
6. Arrange for each group from one half to get together with a group from the other. While the groups listen as their reconstituted story is read aloud, they should make comments and corrections.

Caveats and Options

1. The key to the success of this activity is well-chosen stories. I have collected a number of timeless rescue stories from the newspaper. Short articles that are not narrative based can also be used. For example, I have successfully used articles on subjects such as telepathy, and color and feeling from *Beyond Words* (Maley & Duff, 1976, Cambridge University Press).

2. If a language laboratory is available, the learners can retell their stories onto tapes. With this option, they may want time to make brief speaking notes in Step 3. In the following steps, they listen to other learners' tapes and then regroup to compare notes.

3. Surprisingly different versions of the original stories can emerge, as well as versions that highlight certain details and not others. For these reasons the reconstituting and comparison of stories can be very amusing and involve a lot of interactive language work.

Contributor

Jonathan Newton has taught in China and at the English Language Institute, Victoria University of Wellington, in New Zealand, where he has been for the past 6 years. He recently completed his PhD.

Idioms in Popular Music

Levels
Intermediate +

Aims
Learn idioms in real use
Practice guessing from
context
Get strongly focused
listening practice

Class Time
30 minutes

Preparation Time
30 minutes

Resources
Cloze version of a
popular song

Many kinds of music, both old and new, can be used for this, as long as they meet two requirements: (a) use of English-language idioms and (b) understandable vocals. My criterion for the latter is that if I have to strain to catch the words, it is not suitable for language learners. Some pieces I use are: "Papa Was A Rolling Stone" (The Temptations), "Heard It Through The Grapevine" (Credence Clearwater Revival), "Things That Make You Go Hmmm. . ." (CC Music Factory).

Procedure

1. Make a copy of the lyrics (with idiomatic expressions underlined) and give the students a cloze version. For the first version, delete one or two stressed content words per line, increasing the number slightly as the song progresses. If the lyrics are repetitive, leave blank an entire line on its third or fourth repetition. Consider the proficiency level of the students when choosing the words to omit, and omit fewer words, usually not starting until several lines into the song, for lower-level students. For very low-level students, full lines can simply be scrambled; for those who are advanced, more words and even some phrases can be omitted.
2. Form groups of three or four (from different language backgrounds, if possible) and give each group one copy of cloze lyrics.
3. Let the students simply listen to the song once or twice.
4. Play the song twice again (uninterrupted) while they attempt to fill in the missing words.
5. Play it again, pausing briefly after every few lines.
6. Groups help each other (without the music) fill in the words still missing.

7. Each group tries to determine what words and phrases are used idiomatically and guess at the meanings based on context.
8. The whole class discusses, with groups trying to agree on idiomatic expressions and their meanings. Only if students miss an expression or cannot come close to the meaning do I point out the idiom or define it.

Contributor

Coleman South teaches at the American Language Center in Damascus, Syria. Partial credit for this idea goes to Elena Pavia, a teacher of English who uses popular music to teach U.S. social history and culture in Barcelona, Spain.

The Vocabulary of Newspapers

Levels
Beginning; adults

Aims
Rapidly expand
vocabulary

Class Time
40 minutes

Preparation Time
20–30 minutes

Resources
Simplified current news
items
Full newspaper items

One of the challenges of teaching English to a class of adult beginners is to make the thinking level higher than at first seems possible for their level of vocabulary. A technique I have used is to introduce the language of current news items via simplified versions of newspaper articles.

Procedure

1. For each lesson, prepare a simplified version of news items from that day's paper and attach it to the full news report. Today's paper, for example, would have yielded the following text about one photograph and news item:

   These men are soldiers.
   They are carrying food.
   The food is rice.
   They are putting sacks of rice on to a ship.
   The food is going to Bangladesh.
   The people in Bangladesh are hungry.

   Sometimes I have added quick sketches beside the sentences, for instance of sacks or a ship.

2. Ask the learners to do some simple tasks based on the item. For example:

   Look at the picture. Find   the sacks of rice
                                the soldiers
                                the ship.

   Look at the map. Where is Bangladesh? Why do the people need food?

49

Use half the number of picture stories as there are people in the class, to encourage communication. As the papers are being passed round, read, and discussed, move round responding to questions or adding comments.

3. Next, collect all the accounts, hold them up one by one and ask different people to talk about them. List on the board any words that arise or that students are searching for. As many as 50 new words a day can be generated in this way.
4. For the next lesson, blank out the key words and pass around the same pages for students to try themselves out either orally or in writing on the missing words.
5. The pages can then lie around the classroom for students to use as they wish. Some like to copy them out; others like to take them home.

Caveats and Options

1. Choose a range of topics to cover the interests of as many students as possible.
2. Select items with supporting pictures to provide a context.
3. See the resource as a temporary one that takes very little time to prepare.
4. Keep weaving into the simplified versions as many as possible of the words from recent weeks.
5. Let the context (words and pictures) supply the meaning of more difficult words.
6. Encourage students to use the versions in whatever way they find most helpful.
7. The technique attends to a number of principles of learning: systematic building up of new vocabulary, room for individual differences in learning strategies and a communicative approach to the learning of words. It also reflects the international composition of many ESOL classes.

Contributor

Marilyn Lewis is Senior Lecturer in the English Department of the University of Auckland, New Zealand, where she has responsibility for the Diploma in English Language Teaching. She has also taught in India and Cambodia.

Retelling Texts to Learn New Vocabulary

Levels
High beginning +

Aims
Integrate new
vocabulary into existing
lexicon

Class Time
30–45 minutes

Preparation Time
45–50 minutes

Resources
A short text
Two task cards
Overhead projector
(OHP) and
transparencies

Retelling texts encourages learners to attend closely to the meaning of the text and to draw on their experiences and prior knowledge of a particular situation and topic when reading. This process helps learners activate vocabulary knowledge and enrich the contexts and meanings of partially known words.

Procedure

1. Check texts for their suitability to this task. Prepare a few prereading questions to activate learners' background knowledge. Prepare brief task sheets explaining the situation and the learners' roles. Prepare brief demonstration texts and tasks.
2. Introduce the topic and prereading questions. Elicit responses and discuss.
3. Divide the students into pairs. Put the instructions for Student A (retellers) on the OHP. Ask a volunteer to tell the class what is required in the task. Emphasize the following points:
   - Use your own words when retelling
   - Make sure you include all the important ideas
   - Use your own experience to describe or explain new information
   - Give examples
   - Use context clues and your own knowledge to work out new words
   - Tell all the Student As to start the task
   - Select one student to be timekeeper
4. Put the instructions for Student B on the OHP. Ask a volunteer to tell the class what is required in the task. Tell Student Bs to start the task.

5. Use two volunteers to demonstrate the retelling and the negotiation of vocabulary meaning. Focus students' attention on the use of paraphrase, examples, associated words/contexts/concepts, and personal elaboration.
6. Ask students to practice the demonstration task in pairs. Monitor the activity.
7. Distribute new texts and task sheets to one member of the pair. Distribute new task sheets to the other member. Tell students to time the reading (10 minutes) and to start the activity.

Caveats and Options

1. Write instructions that encourage learners to process information in the text from a different point of view from that presented by the writer. Also, change the genre: If the text reports on treatments for pain control, instruct the student to talk about treatments s/he has tried. When writing tables, charts and so on for Student B, word the information in such a way that none of the target words is used verbatim. Substitute with synonyms, paraphrase, superordinates, and so forth.
2. To follow up the task, students can work in pairs to organize vocabulary into categories. Group according to meaning, physical properties, part of speech, associations, superordinate/subordinate groups, and so on. Use the target words plus words from the text and background knowledge. Compare the categories and discuss.

Contributor

Angela Joe has taught English to Japanese students in Japan and in New Zealand for 4 years. She is currently studying for an MA in Applied Linguistics at Victoria University of Wellington, New Zealand.

Vocabulary in News Broadcasts

Levels
Intermediate +

Aims
Expand and practice
vocabulary

Class Time
20–30 minutes

Preparation Time
30–45 minutes

Resources
Audio- or videotaped
news items

This activity requires either an audio- or videotape of a local or national news show. (National news shows may be better because they highlight events around the world; it may, then, be easier to find topics interesting to foreign students.) News, in contrast to other kinds of programming such as talk shows or situation comedies, contains less slang, fewer colloquial expressions, fewer sentence fragments, and less emotionally charged language. When these factors exist in combination, they can distract from the topic, overwhelm the listener, and make the in-class activity a bigger chore than it needs to be.

Procedure

1. Tape a news show and choose a segment that is appropriate for the particular students.
2. Play the segment in class. Some segments may require two or three playbacks, depending on the level of the students and the complexity of the language.
3. Lead a discussion examining the importance of the topic in the home country/city/state and eliciting cross-cultural information from the students.
4. Have the class examine the difficult vocabulary used in the segment. This list can be prepared ahead of time or the students can point out problem words on their own.
5. Students can act out the role of newscaster, giving their own version of the news using one or more of the vocabulary items.

Caveats and Options

1. The role-play activity is a good follow-up to each lesson, or can be scheduled less often at the discretion of the instructor.

2. Instructors may wish to use this activity in combination with a vocabulary text, if the news shows are not providing enough new words.
3. Teachers may invest more planning time in this activity, but it allows them greater flexibility in adjusting material to the interests of the students. The tapes themselves can provide sentence frameworks within which problem vocabulary can be practiced for both meaning and for pronunciation and can be analyzed in terms of its grammatical function.
4. This technique allows the class to create its own activities as well. For example, students may prepare their own text or may organize an entire news show with weather, sports, entertainment and so on as an end-of-term project (a project that can be videotaped and reviewed for considerable benefit to the students).
5. Instructors may need to check with the broadcast company to see if there are copyright restrictions.

Contributor

Rebecca Setliff is Director of the Language and Culture Institute and Program Manager for the Center for Executive Education at the University of Pittsburgh in the United States.

Find the Technical Words

Levels
Intermediate +

Aims
Increase knowledge of
subject-related words

Class Time
20–30 minutes

Preparation Time
5–10 minutes

Resources
Newspaper or magazine
article on a technical
subject

Contributor

Procedure

1. Choose a technical article such as a sales advertisement, technology update, or sports review.
2. Distribute the article and tell the learners to read it by skimming for content.
3. Tell the learners to list the words or phrases that they believe are technical, or specialized, vocabulary related to the subject matter.
4. Have the learners, in pairs or alone, put as many as possible of the words or phrases into sentences. Set a time limit (maximum 10 minutes).
5. Ask the learners to read their sentences aloud. Tell them whether the sentences are correct or not.
6. Encourage the learners to seek further clarification as needed.

Caveats and Options

Ask learners with expertise in the topic at hand to explain the terms as necessary.

Maria Verivaki studied at Victoria University of Wellington and now teaches English in Greece.

Part II: Establishing Vocabulary

Editor's Note

In this section and the following, a distinction is made between activities that establish the meaning of previously met vocabulary and activities that enrich the meaning of previously met vocabulary.

Establishing and enriching activities are each important for vocabulary learning. *Establishing activities* encourage repetition of what was previously learned. In the activities in this section, repetition is achieved as the learners

- perform an action
- draw the term
- choose synonyms
- define terms
- produce the written form of a word
- make a sentence containing the word.

This last kind of activity takes establishing activities close to *enriching activities*. The reason for placing some of the sentence production activities in the establishing section is that learners could recall previously met sentences to perform the activity.

Baddeley (1990) considers that the most useful research finding on repetition and learning is that spaced recall with increasing gaps between the repetitions (expanding rehearsal) is far superior to massed repetition. This means that after a word has been met for the first time, it should be recalled fairly soon after (within a few minutes), then a little later (an hour or two after), then a few days later, then a month later. This kind of schedule fits easily into classroom activity requiring the teacher or the learners to have a system for keeping a rough check of when to recycle material or arrange for repetitions. Baddeley (1990) points out that recalling the item has a stronger effect on learning than having the item presented again, "it appears that the retrieval route to that item is in some way strengthened by being successfully used" (p. 156). Establishing activities can thus lead to improved fluency of access to the repeated items. For vocabulary learning, this means that the learners should not just see the word along with a representation of its meaning but that the learners should see the form and have a chance to recall its meaning, or have a need for the word and have to recall its form.

Repetition can lead to boredom, so it is useful for a teacher to be able to draw on a variety of activities to repeat old material in a new way. These activities can differ only slightly from those met previously by including a challenge, such as a time limit on an activity that previously did not have a time limit. Another challenge is a challenge to memory. An example of an activity with such a challenge is Kim's Game, where the learners have to view items for a short time and then try to recall all that they have seen.

Activities to provide variety in repetition can also be quite different from each other, and this section is a rich source of these. It is quite useful for a teacher to consider planning a simple syllabus to provide for the repetition of a group of words. This planning involves choosing four or five activities suited to these words and then putting the activities in a sequence that best fits the development of the establishment of the words.

References

Baddeley, A. (1990). *Human memory: Theory and practice.* Hillsdale, NJ: Lawrence Erlbaum.

◆ Revising Words
Calendar Fun

Levels
Beginning; young
learners

Aims
Practice the days of the
week and numbers

Class Time
40–45 minutes

Preparation Time
None

Resources
One unlined piece of
standard size (or larger)
typing paper per child
Crayons, scissors, and
pencils

Procedure

1. Give each child a piece of paper, pencil, scissors, and a few crayons.
2. Give the following directions:
   a. "Fold your paper in half," and model the folding.
   b. "Fold your paper in half again, the same way." The children should now have four folds each going from the top of the paper to the bottom.
   c. "Fold your paper in half again, the same way," and then say, "Unfold your paper. How many parts do you have?" (There should be eight.) "How many days are there in a week?" (Count the days with them, if necessary.)

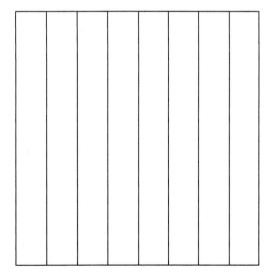

61

"If there are 7 days in a week and we have eight spaces for the days' names, what should we do?" (The children should decide to cut off one strip.)

d. Cut off the last strip and have the children do it.

e. "Now fold your paper in half the other way." Continue until the children have 56 boxes.

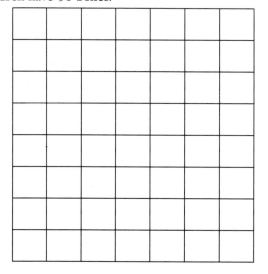

f. Ask, "What month is this?" The children answer.

g. Say, "Write the name of the month across the top row of boxes on your paper."

h. Say, "What is the first day of the week?" The children answer. Say, "Write 'Sunday' (or 'Sun.') in the first box."

i. Continue until all of the days are written.

j. Say, "What day is it today?" and explain that because today is the first day of the month, and it is a Tuesday or Wednesday and so on, the number 1 does not go in the first box (unless the first of the month happens to fall on a Sunday). Model writing the '1' in the correct box under the correct day.

k. Continue saying and writing the rest of the numbers with the children.

2. After the calendar is finished, you may choose to allow the children to color it and draw a small picture on the holidays. For example, they can draw a pumpkin on October 31.

After the calendars are finished, they can be used in many ways:

1. The children can cross off each day as it passes.
2. They can write the weather each day and have a weather calendar. Then they can compare the different seasons at the end of the year.
3. They can pick a favorite "word of the day" each day and write it on the calendar.
4. They can write a noun each day for one month, a verb each day for the next month, and so on
5. This activity can be done in two days by folding and cutting the first day and writing the second day.

Caveats and Options

Appendix: Sample Calendar

J	a	n	u	a	r	y
Sun	Mon	Tues	Wed	Thurs	Fri	Sat
			1	2	3	4
5	6	7	8	9	10	11
12	13	14	15	16	17	18
19	20	21	22	23	24	25
26	27	28	29	30	31	

Contributor

Judi Braverman is a K–5 ESL teacher at Lindell School, Long Beach, New York, in the United States. She has an MA from New York University.

Word Shapes

Levels
Beginning

Aims
Recall words in sets

Class Time
10 minutes

Preparation Time
5 minutes

Resources
Objects to put on an
overhead projector
(OHP) and a cover

This activity encourages beginning students to consolidate and build on their receptive and productive knowledge of nouns. Speculation about different shapes will generate related vocabulary, for example, different kinds of fruits and vegetables.

Procedure

1. Place, or cover, the OHP so that students cannot see what is on it.
2. Put an assortment of objects on the OHP and then switch it on.
3. The students will see an interesting silhouette collage on the screen. Have them work in pairs to try and identify as many of the objects silhouetted on the screen as they can.

Caveats and Options

1. Make silhouette collages for a particular semantic set, for example, a mixed collage of different kinds of fruits and vegetables: bananas, potatoes, pears, onions, grapes, carrots, mangoes, leeks, apricots, radishes, oranges; objects on a dinner table: knife, fork, spoon, chopsticks, salt and pepper shaker, plate, bowl, toothpicks; objects from a bathroom: toothbrush, toothpaste, scissors, nail file, razor.
2. Make a random silhouette collage of objects collected from students in the class.

Contributor

Dino Mahoney is Senior Lecturer in the English Department of the City Polytechnic of Hong Kong. He teaches on BA and MA TESL programs including the teaching of modules on drama in ESL. He has also lived and taught in England, Greece, and the United Arab Emirates.

Repetition Made Enjoyable

Levels
Beginning

Aims
Review known
vocabulary

Class Time
20 minutes

Preparation Time
30 minutes initially

Resources
Set of paired picture
cards

This activity is based on the premise that learning the correct meaning of a word must be followed by sufficient frequency of use. Initial learning should be carried out in the most efficient way possible, and the subsequent practice should be achieved in the most meaningful and diverting of ways. This variation on the game called "Nature Memory" is one way of achieving this goal.

Procedure

1. The game begins with any number of pairs of picture cards about 2 inches square placed face down. Normally, a player turns one card over and then turns over another, hoping it will make up the pair. If it does, the player collects the pair and continues to try and find other pairs. If it does not, the player carefully turns the cards back face down, as near as possible to their original position because an essential part of the game is remembering the configurations of the cards.
2. Because this is a language learning activity, when a student turns over a card, the player must say what the object is, as in, for example, "It's a car."
3. If able to do so, the player turns over another card. If not, the card is turned back down to its original position, and the turn passes to the next student.
4. Continue the game until all the pairs have been picked up, the player with the most pairs being the winner.

Caveats and Options

1. The game is best played in groups of four to six students with the teacher passing from group to group acting as referee to settle problems of pronunciation and correctness of form.

2. The game may be rendered a little more demanding by having the student who had the previous turn ask a question when the first card is turned over. The questions may be as simple as "What color is it?" or more difficult as in "How many wheels has it got?" If the other student is unable to answer the question, the turn passes to the next student. This addition to the game may well require some preparation in terms of the possible questions to be asked.

3. The pictures may clearly cover a wide range of objects, fauna, and flora, thereby allowing the game to be used at all levels.

4. With more advanced students using more difficult cards, one can imagine all sorts of demanding words and questions that might be used. One can also have, for example, pictures of famous people and, in addition to asking the question "Who is this person?" one can ask other questions about the person.

5. The game may be played as a one-off activity. However, ideally, the sets of cards could be designed to accommodate the vocabulary syllabus. Thus as new words are learned, new cards may be added; as words become so well known that they no longer present a challenge, the appropriate cards may be removed. Long-term retention can be facilitated by using the game systematically, say on a weekly basis.

6. The groups may be selected at random or one can increase the competitive element by using the results of each game to decide the composition of the groups, thereby allowing players of comparable ability to be grouped together. However, players may be at any time demoted or promoted depending on the result of the previous game.

7. I have used this activity for some time now with a wide range of students. It has the great advantage of masking what might be boring repetition in the form of an enjoyable game. Furthermore, it engages the students' attention in their desire to do well while at the same time obliging them to expend some energy on remembering the words they must use. I have been amazed at times how playing with up to 50 pairs in the game, students remember the words with apparent ease.

Contributor

Ronald Sheen teaches in the Faculty of Education of Tottori University, Japan.

Secret Word

Levels
Beginning; adults

Aims
Understand
relationships between
words and meanings

Class Time
15–20 minutes

Preparation Time
10 minutes

Resources
Small pieces of paper
with the same word
occurring on two
separate pieces clipped
together

Caveats and Options

This game is a great deal of fun and can be used with any set of vocabulary. The idea is based on "Password," a popular U.S. TV game show.

Procedure

1. Divide the students into pairs. In a large class, have two pairs play against each other. (Suggestions for doing this in a small group follow.)
2. Give one student in each pair one of the pieces of paper. This person is the clue giver. The partner is the guesser. Thus, in each pair, one student has access to the word and one does not.
3. The two pairs (Students A, B, C, D) sit in a small group. Student A begins by giving a one-word clue to help B (the partner) say the word. After A says a clue, B has 5 seconds to guess. If B is unsuccessful, then C will give a one-word clue to D. D has 5 seconds to guess. Continue until either B or D guesses the word. (Example: With the second word *breakfast*, clues could be *eggs*, *meal*, *morning*.)
4. If this activity is scored, one suggestion is to give 10 points if the word is guessed after the first clue, 9 points after the second, and so on In other words, as more clues accumulate and it becomes easier to guess the secret word, the number of points decreases. In the next round, students B and D will be clue givers, A and C will be guessers.

1. In a small class, have two students take turns giving clues while all the other students have to take turns guessing. This alternative is useful if you have an odd number of students.
2. It is important that students be limited to one-word clues. It should go without saying that no language but English should be used in this activity.

Contributor

Keith S. Folse is Principal at Language Academy, in Maebashi, Japan. He is the author of English Structure Practices, Intermediate Reading Practices, *and* Talk a Lot *(University of Michigan Press).*

Playing Tennis

Levels
Beginning–intermediate

Aims
Practice oral and
written production of
activity words and the
verbs they relate to

Class Time
10 minutes

Preparation Time
None

Resources
None

Procedure

1. Ask students to get into groups of six.
   - Each student has to say, "I like . . ." and then mime whatever it is he or she likes, for example, playing tennis, eating a bar of chocolate, watching television.
   - The other students have to say what they think the student is miming.
   - As students mime what they like doing, each student has to remember their peers' preferences. If anyone gets stuck, the other students can help.
2. Have the students then write six sentences about what the other students in their group like doing.

Caveats and Options

1. It is not necessary for an activity to always be matched with a verb. The activity may be a free-standing lexical item. For example, if someone mimes *sleeping*, the target sentence would be, *(Tony) likes sleeping.*

2. This game can be played with higher-level students at a greater level of sophistication using lower frequency count lexical items, *playing squash* (the student mimes a faster racket game than tennis), *eating Chinese or Asian food* (the student mimes eating with chopsticks), *going to the races* (the student mimes looking through binoculars and getting increasingly excited).

Contributor

Dino Mahoney is Senior Lecturer in the English Department of the City Polytechnic of Hong Kong. He teaches on BA and MA TESL programs including the teaching of modules on drama in ESL. He has also lived and taught in England, Greece, and the United Arab Emirates.

Close the Gap

Levels
Any

Aims
Practice vocabulary in
contexts
Practice communication
strategies

Class Time
5–10 minutes

Preparation Time
None

Resources
None

Procedure

1. While talking (explaining/describing something, telling a story and so on) to the students, challenge them by leaving a key vocabulary part blank by pretending you have forgotten it. Pause or ask, "What?", or supply bridging questions like, "Ah, I can't remember that word, can you?" or "What's that word again?"
2. Wait until one of the students can fill the gap with a correct word or phrase.
3. If somebody gives you the correct response, say, "Ah, that's right," repeat the response, and continue on. If nobody comes up with a proper expression in 2 or 3 seconds, cover up the gap saying, "Ah, now I remember."

Caveats and Options

Students can do the same by leaving one or two gaps like this in their speech for other students to fill while listening, either on purpose (for practice of specific vocabulary items) or when they have genuinely forgotten a word or phrase.

Contributor

Jong-Oe Park teaches English in Japan. He has also taught English in South Korea at the secondary and tertiary levels.

ESL Scrabble

Levels
Any

Aims
Use a monolingual
dictionary

Class Time
30–45 minutes

Preparation Time
None

Resources
Scrabble set for each
group of 4–12 students
Monolingual dictionary

The game of Scrabble is an entertaining way to learn and use vocabulary even for native speakers. However, certain adjustments in the rules can improve the teaching value of the game.

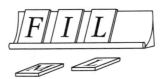

Procedure

1. Using volunteers from the class, demonstrate how the game will be played. Have each volunteer receive seven Scrabble tiles and play one word on the board. Demonstrate how to calculate the score for each word.
2. Divide the students into groups of either 4, 8 or 12 students. Form four teams out of each group. (The higher the level of the students, the smaller the group size should be.) Select one student from each group to keep a record of the scores. Select another student to be timekeeper.
3. Explain the following rules:
   - Students must use the seven tiles they have to add a word connected to the words already on the board.
   - Students have only 1 minute to place their word on the board.
   - Students only score points for words that they can successfully define and use in a sentence. (Reading the dictionary definition does not count.)

- At the end of each turn, a team should replace the letters it has used.
- In the event of any controversy, the teacher will be the sole judge.

Caveats and Options

1. No word of fewer than three letters will be given any score.
2. If one team cannot successfully play or define a word, the next team has the right to complete the task and receive the points.
3. The teacher can replace the letters held by any team to make their task either easier or more difficult.
4. A team receives double points for any word played and defined without using their dictionary.

Contributor

Hugh Rutledge graduated from Boston University in 1988. He has taught in East Asia for several years and is Head of Faculty at Tokyo International College, in Japan.

Vocabulary Bingo

Levels
Beginning

Aims
Review numbers, the alphabet, body parts, or other semantic groups
Improve aural comprehension of previously studied vocabulary

Class Time
10 minutes

Preparation Time
5 minutes

Resources
Bingo grid with 25 squares (5 rows x 5 columns)
One list of words per game

Procedure

1. Give each student a bingo grid sheet or have the students draw their own grid sheet. Each square should be big enough to accommodate one of the words.
2. Put a list of words on the board. The list could consist of numbers, the alphabet, parts of the body, days of the week, or names of fruit. The list should consist of around 15 items. Students should copy any of the items into any of the squares. Students can write any item more than once if they want, but it is best to set a limit, for example, three times per word. Thus, it is all right if the master list on the board has only 15 items because each item may be written up to three times.

BINGO				
7			arm	
		Tues day		
		leg		
pear			11	

3. Have the students work as a class. (If you have more than 20 students, you might want to divide the class into two groups.) Student A begins by choosing one of the words (preferably one of the words on his paper) and then saying any simple sentence with that word. The other students have to listen carefully and put an X or some kind of marker on that word if it appears on their grid. For each time a word is called out, an X or marker can be put on only one word. For example, if *cat* is called out and appears on a student's grid three times, *cat* should only be marked one time when it is called out. If *cat* is called out by another student at another time, then and only then can an X or marker be put on the second *cat*.

4. When any student has bingo in any three rows, he shouts "Bingo." If students have used markers (instead of writing on their papers), the game may be played again and again.

Caveats and Options

For beginning levels, stick with concrete items such as the alphabet, numbers, names of fruit. Make the students use these kinds of patterns for their sentences:

(alphabet)   The first letter of *apple* is A.
(numbers)   I have *10* fingers.
(names of fruit) I don't like *oranges*.

Reviewing vocabulary—not just one time but several—is a necessary part of successfully mastering any language. This game idea has worked well in class. As with any activity, this game should be short and somewhat fast paced to maintain the interest of the entire group.

Contributor

Nadine Battaglia is a French and English instructor at Language Academy, in Maebashi, Japan. She previously taught French as a second language in intensive courses in France.

Computer-Assisted Vocabulary Review With Hangman

Levels
Intermediate

Aims
Review vocabulary met
in a text

Class Time
25 minutes

Preparation Time
10 minutes

Resources
IBM Hangman, Version
4.1

Note

With this on-screen version of Hangman, the computer replaces the letters of the word with dashes and the player reconstructs the word by guessing letters. One part of the human being on the screen is lost (and finally hung) with each incorrect guess.

Computer-assisted language learning (CALL) is a great way to add variety and excitement to lessons as students are generally fascinated by using computer equipment. The following activity is an easy way to introduce students to computers and make them practice a lot of vocabulary.

Procedure

1. For homework ask the students to prepare from the class text up to 10 words with accompanying hints such as definitions, synonyms, opposites, and contexts.
2. Do a classroom activity to review these words, such as pronunciation practice or a spelling test.
3. Practice using the Hangman computer program by getting one student to type in a word or phrase related to the text, such as the name of a character or object. The other student in the pair tries to guess using Hangman while listening to the first student give clues about the character or object.
4. Begin the main Hangman activity. Student A types in one of the prepared words while B is not looking. Student A gives clues (definition, synonyms, opposite) for the word. Once this word has been discovered, the roles reverse.

IBM Hangman Version 4.1 (1983) is available from Eric N. Miller & Norland Software, 10/4A West Badger Road, Madison, WI 53713, USA. This is shareware software.

Contributor

Elizabeth Lange currently teaches at Temple University Japan. She has also taught ESL/EFL in New Zealand, Australia, Singapore, and South Korea.

◆ Working With Definitions Guess My Word

Levels
Any

Aims
Recycle vocabulary

Class Time
15–20 minutes

Preparation Time
10 minutes

Resources
Three words per student
A list of 20 words

This task enables students to revise vocabulary in a lively, interactive manner.

Procedure

1. Select 12 vocabulary items that you would like the students to revise. Divide the students into groups of four; distribute three different words from the list, plus the full list of 20 words to each student in the group. Ask students not to show their particular words to the others.
2. Using two volunteers from the class, demonstrate how to do the task. Have Student A explain, demonstrate, or give an example of the meaning of one of the three words, without using the word. Student B must guess which word it is in the list, then circle the correct word. In turns, each pair of students continues to negotiate the meaning of their six words until all six have been circled. Students C and D do the same with their words.
3. When both pairs have finished, Student A pairs off with Student C, Student B with D. Each person explains the six words circled on their list to their partner.
4. Upon completion, quickly elicit which of the 20 words were chosen. Select some students to share their responses.

Caveats and Options

1. To add an element of competition, time the groups.
2. When students finish, they can continue to explain the other words on the list.
3. If time permits, give each student only two words and expand the full word list. Break students off into new pairs with a new partner each time they finish negotiating their words.

Contributor

Angela Joe has taught English to Japanese students in Japan and in New Zealand for 4 years. She is currently studying toward an MA in Applied Linguistics at Victoria University of Wellington, in New Zealand.

Pair Crosswords With Hangman

Levels
Intermediate +

Aims
Review previously met
vocabulary

Class Time
25 minutes

Preparation Time
10 minutes

Resources
A simple crossword
puzzle with clues

The crossword puzzle can be based on one vertical word or phrase that may be a hidden message, for example, Happy New Year.

Procedure

1. Give each learner in the pair half the crossword puzzle, with clues for every second line in the puzzle.
2. Have learner A tell learner B the definition of the wanted word. If B cannot figure it out from this clue, use the Hangman game with the letters of the word mixed up. If learner B still cannot guess, A says the last letter is _____.
2. Reverse the roles to work on the next line in the puzzle.

Contributor

Elizabeth Lange currently teaches at Temple University Japan. She has also taught ESL/EFL in New Zealand, Australia, Singapore, and South Korea.

Guess the Word

Levels
Intermediate +

Aims
Recycle known
vocabulary

Class Time
15–30 minutes

Preparation Time
5 minutes

Resources
List of words to review

The activity stimulates two sorts of mental processes connected to recalling words or their meanings. The learners acting as prompters have to recognize a word and then think of its meanings, connotations. frequent contexts, or collocations in order to find an efficient way of getting their partners to guess the word. The guessers have to search their mental store of meanings, associations, and contexts for a lexical item that falls within the gradually narrowing semantic bounds suggested by their partner. Both processes seem to parallel processes that are thought to be used in understanding and producing language.

Procedure

1. Have learners sit in pairs, one partner facing the front of the room and one facing the back.
2. Present five of the items to be reviewed on the board or overhead projector. In each pair, the student facing the front chooses one of the items and begins to define it or suggest it in some other way (e.g. by describing a situation, giving a context, miming), so that the partner can guess it.
3. Continue this with pairs working simultaneously until most pairs have finished all five.
4. Then have the partners switch seats and roles, and offer five new items for review.

Caveats and Options

Have the partner who gives the definitions and other prompts draw them instead of saying them. Some high intermediate learners forced this variation upon me against my protests about conveying abstract words. It seemed to be just as effective as the verbal method, producing a lot of semantically relevant guessing. It does help, though, if learners are conscious of the sets of words that might come up for review.

Contributor

Heather Murray teaches at Universität Bern in Switzerland.

Split Vocabulary

Levels
Beginning

Aims
Match vocabulary and
definitions

Class Time
15 minutes

Preparation Time
25 minutes

Resources
Handouts

Procedure

1. Prepare two sheets with approximately 50 items per sheet. For each
   pair of students, prepare sheets mixed with words, true statements
   about the word, and distractors. Here is an example:

Learner A	Learner B
1x We can read it	1 A book
2 Run	2x We sit down and do this
3x Like a circle	3 square
4 It is nice to eat	4x fruit

   The learner with the cross next to the number (1x) says the number
   and reads the sentence aloud. The other learner says the word next
   to the number. The learners decide if their items are the same or
   different and write *S* or *D* on their sheet (In the example, 1 is the
   same, 2 is different, 3 is different, and 4 is the same). The learners
   must not look at each other's sheet.
2. After doing five items, have the learners can change partners and do
   the next 5 items.

Caveats and Options

Use a picture instead of a word. Put the cross next to the item with the
picture so that the learner with the picture has to recall its name.

Contributor

Paul Nation has trained teachers in Indonesia and the United States.

Matching Synonyms

Levels
Beginning–intermediate

Aims
Recognize synonyms

Class Time
15–30 minutes

Preparation Time
20 minutes

Resources
Set of 30 index cards
for each pair of students
Monolingual English
dictionary for each pair
of students

Matching games are popular among English-speaking children and adults and among speakers of other languages, so this activity requires little preteaching.

Procedure

1. On one side of each card, write an English word, making sure that each set of 30 cards contains 15 synonyms.
2. Using volunteers from the class, demonstrate how the game will be played. Place the 30 cards face down in five rows. Ask the first student to turn over two cards. If the cards are synonyms, the student keeps the two cards and takes another turn. Otherwise, both are placed face-down in their original positions. The second student repeats the process.
3. If the students do not know the meaning of one word, tell them to look the word up in the dictionary. If they do not agree whether two words are synonyms, they must ask for the teacher's judgment.
4. Explain that the player with the most cards after all the cards have been matched is the winner of the game.
5. Divide the class into pairs. Give one set of cards to each pair. If time permits, play a second game, making sure each player is using a new set of cards.

Caveats and Options

Instead of pairs, divide the class into groups of four so that two players cooperate as a team. This allows the teacher to monitor the progress of each game more effectively.

Contributor

Hugh Rutledge graduated from Boston University in 1988. He has taught in East Asia for several years and is Head of Faculty at Tokyo International College, in Japan.

Twenty Questions

Levels
Any

Aims
Reinforce vocabulary
groups, such as
occupations, food,
clothing, furniture,
family, hobbies

Class Time
20 minutes

Resources
Slips of paper

Contributor

Procedure

1. Write one item from the target vocabulary group on each slip of paper. Make sure there is at least one slip for each student. Items chosen will depend on the target vocabulary. Examples:

   Occupations: policeman, typist, cleaner, bus driver
   Furniture: bed, chair, wardrobe, chest of drawers

2. Put the folded slips in a container and let each student choose one. The other students must then ask questions. The questions can only be answered Yes or No. For instance:

   Occupations: Do you earn a lot of money?
   Furniture: Is it found in the kitchen?

The class must work out the answer in 20 questions or fewer.

Carol Griffiths is an ESOL teacher in Auckland, New Zealand.

Draw-a-Word Game

Levels
Any

Aims
Make visual
representations of
vocabulary items

Class Time
30 minutes

Preparation Time
5 minutes

Resources
Large sheets of paper
Pencils
Coloring pens

Before doing the following activity, the students should already have been taught the meanings of the words and their pronunciation.

Procedure

1. Divide the students into Teams X and Y. (Let students choose their team names.) Give each team nine review words.
2. Have the members of each team work together (each team on a separate side of the room) to draw pictures representing six of the words. All members are to offer ideas, but the group must decide which is the best idea and who is the best person to draw it.
3. Each picture is drawn on a large piece of paper so that, when shown from the front of the room, all students can see it. The word should be written in the top right-hand corner on the back for the teacher (small letters so only the teacher sees).
4. Circulate among the students. If a drawing is too sloppy or too abstract, make the students redo it.
5. One representative from each team comes up with the drawings. (The same representatives remain at the front of the class for the entire game.) The representative from Team X holds up the first drawing. Inhibit talking (e.g., telling the answers) with a fine of 3 points. Keep a record of points on the blackboard.
6. As the members of Team Y who want to guess the words hold up their hands, call on one of them. If the person guesses correctly, give Team Y 5 points. Then have the representative from Team Y hold up a picture for Team X to guess and continue play.
7. If the answer is incorrect, call on someone else from Team Y. If that person guesses correctly, Team Y gets 3 points. If that person guesses

incorrectly, call on a third person from Team Y. A correct response earns 1 point; an incorrect response results in a loss of 3 points (− 3).

8. Then have the representative from Team Y hold up the team's drawing and continue play as above. The team with the most points at the end wins.

Contributor

Tracy M. Mannon teaches at the University of Neuchâtel in Switzerland. She has also taught in the People's Republic of China and at the University of Delaware in the United States.

Listening/Speaking Crosswords for Vocabulary Practice

Levels
Any

Aims
Recycle vocabulary

Class Time
30 minutes

Preparation Time
10 minutes

Resources
Crossword grid with
down and across clues
Overhead projector
(OHP)

Crosswords are a great way to recycle and reinforce vocabulary. Many texts have accompanying workbooks with crosswords that practice the vocabulary and structures introduced in the text. These, as well as crosswords that make use of general vocabulary appropriate for the students' level, can be adapted to make listening/speaking pair work activities which involve lots of use of the required vocabulary and structures, guessing words from a listening context, and fun. This activity works well with beginning students but can be adapted for other levels.

Procedure

1. Enlarge a crossword grid. You will need one for each pair. Divide the clues into across and down; one of each for each pair.
2. Preteach the following types of phrases:
   - What's 6 across?
   - What's 3 down?
   - Pardon.
   - I'm sorry. I don't understand, could you say that again?
   - How do you spell that?
   - Pass.
3. Have the students sit facing each other. Give the grid to one student and one set of clues, the down clues, to the other. While one student reads the clue, the other tries to guess the answer and write it down. Neither has the answers but as this is not their first time encountering the words, they should between them be able to progress quite quickly.
4. As each pair completes what they can of the first half of the clues, give out the second set, the across clues, then switch their roles and

let them finish. Toward the end, students should be working together to puzzle out the ones they do not know.

The atmosphere is competitive because each pair wants to be the first to finish. The teacher's role is to circulate, offering extra hints if needed, to check that students are being fairly accurate, and to ensure they are using the target language.

5. After most of the pairs have finished, have a quick round-the-class check. Then, leaving students in pairs, give one student the clue sheet to test the other student:

A: I was hungry _____ I ate a hamburger.
B: So.

A: Yes, good. I take a _____ to school.
B: Train.

Encourage them to read and answer quickly. They can change roles and change pairs. I circulate, saying, "Is she perfect?" If they say Yes, I test them and change the clue a little, for example, "I _____ a train to school."

6. When everyone knows the words pretty well, divide the class into two teams and write on the board:

A	B

Have one student keep the score. Read the clue sentences quickly. The first team to answer gets a point. Halfway through, have another student continue reading the clues.

7. At the end of the exercise, collect all the grids and clues, and then hand out complete copies of the crossword to each student, or refer them to the page in their workbooks and have them do it again for homework.

Caveats and Options

1. As a quick review of vocabulary, use one copy of a crossword per pair. Have one student use a red pen and the other a blue pen. Students read the clues and fill in the grid as quickly as they can. When they have finished, they can count up the red and blue letters and see who has the most.
2. Using an OHP, make a large crossword grid on the wall. Divide students into a red group and a blue group. Have each group ask for clues in turn. Read the clue aloud. If the red group guesses correctly, write the word in red. If not, give the blue group a try. When the crossword has been completed, count up the red and the blue squares to find the winner.

Contributor

Sonia Millett teaches at Temple University Japan.

Find the Sentence

Levels
Intermediate +

Aims
Individualize review
vocabulary

Class Time
10 minutes

Preparation Time
20 minutes

Resources
A prepared Find the
Sentence activity

Procedure

1. Prepare exercises similar to the following example.

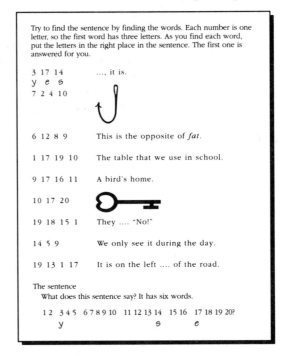

Try to find the sentence by finding the words. Each number is one letter, so the first word has three letters. As you find each word, put the letters in the right place in the sentence. The first one is answered for you.

3 17 14	..., it is.
y e s	
7 2 4 10	
6 12 8 9	This is the opposite of *fat*.
1 17 19 10	The table that we use in school.
9 17 16 11	A bird's home.
10 17 20	
19 18 15 1	They .... "No!"
14 5 9	We only see it during the day.
19 13 1 17	It is on the left .... of the road.

The sentence
  What does this sentence say? It has six words.

1 2 3 4 5 6 7 8 9 10 11 12 13 14 15 16 17 18 19 20?
   y   s   e

2. Have the learners do the exercises in their free time. The work does not need to be corrected.

Contributor

Paul Nation trains ESL and EFL teachers.

Find the Right Definition

Levels
Intermediate +

Aims
Learn vocabulary from classmates

Class Time
20 minutes

Preparation Time
5 minutes

Resources
A sample multiple-choice item

Contributor

Procedure

1. Divide the class into groups of three or four students. Ask each group to choose a word or set of words to define. This should be a word they think other students in the class will not know.
2. Tell each group to prepare one true definition of each word they have chosen and two false definitions. Set a time limit. For example:

   Elation: a feeling of great happiness and excitement (true)
   a cream applied to burns
   a procedure for selecting civil servants

3. Ask the groups to take turns reading their definitions aloud once only. Others try to guess which of the three definitions is the true one.

Ronald Jackup is a freelance teacher and course designer.

Define and Match

Levels
Intermediate +

Aims
Peer teach vocabulary

Class Time
25 minutes

Preparation Time
20 minutes

Resources
Sets of vocabulary cards
Worksheets (see
Appendix below)

Procedure

1. Give half of the class a list of words and the other half a list of definitions.
2. Ask the learners with the words to try to give a meaning in English and the learners with the definitions to try to think of the defined words.
3. Have the learners form pairs, with one learner having a list of words and the other a list of definitions. They match the words with the definitions and see how many they got correct.

Continues on next page

Appendix: Sample Worksheets

WORDS	MEANINGS
a name	
a family name or a surname	
a given name or a Christian name	
a signature	
a title	
an initial letter	
initials	
a monogram	
a vowel	
a consonant	

MEANINGS	WORDS
the word by which an individual person, place, or thing is spoken of	
the name common to all members of a family	
two or more letters, especially of a person's initial, woven together	
a speech sound in which the air stream is partly stopped	
the name of a book or poem	
a way of showing a person's status; it is put before their name	
a speech sound in which the flow of air is not stopped	
the letters at the beginning of a person's names	
a letter at the beginning of a word	
a person's name or initials used in signing	
the name that is chosen for a child to distinguish it from other members of the family	

Contributor

Dorothy Brown has trained teachers and taught English in Australia, New Zealand, and China.

◆ Words and Actions
Total Physical Response
Vocabulary Practice

Levels
Beginning; children

Aims
Recognize known
vocabulary

Class Time
20 minutes

Preparation Time
10 minutes

Resources
A box or bag containing
cards

Procedure

1. Put together a box or paper bag containing cards with commands written on them, for example, *Put the red crayon in the box, Sit on the table, Stand up, Put a book under the chair.*
2. Seat the children in a circle.
3. Ask the first child to select a card from the box, read it aloud, put the card in a pocket chart, and perform the required action.
4. If the child is correct, she or he chooses the next child to pick a card. If the child is not correct, then she or he chooses another child to help perform that action and the two children do it together.
5. Continue the game until everyone has had a chance to pick a card, read it, and do what it says.

Caveats and Options

1. If some children in the group are reading and others are not, the children can be paired so that there is a reader who reads the card and an actor who demonstrates what the words mean.
2. Divide the class into two teams. As each child picks a card, reads it, and does what it says, the child's team gets a point. If a child is not correct, the card goes to the next member of the opposing team.
3. Separate the class into groups of four with a high-achieving child, a low-achieving child, and two average-achieving children in each group. Instead of writing the entire command on one card, separate the words so that one word is written on a card. Give each group all of the cards for one complete command. (For example, one card

has *on,* one card has *sit,* one card has *the,* and one card has *table.*) The children have to get in line in the correct order and then do what the cards tell them to do.

Contributor

Judi Braverman is a K–5 ESL teacher at Lindell School, Long Beach, New York in the United States. She has an MA from New York University. She has trained student teachers from Hofstra University.

Total Physical Response Verb Practice

Levels
Beginning; children

Aims
Recall and recognize
known vocabulary

Class Time
15 minutes

Preparation Time
None

Resources
None

Procedure

1. Seat the children in a circle.
2. Perform an action and ask, "What am I doing?" and call on a child for the answer. The child answers, for example, "You are walking." If the child's answer is correct, the child performs a different action and asks, "What am I doing?" and calls on another child for the answer. This continues until all of the children have had a few turns.

Caveats and Options

1. A child picks a card with an action written on it and then performs that action. The other children guess what she or he is doing. The child who guesses correctly goes next.
2. Separate children into groups of four with a high-achieving child, a low-achieving child, and two average-achieving children in each group. Give each group three cards describing an action. For example, one card has *am*, one card has *I*, one card has *jumping*. Three children have to get in line in the correct order and the fourth child has to perform the action.

Contributor

Judi Braverman is a K–5 ESL teacher at Lindell School, Long Beach, New York in the United States. She has an MA from New York University. She has trained teachers from Hofstra University.

Hit the Word

Levels
Beginning; children

Aims
Practice auditory and
visual discrimination of
words

Class Time
15–20 minutes

Preparation Time
10 minutes

Resources
Words written on cards
or on the blackboard

Procedure

1. Teach students how to sound out words based on the phonics approach. Once they are able to read and identify words through sound, the following activity can be used to reinforce these skills for vocabulary development.
2. Write about 10 words on the blackboard for students to give further practice, for example, 10 verbs in the past tense.
3. Decide on two teams and give them names, for example, Cockroach and Dracula.
4. Draw a line on the floor about one meter (about 39 inches) away from and running in parallel to the blackboard. Ask one student from each team to stand behind the line. Explain (and demonstrate) the rules of the game as follows:

   Listen to the sentence/dialogue and hit a word on the board that corresponds with one in the sentence/dialogue. The first student to hit the correct word gains a point for the team. Example: Write on the board past tense verbs *ran*, *came*, *went*, and so on.
   Then say: "Yesterday, Peter ran to school." A student runs to the blackboard and hits the word *ran*.

Caveats and Options

On a table, put five or six words the students have learned through the phonics method to read and identify through listening. Make two rows of students behind the table, for example, one row of boys and one row of girls. Stand behind the table and sound out one word. Whoever can hit the word first can sit down. The first team to have no members left wins.

Contributor

Elizabeth Lange currently teaches at Temple University Japan. She has also taught ESL/EFT in New Zealand, Australia, Singapore, and South Korea.

Who's My Partner?

Levels
Any

Aims
Decide seating
arrangements while
reviewing vocabulary

Class Time
10 minutes

Preparation Time
None

Resources
Strips of paper
approximately 5
centimeters (about
2 inches) × 10
centimeters (about
4 inches); half of the
paper strips should have
a different color (shape
or size) from the other
half

Every teacher has to contend with the tendency of students always sitting next to or deciding to work with the same person in class. The following is a creative, stress-free and productive way of solving this problem. It simultaneously achieves the aims of warm-up (if used at the beginning of a lesson) and vocabulary review, thus killing two (or three?) birds with one stone.

Procedure

1. Either you or each student (if time allows) should copy part of a sentence containing an idiomatic expression onto a strip of colored paper. Copy the other part of the idiomatic expression onto another colored strip. Choose the sentences from a specified unit of the textbook. If necessary, give students different pages of the textbook to choose from to avoid repetition. If practice of conjunctions, transition expressions, or other connectors used to combine sentences are involved here, include them in one of the two matching strips. Examples of this are:

	Yellow Strips	Blue Strips
1a	Please *call* me	*by* my first name.
1b	Peter *went*	*with* Sally for 2 years before getting married.
2a	I was late for school	*because* my alarm clock didn't work.
3a	Mr. Suzuki worked hard all year;	*as a result*, he was promoted.

2. Collect the strips of paper.

3. Select half of the strip pairs according to the number of students in class. You can use the rest later.
4. Jumble them up, fan them out, and hold them up (or put them in a nontransparent bag) so that students cannot see them. Ask each student to take one.
5. Ask the students to memorize their part in about 30 seconds and not show it to anybody. They should then return it to you.
6. Ask the students to walk around and talk to each other until they find a match.
7. Once they are all seated, ask them to say their part aloud so the others can hear and you can check.

Caveats and Options

1. If there is an odd number of students, the one who cannot find a partner can go to the teacher. (The teacher will have the other part, thus becoming a partner when the situation requires it.)
2. If the sentences are not related to each other, the first pair can choose where to sit together, and so on.
3. However, if the sentences are related in the form of an extended dialogue, the students should sit in the order of the dialogue.

Contributor

Jong-Oe Park teaches English in Japan. He has also taught English in South Korea at the secondary and tertiary levels.

◆ Revising Words in Sentences Back-to-Back

Levels
Beginning

Aims
Consolidate oral and written production of "clothing" and "colors" lexical sets

Class Time
10 minutes

Preparation Time
None

Resources
None

This motivating vocabulary building game gives real beginners active practice in using Color and Clothing lexical sets.

Procedure

1. Ask students to sit back-to-back in pairs. Student A, without turning round, has to describe what articles of clothing Student B is wearing and what color they are, for example, "You are wearing a white T-shirt." Student B then does the same for Student A. Both students turn to face each other and check to see if their descriptions were accurate.
2. Have students write a brief description of the student they played the back-to-back game with.

Caveats and Options

1. If there is enough space, ask students to slowly walk about the room observing what everyone else is wearing. At any given moment ask students to stand back-to-back with whomever is closest to them. Ask these pairs to follow the procedure described above. When everyone has finished, ask the whole class to continue walking about the room and again, at any given moment, ask students to pair up and repeat the procedure. This may be repeated four or five times.
2. To avoid having students shout to each other during the description process, ask them to keep the backs of their heads close together and to talk sideways to each other.

Contributor

Dino Mahoney is Senior Lecturer in the English Department of the City Polytechnic of Hong Kong. He teaches on BA and MA TESL programs including the teaching of modules on drama in ESL. He has also lived and taught in England, Greece, and the United Arab Emirates.

Vocabulary Match-Ups and Sentence Writing

Levels
Any

Aims
Practice vocabulary in
meaningful contexts

Class Time
25–30 minutes

Preparation Time
10 minutes

Resources
Vocabulary cards

Procedure

Before doing the following activity, teach the students the meanings of
the words and their pronunciation. Before class, write all the words to be
reviewed and the matching definitions in blocks on separate sheets of
paper, as below:

predict		to foretell
precede		to go or come before

1. If there are 20 students, give 10 students a word and 10 students
   the corresponding definition.
2. Have students mill about the room, looking for their partners.
3. When students have found their partners, have them sit together and
   write an interesting sentence that clearly shows that they know the
   meaning of the word.
4. One representative from each pair to come up to the board to write
   the sentence. To save time, have three or four students write at the
   same time.
5. Go over the sentences one at a time, first having the other students
   from the pair read the sentence out loud. Have the class correct the
   sentences as necessary.
6. Copy down the sentences to be used later on a quiz or review sheet.

Contributor

*Tracy M. Mannon teaches at the University of Neuchâtel in Switzerland.
She has also taught in the People's Republic of China and at the University
of Delaware in the United States.*

Vocabulary Exchange Game

Levels
Any

Aims
Review vocabulary with
context clues

Class Time
40 minutes

Preparation Time
None

Resources
Strips of paper
approximately 3.5
centimeters (about
1.5 inches) by 18
centimeters (about
7 inches)

This is a highly interactive activity. Because the learners write the hints, they must use their known English to explain unknown English words to someone else.

Procedure

1. Have the students choose one different word from a text all the students have read, by allotting different pages or sections for each student to choose from. Make sure the students do not tell anyone what word they chose.
2. Have them write a sentence or more on their strip of paper containing and explaining the word they chose. They should leave the chosen word blank but can supply hints. You need to supply enough examples so that the students understand exactly what to do when they write their sentences.

The following are two examples to illustrate how to write context clues that leave the key word blank.

Apples, oranges, grapes and *pears* are examples of _____.

(Additional hints might be that it is a noun and consists of five letters.)

Peter got high grades for all his subjects. He will certainly pass. He is much better than a satisfactory-level student. In fact, he is an _____ student.

(Additional hints might be that it is an adjective beginning with *o-* and ending with *-ing*.)

You may also need to check each student's context clues and make sure the students are equipped with expressions such as *Once more*

106

please, Please give me more hints, How many letters are there?, You are getting close!

3. When ready to begin, have the whole class stand up, each person finding a partner to explain their context clues to and give other hints for their particular word. They must use eye contact while explaining and keep giving hints until their partner guesses the word.

4. Then have them exchange roles. When each pair has guessed each other's words, they have to exchange strips of paper and find a new partner. The process continues until each student has exchanged strips of paper as many times as there are students in the class.

5. Finally, test the students on the vocabulary items.

Contributor

Elizabeth Lange currently teaches at Temple University Japan. She has also taught ESL/EFL in New Zealand, Australia, Singapore, and South Korea.

Verb Group Game

Levels
Intermediate +

Aims
Review vocabulary
productively
Practice correct use of
verb groups

Class Time
1 hour

Preparation Time
30 minutes

Resources
Set of 40 verb cards for
each group of four or
five
Set of 40 auxiliary verb
cards for whole class

This activity is an enjoyable way to practice verbs and provide practice in the grammatical accuracy of verb groups. It allows students to try using new words and to discuss whether the use is right or wrong. Some very heated discussions can result. Although the activity has a grammar focus, it contributes to vocabulary learning by encouraging creative use of newly met verbs.

Procedure

1. Prepare vocabulary cards in advance (e.g., on index cards). The requirements may be a little too complex for students to do this preparation, although, if time permits, you could try.
   You need (for each group of four or five students):

   40 auxiliary verb cards: 10 modal verbs
                                     10 forms of *have* (i.e., *have, had, has*)
                                     20 forms of *be* (i.e., *is, was, are, were*)
   40 verb cards using words currently being studied by the students:
                                     10 stem forms
                                     10 *-ing* forms (present participles)
                                     10 *-ed* forms (past participles)

   It is best if the auxiliary verb cards are all on a different color card from the verb cards to avoid confusion.

2. Give groups one set of auxiliary verb cards and one set of verb cards. The auxiliary verb cards are placed face down in the middle of the table. All the verb cards are dealt to the players—an equal number to each player.

3. The first player takes a card from the top of the auxiliary verb pile and places it face up on the table.

- The player then looks at the cards in her hand to see if they include a verb form that can go with the auxiliary verb just turned over.
- If she does, she places the verb card next to the auxiliary verb card so that everyone can see it.
- The player must then say a sentence using the verb group she has created.
- If the group agrees the sentence is correct in grammar and meaning, the player keeps the pair of cards.
- If the sentence is considered incorrect, the player must take back her verb card, and return the auxiliary verb card to the bottom of the pile.
- In either case, the next player then has a turn.

4. Be available to settle disputes and answer questions. The winner is the player with most pairs at the end of the game.

Caveats and Options

1. Some students have changed the rules so that a player keeps playing until she makes a mistake. This can be boring if a player is very good and can lead to nobody else getting a turn. Adult groups seem to be quite happy to decide on their own rules, however.
2. When preparing the cards, some care needs to be taken with the choice of which verbs are presented in the *-ed* or *-ing* form so that sentences are able to be formed that make sense and are plausible.

Contributor

Jo Hilder is Assistant Lecturer in the English Language Institute of Victoria University of Wellington, New Zealand.

Writing Definitions

Levels
Intermediate +

Aims
Develop skill in writing definitions
Learn new vocabulary through defining

Class Time
25 minutes

Preparation Time
None

Resources
Previously studied words

Contributor

This activity helps students explore the meanings of words and helps them practice writing definitions. It also helps students expand their vocabulary.

Procedure

1. Review a unit of your textbook or anything students have studied recently. Select up to 20 words you think students should remember and be able to use. Choose 5 words each from different parts of speech, or all 20 could be from the same part of speech.
2. Divide the class into groups. Give each group 5 words each. It is easier if each group is working with a set of words with the same part of speech. Ask them to write definitions for each word but not to mention the word they are defining. These should be analytical definitions, rather than synonyms. For example, for the word *medicine* they might write:

   > noun. This is a liquid which you take when you are sick. You get it from the drugstore. Sometimes it doesn't taste very pleasant.

   Note that the definitions should be as complete as possible.
3. Tell groups to exchange definitions and try to guess the words which have been defined.
4. Once all the groups have tried to guess the other groups' words, give them the answers and put some of the definitions on the board. Then have students look up the definitions of the words in the dictionary. What are the differences between the dictionary definition and their definition? What other information is included in the dictionary?

Ronald Jackup is a freelance teacher and course designer.

Tic-Tac-Toe for Vocabulary Review

Levels
Intermediate +

Aims
Practice and review vocabulary and lexical sets

Class Time
15 minutes

Preparation Time
5 minutes

Resources
List of words

Tic-Tac-Toe is also known as noughts-and-crosses.

Procedure

1. Divide the class into two teams. Designate one team as O and the other team as X.
2. Draw a tic-tac-toe grid (i.e., 9 squares in a 3 x 3 format; see sample below) on the board and fill each space with vocabulary the students know. (This could be vocabulary studied in the previous lesson.)
3. Demonstrate to the students that the object of the activity is for one team to put three of their team's symbols (O or X) in the grid in a straight line before the other team does the same. The line can be horizontal, vertical, or diagonal but must be straight. Team O starts the activity by choosing a word from the grid. Rather than having students just say the word to indicate which one they want, the teacher may choose to make the students say the location of the word, for example, "top left," "bottom right." When the word has been chosen, the students must create a correct sentence using the word. (Set an appropriate time limit, e.g., 30 seconds.) If the sentence is correct, the word is erased from the grid and Team O's marker is put in that place. The turn then moves to Team X who tries and create a correct sentence. If the team makes an error in forming a sentence with the chosen word, the turn moves directly to Team O who tries and give a correct answer. However, if they are correct, they automatically continue with their next turn. The activity continues in this way until one team is successful in producing a straight line in the grid.

4. Once the students become familiar with the activity, it can be carried out as a pair work activity in which one student is O and the other X. In this activity, the teacher may be called upon by different groups of students to comment on the correctness of a completed sentence.

capital	change	cold
match	benefit	end
watch	label	shop

Caveats and Options

1. To increase the team challenge aspect, let teams choose the space containing the word that the other team has to use to make a sentence. For example, Team X calls out "the top right square" because they know that it will be difficult for the other team to make a sentence with the word in that particular square.
2. For homework, the students can create their own grids for their classmates, choosing vocabulary studied in earlier units of a textbook. At the next class meeting, the grids are given out to different groups of students. This alternative is especially valuable because students actually review more vocabulary more frequently than they would in a traditional review exercise: The students will review vocabulary once when they make out their grids with words they have chosen themselves and once again when they complete the game by reviewing words other students have chosen.

Contributor

Jason D. Halstead teaches at Language Academy, in Maebashi, Japan.

Scrambled Idioms in an Envelope

Levels
High intermediate +

Aims
Practice idioms in a
task-based activity
Review the grammar of
specific idioms

Class Time
20 minutes

Preparation Time
15 minutes

Resources
Cards containing parts
of sentences

Procedure

1. On a sheet of paper, write sentences with various idioms the students know. You may also include a few that you want students to guess from the context. If possible, try to create sentences that use two or more idioms at a time. Leave ample space between the sentences (several lines). Cut the sentences into several pieces. Possible places to cut have been indicated with an asterisk (*).

A class has studied these idioms: *let the cat out of the bag, call on, throw in, put off, call off, about to, be off, show up.* Here are sample sentences with these idioms:

John thought that * Mary knew about the party, *

so he didn't realize that he had * let the cat out of the bag.

The teacher usually calls * on students * who are about to fall asleep.

The sauce was * a little off, so * I decided to throw * in some basil.

113

The game was put * off until * next week * because of the weather.

Mr. Miller called * off the meeting * because the workers * were too busy.

The bride was * about to call * off the wedding, but * the groom suddenly showed * up.

2. Divide the class into pairs or small groups (three to four). You will need one envelope with all 24 pieces per pair or small group.
3. Explain what a scrambled sentence is. If necessary, do an example on the board. (Write a sample sentence in several scrambled chunks. Have the students construct the correct sentence.)
4. Give each pair/group an envelope. Have students empty the contents and count the number of sentence pieces. Using the above sample sentences, there should be 24 pieces. (This step is important. If students don't have all 24 pieces, they cannot complete this task.)
5. Announce a set time limit of 10 minutes. Have the students work as quickly as possible to construct the sentences. Walk around the room and give hints to students who are having some difficulties. Obvious clues should be the capital letters and punctuation. However, the main focus here should be on the meanings of the idioms and any grammatical clues that the students can find.

Caveats and Options

1. Instead of having everyone work on the same set of sentences, prepare five to seven envelopes. Each envelope should have three or four sentences which have been cut up into pieces. On the outside of each envelope, write (in large letters) a number on the envelope and the number of pieces inside (e.g., Envelope Number 4; 13pieces). You will need more envelopes than pairs/groups. For example, if you have five groups, you will need about eight envelopes for this activity. Write the names of the pairs/groups on the board. Have each pair/group choose one envelope and begin working at the same time. When students have finished, they should raise their hands and the teacher should then check their work. If all the sentences are correct, all the pieces should be put back in the envelope. The teacher then writes that envelope number by the students' names on the board (since they have successfully completed that envelope). The students

should then choose one of the remaining envelopes. This task can continue for a certain time limit set by the teacher or until one pair/ group has done all of the envelopes.

2. This alternative has a faster pace than the original exercise and is often more entertaining for the students. However, the advantage of the original exercise is that you can review all of the constructed sentences with all of the students very easily.

Contributor

Keith S. Folse is Principal at Language Academy, in Maebashi, Japan. He is the author of English Structure Practices, Intermediate Reading Practices, *and* Talk a Lot *(University of Michigan Press). The idea for Scrambled Idioms came from a former teaching colleague, Beth Powell.*

Two-Step Recycling Cards

Levels
Advanced

Aims
Recall known words
using context

Class Time
10 minutes

Preparation Time
20 minutes

Resources
Pairs of vocabulary
cards

Two-step recycling assumes that it is easier to recall the meaning of a contextualized word than it is to recall the form of a word from being given its meaning or a context. This learning technique works first on reinforcing comprehension of the word and only afterwards asks learners to supply the word itself as required by a particular context.

This activity has two steps: Learners first only have to recognize new lexical items and remember their meaning in the original context. In a second step, they are required to recall the new items using the context as a prompt.

Procedure

1. Let us assume that the class has read a text on physical exercise. Part of the original text reads:

   Corporations have attempted to improve their employees' health by providing exercise facilities or offering memberships in health clubs.

2. Make a set of about eight cards or slips, each with one or two sentences from the original text containing words thought to be new and worth learning. Leave out some of the words in the sentences. For the first set of cards, use known words that provide the context for the new words. For example, a card for the sentence above might look like this:

   > Corporations have attempted ——————— improve their employees' health ——————— providing exercise facilities or offering memberships ——————— health clubs.

3. Have students, working in pairs on a card at a time, decide on the best way to fill in the gaps and then write their answers on the back of the card so that the gaps remain unfilled and other pairs can use the same card.

4. The new vocabulary is actually *improve*, *health*, and *facilities*, so the second time around (perhaps one lesson later) student pairs would be working on cards like the following one, writing their own solutions on the back, as in the first step:

Corporations have attempted to i_____ their employees' h_____ by providing exercise f_____ or offering memberships in health clubs.

Contributor

Heather Murray teaches at Universität Bern in Switzerland.

Part III: Enriching Activities

Editor's Note

Enriching activities involve learning new information about previously met words. This can occur through

- gaining new input from the teacher
- extending knowledge of the meaning of words through meeting new uses, new collocations, and new associations
- placing the word in a new context.

Placing the word in a new context can occur as the learners create a context or as they retell a text under new conditions that encourage creative use of the target vocabulary.

The distinction between establishing and enriching activities has been made to make teachers aware of the need both to repeat vocabulary and to extend and elaborate knowledge of particular words.

Knowing a word involves much more than being able to recall the meaning (or L1 translation) of a presented word form. The following list covers most of the aspects involved in knowing a word.

1. Being able to recognize the spoken form of the word
2. Being able to pronounce the word
3. Being able to spell the word
4. Being able to write the word
5. Knowing the underlying meaning of the word
6. Knowing the range of meanings of the word
7. Knowing the grammatical patterns the word fits into
8. Knowing the affixes the word stem can take
9. Knowing the words that fit into the same lexical sets
10. Knowing the typical associations of the word
11. Knowing the range of collocations of the word
12. Knowing whether the use of the word is limited by considerations of politeness, gender, age, country, formality, and so on.

13. Knowing whether the word is commonly used or not
14. Being able to use the word receptively and productively.

These various aspects of knowledge are not all equally important, and their relative importance will depend on particular words. For example, some words need only be used receptively. Many words are neutral with regard to politeness or gender.

The list of aspects can provide a source of points for teacher observation during vocabulary activities. For example, the teacher may try to observe the grammatical patterns that the learners are using with some particular words. This may reveal that the learners are quite developed in their use of the word, or that they are not using or are misusing certain patterns. Similarly, the teacher may wish to observe whether a particular activity is achieving its aim or if a word is being enriched across the range of aspects.

◆ Associations and Lexical Sets
Word Maps

Levels
Any

Aims
Show the connections
between words

Class Time
30 minutes

Preparation Time
10 minutes

Resources
Sample word map
Lists of words to put
into the map

Procedure

1. Prepare a semantic map or chart which shows how a set of words
   can be grouped or classified.
2. Tell the students to work individually or in pairs to arrange the words
   on the word map.
3. Ask the students to add further words to each category.

Appendix:
Sample Exercise: Verbs of Communication

1. Add these words to the word map.

doubt	guess	laugh	remember	state	tell
forget	joke	mention	remind	tease	think

Humor	Beliefs
....	....
....	....
....	....

Communication

Memory	Reporting
....	....
....	....
....	....

2. Can you add two more verbs to each category? (Work in pairs)

This kind of activity enables learners to see connections between words. This is often a useful device in helping to remember new words.

Contributor

Ronald Jackup is a freelance ESL teacher and writer.

Understanding Occupations

Levels
Any

Aims
Develop the vocabulary
related to occupations

Class Time
25 minutes

Preparation Time
5 minutes

Resources
None

Procedure

1. Prepare a sheet with the following headings.

Skills needed:	Clothes usually worn:	Tools or equipment used:

    Add other categories as appropriate.
2. Divide the class into groups. Give each group a worksheet.
3. Write a list of occupations on the board or ask students for a list of five interesting or unusual occupations.
4. Have students provide as much information as they can about each of the occupations, under the categories on the sheet. Set a time limit (10–15 minutes).
5. Ask a student from each group to present their information. Which group has the most information?

Contributor

Ronald Jackup is a freelance ESL teacher and writer.

Flexible Odd Man Out

Levels
Any

Aims
Practice explaining
orally relationships
between words

Class Time
15–20 minutes

Preparation Time
15 minutes

Resources
Minilists of four items,
each word on a card

This is a good exercise to review vocabulary. It is especially useful for low levels where students' oral fluency is rather weak. Students at low levels tend to learn vocabulary through translations, but in multilingual classes teachers cannot do review exercises that depend on the L1. This exercise lets students demonstrate their knowledge of vocabulary at their own level.

Procedure

1. Prepare several minilists consisting of four items: Two should belong to one group and two to another group. For example, the list might consist of *tree, flower, red, green*. Write each word on a small piece of paper (5 centimeters (about 2 inches) x 5 centimeters (2 inches)) and then clip them together with a paper clip. The students must work in trios for the exercise, and you will need to prepare about 10 of these clipped lists per group of students.
2. Explain how an odd man out exercise works: In a given group of words, the goal is to find which of the words does not belong. On the board, write *tree, flower,* and *red.* Ask the students which is the odd man out. Then have someone tell why. Next, erase *tree* and substitute *blue.* Again ask which is the odd man out and why.
3. Once students understand the basic idea of odd man out, have them work in trios.
4. Pass out about 10 of the clipped minilists to each trio. (For classroom logistics, put each set of 10 minilists in a large envelope. Make sure the students reclip the four pieces of paper as they finish. In this way the game can be reused many times.)
5. Start the students in a given trio with any one of the 10 minilists. In each minilist there are four pieces of paper, but they each take only

126

one of the papers so that there is always one extra piece. Each student should read aloud the word on the paper. When all three students have done this, then the one student who has the odd man out word should explain why the word is different.

Caveats and Options

With many oral/aural pair or group work activities, students often overhear and are distracted by what the other students are saying. This problem has been eliminated in this exercise due to two important features: (a) Students will do the 10 minilists in random order and the odds of two groups who are sitting near each other doing the same item at the same time is only 1 in 10 or 10%. (b) In flexible odd man out, there are four papers that three students must choose from; thus, there are four possible combinations (abc, abd, acd, bcd), and this reduces the odds of any groups doing the same item at the same time to almost nil.

Contributor

Keith S. Folse is Principal at Language Academy, in Maebashi, Japan. He is the author of English Structure Practices, Intermediate Reading Practice, *and* Talk a Lot *(University of Michigan Press), from which this activity was adapted.*

Vocabulary Enrichment Through Word Association

Levels
Intermediate +

Aims
Raise awareness of
word associations
Explore words in
greater detail

Class Time
15–30 minutes

Preparation Time
10–20 minutes

Resources
List of high frequency
words
Charts

Students cannot always give definitions for words for which they have a good sense (at least receptively). Likewise, they may be able to give a definition of a word quite easily, but not be able to use the word. Having students give as many associations as they can provides insight in both these areas and can indicate to students where they may need to explore words further.

Procedure

1. Prepare charts with 10 words for associations, such as the following:

   Word   Associated Words (in 30 seconds)
   1. drink
   2. store
   3. etc.

2. Put students into a circle, and for a few minutes play a word association game. In this game, say a word and then ask each student to say the first word to come to mind. Students can listen to each other's first words and try to understand how the association was made. (An option would be to have students write the first word that comes to their minds for each of 10 words the you say. In either case you may want to have students share their answers, to raise awareness of varied associations made.)

3. Pass out a sheet with 10 words, and tell students you will give them 30 seconds for each word, in which they should write as many words associated with the given word as they can.

4. Tell the students to begin, and at the end of 30 seconds call out, "Next word." Continue to do this until all 10 words have been covered.

5. Have students go back through the list and circle any words for which they could not get many associations. Tell them that these words are ones that warrant spending time with their dictionaries (e.g., noting alternate meanings, phrasal uses, collocations). You may want to allow class time for this.

Some words lend themselves to alternate meanings and a large variety of associations, while others are much more limited. Therefore, it is advisable to have a native speaker (or other successful user of the language) do this exercise with each sheet of 10 words before you give them to the students, to give yourself an idea of reasonable expectations for each word in the list.

Contributor

Kenny Harsch is Director of English Education at Kobe YMCA College, Japan. He is interested in learner autonomy, student-centered curriculum development, and helping students discover their own uses for English. He also believes in developing students' ownership of the direction their learning takes. The idea for this activity came from a discussion with Norbert Schmitt, who is currently doing his doctoral dissertation on a related aspect of vocabulary acquisition.

Connections

Levels
Intermediate +

Aims
Develop a deeper
understanding of word
meanings

Class Time
25 minutes

Preparation Time
5 minutes

Resources
List of words to review

This activity involves students working with a group of words and trying to find connections between them.

Procedure

1. Choose a group of 10–15 words that you want students to review. These could be taken from anything the students have been studying. The words should be of a similar part of speech to enable students to make connections more easily. For example: *style, comfort, sample, combination, service, guarantee, advertisement, parade, index.*
2. Divide the class into groups. Ask groups to think of connections between the words on the list. Can they arrange the words into groups, and explain the connections between them? Give an example to help them get started, such as one from the list above:

   Comfort and *service* can go together. They can both be used to describe a hotel. A hotel should provide comfort, and the service should be good.

   Sample and *advertisement* can go together. When you want to buy something in a store, you will see advertisements for different things (paint, carpets, curtains), often with different samples for you to choose from.

3. Set a time limit for the activity: 10–15 minutes.
4. Ask group leaders to present their group's combinations to the class. Who could make the most connections between the words on the list?

Contributor

Ronald Jackup is a freelance ESL teacher and writer.

Missing Words

Levels
Intermediate +

Aims
Develop prediction
skills
Practice guessing from
context
Learn collocation
patterns

Class Time
25 minutes

Preparation Time
15 minutes

Resources
Cloze text

Procedure

1. Select a paragraph or short text at a suitable level for your class. Delete selected words from the text. Number the blanks in the text. Select words that cannot be predicted too easily but allow prediction.
2. Divide the class into groups, and give each group a copy of the text. Ask them to think of as many words as possible that could go into the missing sections of the text.
3. Ask a member of each group to come to the board and write up their suggestions for each blank.
4. Ask students to compare their suggestions. Are they all acceptable? Would they reject any? Why?
5. Give the class feedback on their suggestions. Use this phase of the activity to develop the students' awareness of lexical choice, vocabulary restrictions, and collocation.

Contributor

Ronald Jackup is a freelance ESL teacher and writer.

Sorting Words as Review

Levels
Intermediate +

Aims
Develop and extend
semantic networks

Class Time
20–30 minutes

Preparation Time
15 minutes

Resources
List of items

This activity helps learners remember the meanings of recently encountered lexical items. In a first step they are asked (indirectly) to examine the semantic network they have constructed for the item. The second step, which consists of comparison and discussion with other learners, serves to make them aware of gaps and misunderstandings as well as to extend their semantic networks. The activity can therefore be classified as a review exercise for "passive" control, in other words, for recognition and comprehension.

Procedure

1. From the lexical items to be reviewed or recycled, select between 10 and 15 and either dictate them to the class or present them on the board or overhead projector.
2. Ask the learners to think of three categories into which they could sort the words according to their meanings. It is up to them to decide on categories.
3. When they have done this, they sit in small groups and compare categories and how they sorted the words, justifying their categories and discussing meanings. The discussion may be either in the L1 or L2, depending on class level.

Caveats and Options

1. Give the categories as well as the words, but this is only interesting when it does not look like a test, that is, when there are a number of plausible sortings for learners to discuss afterwards. Here is an example. Let us say that the lexical items selected for review come from a reading text and subsequent discussion on physical fitness.

They are:

daily exercise	*health clubs*	*exercise facilities*
gym outfits	*stress*	*consumer society*
equipment	*body building*	*leisure time*
urban life	*aerobics*	*advertising campaigns*

2. After re-presenting the lexical items, ask the learners to sort them into categories labeled Luxury, Normal, and To be avoided. Another set of categories might be Expensive, Cheap, and Free. Categories like these introduce a new perspective and, at the same time, clearly indicate that sortings will depend on opinion and not fact.
3. The small-group discussion after the sorting phase is essential because this is the time when the known meanings and connotations of the lexical items are discussed. The teacher will want to circulate among the groups, answering questions and listening for misunderstandings.

Contributor

Heather Murray teaches at Universität Bern in Switzerland.

Odd Man Out and Nonverbal Communication

Levels
High intermediate +

Aims
Learn cultural
connotations of words
associated with the
body

Class Time
30–45 minutes

Preparation Time
15 minutes

Resources
Lists of items (see
Appendix below)
English-English
dictionary

Students are often confused by semantically similar words for gestures, facial expressions, and other forms of nonverbal communication. Furthermore, they are frequently only incidentally made aware of the cultural connotations of these words as well as the behavior to which they refer.

This adaptation of an activity known as Odd Man Out can be carried out by students working in groups or individually and then in small groups. Depending upon the level of the class, students may be allowed to work with an English-English dictionary. A time limit should be set in advance and will vary with the level of the class.

Procedure

1. Compile sets of three or four words referring to a gesture, facial expression, sound, or body movement. One of the words should differ from the others in terms of how it is regarded in a specific English-speaking culture, for example, the United States or Australia, or for the part of the body to which it refers. A thesaurus may be useful for this purpose.
2. Reproduce the list on a handout to be given to each student or group. The list can also be written on the blackboard.
3. Ask the students to study each set of words and select the one word that differs from the others.
4. At the end of the time allowed, ask students to compare and discuss their choices with other groups and, finally, as a class. Reasons for making their choices should also be discussed.
5. You or the students should then define or explain the words in each set.

Caveats and Options

1. Ask students to indicate whether a word carries a positive, negative, or neutral connotation in their culture by marking a + (plus),

— (minus), or / (slash) above each word in a set. Compare their answers with the cultural connotations of the word in the target culture. The instructor should be prepared to describe a situation in which the action or sound occurs.

2. A similar activity can also be carried out using sets of words that describe personalities or physical appearance.

Appendix: Sample List of Nonverbal Forms of Communication

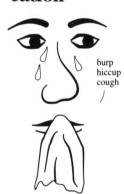

burp
hiccup
cough

Contributor

1. slap, caress, pat, spit
(The odd word is *spit* because it is not done with the hand.)
2. burp, hiccup, cough, sneeze
(The odd word is *sneeze* because it is the only one done with the nose.)
3. wave, clap, wink, salute
(The odd word is *wink* because it is not done with the hand.)
4. shrug, kiss, pout, smack
(The odd word is *shrug* because it is not done with the lips.)
5. wink, roll, stare, lick
(The odd word is *lick* because it is not done with the eyes.)
6. slurp, swallow, chew, sip
(The odd word is *chew* because it is the only one done with the teeth.)
7. giggle, sob, snicker, chuckle
(The odd word is *sob* because it is not a form of laughter.)
8. sniff, gasp, pant, groan
(The odd word is *sniff* because it is the only one done with the nose.)

Kathleen S. Foley received her MA in Applied Linguistics from Indiana University. She has taught in the United States and the People's Republic of China. She currently teaches at Aoyama Gakuin Women's Junior College in Tokyo, Japan.

The Story Behind the Picture

Levels
Intermediate +

Aims
Use words in context

Class Time
25 minutes

Preparation Time
10 minutes

Resources
Picture
List of verbs

Caveats and Options

Contributor

Procedure

1. Select an interesting picture, around which an unusual story could be developed.
2. Give students a list of about 10 verbs to use in the story. Choose words that are a little unusual and not too obvious.
3. Ask the students to work in groups and to develop a story around the picture, one that uses the words you have given them. Tell them their story should involve at least two people. They should make notes to use in telling their story. They must use all the words on the list at least once.
4. Set a time limit. Then have a student from each group tell the group's story. Other groups can ask questions. Which group has the best story?

Have groups write out their stories and attach them to the wall.

Ronald Jackup is a freelance ESL teacher and writer.

Multiple Meanings

Levels
Intermediate +

Aims
Develop awareness of
the multiple meanings
of words
Develop a strategy for
selecting the relevant
meaning for a particular
context

Class Time
30 minutes

Preparation Time
5 minutes

Resources
List of words

Caveats and Options

Procedure

1. Write on the board a list of 5–10 words that could be used in various contexts, for example: *court, decision, king, foul, rival, strategy.*
2. As the students, with the aid of a dictionary if necessary, supply the various parts of speech and meanings, write them beside each word on the board.
3. Ask the students in pairs or small groups to create a scenario or describe a situation using all of the words. With the above list, students could imagine a scene from a tennis match, a basketball game, or a castle in ancient times, among others.
4. Have each pair or group describe its scenario to the class. With the above words, one group might describe a scene of *court* intrigue: The good *king* has a *rival* who has performed *foul* deeds. The king needs a *strategy* to defend his throne and must make a *decision* soon.
5. Add two or three more words to the list and ask the students to define these words and explain how they affect the scenarios described. For instance, adding the words *referee* and *overtime* to the list above narrows the possible scenarios to one involving a basketball game.

This optional activity can be used alone or adapted to make an excellent prereading exercise:

1. Select several key words from the reading and ask students to find the various meanings. With these words, students guess the topic of the reading. Add more key words, and ask the students to determine if the added words change their hypotheses.
2. Have the students explain the relevant meaning of each word for the topic of the reading.

In either of these variations, the activity promotes students' awareness of the multiple meanings of words. Students not only increase their vocabulary of certain words but, more importantly, they learn about the interdependence of word meanings: The meaning of a word relevant to a particular use depends on and affects the other words in the discourse. This provides students with a strategy for selecting the appropriate meanings for words they encounter in communication.

Contributor

Christine Schuler Alvarado teaches at the University of Panama in Chiriquí.

Creating Minidomains

Levels
Any

Aims
Relate new words to semantically similar ones

Class Time
5–10 minutes

Preparation Time
None

Resources
None

Psycholinguistic studies show that related words, such as words for colors, are stored together in the mind. Adjective opposites (*hot*, *cold*) and words that are semantically related to them (*tepid*, *fiery*) are also stored in clusters. Teaching techniques that use the natural storage and retrieval systems of the mind are more effective and efficient. One such technique is described below.

Procedure

1. When a student asks about the meaning of a word, for example, *ecstatic*, elicit from the class other words with similar meanings (*glad*, *cheerful*, *overjoyed*).
2. Write them on the board. Then add other level-appropriate words, phrases, and idioms that you think of on the spot (*elated*, *joyous*, *in hog heaven*). This is a minidomain.
3. While or after generating the domain, ask meaningful questions using the vocabulary. (e.g., *What makes you feel sunny? How would you feel if you won the lottery?*)

Caveats and Options

1. Expand the minidomain. You and your students can add words that are opposite in meaning or that express gradients of meaning (*elated*, *sunny*, *sad*, *depressed*). Some domains can be greatly expanded; others are more limited.
2. Help students understand important differences among the words (*happy* is a rather neutral word, *ecstatic* is a strong word, *on cloud nine* is informal/conversational).
3. Have students work in small groups to put the words from the minidomain into categories. This works especially well with noun domains.

Words for bodies of water (e.g., *pond, puddle, sea, lake, ocean*) group into categories (e.g., *large/small, salt/fresh, moving/stagnant*).

4. After class, use a thesaurus to further develop the minidomain. Create a chart that illustrates the relationships among the words to clarify meaning for the students.

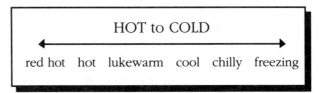

5. Create follow-up exercises to help students learn and retain the words.

The more you work with minidomains, the easier it becomes to create them. Don't give up if it seems difficult the first time you try it. Teaching vocabulary through minidomains helps students learn many new words quickly and easily. Students connect new words to words they already know. They also learn the differences among similar words, which helps them make appropriate word choices. Finally, students learn to view words as components of a lexical network rather than as isolated items.

Contributors

Dee Ann Holisky, Sherry Trechter, and Kathryn Trump all teach at George Mason University in Virginia, in the United States. They are the authors of a vocabulary text, Walk, Amble, Stroll, *published by Heinle & Heinle.*

Teaching Vocabulary Through Word Domains

Levels
Any

Aims
Study by using semantic fields

Class Time
1 hour

Preparation Time
1 hour

Resources
None

Teaching vocabulary effectively begins with building on what students already know. By opening a concept in the students' minds and having them call up familiar words related to the concept, you are preparing them to add new words to their lexical networks. The new words can be presented in the form of a word domain. A sequence of exercises will then help students store the words in long-term memory and finally use the words as their own. This progression of activities based on a word domain (semantic field) is a great leap beyond giving students lists of unrelated words.

Procedure

1. Choose a theme or concept from a reading passage. Decide what the focus word for this concept will be. For example, if you are going to talk about horror movies or read about phobias, the focus word might be *afraid*.
2. Before class, create a domain for this focus word using a thesaurus. Depending on the level of your class, present as many or as few of the words that mean *afraid* as you think are appropriate. Illustrate the degrees of being *afraid*. An example of a word domain for *afraid* is given below.

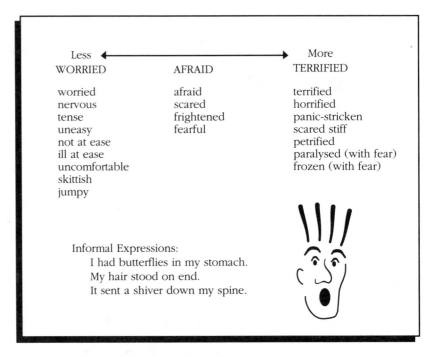

Less ←	→ More	
WORRIED	AFRAID	TERRIFIED
worried	afraid	terrified
nervous	scared	horrified
tense	frightened	panic-stricken
uneasy	fearful	scared stiff
not at ease		petrified
ill at ease		paralysed (with fear)
uncomfortable		frozen (with fear)
skittish		
jumpy		

Informal Expressions:
I had butterflies in my stomach.
My hair stood on end.
It sent a shiver down my spine.

3. Before handing out copies of the domain to your students, get them ready to focus on the concept *afraid* by asking questions such as: *When do you feel afraid? What happens to your body when you feel afraid?* Then present the domain to the class.
4. To help students put the new words into short-term memory, create one-step manipulative exercises: multiple choice, Hangman Game, scrambled letters, categorizing words (e.g., by degrees of being *afraid*), or recreating the domain.
5. At this point, students are ready for some problem-solving activities. To put a new word in long-term memory, they need to understand its meaning and use it to solve a problem. Problem-solving activities include matching words and situations, fill-in-the-blank, multiple choice, or vocabulary games. They should require students to go beyond simply matching the word to its meaning. Example: Hiro thought he saw a ghost. His face turned white and he was speechless.

Was he *uncomfortable* or *frozen with fear*? (See also Sense or Non-sense, the activity following this one). These exercises lead to class discussions that clarify word meanings.

6. Now that students have handled the words and made decisions using the words, they are ready to make the words their own. You and your students can generate some communicative, open-ended questions and activities for writing, discussion and interviewing. For example, ask students to write or talk about how they feel just before they have to take the TOEFL test. They can interview classmates and/or native speakers about some cultural aspects of fear. For example: *How do you feel about the number 13 or black cats?*

7. Periodically review the words with games, practice, and discussion.

Contributors

Dee Ann Holisky, Sherry Trechter, and Kathryn Trump all teach at George Mason University in Virginia, in the United States. They are the authors of a vocabulary text, Walk, Amble, Stroll, *published by Heinle & Heinle.*

Sense or Nonsense?

Levels
Any

Aims
Store newly learned
words in long-term
memory

Class Time
10 minutes

Preparation Time
20 minutes

Resources
None

Students easily forget newly learned vocabulary. This exercise promotes retention by asking the students to use the new words to solve a problem. Research has shown that this helps put the new items into long-term memory.

Procedure

1. Before class, create sentences using new vocabulary items. These sentences should either make sense or be nonsense. For example, if the students have learned words for *hot* and *cold* (see the previous activity, Creating Minidomains), you can create the following sentences. (The sentences can be as humorous or serious as you want them to be. A little whimsy makes the exercise more fun for students and teachers.)

SENSE NONSENSE   1. It's chilly in here. I think I'll take
off my sweater.

SENSE NONSENSE   2. The water in the bathtub is lukewarm.
It won't burn your skin.

SENSE NONSENSE   3. The fire in the fireplace is red hot.
It's not keeping us warm.

SENSE NONSENSE   4. It's freezing outside. I want to eat
some ice cream and drink a tall glass
of iced tea.

---

2. Hand out the sentences in printed form for homework or for small-group or individual work in class. You may want to read them aloud by the teacher for listening practice.

   This activity leads to productive discussions. For example, in Number 1, the difference between *chilly* and *warm* can be discussed as well as the verb phrases *take off* and *put on*.
3. When the students have become familiar with this type of exercise, ask them to create their own sense-nonsense sentences. These student-created sentences can be used in class or collected, typed, and handed out the next day as an exercise or even a quiz.

Contributors

Dee Ann Holisky, Sherry Trechter, and Kathryn Trump all teach at George Mason University in Virginia, in the United States. They are the authors of a vocabulary text, Walk, Amble, Stroll, *published by Heinle & Heinle.*

◆ Collocations
Containers

Levels
Any

Aims
Review names of such things as substances, foods, drinks as well as the phrases used to refer to containers of each thing, such as a vase of flowers, a box of matches

Class Time
20 minutes

Preparation Time
10 minutes

Resources
Pictures or worksheet

Procedure

1. Find pictures of things for the students to work with, or prepare a worksheet with a list of nouns for different kinds of familiar things. For example: *flour, coffee, flowers, shirts, oil, toothpaste, sugar, paper, paint, milk, shampoo.*

2. Give students a list of container words. For example: *tube, jar, carton, vase, pile, bowl.*
3. Ask students to work in groups and make as many combinations as they can, using container phrases and names of things. Set a time limit of about 5 minutes.
4. Check around the class to see what combinations the students have produced. Correct any unacceptable or unusual combinations they may have come up with.

Contributor

Ronald Jackup is a freelance ESL teacher and writer.

Matching Activity

Levels
Any

Aims
Study new vocabulary
in useful contexts

Class Time
20–30 minutes

Preparation Time
15 minutes

Resources
Small cards

This matching activity provides learners with an enjoyable way to practice using newly learned words in sentences. The competitive nature of the activity ensures that valuable verbal interaction occurs over the correct meanings of words.

Procedure

1. Divide the students into groups of four.
2. Each group receives two sets of 16 cards. One set consists of cards with a newly learned word written on one side. The other set consists of cards with a sentence with a missing word. Each word from the first set fits one of the sentences in the second set.
3. The students place the two sets of cards face down on a table in two separate blocks of 16 cards.
4. Explain the following rules to the students.
   - The first student turns over one card from each set.
   - If the group agrees that the word fits the sentence, the student keeps both cards and takes another turn. If the group agrees that the word does not fit the sentence, the student returns the two cards to their original position face down.
   - The second student takes a turn.
   - The activity ends when all the pairs have been found.

Caveats and Options

1. Take care to think up sentences that give contextual clues to the identity of the missing word. Each sentence must be able to match with only one word.
2. Substitute dictionary meanings for the incomplete sentences.

Contributor

David Hirsh gained an MA from Victoria University of Wellington, in New Zealand, in 1993. He has taught in New Zealand and Thailand.

Collocation Bingo

Levels
Intermediate +

Aims
Extend collocational
knowledge

Class Time
20 minutes

Preparation Time
15 minutes

Resources
Bingo cards
Prepared word lists

Nearly every kind of collocational activity involves a matching task of words that collocate. In this case, the collocational task has been embedded in a bingo game to improve motivation and also to increase the number of collocational pairs that can be covered. For every *called* prompt word, students have to consider collocational possibilities with most of the 25 words on their bingo card. Also, the class has to judge the validity of the winner's pairs of words. This kind of attention can lead to the type of deeper cognitive processing that promotes learning. If there is any debate about the fitness of a collocational pair, so much the better, because negotiation also leads to deeper processing and fosters information retention.

Procedure

1. Develop a list of 30 or more pairs of words that collocate. Collocational word pairs can be taken from a passage that has been read or from words that have already been taught, but take care to limit the number. One side of this list becomes the "called" word list, and the words on the other side are "card" words to be written on the blank bingo cards. Bingo cards with 25 empty squares should be prepared before class.
2. Give each student one card.
3. Write the card word list on the blackboard and ask the students to fill in their squares with those words in a random order. This should ensure that every bingo card is slightly different.
4. Read words from the called list, and if a student thinks that it collocates with a word on their card, they write it in the same square under that word.

5. When a student gets a bingo, read the five winning word pairs and let the class decide if they match well. If a majority of the class agrees, that student wins. A winner can also be required to use the word pairs in a sentence.
6. The game is then played for second and third places.
7. Finally, the object is to get a "blackout bingo," where every square is filled. This guarantees that almost all of the collocational pairs will be used.

Caveats and Options

Prepare several versions of bingo cards with the card words already written in the squares. This method saves writing time in class, and also allows you to fix the arrangement of the words on the cards so that almost all of the collocational words can be called before someone gets the first bingo.

Appendix: Sample List

The following example shows a list with 30 collocational pairs and two possible game cards. The 25 words on each card vary and are in a different order. Note that the arrangement of the words on the cards is designed to prevent a bingo until relatively late in the game.

Called List	Card List	Called List	Card List
ice	cream	tie	tightly
fire	truck	spend	foolishly
guitar	string	strong	coffee
color	photograph	heavy	weight
cassette	tape	wind	blows
knife	cuts	pen	writes
ball	bounces	bright	sun
green	leaf	furry	animal
nylon	stockings	cold	winter
argue	loudly	pretty	baby
aeroplane	flies	brake	stops
whisper	softly	candle	lights
front	door	tall	building
shirt	sleeve	chef	cooks
telephone	booth	clear	glass

Card 1

bounces	cooks	stockings	animal	cuts
sleeve	cream	writes	foolishly	stops
blows	winter	building	tape	sun
glass	photograph	baby	weight	string
door	tightly	truck	lights	flies

Card 2

animal	photograph	softly	glass	bounces
loudly	sun	writes	cream	building
cuts	foolishly	cooks	door	tightly
lights	truck	coffee	blows	string
baby	stops	stockings	winter	sleeve

Contributor

Norbert Schmitt is a lecturer at Minatogawa Women's College in Hyogo, Japan. His main interests are L2 vocabulary acquisition and vocabulary testing. He is currently researching the effects of various types of word knowledge on vocabulary acquisition.

Collocation Dominoes

Levels
Intermediate +

Aims
Develop knowledge of
and practice in using
collocations

Class Time
20 minutes

Preparation Time
30 minutes initially

Resources
A set of collocation
dominoes

Collocation might be described as an instinctive reflex of the native speaker, but for the nonnative speaker, it involves difficult decisions concerning word coverage and relies on extensive exposure to the language. The element of competition in a game of collocation dominoes will encourage the quick reactions necessary for fluent use.

Procedure

1. As the name of the game suggests, collocation dominoes operates in a similar way to the traditional game so first you need to make the dominoes. There are two types of dominoes needed. One type is marked with words that can function as either nouns or verbs. Here are some examples:

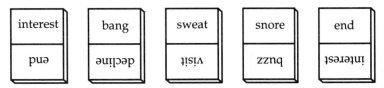

The other type of domino is marked with one adjective and one adverb. Here are some examples:

Compile a stock of about a hundred dominoes because this gives a wide range of words. I originally collected these words by drawing

151

up a list of nouns/verbs from the indexes of current course books and then asking native speakers to provide collocating adverbs and adjectives for those nouns/verbs. The two types of domino can be color differentiated in some way, and it is worth taking steps to make the dominoes durable for repeated use.

2. To start a game, place the dominoes face down and shuffle them. The players each take 10 dominoes. The way the game proceeds is for each player in turn to place one domino next to another so that adjacent words collocate correctly; the dominoes should be placed end to end.

3. Every time a player puts down a domino and claims a collocation, they have to justify their claim by using the collocation correctly in a sentence. Enforce a 60-second time limit when players cannot make up their mind which domino to use. If the time limit is exceeded, the collocation or the justification incorrect, the player must take a domino from the general stock. The winner of the game is the first to use up all the dominoes in his or her possession.

Contributor

Wendy E. Ball is a tutor at the Institute for Applied Language Studies at the University of Edinburgh in the United Kingdom.

Using Shareware Software to Enhance Vocabulary Knowledge

Levels
Any

Aims
Reinforce knowledge of
collocations

Class Time
2 hours per week

Preparation Time
Initially high

Resources
An IBM compatible PC
for every two students
Eclipse Shareware disk

Caveats and Options

In this activity, students have to guess at the missing words in a text in much the same way as in a cloze exercise. The students have to use their knowledge of collocation to predict the missing words. To test a prediction, they type in words to fill the available gaps.

Procedure

1. Type the text into *Eclipse* and print out a copy of the full text. Give a photocopy to each student, then read and discuss the text in class. The texts should consist of no more than 19 lines (approximately 250 words) and should contain vocabulary items being taught at that level. Students often type their own texts on to the computer and challenge other students to rebuild them.
2. Choose how much of the text is going to be visible to the students on the computer screen. Then have the students compete in pairs to see who can correctly predict the greatest number of words. Display the results for each student when the exercise is finished.

1. *Eclipse* is a text rebuilding program written by John and Muriel Higgins, similar to commercial versions, but with some additional features. It is a piece of shareware: cheap computer software available for about $5 a disk. This is the cost of a trial copy. If you are satisfied with it you may then register for a further fee which is very reasonable. One distributor is Seltec. *Eclipse* is on disk MGH1289.
2. The great strength of *Eclipse* is its flexibility. You can leave or omit function words, first and last letters, long words, short words, determiners and pronouns, capitalized words, numbers, prepositions and conjunctions, and auxiliary verbs. You can choose to display dashes

for the missing letters or may prefer to not indicate the size of the words.

3. Students can play against the computer, against another student, or by themselves. They can see the whole text at any time or ask for free words.

4. The optional analysis displays the time spent, the amount of time the text was revealed to the student, and how many words were correctly predicted.

5. The texts that students rebuild need not be the same as the texts they have previously read. In this case the exercise will be more demanding.

6. Please note that texts should always be added to a master copy and then transferred to other machines, otherwise the menu of texts will not be the same on each machine.

7. Another useful shareware program, also available from Seltec, is *DoubleUp* which reinforces knowledge of collocation and sentence order. A knowledge of MSDOS editing is needed to tailor it to your students' needs.

Seltec Addresses:

In The United Kingdom: Britsel Data Services, Albert House, 10 Albert Rd, Bournemouth, BH1 1BZ.

In Australia: Box 15/2B Grosvenor St, Bondi Junction, NSW 2022.

In New Zealand: Box 943, Nelson.

Contributors

Stuart Hudson is a secondary school teacher in New Zealand.
Simon Jenkins is studying for an MA in Applied Linguistics at Victoria University of Wellington in New Zealand. He has taught in the Solomon Islands.

◆ Enriching Meaning and Productive Use
Mind Benders

Levels
Intermediate +

Aims
Become familiar with
lateral thinking and
phrasal verbs

Class Time
5–10 minutes

Preparation Time
How clever are you?

Resources
Overhead projector
(OHP) and
transparencies

Mind Benders are a useful way to get students thinking in English. They can be used as warm-ups or when waiting for the class to start. They are a good way to get intermediate level students experimenting with vocabulary and can also be used as an introduction to idioms to demonstrate how we do not have to take words literally. They also encourage students to develop their visual memory.

Procedure

Some examples of mind benders are as follows:

Mind Bender		Meaning
LE EL	=	split level
<u>KNEE</u> LIGHT	=	neon light
R\E\A\D\I\N\G\	=	reading between the lines
DEATH — LIFE	=	life after death
<u>STAND</u> I	=	I understand

1. Prepare five or six Mind Benders on a transparency or write them on the board (without the meaning).

155

2. Give an example of the first one or two and show how the words have been written according to their literal meaning.
3. Ask the students to think what the others could mean. After a few minutes, take some suggestions from the class before telling them what the meaning is.

Some other examples are:

Mind Bender		Meaning
MIND MATTER	=	mind over matter
HE'S/HIMSELF	=	he's beside himself
R ROAD A D	=	crossroads
LOOK/LEAP	=	look before you leap
CYCLE CYCLE	=	bicycle

Caveats and Options

1. Once the students get used to the idea of trying to find the expression through the words, they get very interested in this activity. But they do need some examples and some time to get started.
2. It is useful to try out your Mind Benders with colleagues first to see how easy or difficult they are. Once the students get used to the activity you can ask them to give you some ideas of Mind Benders and use them at the beginning of each lesson.

Contributor

Lindsay Miller is a lecturer in the English Department at City Polytechnic of Hong Kong. He has taught English in Europe, the Middle East, and Southeast Asia for the past 14 years.

What Is It?

Levels
Intermediate +

Aims
Individualize the
revision of vocabulary

Class Time
10 minutes

Preparation Time
20 minutes

Resources
Activity sheet

Procedure

1. Prepare a sheet containing several sets of sentences such as:

   It is like water.
   Everybody has it.
   It is warm when it belongs to people.
   It is cold when it belongs to a fish.
   It is usually red.
   It is in your body.
   What is it?

2. The learners work on the sheets in their own time and at their own speed. They mark their work from an answer key.

Caveats and Options

1. Arrange the sentences in a set so that the first sentences do not give a lot of information.
2. This activity can be used to teach vocabulary if the actual word is used instead of *it*. The learners respond by writing the L1 translation of the word.

Contributor

Paul Nation is Reader in Applied Linguistics at Victoria University of Wellington, New Zealand.

More Than Meaning

Levels
Intermediate +

Aims
Develop awareness of
the range of
associations a word can
have

Class Time
30 minutes

Preparation Time
5 minutes

Resources
Grids

There are many other kinds of word knowledge besides meaning. This activity is designed to have students focus on other kinds of word knowledge that are not often given attention. It is intended as an enrichment activity for words that have already been introduced. To fill in the blanks, students must carefully consider and analyze the connections the target word has with other words. This should lead to the kind of deeper processing that facilitates learning. It is organized as a group activity to encourage cooperative learning where weaker students can learn from better ones. Although this activity can use a considerable amount of class time, students are learning much more than the selected target words. They are considering numerous words as answer possibilities. Also, this activity encourages students to think more broadly about what it means to "know" a word, giving them a better sense of the kinds of word knowledge they should be trying to develop.

Procedure

1. Before this activity can be used, teach the students about the different kinds of word knowledge. It is probably necessary to use nontechnical definitions when explaining these concepts:

   Meaning: The general meaning of a word
   Part of speech: Is the word a noun, verb, adjective etc.?
   Derivative forms: Other members in a word family (e.g., *act*, *active*, *actively*, *action*)
   Synonyms: Words with a similar meaning
   Antonyms: Words basically opposite in meaning
   Collocates: Words that frequently appear together
   Superordinate: The name or description of a group of things (e.g., *anger*, *jealousy*, *hate*, *love* → *emotions*)

Coordinates: Members of a concept group, such as the four emotions above

Subordinates: Types or varieties of whatever the word is (e.g., *vehicles* → *cars*, *buses*, *trucks*)

The last three categories may best be taught with some type of tree diagram to illustrate their interrelationship.

2. For each group, make a worksheet by drawing a cross-hatch design on a piece of paper. In each section, write as many numbers as there are groups. If you will have a large number of groups, you may want to limit the answer spaces in each section to five. Write a different target word at the top of each sheet. In class, draw a master chart on the blackboard to show the students which category of word knowledge goes in each worksheet section. It will look something like this, although the definitions should be the same as you used in your explanations:

meaning	coordinates	part of speech
superordinates	synonyms	derivative forms
subordinates	antonyms	collocates

3. Divide your students into groups.
4. Then give each group one worksheet and tell them they have a set amount of time (e.g., 5 minutes) to complete as many sections as possible. They can put more than one answer in each section.
5. When that time is over, rotate the sheets between the groups. Ask each group to try to answer as many sections as possible, writing on Line 2. They may of course look at the answers on Line 1 and agree with them or try to come up with better ones. When time is up, rotate the sheets again, the answers going on Line 3 and so forth. If there are more than five groups, there will be some sheets that every group will not have a chance to work on. Having every group use a different colored pen is helpful in keeping the answers separate.

6. When the answer sheets are completed, have each group in turn read off the answers written down on the sheet they last worked on, section by section.
7. The class decides which answers are correct, but you have the final say if there are any problems.

Caveats and Options

If the activity is to be played as a game, then points can be given with the teacher keeping a running tally on the blackboard. If two or more different answers are correct, the groups who wrote them get points. When a correct answer is duplicated, the first group to have written it gets the point. The winning group is the one with the most points after all the sheets have been evaluated.

Appendix: Sample Worksheet

SHY

1. 2. 3. 4. 5.	1. 2. 3. 4. 5.	1. 2. 3. 4. 5.
1. 2. 3. 4. 5.	1. 2. 3. 4. 5.	1. 2. 3. 4. 5.

Contributor

Norbert Schmitt is a lecturer at Minatogawa Women's College in Hyogo, Japan. His main interests are L2 vocabulary acquisition and vocabulary testing. He is currently researching the effects of various types of word knowledge on vocabulary acquisition.

Demonstrating Nuances

Levels
Intermediate +

Aims
Examine positive,
negative, and neutral
connotations of words

Class Time
30 minutes

Preparation Time
20 minutes

Resources
Lists of synonyms (see
Appendix below)

The value of this exercise is that students see that no two words ever have the exact same meaning; rather, each word has its own connotations depending on situations and cultural contexts. For example, most U.S. women would probably rate *thin* as positive, but students from other cultures could consider it negative. As a result, differing cultural attitudes can be explored in relation to these concepts.

Procedure

1. Give the students a list of synonyms.
2. Tell them to work together in groups to decide if the synonyms have a positive, negative, or neutral connotation.

Appendix: Sample List

Look at the following synonyms and decide if each word has a negative, positive, or neutral connotation:

1. slim	skinny	thin	slender
2. old	elderly	ripe	wrinkled
3. ignorant	uninformed	illiterate	unaware
4. poor	needy	broke	homeless
5. nurse	servant	slave	maid
6. strange	unusual	rare	odd
7. cheap	thrifty	careful	frugal

Contributor

Vickie Safari has an MS in TESL and teaches in Georgia State University's Intensive English Program. She was a Fulbright Lecturer in Pakistan during the 1991–1992 academic year.

Follow Your Character

Levels
Intermediate +

Aims
Focus on a particular
type of vocabulary

Class Time
30 minutes

Preparation Time
15 minutes

Resources
Video segment

Students pool their knowledge of vocabulary and create a coherent passage describing one character's activities in a video passage. When video is used for language learning purposes, students' often focus on just the dialogue. This activity is a way of focusing students' attention on a different set of vocabulary items. By reducing the volume and giving each group a specific character and giving each group member a specific part of speech, the cognitive load is significantly reduced. This enables students to focus on aspects of the video passage and hence vocabulary that they would not focus on with more listening-based approaches.

This type of cooperative group work encourages students to pool their knowledge of vocabulary and teach each other. There is a considerable amount of interaction and negotiation of meaning that takes place as students work to create a paragraph to present to the class.

Procedure

1. Choose a section of video from 20 seconds to 1 minute in length that has a lot of action and several characters.
2. Split the class into enough groups so that each group has one character to watch.
3. Each person in the group should watch the character and be in charge of taking note of the vocabulary related to one of the following categories: (a) actions, (b) objects, (c) descriptions of objects or people, and (d) descriptions of actions.
   Play the video two or three times. Turning the volume off might help the students focus on the task.
4. The students' task will be to pool their vocabulary and from this group of words create a complete description of their character's role in the scene.

5. Have them write a paragraph for one of the group members to then read to the class.

The following is an example from the introduction to "The Simpsons," a popular U.S. TV show, which I have used in my class.

Appendix: Sample Student Text

First Bart leaves school on his skateboard. He is wearing a yellow striped shirt and short pants. He drives dangerously past three people on the sidewalk. Homer throws away a green radioactive rod that almost hits him. Finally, Bart jumps over the car and goes into the house and sits on the old couch with the family.

Contributor

Eric Bray is Academic Director at the Kyoto YMCA English School, in Japan.

Story Retelling

Levels
Intermediate +

Aims
Turn receptive
vocabulary into
productive vocabulary

Class Time
20 minutes

Preparation Time
10–15 minutes

Resources
Story

This activity allows teachers to create interesting vocabulary lessons that incorporate the language skills of reading, writing, speaking, and listening. Students focus on a topic while gaining productive vocabulary knowledge.

Procedure

1. Choose a true, interesting, and short story. Consider all available forms of the media as possible sources. Do not write the story and plan to read it; natural language and spontaneous elaboration aid comprehension.
2. Select 5–10 useful target words from the story that the students might know receptively but not productively. The words should be relevant to the central meaning of the story.
3. Write the target words on the board in the order you will use them. Answer any questions about the meanings of words briefly. At this point the students should have a basic receptive knowledge of the words.
4. Send half the students (Group 1) outside the room or out of earshot. Tell the story to the remaining students (Group 2), using the target words in the order listed. If the story includes names, dates, or other specific pieces of information, write them on the board. Clarify as needed. Direct student attention toward the words on the board as you use them. Let the list serve as a reminder of the sequence of the events in the story.
5. Group 1 returns and each student is assigned a partner. Partners from Group 2 tell the story, using the words on the board as a guide for both speakers and listeners. Group 2 tries to pass on the same meaning as the teacher's version of the story, using the target words and explaining as needed.

6. When the pairs are finished, review the story to check comprehension. Follow up with activities based on the message of the story. Encourage students to use the target words in all phases of the activity.

Caveats and Options

Story Retelling can be followed by any of these activities.

1. Mock interviews: Students ad lib TV news interviews with one or more witnesses of this event.
2. Letter writing: Students write imaginary letters (a) to an investigator from the FBI, seeking further information, or (b) to one character in the story from another.
3. Next Chapter: Students speculate in a discussion or in writing about what happened next.
4. Discussion: What can be done to protect public places like the World Trade Center from terrorist attack?

The value of this technique is that students can be guided from a receptive to a productive knowledge of a word while focusing on a topic of general interest. The activity might be used as preparation for a related activity or adapted to use with a given vocabulary list. If the activity is working well, the students will be busily using the target words in original expressions while focusing on the content.

Appendix: Sample Story Assignment

Directions: Tell the story in your own words. Target words are italicized.

In February of 1993 the World Trade Center in New York was the *site* of the most *destructive terrorist* act yet to occur on United States soil. An *explosion* occurred near noon on a busy work day, leaving a five-story crater. The 110-story Twin Towers swayed as windows exploded, ceilings *collapsed* and fires broke out. At least 6 people were killed. Over 1,000 were injured. Thousands of businesses were *paralysed* for several weeks while the *investigation* and cleanup took place. This attack occurred when a rented moving van carrying *sophisticated* explosives was left in a lower-level parking garage by a group of *terrorists*.

Contributor

Cheryl Boyd Zimmerman teaches at the American Language Institute at the University of Southern California in the United States.

Discovering Meaning Constraints

Levels
Intermediate +

Aims
See the differences in
L1 and L2 use of
particular words

Class Time
20 minutes

Preparation Time
10 minutes

Resources
List of uses of a word

A major obstacle to learning vocabulary well is the understanding of the constraints on the uses of a particular word. Unsophisticated learners have a tendency to give to a newly acquired word all the meanings of the word their L1 associates with it. Thus, Japanese learners of English, having learned *osieru* means "to teach," will then tend to overgeneralize its use and produce incorrect sentences such as "I *taught* him that there was a meeting" because *osieru* is also used for "tell" in the sense of give information.

With groups of students sharing a common L1, the problem is easily overcome if one has no objection to using explicit contrastive analysis. One can simply explain the constraints on the use of a particular word compared to those of its acknowledged counterpart in the L1. However, if the class is heterogeneous in terms of the L1, this solution is not practical. One can still, nevertheless, exploit the principles of lexical contrastive analysis by encouraging students themselves to use it.

Procedure

1. Explain the principles of lexical contrastive analysis at the beginning of the course by using such examples as that of *osieru* and *teach* as discussed above. This teaches students to be wary of overgeneralization and also prepares them for comparing the constraints on the meaning of the target language words with those of the counterpart word in their L1.
2. Choose a word and prepare a list of sentences that contain a range of uses of that word.
3. Instruct the students to examine the uses and work out the constraints compared with those of the counterpart word in the L1.

Caveats and Options

1. It is a good idea to have students check their answers in a bilingual dictionary.

2. If this problem solving is done as a regular activity, students are able to build up their own minidictionaries and put their acquired knowledge of constraints into practice, providing you offer opportunities for regular use.

Appendix: Sample Sentences With the Verb *see*

I *saw* a man biting a dog yesterday.
I can *see* the sea from my house.
The boss wants to *see* you tomorrow at 2.
Ah, yes, now I *see* what you mean.
Has she been *seeing* anyone since her divorce?
I can't *see* him as president; he's too inexperienced.
I could *see* there was trouble in store for the newlyweds.
I'll *see* you home after the dance if you like.
We *saw* them off at the station.
I'll *see* you. (as in poker)

After you have made sure that all the students understand the meaning of all the sentences, ask them to think of the L1 word they associate with *see* in the first sentence. They should then find the other uses of *see* which correspond with their L1 word and write a summary as follows:

See may only be used as an equivalent of my L1 word in the following contexts: . . .

You can extend the scope by also having the students deal with those cases where *see* is not equivalent to their L1 word.

Contributor

Ronald Sheen teaches in the Faculty of Education of Tottori University, Japan.

Vocabulary Ranking

Levels
Intermediate +

Aims
Explore word meanings

Class Time
10 minutes

Preparation Time
20 minutes

Resources
Ranking activity

Procedure

1. Make a ranking activity based on a word that is useful for the learners. The word may be one from a text that the learners are working on. Here are some examples:

   The word *journey* has many parts to its meaning. Rank the following ideas according to their importance for the meaning of *journey*.
   - Traveling for a long time
   - Going from one place to another
   - Going a long distance
   - Going to another country
   - Involving difficulty
   - Involving mechanical transport

   Collapse. When things collapse, they may affect a lot of people's lives both directly and indirectly. Rank the following items according to the number of people they would affect if they happened in your country.
   - collapse of the transport system
   - collapse of the banking system

168

- collapse of the government
- collapse of law and order

2. Give the activity to the learners to do in small groups.
3. Get the groups to report and justify the result of their ranking to the rest of the class.

Contributor

Paul Nation has taught in Indonesia, Thailand, the United States, and Finland.

Part IV: Developing Vocabulary Strategies

Editor's Note

Strategies for coping with vocabulary include guessing from context clues, using word parts, learning vocabulary in isolation using cards and mnemonic techniques, using dictionaries, and using paraphrase and other procedures to make up for gaps in production.

These strategies enable learners to be independent of teachers and specially prepared texts. They are very important in dealing with the thousands of unknown low frequency words that the learner of English may encounter. This gives these strategies an importance that justifies spending a lot of time on making sure that they are well learned.

Guessing from context is the most important of the strategies. It is the way native speakers most often expand their vocabulary. Research on the strategy makes the following points:

1. Second language learners need to know at least 95% of the running words in a text for guessing to be largely successful (Liu Na & Nation, 1985).
2. Guessing correctly does not necessarily lead to learning (Mondria & Wit-de-Boer, 1991).
3. Learning through guessing is probably a cumulative process for most words, with successful guesses generally resulting in small increments of word knowledge (Nagy, Herman, & Anderson, 1985).
4. Wrong guessing does not seem to inhibit or interfere with later learning of a wrongly guessed word (Mondria & Wit-de-Boer, 1991).
5. Guessing that results from interpreting the language context of an unknown word probably leads to more learning than guessing from background knowledge of the topic (Haastrup, 1989).

The first three activities in this section focus on guessing from context. According to Roberts (1965), about 60% of the low frequency words of English come from French, Latin, or Greek. A large proportion of these words can be broken into parts consisting of affixes and stems. Some of the affixes occur very frequently in English words and thus deserve special attention (Bock, 1948; Stauffer, 1942). It is generally dangerous to use word parts to guess the meaning of a word, but a knowledge of word parts is particularly useful for checking if a guess from context is correct, and for helping fix a newly met word in memory. Awareness of word parts also has the effect of reducing the number of new words to learn. If *destine* and *pre-* are already known, then *predestined* requires much less learning effort. To make effective use of word parts, learners must be able to recognize and know the meanings of the most frequent affixes, and they must be able to see how the meaning of the affixes is related to the meaning of the whole word.

The development of vocabulary learning strategies requires increasingly spaced practice over a period of time. It is of little use to teach a strategy that is poorly understood and has not reached the level of fluent use. Guessing from context for example requires practice over several weeks so that learners are able to use it without causing a major interruption to their reading. The benefits from being able to use this strategy well are so great that the time given to learning is well repaid.

It is useful to have a systematic and organized approach to vocabulary knowledge. The activities in this section that focus on keeping a vocabulary notebook and getting students to teach each other are very good steps toward this.

References

Bock, C. (1948). Prefixes and suffixes. *Classical Journal, 44,* 132–133.

Liu Na, & Nation, I. S. P. (1985). Factors affecting guessing in context. *RELC Journal, 16*(1), 33–42.

Mondria, J-A., & Wit-de-Boer, M. (1991). The effects of contextual richness on the guessability and the retention of words in a foreign language. *Applied Linguistics, 12*(3), 249–267.

Nagy, W. E., Herman, P., & Anderson, R. C. (1985). Learning words from context. *Reading Research Quarterly, 30,* 233–253.

Roberts, A. H. (1965). *A statistical linguistic analysis of American English.* Janua Linguarum, Series Practica 8, The Hague: Mouton.

Stauffer, R. G. (1942). A study of prefixes in the Thorndike list to establish a list of prefixes that should be taught in the elementary school. *Journal of Educational Research, 35*(6), 453–458.

◆ Guessing Words in Context

Nonsense Words

Levels
Intermediate +

Aims
See the value of using
contextual clues

Class Time
15 minutes

Preparation Time
None

Resources
Passage with nonsense
words and questions

Teachers often try to convince students that they do not need to resort to the dictionary for every unknown word they encounter; however, students are often not easily convinced of this fact. The value of this exercise is that students see for themselves that it wastes time to look up every unknown lexical item because a reader can get an approximate meaning based on contextual clues. Most students also find this exercise lots of fun.

Procedure

1. Introduce the concept that it is often possible for readers to understand the approximate meaning of new words from contextual clues, and it is thus unnecessary to look up all new words in the dictionary.
2. Students then read a short narrative that contains "nonsense" words. It is usually necessary to emphasize that the text contains made-up words that are not real and that it is impossible to look them up in a dictionary.
3. Give the students some questions after the reading to allow them to use the nonsense words as if they were real.
4. Allow the students to discuss the questions and their answers in small groups. The students should understand that the questions must be answered using the nonsense words because the objective is not to translate the nonsense words but to use them naturally as any new lexical item is used.

Contributor

Vickie Safari has an MS in TESL and teaches in Georgia State University's Intensive English Program in the United States. She was a Fulbright Lecturer in Pakistan during the 1991–1992 academic year.

Learning From Examples

Levels
Intermediate +

Aims
Develop skill for
guessing from context
Develop productive
knowledge of
vocabulary

Class Time
20 minutes

Preparation Time
5 minutes

Resources
None

Very often, students find it hard to understand the meaning of a new word (particularly a word that entails abstract concepts) without looking it up in a dictionary. Even when the dictionary provides an explanation, learners may still be unable to grasp the full sense of the word and use it appropriately. The technique suggested here helps to address such problems.

Procedure

1. Provide several sample sentences containing the same unknown word.
2. Tell the students to guess meaning from the context provided by the examples. Here is an example teaching *accident*:
   a. Yesterday an *accident* happened to him. A car ran over him when he was crossing the road.
   b. Last week, an *accident* took place in a construction site. The crane suddenly fell down and hit two workmen who were passing by.
   c. Children easily become victims of *accidents* that occur at home. Every year, among hundreds of patients in the children's hospitals, there are those who have been burned by boiling water carelessly placed in the kitchen, those who have swallowed chemicals mistaken for soft drinks and those who have nearly been electrocuted after poking their little fingers into the plugs.
3. Keep on giving examples until the students can respond by saying the word in their first language or show their comprehension by providing further appropriate examples.

Caveats and Options

1. Summarize either orally or by writing on the blackboard all the useful information related to the word, such as part of speech, semantic

properties, register, collocated words, and other features so that students may enter the information into their vocabulary notebooks for future reference.

One of the advantages of using this technique is that it allows the learners to make intelligent guesses from a meaningful context. This will make the learning task much more active, interesting, and challenging than direct explanation of words. Another advantage is that the examples provide input on the semantic properties, register, and even collocation of the word taught. In the above example, the teacher may help the students to draw their own inference that *an accident* normally entails an element of suddenness, unexpectedness, and misfortune. It is used both in spoken and written English, but more often in a serious tone. The collocated words are *happen*, *take place*, *occur*. This will give the learners a better understanding of the usage and use of the word taught. It could be particularly useful in teaching abstract words. The second part of the technique, that is, asking students to offer more examples, is an effective way of checking comprehension and interpretation and provides a smooth transfer from reception to production.

Contributor

Judy Ho teaches in the English Department of the City Polytechnic of Hong Kong.

If You Know What It Means, Prove It

Levels
Any

Aims
Guess the meaning of
words from their use in
context and then use
words in original
sentences

Class Time
10–20 minutes

Preparation Time
10–20 minutes

Resources
List of high frequency
words
A few sentences for
each word

It is very easy for learners to look up words in a bilingual dictionary and restrict their understanding of a word to the first entry in the dictionary. Understanding additional meanings, collocations, and uses of the word in idioms is important for developing depth and breadth in learners' vocabulary.

Procedure

1. Divide the students into teams and explain the rules of the game.
2. Write a word on the board and then use it in a sentence or two. For example: *Waste: It is a waste of money to buy expensive shoes for a baby. Don't waste your time watching TV when you should be studying.*
3. Tell students to raise their hands if they think they know the meaning of the word and, when called on, to use the word in an original sentence. If the sentence uses the word correctly, the respondent's team receives two points. If the use is incorrect, or too ambiguous, the team receives nothing and the game continues until someone uses the word correctly.
4. Continue until you have used all the words, or until a designated amount of time is up. Tally the points and declare a winner.

Because this activity spends a lot of time on each word, it is a good idea to limit its use to high frequency words or words that your particular group of students need for specific purposes.

Contributor

Kenny Harsch is Director of English Education at Kobe YMCA College, Japan. He is interested in learner autonomy, student-centered curriculum development, and helping students discover their own uses for English. He also believes in developing students' ownership of the direction their learning takes.

Guessing From Context

Levels
Intermediate +

Aims
Practice a guessing
strategy

Class Time
30–40 minutes

Preparation Time
None

Resources
Text
Strategy guide sheet
(see Appendix below)

I decided to focus on guessing meanings from context with my reading class. Instead of asking my class to copy the meanings from the dictionary of words they do not know and write sentences using these words, I started to talk to them about using their "microscopic eyes," "microscopic minds," and "strategies."

The goal of this exercise is to figure out the approximate meaning of the unknown word by using different strategies with the aid of their microscopic eyes and minds. Of course, I do tell my students that sometimes they will have to use the dictionary.

Procedure

1. Assign an article. Then, in class, ask the students to point out some words they do not know. Do not allow them to look into the dictionary before doing this exercise.
2. Distribute a vocabulary strategies handout (see below), talk about each strategy, and give ample examples. Some students start to divide words in any way they want to, such as (the purported) suffix *-us* in *unconscious* or prefix *glan-* in *glance*. This discussion helps them to understand what affixes are.
3. In the exercise, have students follow very explicit instructions. Ask them to
- copy the sentence where the word is
- underline the word that they do not know the meaning of
- explain in at least five sentences what strategies in the text guide them to the approximate meaning of the word
- give the meaning
- check the dictionary to see if their approximate meaning is close or not.

Do this exercise with groups, pairs, and individuals.

4. As a group activity, have them write their responses on the board and then review each group's work. Sometimes each group discusses a different word from the article; at other times, they may have the same word. One group may discover strategies that the other groups do not.

Caveats and Options

1. Students tend to look at the general picture; they sweep through an article so fast that they fail to look at certain details for all kinds of reasons. But they should be able to do both—to start asking questions about what they "see" in what they read.

2. This exercise also helps students in another way. Students often say, "I know what it means, but I cannot explain it." Their use of the English language is limited to words, phrases, or short sentences. This exercise forces them to "explain" what is in their minds.

Appendix A: Samples of Student Work

"Five minutes after the bell rang for afternoon class, the Middle-Aged English teachers gradually trickled into the classroom and argued with each other for a few minutes" (from *Iron and Silk* by Mark Saltzman, p. 53). The words I don't understand are *middle-aged* and *trickled into*. Middle-aged is an adjective. I think that *middle* means centre. Human beings could live for one hundred years. Therefore *middle-aged* means 50 years old. *Trickled* is a verb in this sentence. Because of the preposition *into* after the word *trickled* this indicates to me that the person is coming into the classroom. I think that *trickled* means to enter.

(A Haitian-Creole-speaking student)

"When the Communists came and liberated our village, I remember our village people welcomed the soldiers" (from *Iron and Silk*, p. 57). The word is *liberated*. In this case it is a verb. Because of the conjunction *and* between *came* and *liberated* this shows me that those two words are synonymous. But the *liberate* meaning in this sentence is more complex. I think that *liberated* means to free because the village was happy to welcome the soldiers.

(A Spanish-speaking student)

Appendix B: Strategy Guide Sheet

Strategy Guide Sheet

1. Use your "microscopic eye" and "microscopic mind" to look for details.
2. Look for affixes (prefixes and suffixes) in the word.
3. Look at punctuation marks.
4. Look at parallel structures.
5. Look at parts of speech.
6. Look for clause connection clues (conjunctions, transitional words, etc.).
7. Look for meaning relationships in sentences (cause-effect relationships,definitions, cohesive markers).
8. Read the sentences before and after.
9. Read the whole paragraph for context.
10. The more strategies you have in your hands, the more chances you will be able to guess the meaning.

Reference

Saltzman, M. (1986). *Iron and silk.* New York: Vintage Books.

Contributor

Nancy Duke S. Lay, Professor of ESL, teaches at City College, City University of New York, in the United States.

◆ Word Building
Word Family Practice

Levels
Intermediate

Aims
Extend use of
derivational suffixes

Class Time
5–10 minutes

Preparation Time
None

Resources
None

It is useful to make learners aware of regular rules and features that can be generalized in the future, thus making subsequent learning easier for the student. If the main derivational suffixes of English are learned, this can help give the student access to the other members of a word family, even though only one member may be initially learned. This simple activity is intended to raise students' consciousness about this fact, and to give them practice in manipulating the parts of speech of different members of a word family.

Procedure

1. When a new word is introduced, write it on the blackboard along with its part of speech.
2. Ask the students to give (or guess if they don't know) the other related words in the word family along with their parts of speech and write them on the blackboard also. Point out the regular suffixes that signal different parts of speech.

After this activity is used a few times, some students may begin to realize that they already know many words that are related to the newly introduced words. This should encourage them to look for derivational relationships in the future. When the students can formulate the derivations on their own, this activity can be used occasionally to remind them to continue thinking in terms of word groups.

Contributor

Norbert Schmitt is a lecturer at Minatogawa Women's College in Hyogo, Japan. His main interests are L2 vocabulary acquisition and vocabulary testing. He is currently researching the effects of various types of word knowledge on vocabulary acquisition.

Peer Teaching Prefixes

Levels
Advanced

Aims
Learn important
prefixes

Class Time
20 minutes

Preparation Time
15 minutes

Resources
List of prefixes with
their meanings and
example words
List of meanings of the
prefixes in a different
order

Procedure

1. Form the learners into pairs. One person in a pair will be the teacher and the other will be the learner.
2. Give each learner who is acting as the teacher the list of prefixes with the meaning and the example words. Here is an example of part of a list.

ad-	to(ward)	admit, advance
com-	together, with	composition, concentrate
dis-	not	disagree
ex-	out, beyond	extract

3. Give each learner who is acting as a learner the list of meanings. Here is an example of part of a list.

   not
   to
   out
   with

4. Show the "teachers" the following procedure for teaching the other learner.
   - Say the prefix two or three times and then say an example word.
   - The learner has to look at the list of meanings and choose the right meaning.
   - If the learner does not choose the right meaning by the third attempt, the teacher tells the answer.
   - Before moving on to a new prefix, revise the ones just practiced.

Contributor

Paul Nation is Editor of this volume.

Word Building

Aims
Develop knowledge of
word forms
Extend the range of
meanings for known
words

Class Time
20 minutes

Preparation Time
5 minutes

Resources
None

Procedure

1. Choose a set of words or forms to work with. These could be prepositions, prefixes or suffixes, phrasal verbs (e.g., the preposition *against*;
or the suffix *-ful*).
2. Ask students to form groups and to think of many ways in which the
word can be used. In the case of *against*, for example, students might
produce:
> Lean against the wall.
> I'm against your suggestion.
> For and against.
> It's against my expectation.
> I'm not against what you say.
> It's against the law.
3. Set a time limit and let students use their imaginations. By pooling
their resources, they should be able to generate at least six or more
examples.
4. Ask groups to read out their examples. Give further explanations
concerning usage. Correct any unacceptable explanations and give
reasons.

After all the examples have been gathered, get the class to classify them
into meaning groups or to find the underlying meaning of the item.

Caveats and Options

Contributor

Ronald Jackup is a freelance ESL teacher and writer.

Prefixes: A Word Game

Levels
Beginning

Aims
Learn prefixes

Class Time
10 minutes

Preparation Time
1 hour

Resources
Cardboard, scissors, felt-tip pens

This game helps in follow up work in guessing meanings of words from context, in using the meanings of prefixes to confirm a guess. The game also helps beginners review parts of speech.

Procedure

1. Cut up cardboard into equal sizes about 5 centimeters x 3 centimeters (about 2 inches x 1 inch). The number of pieces depends on the size of the class, but there should be 16 pieces for every group of four.
2. For each group, print on the cards:
   - four words beginning with prefixes you want learners to know
   - the meanings of the words
   - the parts of speech of the words
   - the meanings of the prefixes
3. Tell each member of the group to take four cards, one from each of the categories above. The aim for the group is to make four sets of four cards.
4. Have each learner contribute a card from each of the categories above in order to complete each set. Learners do not look at each other's cards but describe them to each other.

Caveats and Options

When the set is complete, learners can place the word in context by making up sentences using the words. Groups can also exchange cards with other groups who may have other words and prefixes. When learners become familiar with the prefixes, the class can have a competition as to which group is able to make up the set and write four correct sentences, either first or within a limited period of time.

Contributor

Nikhat Shameem teaches at the English Language Institute, Victoria University of Wellington, New Zealand. She is researching the maintenance of the Fiji Hindi language in New Zealand.

Word Formation Game

Levels
Intermediate +

Aims
Study four processes of
word formation in
English
Practice creating words

Class Time
45–60 minutes for
15–20 students

Preparation Time
None

Resources
Optional handout (see
Appendix below)

Students have no difficulty understanding the patterns of word formation, and in fact frequently invent existing but unfamiliar words. This game requires students to work in teams which are told they cannot use real words as game entries. To comply with this rule, team members are forced to exchange information about existing vocabulary in the process of producing new words.

Procedure

1. Divide the class into teams. The game works most effectively if teams have equally mixed English proficiency levels.
2. Explain the following word formation processes (McManis, Stollenwerk, & Zheng-Shen, 1987) to the class:
   a. An acronym is the result of combining the first sounds or letters of principle words in a phrase. *Radar* is an acronym for "radio detecting and ranging," while *scuba* represents "self-contained underwater breathing apparatus."
   b. Blending is a process that combines parts of existing words to produce new words. *Clash* is derived from "clap" and "crash"; *because* came from "by" and "cause."
   c. Compounding combines entire words to produce new vocabulary items, such as *flashlight*, *doorknob*, and *headache*.
   d. Clipping produces short words from longer words, such as *phone* from "telephone" and *gas* from "gasoline."
3. Have each team gather and make as many words as possible using the processes. After approximately 20 minutes of deliberation, one member of each team writes the team's entries on the blackboard.
4. Ask the class as a whole to decide if each entry follows a rule of word formation. Teams must supply definitions. The teacher or any

class member may note whether the entry is an existing word. A team wins by making up the largest number of new words. Students usually need to be reminded that the point of the game is to create words, not to list familiar vocabulary. A team must have entries in all categories and be able to give definitions for each entry.

Caveats and Options

Give one point for known words and two points for well-made created words.

Appendix: Optional Handout for Students: Word Formation Game

Directions

1. The purpose of this game is to explain some of the ways that new words enter the English language. You can increase your vocabulary by understanding the patterns of word formation.
2. The teacher will divide the class into teams.
3. Team members make up new words to fit the word formation rules. The team that makes up the most words wins. Every word must follow a rule of word formation. (Some of the words will turn out to be real words anyway.)
4. A team cannot win unless it has made up at least one word for every category.
5. Be prepared to give a definition for each word your team creates.
6. After you have worked with your team for 20 minutes, one person from each team will write its list of words on the blackboard. The class as a whole will decide if each entry conforms to a rule. The teacher is the judge in case of a difference of opinion. Real words will be identified at this time.

Category A—Compound words are new words created by combining two existing words, such as *flashlight* (flash + light), *rainbow* (rain + bow), *toothbrush* (tooth + brush), and *doorknob* (door + knob).

Category B—Acronyms are the result of combining the first sounds or letters of important words in a phrase. *Radar* is an acronym for "radio detecting and ranging." *Scuba* comes from "self-contained underwater breathing apparatus."

Category C—Blending is a process which creates new words by combining parts of other words. *Clash* is derived from "clap" and "crash." *Because* is a blend of "by" and "cause."

Category D—Clipping produces new words by shortening an existing word, such as *phone* from "telephone" and *gas* from "gasoline."

Reference

McManis, C., Stollenwerk, D., & Zheng-Sheng, Z. (Eds.). (1987). *Language files* (4th ed.). Reynoldsburg, OH: Advocate Publishing Group.

Contributor

Michele Kilgore is an ESL instructor at Georgia State University in the United States. She has a MS in Applied Linguistics and is working on her doctorate.

Find the Prefixes and Suffixes

Levels
Intermediate +

Aims
Recognize suffixes and prefixes

Class Time
10–15 minutes

Preparation Time
None

Resources
A variety of short (five-paragraph) newspaper articles

Lists of prefixes and suffixes can help students to build up their vocabulary and are especially useful for "creating" words needed in composition writing.

Procedure

1. Give each learner a different newspaper article.
2. Tell the learners to make a list of all the prefixes and suffixes they find in their article. The affixes must be put under appropriate headings of noun, verb, adjective and adverb.
3. When they finish, tell them to swap articles with each other.
4. Organize the learners into pairs to compare notes on the suffixes and prefixes found. Points in dispute may be clarified by the teacher.
5. At the end of the exercise, tell the learners to add any new suffixes or prefixes learned from the exercise to their own personal record of suffixes and prefixes, under appropriate parts of speech.

Caveats and Options

1. It helps if students know some prefixes and suffixes from previous learning.
2. Get all the learners to use the same article and compare notes. The exercise may take less time to finish, and the teacher may go over it with the class, rather than use peer tutoring.

Contributor

Maria Verivaki studied at Victoria University of Wellington in New Zealand and now teaches English in Greece.

♦ Using Dictionaries

Using the Dictionary: Common Words, Uncommon Usage

Levels
Intermediate

Aims
Practice using a
dictionary

Class Time
20 minutes

Preparation Time
10 minutes

Resources
A learners' dictionary,
such as *Collins
COBUILD*, or the
*Longman Dictionary of
Contemporary English*

This activity draws attention to words with an easy, or frequent, surface meaning, but which are being used with a less frequent, unusual, or rare meaning in a text. Learners are likely to be aware of the common or frequent meaning of the word but unaware of the special usage. The activity combines two independent learning strategies: guessing from context, and, using a dictionary.

Procedure

1. Draw attention to a common word that is being used in an uncommon way in a text. For example, from a magazine on home decorating: *The walls were painted in pale terracotta, with the door mouldings* picked out *in a rich shade of aqua*. The learner identifies a similar example in a reading text.

2. Model the procedure for dealing with these for the learner.
   - Use the guessing from context procedure (Nation, 1990) to come to an estimate of the meaning.
   - Check the guess by looking up the unusual usage in a learner dictionary under the common form. Read through the various entries under the common form until a matching meaning is found.
   - Other examples that the teacher might model are:
     He was *picked up* by the police for questioning.
     She entered the church, and felt the cold *flags* under her hot and tired feet.
     He came home *plastered* after the party.
     This year, Wimbledon was won by the number three *seed*.

3. The learners follow the teacher's model independently.
   - The learners apply the procedure for guessing from context to the unfamiliar item.
   - Once they have reached the stage of guessing the meaning, they check their guess by looking the word or phrase up in a learner dictionary. In the above example: *The walls were painted in pale terracotta, with the door mouldings* picked out *in a rich shade of aqua. Picked out* can be found on p. 1078 of *COBUILD* as a separate entry under *pick*. The appropriate meaning is the second listed under *pick out*: "If part of something that is painted is *picked out* in white or in a bright colour, it is painted in that colour so that it can be clearly seen beside the other parts. e.g. . . .*mouldings picked out in white.*"

Caveats and Options

Ask the learners to prepare an example of these types of word usage for sharing with their classmates.

Reference

Nation, I. S. P. (1990). *Teaching and learning vocabulary.* New York: Heinle & Heinle.

Contributor

Mary Boyce teaches at the English Language Institute, Victoria University of Wellington, New Zealand.

Think, Consult, Compare

Levels
Intermediate +

Aims
Develop dictionary
skills

Class Time
20 minutes

Preparation Time
5 minutes

Resources
Dictionaries

Procedure

1. Give the learners a list of words and get them to write them done one side of a page with four additional columns drawn across the page.
2. Tell them to write their meaning for the word in the first column, an example using the word in the second column and the dictionary definition in the third column. They should not fill the third column for a word until they have filled the first column.
3. Tell the learners to look carefully between the meaning they gave in the first column and the dictionary meaning.

Caveats and Options

1. Add another column for the first language translation(s).
2. Set out the first column like a definition, for example

   An *octagon* is a _____ that _____ .

Contributor

Dorothy Brown has trained teachers of English and taught English in New Zealand, Australia, China, Malaysia, and Samoa.

Using the Dictionary to Produce Sentences

Levels
Intermediate +

Aims
Develop dictionary
skills

Class Time
10 minutes

Preparation Time
5 minutes

Resources
English-English learner
dictionaries

Dictionaries are usually used to find out the meanings of unknown words. However, learners' dictionaries contain a great deal of information that learners can use to use vocabulary productively. This activity develops this skill.

Procedure

1. Write an unfamiliar word on the blackboard and tell the learners to form groups.
2. Tell the learners to follow these steps to gather information about the word that will help them write an original sentence containing the word.
   a. Find the meaning of the word
   b. Use the grammar notes and examples in the dictionary to find out about the grammar of the word.
      - What part of speech is it?
      - If it is a noun is it countable or uncountable?
      - If it is a verb, does it take an object?
   c. Look at the examples and note the similarity in their sentence patterns.
   d. Copy these patterns to write a new sentence.
4. Have each group write its sentence on the board and discuss the results.

Contributor

Paul Nation's interests include the teaching and learning of vocabulary and teaching methodology.

Using a Dictionary of Synonyms

Levels
Intermediate +

Aims
Distinguish synonyms
Use a monolingual
dictionary

Class Time
30–45 minutes

Preparation Time
10 minutes

Resources
Dictionary of synonyms
Page from a reading
text or previous student
writing assignment
worksheet (see
Appendix below)

This activity is to introduce the students to a helpful vocabulary learning tool, a dictionary of synonyms. The students will also be made aware of the need to make distinctions among largely synonymous words.

Procedure

1. Show the students a dictionary of synonyms. Invite the students to suggest one English word to look up.
2. Ask one student to look up the word the others suggested. Write four or five synonyms for the word on the blackboard. Ask the students to suggest any differences between the synonyms.
3. Pass out a text (either a previously completed student writing assignment or a short selection from a reading task) with one key word marked. Have the students complete the worksheet on the word marked.
4. After completing the activity, ask the students to repeat the same procedure with other words from the text.

Caveats and Options

Instead of working alone, the learners can be divided into groups of three or four. Ask them to work together on a key word.

Appendix: Sample Worksheet: Distinguishing Synonyms

1. Write down the key word from the reading text that you will look up in the dictionary of synonyms. Next to it, write at least three words of which this key word reminds you.

   _____   _____

   _____

2. Look up the word in a dictionary of synonyms. Write four synonyms on the lines below. Next to each word, explain the difference between it and the key word written in No. 1.

   A _____   _____

   _____

   B _____   _____

   _____

   C _____   _____

   _____

   D _____   _____

   _____

3. Write down one of the five words above that you feel best fits the context. Explain why.

   _____

Contributor

Hugh Rutledge graduated from Boston University in 1988. He has taught in East Asia for several years and is Head of Faculty at Tokyo International College in Japan.

◆ Giving Learners Control

Learners' Choice

Levels
Intermediate +

Aims
Become involved in
lesson planning

Class Time
None

Preparation Time
5 minutes

Resources
Small pieces of paper

The ideas behind this procedure are that learners, particularly at intermediate levels and above:
- differ with regard to their knowledge of words
- differ with regard to their vocabulary needs
- are capable of deciding which words they want to know and how
  well they want to know them
- are more receptive to words that they themselves have chosen for
  review

Procedure

1. Place small piles of cut up scrap paper within easy reach of all learners.
2. Tell the learners to write words or phrases that occur in the lesson
   and that they would like to review in class on these small slips of
   paper, one word or phrase per slip. If appropriate, they can also be
   asked to indicate (with an *A* or a *P*) whether they would like this
   item to become part of their active or passive vocabulary.
3. Collect accumulated slips at any time and incorporate them in the
   ongoing lesson, or else use them as the raw material for a vocabulary
   recycling/review activity in some later lesson.

Contributor

Heather Murray teaches at Universität Bern in Switzerland.

Keeping a Vocabulary Book

Levels
Any

Aims
Learn how to keep a
useful record of new
vocabulary

Class Time
20 minutes

Preparation Time
None

Resources
A blank pocket-sized
book with strong covers

Students often have difficulty remembering new words or phrases they encounter in their reading or in other language classes. Many students find it useful to keep a vocabulary book in which they record and classify words which they want to remember.

Procedure

1. Show the students how to organize the new vocabulary that they put into their book. Words can be organized in three ways.
   - Write down all the new words from one unit of a book together on the same page.
   - Organize the words alphabetically, like a dictionary.
   - Keep sections of the book for different topics or areas, such as hobbies, sports, or for phrases.
2. Encourage the students to record more than just a word's meaning, or translation. These points can be considered.
   - Is it a noun, verb, or adjective etc.?
   - If it is a phrase, has the whole phrase been entered?
   - Will an example of the word in context be helpful?
   - Is there any other useful information about the word?
3. Provide time for the students to review their entries regularly, to help remember new words.

Ronald Jackup is a freelance ESL teacher and writer.

Contributor

Student-to-Student Vocabulary Teaching

Levels
Intermediate +

Aims
Take responsibility for
own learning

Class Time
10 minutes

Preparation Time
None

Resources
None

Procedure

1. In the first lesson, demonstrate how students should keep a vocabulary notebook. While there are numerous techniques for doing this, for the purposes of this activity it is suggested that a word with one or two roots and several different forms be used. For example, *manipulate* can appear like this:

   Forms

V	N	person	adjective	adverb
manipulate	manipulation	manipulator	manipulative	
	manipulatively			

   Roots
   man(i) = hand, by hand   pul = to pull
   Words using the root
   manufacture
   manage
   manual

   Context of occurrence

   People manipulate the movements of puppets by pulling strings attached to the puppet.
   Lobbyists try to manipulate the political process from behind the scenes.

2. Assign students words and ask them to replicate the analysis you modeled.

3. As homework, assign one or two students for each lesson to bring in two words to teach their classmates using the techniques above.

There are two differences, however, in how they are to teach their classmates. Firstly, the context of occurrence should be the actual occurrence, in other words, where the students actually came across the words. This may be in an advertisement, a graded reader, or the newspaper. The point is that students make the effort to expose themselves to authentic English outside the classroom. Secondly, students report the following information when teaching the word:

- Where they were when they found the word
- What they were doing at the time
- Who they were with
- What the date and time were
- Where they first recorded the word
- Why they thought the word was valuable

4. The students teach the words, roots and context as a minipresentation in front of the class. It works well as a warm up and before and after breaks.
5. Keep a record of the words taught and periodically give quizzes. The students can often be helped into remembering the words by reminding them of the context in which they were learned.

Contributor

Patrick Colabucci teaches and develops curricula for Japanese companies.

Vocabulary Cards

Levels
Any

Aims
Learn new vocabulary

Class Time
15 minutes

Preparation Time
None

Resources
Small cards

Using vocabulary cards is a word learning strategy for independent learning in or out of class. On one side of the card is written the word to be learned. On the other side is the word's meaning, usually in the form of a first language translation.

Procedure

1. Show the learners how to make and learn from cards. When learning from cards they should keep changing the order of the cards, use mnemonic tricks to fix the meaning in their mind, look at the cards at spaced intervals rather than spending a long amount of time in one go, and make sure that similar words are not in the same group of cards.
2. The learners make 10–15 cards each day and keep a record of their progress.

Caveats and Options

1. If learners prepare their own cards, you may wish to check the words they choose and the translations.
2. The students can exchange cards they have already studied.
3. In addition to a translation, the cards could contain a context for the word.

Contributor

David Hirsh gained an MA from Victoria University of Wellington, New Zealand, in 1993. He has taught in New Zealand and Thailand.

The Keyword Technique

Levels
Any

Aims
Discover a way to
improve the learning of
new vocabulary

Class Time
20 minutes

Preparation Time
None

Resources
None

The keyword technique involves associating the new word with a similar sounding word in the L1. The technique works in this way. Imagine the learner wants to learn the English word *salary*. The learner thinks of a word in the L1 which sounds like *salary* or sounds like the beginning of the word *salary*. For an Indonesian learner of English, this L1 word might be *salah*, which means "mistake, error, or wrong." This first language word is the keyword. The learner now imagines the meaning of the English word *salary* and the meaning of the Indonesian keyword *salah* joined together. For example, the learner might think of someone being paid the wrong salary, or being paid a salary for doing things wrongly.

Procedure

1. Describe the technique and demonstrate its use with a personal example in a language you have learned.
2. Select several words and write them with their meaning on the blackboard. Have the students think up their own keywords and images.

Caveats and Options

1. This technique can take time and practice to develop. Learners may need encouragement if they have difficulty in choosing keywords or making associations.
2. Keywords can be made from known L2 words instead of only L1 words.

Contributor

David Hirsh gained an MA from Victoria University of Wellington, New Zealand, in 1993. He has taught in New Zealand and Thailand.

In Other Words
(A Paraphrasing Game)

Levels
Any

Aims
Practice paraphrasing

Class Time
10–30 minutes

Preparation Time
20–30 minutes

Resources
Word cards

Paraphrasing is a very useful strategy for learners of a second language. It helps them to explain to their interlocutor what they mean when they cannot think of the right word in the second language or are trying to explain the meaning of a word of their native language.

Procedure

1. Write some of the following on the board (whichever you feel are useful for your class):
   It's a THING that . . .
   It's a PERSON who . . .
   It's a PLACE where . . .
   It's an IDEA that . . .
   It's a GROUP of . . .
   It's a KIND of . . .
   It's SOMETHING you do when . . .
   It's THE WAY you feel when . . .

   Tell the students they can substitute a more accurate word for the word in capital letters (e.g., "It's a book that has words" instead of "It's a thing that has words"), but the capital letter words are there to fall back on if they can't think of a substitute word.

2. Show students the word cards and explain that each card has a word on it. You will describe a word from a card, using one of the openers on the board, and they have to try to guess the word.

3. Put students into teams, draw a card and paraphrase it. If nobody can guess correctly, give further paraphrases of the word until someone guesses. Give that student's team one point, and go on to the next card.

4. After you feel the students are comfortable with the game, have the student who guessed the last card come up and give a paraphrase of the next card, and so on until time is up. (An alternative would be to have each student come up in turn and paraphrase a word from a card.)
5. Count the points for each team and declare a winner.

Contributor

Kenny Harsch is Director of English Education at Kobe YMCA College, Japan. He is interested in learner autonomy, student-centered curriculum development, and helping students discover their own uses for English. He also believes in developing students' ownership of the direction their learning takes.

Part V: Developing Fluency With Known Vocabulary

Editor's Note

It is not sufficient to have a large vocabulary. Learners must be able to access and use this knowledge fluently. Fluency is being able to make the most effective use of what is already known. This comes from having a well-organized system of knowledge that has been well practiced in meaningful activities. For vocabulary learning, this means that learners should have plenty of opportunity to make use of known vocabulary over the range of language skills and in a range of contexts.

The most suitable activities for fluency practice are ones in which a substantial part of the requirements of the task are already within the experience and capability of the learner. This happens if

1. the activity uses familiar language items. That is, the vocabulary and grammatical constructions required in the activity are already known by the learner.
2. the content matter of the activity is familiar. That is, the learner is quite at home with the ideas that are involved in the activity. This can occur if the learner is drawing on knowledge from the learner's own culture, from previous experience, from preparation before the activity, or from planned experience activities such as visits, watching films, or project work before the main activity.
3. the organization of the discourse and the activity itself are already familiar to the learner.

When the language, ideas, and discourse in an activity are already familiar to a learner, and when the activity itself is already familiar, learners are able to give their attention to improving the level of skill with which they perform the activity. This enables them to make use of the vocabulary in the activity with a higher than normal level of fluency.

Activities that contain many unfamiliar elements are likely to produce hesitant, uncertain language use.

This section is the shortest one in this book because it is here that vocabulary learning overlaps most of all with developing the skills of listening, speaking, reading, and writing. For a much wider range of activities to develop fluency with vocabulary through use, it is necessary to look at the other volumes in the New Ways series.

Vocabulary Exercises

Levels
Beginning

Aims
Develop familiarity with
the written form of
known words

Class Time
10 minutes

Preparation Time
20 minutes

Resources
Prepared exercises

The acquisition of new words is only the first step in the process of vocabulary learning. The students must subsequently learn to recognize these words in another context and learn to use them on proper occasions. Whether one can remember and use words learned previously largely depends on frequent practice. For this reason, teachers must give ample practice in using the words they teach in drills.

Sample Exercises

1. Recognition of the right word

Look at the following word list. A "test word" is followed by four other words, one of which is exactly the same as the test word. Read as fast as you can and underline the word which is the same as the test word.

quiet: quite quilt quill <u>quiet</u>
mild: mile milk mild mill
beer: peer beer deer dear

2. Word-pair recognition

Look at the following list of phrases. They are in pairs. Some of them are exactly the same, some are not. Read them quickly, write S if the two phrases are the same, and D if they are different.

a.   poor man   poor men (D)
b.   next stop   next stop
c.   good book   good boot

3. Word matches

Find the words that are exactly the same in spelling in the two columns, linking the word pair with a pencil:

either   whether
neither   /   whither
whether   either

        weather   wither
        wither   neither
        whither   weather

4. Recognition of the meaning of words

Look at the following word list. A "test word" is followed by four other words. Underline the word that is nearest in meaning to the test word.

        easy: busy   lazy   <u>simple</u>   ready
        big: small middle large   little
        ship: boot   boat   sheep   bus

5. Recognition of words according to their prefixes and suffixes

   a. Mark the parts of speech of the following pairs of words:

   (v)   (n)

        sing—singer   each—teacher   weak—weakness
        dark—darkness   quick—quickly   slow—slowly
        translate—translation lock—unlock   tell—retell
        care—careful   meaning—meaningless

   b. Match the words in the two columns that are most closely related:

        sing   swimmer
        dance   teacher
        teach   singer
        write   traveller
        play   dancer
        swim   writer
        travel player

Even at the earlier stages of reading, some idea about word formation would be helpful to increase the students' word power. The temptation to talk systematically and volubly about word formation, however, should be resisted at this stage of learning.

6. Filling the blanks with the appropriate words

   I first met Mr. Lee _____ he was working at the Central TV University, _____ at the time was the _____ important educational center in China. Mr. Lee introduced me to some of his colleagues _____ were working with him on the new English course. I looked at the work _____ Mr. Lee's colleagues were doing. Since then, Mr. Lee and I _____ met several times, and he _____ shown me some books _____ have helped me in my own work. Mr. Lee is one of the _____ helpful people _____ I have ever met.

Contributor

Zhang Decong is Lecturer in English and Dean of the English Department at Hanzhong Teacher's College, China. He has taught English for more than 30 years and has published widely in China. His interests include research on grammar, lexicology, pragmatics, and applied linguistics.

What Did They Say?

Levels
Intermediate

Aims
Practice the spoken language

Class Time
20 minutes

Preparation Time
15 minutes

Resources
Dialogue of 20–30 lines

Caveats and Options

Contributor

Procedure

1. From the dialogue, choose 12–15 segments of remarks. Then omit the selected segments and write out the passage.
2. If it is necessary, write a few lines to give the students a guide to the context and the characters concerned.
3. Make enough copies for the whole class.
4. Distribute copies of the dialogue to the students. Tell them to read it through and put down suggestions for the missing segments.
5. After 10 minutes, ask them to form small groups and compare the suggestions they have noted. They should also record any new ideas that come up in their discussion.
6. Invite each group to call out its suggestions. Put these on the board.
7. Review the different suggestions and correct any mistakes or inappropriate ideas.
8. Reveal the original wording.

In preparing the material, there are many ways of giving a particular language focus to the activity. You could, for instance, concentrate on the use of correct vocabulary, the use of correct verbs/verb tenses, or other structures relevant to the focus of your class.

Matilda Wong teaches in the Department of English in the City Polytechnic of Hong Kong.

Say That Again

Levels
Intermediate

Aims
Practice known words
in context

Class Time
20 minutes

Preparation Time
15 minutes

Resources
Two lists of sentences

The Say That Again game has proved extremely popular and effective with diverse groups of learners.

Procedure

1. Divide the class into two teams.
2. Choose representatives of both teams to read the sentences, each of which forms half of a simple conversational exchange. Put numbers corresponding to the sentences in a grid on the board.
3. Select a number and have the student representative read the corresponding sentence.
4. Select a second number. If the two sentences "match" (i.e., form a logical pair), award a point, cross off the numbers, and allow the same team to continue. If they do not match, the other team gets a turn. (No writing is allowed as this would enable players to simply reproduce the answer key, thereby defeating the purpose of the game.)
5. Play continues in the above manner until all pairs have been found and successfully matched; if one team is trailing by several points, the last play can be made a "bonus" to allow for a dramatic, come-from-behind victory. (Awarding a million points heightens the dramatic effect and ends the game on a delightfully silly note.)

Caveats and Options

If decontextualized practice of individual words is desired, the same format lends itself equally well to this purpose; pairs consisting of L1 and L2 equivalents or of L1 words and L2 definitions simply replace the sentences in the above procedure.

Contributor

Richard Dean teaches in Japan.

Using Maps for Practice

Levels
Intermediate +

Aims
Practice prepositions
and other vocabulary

Class Time
20 minutes

Preparation Time
10 minutes

Resources
Large town plan or map
Smaller copies of the
map
Counters representing
objects

Introduced as a teacher-directed activity, the exercise is easily used in pair and group work.

Procedure

1. Provide the students either with a large-scale town plan indicating names of buildings, streets, and other features or a large-scale ordnance survey-type map marked with geographical features such as rivers, hills, roads, and villages. Also give the students counters or chips marked with the names of the objects they represent, such as *car, horse, house, village, shop.*
2. Pin the map on the board or wall so the class can see it.
3. Ask questions based on the map. The learners write the answers.
    - What is the name of the highest mountain?
    - Which is the nearest village to the mountain?
    - Which river is . . . village on?
    - Which store is opposite the bank?
    - How many traffic lights are there on . . . Street?
4. Get the students to place the counters on the map according to instructions, such as the following:
    - Park two cars on . . . Street.
    - Put a horse in the field behind the church.
    - Place a house next to the library.
    - Position a village where the River . . . and the River . . . meet.
    - Place a village between the two highest mountains.
5. Students can then come to the front to carry out the instructions on the wall map in order that all the class may check what they have done.

Caveats and Options

1. For a variation on this exercise, give the students a blank piece of paper with which to create a map. The points of the compass are assumed to be conventionally placed. Give instructions as to where to draw features; however, if the class is sufficiently advanced, students may also take turns in giving instructions. Examples might be:
   - Draw a coastline at the eastern edge of the map and color the sea blue.
   - Draw a river (A) across the map from west to east. The river is going to the coast in the east.
   - Draw another river (B) starting from the northwest, meeting the other river in the middle of the map.
   - Show a mountain with a circle between the two rivers on the western edge of the map.
   - Place a bridge just below where the rivers meet.
   - Place a village where the two rivers meet.
2. As this task is quite demanding, and subsequent instructions depend on the accuracy of carrying out the previous ones, it is useful to have a large blank piece of paper on the wall or board, in order to place each feature accurately after the students have had a chance to do it themselves on their own maps.

Contributor

Ronald Sheen teaches in the Faculty of Education of Tottori University, Japan.

Listen Very Carefully

Levels
Beginning +

Aims
Become involved in producing descriptive vocabulary

Class Time
20 minutes

Preparation Time
None

Resources
Campus area outside the classroom to accommodate 10–40 people

Procedure

1. Ask the class bring paper and pencils with them as they move from the regular classroom to elsewhere on campus.
2. Ask them to sit down, close their eyes for 2 minutes, listen very carefully, and try to remember what they hear, so that they can write out five things later on.
3. Time the exercise, and tell the class to open their eyes and in 2 minutes list five things they heard, for example: *wind blowing, noisy classrooms.*
4. Have the learners walk around for a few minutes and pay attention to the surroundings. They should note on paper five things they saw, for example: *a physical education lesson, birds resting on a tree.* Then have the learners write out five words or phrases to describe the atmosphere: how they feel and how they think living things around them feel at the time of observation, for example: *hot, very excited.*
5. When the learners have returned to the classroom, have them call out what they heard, what they saw, and how they and others felt, while you write it down on the board.
6. Suggest related vocabulary, based on the learners' descriptions.

Caveats and Options

For intermediate learners, focus explicitly on parts of speech (with the additional purpose of reviewing parts of speech):

- What they hear: List five nouns and five adjectives.
- What they see: List five nouns and five verbs or adverbs.
- Mood: how they or others feel: List five adjectives or adverbs.

Contributor

Wai-king Tsang teaches in the English Department of the City Polytechnic of Hong Kong.

Also available from TESOL

All Things to All People
Donald N. Flemming, Lucie C. Germer, and Christiane Kelley

A New Decade of Language Testing Research:
Selected Papers from the 1990 Language Testing Research Colloquium
Dan Douglas and Carol Chapelle, Editors

Books for a Small Planet:
An Multicultural/Intercultural Bibliography
for Young English Language Learners
Dorothy S. Brown

Common Threads of Practice:
Teaching English to Children Around the World
Katharine Davies Samway and Denise McKeon, Editors

Dialogue Journal Writing with Nonnative English Speakers:
A Handbook for Teachers
Joy Kreeft Peyton and Leslee Reed

Dialogue Journal Writing with Nonnative English Speakers:
An Instructional Packet for Teachers and Workshop Leaders
Joy Kreeft Peyton and Jana Staton

Directory of Professional Preparation Programs
in TESOL in the United States, 1992–1994
Helen Kornblum, with Ellen Garshick, Editors

Discourse and Performance
of International Teaching Assistants
Carolyn G. Madden and Cynthia L. Myers, Editors

Diversity as Resource:
Redefining Cultural Literacy
Denise E. Murray, Editor

New Ways in Teaching Reading
Richard R. Day, Editor

New Ways in Teacher Education
Donald Freeman, with Steve Cornwell, Editors

Students and Teachers Writing Together:
Perspectives on Journal Writing
Joy Kreeft Peyton, Editor

Video in Second Language Teaching:
Using, Selecting, and Producing Video for the Classroom
Susan Stempleski and Paul Arcario, Editors

For more information, contact
Teachers of English to Speakers of Other Languages, Inc.
1600 Cameron Street, Suite 300
Alexandria, Virginia 22314 USA
Tel 703-836-0774 ● Fax 703-836-7864

FRESH FOOD NATION

Simple, Seasonal Recipes *from* America's Farmers

FRESH FOOD NATION

Simple, Seasonal Recipes *from* America's Farmers

Martha Holmberg

The Taunton Press

 The Taunton Press
Inspiration for hands-on living®

The Taunton Press, Inc.
63 South Main Street
PO Box 5506, Newtown, CT
06470-5506
e-mail: tp@taunton.com

EDITOR: **CAROLYN MANDARANO**
COPY EDITOR: **VALERIE CIMINO**
INDEXER: **HEIDI BLOUGH**
DESIGN & LAYOUT: **CAROL SINGER | NOTICE DESIGN**
PHOTOGRAPHER: **KATHRYN BARNARD**
FOOD AND PROP STYLIST: **CALLIE MEYER**

The following names/manufacturers appearing in *Fresh Food Nation* are trademarks:
Barilla®, Bob's Red Mill®, King Arthur®, Mae Ploy®, Old Style®, Pabst Blue Ribbon®, Thai
Kitchen®, Tinkyada®

LIBRARY OF CONGRESS CATALOGING-IN-PUBLICATION DATA IN PROGRESS

ISBN # 978-1-60085-714-0

PRINTED IN THE UNITED STATES OF AMERICA
10 9 8 7 6 5 4 3 2 1

To farmers everywhere, who do such important work and who get to participate in the miracle of tiny seeds becoming delicious food.

If I've learned one thing from this project, it's that it takes masses of people to run a farm—from the farm family to the field workers, washers, and packers; people with great handwriting to create the adorable chalkboards listing "Today's Produce"; the CSA members and farmer's market customers who commit to buying the wonderful food and who frequently volunteer to work at the farm itself; to the whole community, which benefits from the preservation of farmland, whether in the rural countryside or in a green oasis in the city.

And so it was with this book. Masses of friends and colleagues helped me by recommending farms in their regions. In particular, thanks to Hugh Acheson, Brigid Callinan of Idaho State University College of Technology Culinary Arts, Piper Davis, Meredith Deeds, Rebekah Denn, Naomi Duguid, Laura Ford, Dabney Gough, Kathy Gunst, Sarah Hart, David Joachim, Janet Keeler, Amanda Levin, Susie Middleton, Jan Newberry, Susan Puckett, Catherine Ryan, Amelia Saltsman, Molly Stevens, Andrea Weigl, Dawn Woodward, the people at various Edible Communities and Slow Food chapters, and, of course, localharvest.org. I'm so sorry if I'm leaving someone out!

Special thanks to Ashley Gartland and Caroline Ford for their great support in the kitchen and beyond, and to awesome new intern TaMara Edens. And, of course, huge thanks to Carolyn Mandarano, Alison Wilkes, Carol Singer, and my other good friends at my "alma mater," The Taunton Press. And gratitude, along with big hugs, to the photo team of Kathryn Barnard and Callie Meyer for their gorgeous photography and for introducing me to the best prop store ever.

Contents

Eating with the Harvest

Fresh Food Nation is a book about cooking with seasonal vegetables and fruit. You may be getting yours from a CSA (Community Supported Agriculture organization), from your local farmstand or farmer's market, from your own garden, or simply from the supermarket. Where you get your produce doesn't matter—what counts is that you're cooking from scratch with fresh, wholesome ingredients.

The recipes in this book were contributed by people whose lives are literally dedicated to fresh produce: farmers. While most farmers don't have a lot of time for leisurely cooking (in case you're harboring fantasies of ditching the 9-to-5 and starting your own little farm, read a few farmers' blog entries . . . it's hard work!), they do have a deep understanding of what food tastes like when it's fresh from the earth. They know how to prepare ingredients in ways that show off all their aliveness.

Most of the recipes in the book come from the farm families themselves, but some are from CSA members—some who are actually chefs and others who simply love to cook and have shared recipes with their fellow CSA members via the farm's Web site or recipe fliers, which are a frequent bonus in a weekly CSA delivery box.

Part of what you learn when you become a CSA member is how to be flexible and respond to the harvest, so all of these recipes have quite a bit of flexibility built in. No green beans for the Lemon and Dill Green Beans (p. 179), but plenty of wax beans?

No problem. Not quite enough beets for the Siberian Borscht (p. 80), but have some extra turnips? Sounds delicious. Love the idea of the Artichoke and Herb Frittata with Parmesan (p. 124), but your farmer doesn't grow artichokes? Make the recipe using chunks of sautéed zucchini, potatoes, or broccoli.

The more you cook with the seasons, following the gentle but sometimes unpredictable rhythms of the farm, the more you'll develop a sense of how to improvise, deliciously.

What is a CSA and how does it work?

At its simplest, a CSA is an arrangement in which consumers become members, or subscribers, to a farm. The members pay the farmer at the beginning of the season for a "share" in that year's future harvest. The farmer gets cash early in the year, when the farm has intense expenses—seeds, soil amendments, supplies, and prepping and planting labor. The members then get a box of fresh-picked produce once a week throughout the growing season.

At a deeper level, however, a CSA is a way for us non-farmers to connect with the reality of growing food, not just in the manner of knowing where our food comes from, but also by sharing in the risks and the substantial rewards of the farming life.

We take a risk on the agricultural cycle, in the same way a farmer does: Bet a lot up front and hope that it turns out okay later. And, of course, not every bet pays off as expected. Every season is a wager against weather, pests, and other unforeseen events. The amount of the crops, their quality, and the timing of harvests can be different from year to year. That's where the skill of the farmer comes into play—an experienced farmer knows how to manage risk and rebound from disaster.

The rewards of being a CSA member, on the other hand, are plentiful. Most tangible is the selection of wonderfully fresh vegetables and fruit that you get every week. Most CSAs offer produce only, with vegetables dominating and a bit of fruit, depending on the farm. But as the CSA movement develops, farms are beginning to offer a wide range of food—fresh meat, cured meat, eggs, and even bread, jams, honey, cheeses, and other prepared food (flowers, too!).

The contents of a multiproduct CSA box may all come from one farm, but usually a wide range of products is the result of several farms cooperating and grouping their offerings—another dimension to the concept of strength through community.

An intangible benefit of CSA membership is the sense of belonging and ownership. You feel as though you are an integral part of the cycle. You and your fellow members collectively share the disappointments, feel proud of the victories, delight in the pleasures at the table . . . because it's *your* farm.

The earliest CSA models in North America were inspired by the biodynamic farming movement, pioneered by Rudolf Steiner in Austria and Switzerland in the years after World War I. Community farming models based on Steiner's agricultural and philosophical principles were being developed in Europe in the 1950s, '60s and '70s. In the mid-'80s, two American farming communities independently but simultaneously launched CSAs of their own. In 1986, Temple Wilton Community Farm in New Hampshire and Indian Line Farm in Massachusetts began offering farm shares to their local communities. Both of those farms are still in operation.

Is a CSA right for you?

Just being a local-food fan or an avid from-scratch cook doesn't mean you should join a CSA. You need to be a certain kind of cook to make it work, so before signing up for a CSA share, ask yourself the following questions:

- **AM I ABLE TO GIVE UP CONTROL OVER WHAT I'M GOING TO EAT?** Can you adjust your mood to match the contents of your weekly box? You might not have had asparagus in mind for dinner, but when a pound of it is waiting for you in the box, you need to adapt.

- **WILL I BE ABLE TO USE ALL THE PRODUCE?** If your consumption levels vary from week to week, because of frequent travel or kids coming and going, you may find that the steady stream of produce is hard to handle.

- **WILL I BE EXCITED TO MEET UNFAMILIAR VEGETABLES?** Much of your CSA share will consist of familiar favorites, but you're likely to receive a few items you've never cooked before. Of course, learning about new ingredients is one of the benefits of a CSA, too, giving you the chance to expand your cooking repertoire.

- **DO I HAVE ENOUGH TIME TO MANAGE ALL THIS FRESH "INCOMING"?** Fresh food means perishable food, and the only way to keep it all pristine and delicious is to prep, package, and store it properly as soon as you receive your share. You're not buying lettuce in a plastic bag, so you can't just sling stuff into the fridge and deal with it later. Discipline is definitely required.

- **DO I HAVE AN ESCAPE VALVE?** Inevitably, you'll have weeks in which you just can't eat everything fresh, so do you have friends or neighbors who will welcome a gift of zucchini, dandelion greens, or buttercup squash? Even better, can you find the time to "put up" the excess? Freezing is usually the simplest way to preserve fruits and vegetables, and it generally gives you the most flexibility on the other end. But most items need some prep or brief cooking before being wrapped and frozen, and that takes time (and know-how; see p. 9 for freezing ideas). Another wonderful way to preserve your share is by pickling, preserving, and other canning processes. What could be better than having so many ripe, delicious summer tomatoes that you have enough to can some for the winter months?

To learn more about CSAs in your area, starting a CSA, or about the history of CSAs, here are some resources:

LOCAL HARVEST
www.localharvest.org

CSA LOCATOR IN QUEBEC (CANADA)
www.equiterre.org

CSA LOCATOR IN ONTARIO (CANADA)
www.csafarms.ca

COMMUNITY SUPPORTED AGRICULTURE (CSA)
www.nal.usda.gov/afsic/pubs
/csa/csa.shtml

BIODYNAMIC FARMING AND GARDENING ASSOCIATION
www.biodynamics.com

ROBYN VAN EN CENTER FOR CSA RESOURCES
Fulton Center for Sustainable Living
www.csacenter.org

DEMETER ASSOCIATION
(the biodynamic certifying entity)
www.demeter-usa.org

How to find and choose the best CSA for you

Finding a CSA in your region is a lot easier than it used to be—the number of CSAs is growing like, well, the weeds the farmers are trying to get rid of.

A good starting point is www.localharvest.org, a clearinghouse Web site with listings and details about literally thousands of CSAs around the United States. In Canada, you can start with www.csafarms.ca. In some regions, there may only be one or two CSA farms, but in areas of the country where the agricultural regions are close to dense populations, dozens of farms may offer CSAs. Those farmers have access to city dwellers who are looking for sources of great food and for a connection to rural life.

Ask friends and neighbors if they know of local CSA farms, or go to your farmer's market, find vendors whose offerings you like, and ask them if they offer a CSA.

While the general structure of the farmer-member relationship is the same across the board, each CSA has its own terms, offerings, and personality. Do your research to find a farmer who fits your needs and desires. Here are the key factors to consider:

- **MEMBERSHIP COST VS. AMOUNT OF HARVEST.** You want to be sure that you're happy not only with the overall price but also with the overall volume of food. Many CSAs offer a half share, which is good for smaller

households and for first-timers, allowing you to gauge your consumption before committing to a full share.

■ **WHAT'S ON OFFER?** Farms usually list what they grow throughout the year, so you can see who has the types of ingredients you like best. Some farms will focus on the basics, others specialize in heirloom varieties, and many now offer meat, eggs, and other farm-raised food. In many cases the "extras"—flowers, grains, honey, bread, wine—will come from neighboring producers, so it's good to know who those partners are as well.

■ **WHERE AND WHEN IS THE PICKUP?** Being a CSA member requires active engagement, meaning you can't just sit back and receive the food; you need to pick it up yourself. Some CSAs have pickup at the farm itself, which is a fun excursion, and many have pickup locations closer to town. You can also arrange with neighbors to share the duties, but whatever the arrangement, you need to be sure it fits with your schedule and that you understand the "no-show" policy of the farm. Most farms are way too busy to make special arrangements for people who aren't able to make the pickup in a given week.

■ **WHAT'S THE DURATION OF THE SEASON?** This will vary by geography as well as the farm's growing strategy. Some people enroll in a summer CSA and a winter one, to ensure a year-round supply of deliciousness, but most people restrict participation to the spring through fall.

What to do when you bring your CSA box home

Depending on your point of view—and your list of daily chores—the arrival of the weekly CSA box can be a time of joyous activity or simply one more looming obligation. But no matter your mood, there it is, and you can't just leave it on the counter. Thirty minutes spent sorting, cleaning, and processing will make it easy and appealing to cook with your vegetables throughout the week. Here are a couple of tips to make the process more of a joy than a burden.

■ **LEARN WHERE THINGS ARE ON THE PERISHABILITY CONTINUUM.** You want to eat the most perishable items first: tender salad greens, tender herbs, asparagus, berries, ripe stone fruit, melons, certain summer squashes. The hardier categories, such as

Dirty Prep Suggestions

■ Rinse anything that's dirt-caked. Generally the farm will have done a nice preliminary cleaning, but in rainy weather the mud can sometimes linger.

■ Trim off hairy roots and dark green parts of leeks and spring onions.

■ Wash and dry leafy herbs, wrap in paper towels, and store in an airtight plastic bag or box in the fridge.

■ Wash your salad greens, dry well in a spinner, and store in an airtight plastic bag or directly in the salad spinner in the fridge. Then salad for dinner involves no more time than it takes to whip up a vinaigrette.

■ Cut off leafy greens on beets, turnips, kohlrabi, and carrots. If they're very fresh, they are delicious cooked in the same manner as you would spinach or Swiss chard. Wash well in cool water, spin in the salad spinner, and bag.

■ Do a basic cooking of leafy greens to save space in the fridge. Kale, collards, spinach, and chard should be washed and wilted by steaming in a bit of water or chicken broth or by sautéing in olive oil. Season very simply so that you can adjust the flavorings according to your final preparations. Squeeze out excess moisture, chop coarsely, and package up in airtight containers to use during the week.

beets and other root vegetables, potatoes, cabbages, broccoli and cauliflower, and apples, can patiently wait until the end of the week.

■ **BALANCE CONVENIENCE WITH PERFECTION.** Many cooks feel that you shouldn't wash vegetables or fruit until right before you cook with them, because moisture will encourage spoilage. However, there's a trade-off between shelf life and convenience. If you can do a lot of the "dirty prep" right when you bring home your goodies, you will be much more likely to use the produce during the week, for quick family meals, snacks, and other daily cooking opportunities. And you'll be feeding your compost a nice big meal of trimmings as well!

How to preserve your produce by freezing

LEAFY GREENS (such as kale, collards, chard, mustards, spinach, turnip greens, and beet greens) need to be blanched before freezing in order to deactivate the enzymes that promote continuing maturity. If the enzymes aren't killed, the greens can become tough and unpleasant tasting, even though they are frozen. Blanching also "shrinks" the greens, so that you can fit more in the freezer!

1. Trim off tough stems, cut out thick ribs, and wash the greens well in several changes of water.

2. Bring about a gallon of water to a boil in a large pot. Dunk about 8 ounces raw greens into the water, swishing them around with tongs so they are all immersed. Once the water returns to a boil, start counting. Collard greens take 3 minutes, other hearty greens 2 minutes, and very tender spinach leaves 1½ minutes.

3. Lift the greens from the water and plunge into a bowl of ice water to stop the cooking. Continue with the rest of your greens—you can reuse the blanching water for many batches.

4. Drain the cooled greens and package them in freezer-safe containers (bags or snap-lid containers). Add a thin layer of water to the package so the greens are just covered by what will become an ice barrier. Freeze immediately, preferably in a 0°F freezer.

THE SAME HOLDS TRUE FOR ALL VEGETABLES: They need some form of cooking to stop enzymes from spoiling them while frozen. Prepare the vegetables as though you were going to cook them—washing, trimming, cutting into smaller shapes—and then blanch them in boiling water.

Bring about a gallon of water to a boil in a large pot. Add the vegetables, stirring so they don't clump together. Once the water returns to a boil, start counting. The timing is about the same for all vegetables. For smaller items, such as cut-up asparagus spears, slender green beans, or small Brussels sprouts, plan on 2 minutes. Larger, denser items, such as thick broccoli florets and cubes of rutabaga, need 3 minutes. Winter squash and sweet potatoes should be cooked and mashed before freezing.

FRUIT, unlike vegetables, doesn't need to be cooked before freezing (though it can be). Some food experts suggest freezing fruit in a sugar syrup to preserve the

Freezing Information

A handy resource for freezing techniques is at a Web site created by the National Center for Home Food Preservation, a project whose goal is to update and verify methods for canning, freezing, drying, and other food-preserving techniques.

The group was established with funding from the Cooperative State Research, Education and Extension Service (CSREES-USDA) in 2000 as a multi-institutional effort with the University of Georgia and Alabama A&M University as the primary institutions.

Visit the Web site at http://nchfp.uga.edu/index.html.

color and texture, but you can also keep things simple and natural and just freeze the fruit as is, which gives you more flexibility when you're ready to cook with it.

For larger fruit, cut into the size and shape you'll eventually want, for example diced pineapple for a cake or sliced peaches for a pie. Pack the fruit into freezer-safe containers (bags or snap-lid containers), measuring out amounts that make sense for recipes, such as 2 cups, 1 pound, and so forth.

Another option for fruit that will give you flexibility is to spread it on sheet pans (individual berries or cut-up pieces of larger fruits), freeze until just firm, and then pile it into freezer bags or containers. With this method, the individual pieces of fruit or the berries will stay separate rather than freezing together in a block. You can then simply scoop out the amount you'd like to use and return the rest to the freezer.

Typical contents of CSA boxes throughout the year

The contents of an individual CSA box are as varied as the people and the land who produce the food. What you get in any given week is a function of the climate, the soil, the water, and the ambitions and strategies of your local farmer. Despite so many distinct geographies across the continent, most areas grow a core group of vegetables and fruit and follow the approximate seasonal pattern.

What to expect and when to expect it

It's not possible to provide absolute information on what produce will be ripe and ready in every part of the country. Between the various climates and microclimates, as well as farming technology—cold frames, hoop houses, and hydroponics—fruits and vegetables are available at different times depending on where you live.

The chart on the facing page will give you a sense, however, of how the produce from your CSA or farmer's market might flow. You'll see that some types of vegetable grow all season long; for example, carrots may show up in every CSA box from June through November. Each farm usually has its own harvesting schedule that it will share with members each season.

Enough already!

An overflowing CSA box—or prolific backyard garden plot—can tax the resourcefulness of even the most creative cook, especially with regard to vegetables that show up in every box throughout the season or in large quantities in any given week. The following produce are items that have often caused CSA members to say "Again, really?", along with a few mini-recipes for inspiration.

Carrots

- CARROT SALAD: Toss grated carrots with chopped fresh tarragon and lemon vinaigrette.

- CURRIED CARROT SOUP: Sauté chopped carrots in olive oil with sliced onions, garlic, and curry powder until the vegetables begin to soften. Add chicken stock and continue cooking until the carrots are quite tender. Purée in a blender until smooth and reheat.

- ROASTED CARROTS: Cut into chunks, toss with olive oil and fresh thyme, spread in a single layer on a baking sheet, and cook in a 375°F oven until browned.

- QUICK CARROT PICKLES: Peel carrots and cut into sticks, then blanch in a large pot of boiling salted water. Make a brine (1¼ cups water, 1 cup apple-cider or white-wine vinegar, ¼ cup granulated sugar, and some garlic, dill seeds, salt, and bay leaves for each pound of carrots). Bring to a boil and simmer for about 2 minutes. Remove from the heat, add the carrots, and let cool. No need to pack into jars; just refrigerate until ready to use.

- CARROTS WITH CUMIN BUTTER: Toss steamed sliced carrots with cumin, mustard, lemon juice, and butter.

Fruits and vegetables through the year

Produce	June	July	Aug.	Sept.	Oct.
Arugula	■				
Beets			■		
Bell peppers (green)			■		
Bell peppers (red and yellow)					■
Black kale				■	
Blueberries		■			
Broccoli		■		■	
Brussels sprouts					■
Butternut squash					■
Carrots	■	■	■	■	■
Cauliflower				■	
Celery root					■
Chard				■	
Cilantro		■			
Collards	■				
Corn	■	■	■		
Cucumbers	■		■		
Dill			■		
Eggplant			■	■	
English peas	■				
Fennel	■				
Gala apples				■	
Garlic			■	■	
Garlic scapes	■				
Green beans		■			

Produce	June	July	Aug.	Sept.	Oct.
Hot chiles				■	
Leeks		■			
Lettuces	■	■	■	■	■
New red potatoes	■				
Onions			■		
Parsnips					■
Potatoes			■	■	■
Radishes	■				
Raspberries		■			
Red cabbage	■				
Red onions		■	■		
Red potatoes		■			
Shallots				■	
Snap peas	■				
Spinach	■			■	■
Strawberries	■				
Summer squash			■	■	■
Sweet onions	■	■	■		
Tomatoes		■	■	■	
Turnips				■	■
Watermelon				■	
Zucchini		■			

Kale and other hearty greens

- **FRITTATA:** Add beaten eggs to a pan of braised greens and cook over low heat until the eggs are set.

- **VEGETABLE TART:** Spread braised greens over a par-baked tart shell. Pour a mixture of beaten eggs and milk on top, and sprinkle with crumbled feta. Bake at 350°F just until the eggs are set.

- **GRILLED GREENS AND GOAT CHEESE SANDWICH:** Layer braised greens and goat cheese between slices of buttered bread. Grill until the cheese is melted and the bread is toasted.

- **KALE CHIPS:** Tear kale into large pieces and toss with olive oil and salt. Spread on a baking sheet in a single layer and bake at 325°F, turning the leaves occasionally to make sure they don't burn, until crisp.

- **KALE AND PECORINO SALAD:** Tear kale into large pieces and combine in a large bowl with toasted almonds and cubes of toasted bread. Dress with a lemon and mustard vinaigrette and top with shavings of pecorino.

Onions

- **ONION SANDWICHES:** Cut sweet onions into very thin slices and layer between slices of bread spread with mayonnaise.

- **ROMANESCO SAUCE:** Grill thick slices of onions along with sweet red peppers and tomato halves. Purée the charred, softened vegetables with some raw almonds and crushed red pepper flakes to make a sauce for grilled meats.

- **ONION CONFIT:** Sauté thin slices of onions in olive oil with red wine, salt, and fresh thyme over very low heat until the onions are thick and jam-like. Use as a topping for pizzas and in sandwiches.

- **ROASTED ONIONS:** Bake thick slices in a 375°F oven until soft and beginning to brown. Transfer them to a serving dish, cover with vinaigrette, season with crushed red pepper flakes, and let stand for about 20 minutes before serving.

- **STUFFED ONIONS:** Cut the tops and bottoms off the onions and remove the cores with a melon baller. Season with salt and bake at 400°F until the onions are just starting to soften, about an hour. Stuff the onions with a mixture of grated tomatoes, breadcrumbs, feta, crushed garlic, and fresh flat-leaf parsley. Brush the tops with olive oil and continue baking until the tops are crisp and brown, about 20 minutes longer.

Winter squash

- **SQUASH AND PEAR SOUP:** Cook cubes of peeled squash with onions in butter until the onions begin to caramelize and the squash is tender. Add sliced pears and cook for another 5 minutes, then add white wine and simmer for 10 minutes longer. Purée until smooth, thinning with chicken stock as needed. Return the soup mixture to the stove and heat gently. Stir in a bit of yogurt and serve.

- **ROASTED SQUASH WITH FARRO:** Toss 1/2-inch cubes of peeled squash with onions, fresh thyme, olive oil, and sherry vinegar. Spread on a baking sheet and roast at 400°F until tender and beginning to brown. Combine with squash with cooked farro. Season with salt and pepper and garnish with chopped fresh flat-leaf parsley.

- **SQUASH AND CHICKPEA SALAD:** Toss cubes of roasted squash with chickpeas, thin slices of red onion, and chopped fresh cilantro. Make a dressing of tahini, lemon juice, and olive oil and combine with the squash and chickpeas.

- **MAPLE-MISO ROASTED SQUASH:** Brush thick slices of squash with a mixture of miso, maple syrup, and canola oil. Spread on a baking sheet in a single layer and roast at 400°F until the squash is tender.

- **ROASTED SQUASH WITH LIME-GINGER YOGURT:** Brush thick slices of peeled squash with olive oil and sprinkle with a mix of salt and ground coriander; roast at 400°F until tender. Stir the grated zest and juice of 2 limes and some freshly grated ginger into some yogurt. Season with salt and drizzle over the roasted squash.

Zucchini

- **GRILLED ZUCCHINI:** Cut the zucchini in half lengthwise, brush with olive oil, and season with salt and pepper. Grill until tender, and top with herb butter.

- **QUICK ZUCCHINI PICKLES:** Toss sliced zucchini with salt and let drain for several hours. Rinse and squeeze dry. Put the zucchini slices in a jar with fresh dill sprigs, mustard seeds, and some crushed red pepper flakes. Make a brine with equal parts white-wine and apple-cider vinegar and some granulated sugar. Boil the brine until the sugar dissolves, then pour over the zucchini in the jars. Let cool, and refrigerate until ready to use.

- **ZUCCHINI SALAD WITH MINT:** Slice a zucchini lengthwise into long ribbons, toss with salt, and let drain. Rinse and pat dry. Toss with lemon juice, olive oil, pitted black olives, and chopped fresh mint and flat-leaf parsley. Arrange on a platter and top with shavings of pecorino.

- **ZUCCHINI AND RADISH SLAW:** Cut zucchini into matchsticks, toss with salt, and let drain. Rinse and pat dry. Toss with thinly sliced radishes, and season with lime juice, salt, and pepper.

What the heck am I supposed to do with this?

One of the pleasures of being a CSA member is being introduced to wonderful produce that you've either never seen before or have seen but never tried in your own kitchen. Of course, the flip side of all that discovery is that you're often not quite sure what to do with unfamiliar items. While one person's oddball vegetable is another's favorite treat, the vegetables included here are frequently misunderstood; look at the suggestions for transforming them from weird to wonderful.

Cardoons

- **CARDOON AND ARTICHOKE STEW:** Cook 4-inch pieces of trimmed cardoons in a bit of olive oil until tender, adding water to the pan if it begins to dry out. When cool enough to handle, peel the strings from the cardoons and cut them into ½-inch pieces. Return the cardoons to the pan along with some cooked white beans, stewed artichoke hearts, and a few sprigs of thyme. Moisten with chicken stock and cook until everything is warmed through. Stir in some chopped garlic and fresh flat-leaf parsley, and drizzle with olive oil.

- **CARDOONS IN VINAIGRETTE:** Peel off the bitter skin and boil the cardoons in salted water until tender. Slice the cooked stalks into diagonal pieces and dress in a vinaigrette made with anchovies, garlic, lemon juice, and olive oil. Garnish with slices of hard-cooked egg.

- **BRAISED CARDOONS:** Peel off the bitter skin and cut the cardoons into ½-inch pieces. Put in a buttered gratin dish, cover with boiling chicken stock, dot the surface with butter, and sprinkle with salt and pepper. Cover with foil and bake at 425°F until tender.

- **CARDOONS WITH PENNE AND OLIVES:** Peel off the bitter skin and boil the cardoons in salted water until tender. Slice the cooked stalks into diagonal pieces and

All produce is for + U-Pick
Jubilee CSA
members only
Pro-rated memberships are still available, please take a Jubilee Farm Brochure for more info!
Couple Share
1 choice table item
1 lb. apples or 1/2 lb broccoli/cauliflower
1 cucumber
1 bunch carrots or 1 bunch parsnips
2 corn
1 lb. onions or shallots
1 celery
1 1/2 lb. peppers
2 watermelon
1 cantaloupe
Outside on Trailer
3 pints tomatoes
3 summer squash
1 bunch chard
Week 14
CARROTS
CUCUMBERS

cook in olive oil with onions and garlic until tender. Toss with cooked penne and sliced pitted green olives and top with grated Parmesan.

- FRIED CARDOONS: Peel off the bitter skin and boil the cardoons in salted water until tender. Slice the cooked stalks into diagonal pieces. Dip the cardoon pieces in a mixture of 2 egg yolks and 1 egg, and then dredge in dry breadcrumbs tossed with Parmesan, salt, and pepper. Fry the cardoons in ½ inch of very hot olive or vegetable oil until golden and crisp. Serve hot with fresh lemon wedges.

Celery root

- CELERY ROOT AND FENNEL SOUP: Sauté cubes of peeled celery root, slices of fresh fennel, and sliced onions in olive oil until the vegetables are beginning to brown. Cover with chicken stock and continue cooking until the vegetables are tender. Remove from the heat and purée in a blender or food processor until smooth. Return to low heat and thin with a bit of cream. Garnish with chopped fennel fronds.

- CELERY ROOT AND POTATO GRATIN: Layer thin slices of celery root, potatoes, and sautéed onions in a buttered gratin dish. Sprinkle each layer with fresh thyme leaves and season with salt and pepper. Pour white wine and chicken stock over the vegetables. Drizzle with olive oil and dot with butter. Cover and bake in a 400°F oven for 30 minutes. Uncover and continue baking until the juices are bubbly and the potatoes are cooked through.

- CELERY ROOT REMOULADE: Toss julienned strips of peeled celery root with a dressing made from lemon juice, Dijon mustard, mayonnaise, heavy cream, and salt. Sprinkle with parsley leaves before serving.

- CELERY ROOT WITH FRESH PEAS: Boil cubes of peeled celery root just until tender. Sauté a large shallot in butter, then add the celery root and fresh peas.

Season with celery salt and garnish with chopped fresh flat-leaf parsley.

- CELERY ROOT WITH STEAMED MUSSELS: Sauté finely chopped celery root with leeks, carrots, garlic, and fresh flat-leaf parsley. When the vegetables are quite tender, add mussels, white wine, and Pernod. Cover and steam until the mussels open. Serve with saffron aïoli.

- BRAISED CELERY ROOT: Peel the celery root and cut into chunks, add to a pan of water and lemon juice, bring to a boil, and cook for 10 minutes. Warm some olive oil in a sauté pan and cook chopped onions until tender; add the celery root, some diced carrots, and a bit of granulated sugar. Cover with hot water and let simmer until the vegetables are tender. Transfer to a serving platter; season with salt, pepper, and lemon juice, and garnish with chopped fresh flat-leaf parsley.

Daikon

- PICKLED DAIKON SLAW: Grate daikon, toss with salt, and let stand for about 15 minutes. Rinse, drain, and pat dry. Then combine with rice vinegar, granulated sugar, and salt and let stand for another 15 minutes. Drain and pat dry. Use in sandwiches and salads.

- FRIED DAIKON CAKES: Grate daikon, toss with salt, and let stand for about 15 minutes. Rinse, drain, and pat dry. Stir in garlic, minced onions, 1 egg, breadcrumbs, salt, and Asian hot sauce. Shape into patties and cook in a pan of hot oil until browned on both sides. Drain on paper towels before serving.

- SHRIMP AND DAIKON SALAD: Soak thin slices of daikon in iced saltwater for 30 minutes. Drain and pat dry. Toss cooked shrimp in a dressing made from mirin, rice vinegar, soy sauce, and untoasted sesame oil. Serve the shrimp on top of the daikon and drizzle with any remaining dressing.

- **DAIKON AND POTATO SALAD:** Add steamed slices of daikon to boiled potatoes along with shredded carrots and sliced cucumbers. Dress with mayonnaise mixed with lemon juice and top with thinly sliced red onions and torn fresh flat-leaf parsley leaves.

- **VIETNAMESE NOODLES WITH SHREDDED DAIKON:** Toss shredded daikon and carrots with granulated sugar and salt and let drain. Rinse and pat dry. Serve with cooked rice noodles topped with strips of grilled pork and a Vietnamese dipping sauce made from garlic, hot chiles, fish sauce, red-wine vinegar, and granulated sugar.

Garlic scapes

- **GARLIC SCAPE PESTO:** Briefly cook the scapes in a frying pan with a bit of oil until softened. Cool and then combine in a blender with olive oil, toasted pine nuts, and Parmesan.

- **GARLIC SCAPE AND POTATO SOUP:** Sauté chopped onions in butter until softened, add garlic scapes and chunks of peeled potato, and cook for about 5 minutes longer. Season with salt, cover with chicken stock, and continue cooking until the potatoes are tender. Purée in a food processor or blender and reheat before serving.

- **GARLIC SCAPE BUTTER:** Stew sliced garlic scapes in olive oil and a little water until very tender. Put a stick of softened butter in the bowl of a stand mixer; add the stewed scapes and some chopped fresh flat-leaf parsley, thyme, sage, chives, and chervil. Add a bit of coarse salt and lemon zest and mix until well combined. Use this to make the world's best garlic bread.

- **GARLIC SCAPE AND GREEN PEA DIP:** Combine garlic scapes, peas, lemon zest, fresh tarragon, salt, and pepper in a food processor and blend to make a coarse paste. Add olive oil and blend until fairly smooth.

- **GARLIC SCAPE RISOTTO:** Sauté chopped garlic scapes with leeks in a mixture of butter and oil. Stir in rice, and cook until the rice becomes translucent. Add white wine and cook until the wine is absorbed. Add a bit of hot chicken stock and cook, stirring, until most of the stock has been absorbed. Continue adding small amounts of stock in this manner until the rice is tender. Stir in grated Parmesan and season with salt and pepper.

Kohlrabi

- **KOHLRABI AND APPLE SLAW:** Combine equal parts shredded kohlrabi and apples with a bit of mayonnaise thinned with lemon juice. Stir in chopped fresh mint and season to taste with salt and pepper.

- **KOHLRABI FRITTERS:** Combine shredded kohlrabi and celery root with chopped fresh flat-leaf parsley, a bit of flour, 1 beaten egg, and some salt and pepper. Form into patties and cook in a hot, oiled pan until browned on both sides.

- **KOHLRABI FRIES:** Toss thick sticks of peeled kohlrabi in rice flour seasoned with salt. Heat about 2 tablespoons of oil in a large skillet and when hot, add the kohlrabi. Cook until well browned on all sides. Sprinkle with smoked paprika before serving.

- **KOHLRABI AND SPINACH WITH PISTACHIOS:** Toss thin slices of kohlrabi in a dressing made from lime zest and juice, vegetable oil, salt, and pepper. Combine with sautéed spinach and top with chopped pistachios.

- **ROASTED KOHLRABI:** Toss cubes of peeled kohlrabi with olive oil, salt, and pepper, and spread in a single layer on a baking sheet. Roast in a 400°F oven, stirring occasionally, until well browned.

STARTERS & SALADS

Sugar Snap Pea and Radish Slaw with Sesame Seeds

Sugar snap peas are so wonderfully crunchy that even when sliced into skinny julienne, they retain their texture. The finer you slice the peas and radishes, the prettier the salad, but if you're in a hurry, you could simply chop the vegetables. Umi plum vinegar adds a lovely salty-sour note, but it isn't mandatory. This dish is salty, though, so taste before you adjust the seasoning. SERVES 4

8 ounces sugar snap peas, tough strings removed

1 bunch radishes (about 8 ounces), tops and bottoms trimmed

1 tablespoon plus 1 teaspoon seasoned rice vinegar (also called sushi vinegar); more as needed

1½ teaspoons toasted sesame oil; more as needed

½ teaspoon umi plum vinegar

Kosher salt

1 teaspoon black or white sesame seeds

CSA Snapshot

Bluebird Meadows
Hurdle Mills, North Carolina
www.bluebirdmeadowsnc.com

THE FARMERS: Stuart and Alice White and their baby girl, Ruth

THE CSA LIFE: The Whites farm their 30 acres in the rolling foothills of north-central North Carolina using natural growing practices—no synthetic fertilizers or chemicals, lots of compost rich with worm castings ("black gold"), and cover crops. Each of their six fields has its own character and microclimate, which is part of why they stay so excited about farming. They host an annual CSA potluck with members, to continue cultivation of their special bond.

With a sharp knife, cut the snap peas lengthwise into fine julienne (about ⅛ inch thick), so they look like skinny matchsticks. Cut the radishes into thin disks, then stack the disks and cut across into matchsticks. Toss together in a bowl.

Whisk the vinegar, sesame oil, and plum vinegar together. Pour over the peas and radishes and toss well. Let sit for about 5 minutes, then taste and adjust with more rice vinegar, sesame oil, or a pinch of salt.

Sprinkle the sesame seeds over the top of the salad just before serving.

Prep School

Turning a roly-poly round radish into skinny julienne strips may seem like a challenge, but with an engineer's approach and a bit of knife skill, it's easily done. The method is the same for any fruit or vegetable of this shape.

1. Trim off the tops and tails, and cut a thin slice off one side to create a flat spot. Turn the radish so it's resting on the flat spot, making it secure. Carefully cut the radish vertically into slices as thin as you'd like the julienne to be.

2. Turn the slices 90 degrees so they're stacked horizontally and again slice vertically, so the slices become strips.

Creamy Radish Dip

This is a wonderful thing to serve with drinks when friends drop by. The flavors are addictive but fresh and delicate, so you feel good about dipping in for more. The dip is fairly stiff, so it works nicely as a spread for sandwiches, too. You may see some liquid weeping from the radishes on the second day, but don't worry; just pour it off or stir it back into the cream cheese.   MAKES ABOUT 2 CUPS

One 8-ounce package cream cheese, softened

4 tablespoons unsalted butter, softened

1 to 2 cloves garlic, minced (optional)

1 teaspoon Worcestershire sauce; more as needed

½ teaspoon fresh lemon juice

½ teaspoon celery salt

⅛ teaspoon paprika

Dash of hot sauce (optional)

Kosher salt

1 cup finely chopped radishes

¼ cup finely chopped scallions, white and light green parts only

Fresh vegetables and crackers, for serving

Put the cream cheese, butter, garlic (if using), Worcestershire sauce, lemon juice, celery salt, paprika, hot sauce (if using), and salt to taste into a medium bowl. Mix with a wooden spoon until well combined (you can also use a mixer on low speed, if you like). Stir in the radishes and scallions. Chill for several hours to allow the flavors to blend.

Taste and add more salt, Worcestershire sauce, or hot sauce, if needed, but be careful not to let the Worcestershire sauce overwhelm the delicate flavors. Serve with fresh vegetables and crackers.

CSA Snapshot

The Good Earth
Lennox, South Dakota
www.thegoodearth.us

THE FARMERS: Nancy and Jeff Kirstein

THE CSA LIFE: Located in the wide open spaces of eastern South Dakota, this natural farm consists of 26 acres of pastures, creek, and farmland, as well as plenty of birds and frogs. The Kirsteins intended the Good Earth to be more than just a farm. For visitors, it's become a place to get away from daily life and experience the simplicity of rural living—if only for an afternoon spent wandering along the creek or picking fresh fruits and vegetables on the farm.

Turnip Salad Two Ways

Hakurei turnips, sometimes called Japanese turnips, are small, white, and very sweet, with only a hint of the bite you sometimes find in larger turnips. This sophisticated salad is a lovely way to serve these tender bulbs. The recipe works nicely with grated beets and carrots, as well. In autumn, make both separately, and then serve on a platter of lettuce for a beautifully presented buffet dish. SERVES 4

For the Asian dressing

2 tablespoons olive oil

2 tablespoons soy sauce

2 teaspoons honey or brown sugar

½ teaspoon grated fresh ginger

Dash of hot sauce (optional)

⅓ cup chopped peanuts, or
   2 tablespoons sesame
   seeds, toasted

For the honey-mustard dressing

2 tablespoons olive oil

2 tablespoons apple-cider vinegar

2 tablespoons honey

½ teaspoon kosher salt

2 teaspoons Dijon or grainy mustard

⅓ cup sunflower seeds, toasted

1 bunch Hakurei turnips (8 ounces),
   julienned or grated

1 small head butter or leaf lettuce,
   or 4 ounces salad mix

Choose either the Asian or honey-mustard dressing, and whisk together all the ingredients except the peanuts or sunflower seeds.

Put the turnips in a medium bowl and pour the dressing over the top; stir well to coat. Let the salad sit for at least 10 minutes so the turnips can absorb the dressing.

Arrange a bed of lettuce on each plate and top with the turnip salad. Sprinkle with either the peanuts or the sunflower seeds (based on your dressing) and serve right away.

"I invest in something I believe in—I put my money where my mouth is, so to speak."

—Kay, Richfield, MN

CSA Snapshot

**Quiet Creek Farm
Kutztown, Pennsylvania
www.quietcreekfarmcsa.com**

THE FARMERS: John and Aimee Good

THE CSA LIFE: This 8-acre certified organic farm is part of the 300-acre Rodale Institute property in the Pennsylvania Dutch community of Berks County. Rodale's organic apple orchard and grain fields and a neighboring organic dairy farm's grazing cows border the farm, and farm visitors are invited to enjoy some peaceful time by the namesake creek behind the harvest barn. The Goods focus on the most flavorful and nutritious varieties, and grow close to 20 types of tomato alone. They enjoy showing members how the weather and environment relate to the triumphs and failures of each year's harvest and the ways the farm operates within nature, not independently of it.

Cook's Tip

When you have access to really fresh root vegetables, you learn that the roots aren't the only delicious part. As soon as you get your turnips home, cut off the greens, wash in cool water, and dry well in a salad spinner. Use them in the same way you would spinach or chard, or even turn them into a pesto (see p. 203).

Rabbit Rillettes with Oven-Stewed Rhubarb and Aged Goat Cheese

This dish takes some planning ahead, but the actual steps of making the rillettes and rhubarb are quite simple. It's a rustic yet truly impressive dish to share with friends as a first course to a spring dinner. Fulcrum chefs Gabrielle Rysula and Chad Hahn use delicately flavored rabbit as the meat for the rillettes, but you could also make more traditional pork rillettes using the same basic technique, substituting pork shoulder for the rabbit. And the oven-stewed rhubarb is a lovely accompaniment to many meats and cheeses. SERVES 12

For the rillettes

One 2-pound rabbit, cut into pieces

8 ounces fresh lard or pork fat you've rendered yourself (don't use the commercially processed lard from the grocery store)

½ cup olive oil

3 large sprigs fresh thyme

10 whole black peppercorns

5 bay leaves

Kosher salt and freshly ground black pepper

Quatre épices or a mix of equal parts ground cloves, ginger, nutmeg, and white pepper

Few drops of white balsamic or other sweet white vinegar

2 to 3 tablespoons unsalted butter, melted (optional)

12 to 24 thin slices baguette

Oven-Stewed Rhubarb (recipe on the facing page)

12 thin wedges aged Tomme-style goat cheese (such as Pholia Farms Elk Mountain)

MAKE THE RILLETTES

Heat the oven to 300°F. Put the rabbit in a large ovenproof Dutch oven with the lard, olive oil, thyme, peppercorns, and bay leaves. Heat over medium heat until you see a few little bubbles of a simmer, then cover and put into the oven. Bake until the meat is totally tender and falling off the bone when pulled with a fork, 2 to 3 hours.

When the rabbit is cool enough to handle, remove it from the pot and pour off all the juices and fat into a tall container or a gravy separator. Let the fat settle to the top.

Pull off all the meat and put it in the bowl of a stand mixer fitted with the paddle attachment. Beat on low speed for a few seconds to start crushing and smearing the meat a bit. Continue beating, and as you do so, drizzle in some of the cooking liquid and a few spoonfuls of the cooking fat. You want the consistency to be moist and blended but not

wet. Season generously with salt, pepper, and some quatre épices (start with just ¼ teaspoon because it can be overpowering); taste and adjust seasonings, adding a few drops of the vinegar for balance.

Pack the rillettes into a crock or container, pour a thin layer of cooking fat or some melted butter on top, cover tightly, and store in the fridge. The rillettes are best after a day of aging and will keep for up to 1 week.

ASSEMBLE THE DISH

Spread some rillettes on one or two thin slices of baguette, arrange on a small plate, nestle some rhubarb chunks alongside, and finish with a piece of goat cheese.

Oven-Stewed Rhubarb

SERVES 12

1 cup granulated sugar
Pinch of kosher salt

1½ pounds rhubarb stalks, tough or browned ends trimmed

Heat the oven to 375°F. Stir together the sugar and 1 cup water in a small saucepan, add the salt, and bring to a boil to let the sugar dissolve.

Arrange the rhubarb in a large baking dish or rimmed sheet pan (the rhubarb should be in a single, slightly snug layer). Pour the sugar syrup over the top, and roast the rhubarb in the oven until very tender but not yet falling apart, about 25 minutes, depending on the size of your stalks.

Let the rhubarb cool in the syrup. When ready to serve with the rillettes, cut the stalks into 1½-inch pieces.

> "My favorite thing to do is just make a big frittata with whatever's left from last week's pickup, the night before the next box will arrive."
>
> —Jessica B., Crow, OR

Cucumber-Lime Cooler

This super-refreshing drink is an unexpected and delightful way to use up extra cucumbers. Reminiscent of a Mexican *aqua fresca*, the cooler is highly adaptable. Honeydew, cantaloupe, or watermelon would be a delicious companion to the cucumber, and other herbs such as cilantro, lovage, or parsley can team up with the mint. SERVES 2

1 large cucumber, chilled, peeled, seeded, and coarsely chopped
½ cup fresh lime juice, chilled
3 tablespoons honey or stevia; more as needed

6 large fresh mint leaves
10 ice cubes
2 lime wedges, for garnish

Put the cucumber in a food processor or blender with the lime juice, honey, and mint. Add the ice cubes and process until smooth, adding a little water if needed to get the right consistency. Pour into chilled glasses, garnish with the lime wedges, and serve immediately.

CSA Snapshot

**Earth Spring Farm
Gardners, Pennsylvania
www.earthspringcsa.com**

THE FARMER: Mike Nolan

THE CSA LIFE: This CSA farm serves both the Harrisburg area in Pennsylvania and the Washington, D.C., area from their land at the northern end of Michaux State Forest in Cumberland County, Pennsylvania. With the South Mountains always in view, this family works the land in an area steeped with rich agricultural history. Growing up as a 4-H member, Mike was surrounded by this culture. He became more committed to sustainability later during study in Denmark, where he was exposed to progressive ideals of controlling urban sprawl, biking as transportation, and small-scale urban farm production. After an extensive hands-on farming education, Mike returned to the East to put this knowledge to use on his own farm.

Cook's Tip

Lemon cucumbers, which are round, pale yellow, and slightly bumpy, are very sweet and clean tasting, with no trace of bitterness—perfect for this summer drink.

Solar Dill Pickles

You've probably heard of sun tea. Here's the pickle equivalent! Kenneth L. Bowie, a member of the CSA from Lattin Farms in Nevada (where there is lots of sun), shares this easy method for a quick cucumber dill pickle. In late summer, you'll see big bunches of dill flowers laden with seeds, just waiting to flavor cucumbers. Grape leaves aren't as easy to find, but chances are there's someone in your neighborhood with some grapevines, so just knock on the door and promise some garlicky dills in return. MAKES 1 GALLON

9 cups distilled water
⅓ cup pickling salt
1 cup apple-cider vinegar
Lots of fresh dill, preferably flowering heads
Lots of cloves garlic, peeled

About 4 pounds pickling cucumbers, such as Kirby
Fresh red chiles (optional)
1 teaspoon pickling spices
2 large fresh grape leaves, rinsed

Put the water, pickling salt, and vinegar in a pot, bring to a full boil, and then leave the brine to cool.

Put some dill and a few garlic cloves on the bottom of a sterilized 1-gallon jar, then add a layer of cucumbers and another layer of garlic and dill; repeat until the jar is full. If you want a spicy pickle, add red chiles with each layer. Cover with the brine. Add the pickling spices and arrange the grape leaves on top (this will keep the pickles crisp). Screw on the lid.

Leave the jar in strong sun for 4 days, turning it one-quarter turn each day. Don't leave the jar on sand or cement, which would conduct too much heat to the jar; instead, put it on something made of wood.

After 4 days, the pickles should be ready to eat. Store in the refrigerator (you can transfer into smaller containers). The pickles will keep for 2 to 3 months.

CSA Snapshot

Lattin Farms
Fallon, Nevada
www.lattinfarms.com

THE FARMERS: Rick Lattin and B. Ann Lattin

THE CSA LIFE: One of the largest corn mazes in the United States can be found on Lattin Farms, and when viewed from above, it loudly proclaims, "Know your farmer, know your food." Rick and B. Ann have been mixing fun with a passion for agriculture and reconnecting with the earth for the past 35 growing seasons, following in the footsteps of their ancestors—Rick's great-grandparents began farming in the region in the very early 1900s. The Lattins' CSA is the largest in northern Nevada.

Cook's Tip

The method used in this recipe is a "quick pickle," meaning both the preserving and the flavoring come from a vinegar brine, along with other ingredients. The brine gives the characteristic tangy flavor and also prevents the growth of bacteria.

The other method of making a sour cucumber pickle is by fermentation, in which the cucumber is left in a salty brine (with no vinegar), which produces lactic acid that makes it sour and preserves it.

Garden Summer Rolls with Shrimp and Peanut Sauce

Unless you already have experience with rice paper wrappers, making these light and fresh salad rolls might seem a touch tricky the first time. But you'll get the hang of it very quickly and then will find yourself wrapping up all your fresh tender garden greens, vegetables, and herbs.

These rolls are lovely as a starter to a summer meal or as a light meal or snack on their own, and kids love them, too. MAKES 10 ROLLS

For the peanut dipping sauce

1 tablespoon soy sauce

½ cup smooth peanut butter

1 tablespoon toasted sesame oil

1 tablespoon fresh lime juice

1 teaspoon grated fresh ginger

For the rolls

10 small shrimp, peeled and deveined, or twenty ¼-inch strips firm tofu (1 pound)

2 tablespoons toasted sesame oil

5 rice paper wrappers

1 small cucumber, peeled, seeded, and cut into long, thin slices

2 small carrots, peeled and cut into long, thin slices

1 small avocado, pitted, peeled, and sliced

A handful of small lettuce or mizuna leaves

3 radishes, raw or pickled, cut into thin slices

10 fresh mint leaves or Thai basil leaves

MAKE THE DIPPING SAUCE

In a small saucepan over low heat, whisk together the soy sauce, peanut butter, sesame oil, lime juice, and ginger. Whisk in a few tablespoons of water until the mixture is creamy. Let stand while you prepare the rolls.

MAKE THE ROLLS

Gently sauté the cleaned shrimp or tofu pieces in the sesame oil in a frying pan on low heat. (Sesame oil can burn easily, so keep the heat low.) The shrimp will turn completely pink when done; the tofu should be golden brown. Set aside to cool.

Fill a shallow dish with cool water and place 1 rice paper wrapper in it so that it's completely submerged. It will soften in about 1 minute. (If you put more than one in the water, they may stick together.)

To assemble the rolls, gently remove the wrapper from the water, let the excess water drip off, and place it on a flat dish. Add another wrapper to the water and let it soak as you finish making the first roll. Each time you remove a paper, replace it with another one.

CSA Snapshot

**Kitchawan Farm
Ossining, New York
www.kitchawanfarm.com/
backtothegarden**

THE FARMERS: Nicole Porto, Linsay Cochran, and Alexander Cochran

THE CSA LIFE: This family farm boards horses and grows vegetables, herbs, and flowers for a small farmshare/CSA as well as by order. They are stewards of their inherited home, caring for the soil and water by growing crops organically and employing sustainable land management practices.

Lay 2 or 3 slices of cucumber, carrot, and avocado in the center of the wrapper, leaving about an inch of space at the top and bottom. Top with the shrimp or tofu, a few lettuce leaves, 3 or 4 slices of radish, and 2 whole herb leaves. Fold in the top and bottom of the rice paper, then fold one side over the filling and tightly roll it up. Repeat with the remaining wrappers. Cut in half and serve with the peanut sauce.

"One of our CSA customers giddily said the other day, 'Oh, it's so wonderful to shop and not have to spend money.' We both laughed, knowing that she did spend money earlier—it just feels that way during the season."

—Freida Lansing, Windermere Farms & Apiaries

Cantaloupe-Lime Salsa

Cantaloupe is a sweet fruit that is very much at home in the savory world, especially when paired with chiles and lime juice. Here, the overall brightness of the salsa is dialed up by adding fresh orange juice and zest, too. Perfumey basil is lovely, but feel free to use cilantro, parsley, or fresh mint instead. This salsa is gorgeous on halibut or shrimp or next to grilled pork tenderloin. SERVES 4 TO 6

2 cups ½-inch-dice cantaloupe

2 cups ½-inch-dice cored and seeded tomatoes

¼ cup minced onions

1 to 2 tablespoons minced fresh jalapeños

2 tablespoons fresh lime juice; more as needed

2 tablespoons fresh orange juice

1 tablespoon grated orange zest

1 tablespoon granulated sugar; more as needed

¼ teaspoon kosher salt; more as needed

⅛ teaspoon freshly ground black pepper

¼ cup chopped fresh basil (don't chop too finely)

Put the cantaloupe, tomatoes, onions, and 1 tablespoon jalapeños in a large bowl. Add the lime juice, orange juice, zest, sugar, salt, and pepper and toss thoroughly so all the flavors are well distributed.

Add the basil right before serving and toss again. Taste for balance, adding more jalapeños, lime juice, sugar, or salt as needed.

Cook's Tip

Choosing a ripe cantaloupe is a matter for multiple senses. First, look at the color—the skin underneath the netting should be a rich sandy brown, not green or yellow. Next, hoist a few melons to feel for the heaviest one for its size, an indication of juicy flesh inside. Then thump the melon with your fingers and listen for a hollow sound, like a drum. And last, take a deep sniff, especially at the stem end. If a sweet perfume isn't obvious, the melon probably isn't ripe. And if the perfume is slightly fermented, the melon is probably overripe.

CSA Snapshot

Lattin Farms
Fallon, Nevada
www.lattinfarms.com

THE FARMERS: Rick Lattin and B. Ann Lattin

THE CSA LIFE: One of the largest corn mazes in the United States can be found on Lattin Farms, and when viewed from above, it loudly proclaims, "Know your farmer, know your food." Rick and B. Ann have been mixing fun with a passion for agriculture and reconnecting with the earth for the past 35 growing seasons, following in the footsteps of their ancestors—Rick's great-grandparents began farming in the region in the very early 1900s. The Lattins' CSA is the largest in northern Nevada.

Hot-Summer-Day Cucumber Salad

Just about every cuisine features a version of this simple marinated cucumber salad, probably because it's so tangy and refreshing. Serve it alone as a side dish, especially with dishes from the grill such as barbecued chicken, or as a topping to a burger or pulled pork sandwich. If you have interesting varieties of cucumber, such as lemon cukes, this recipe is a perfect showcase for them. SERVES 4

½ cup white vinegar (distilled white or a mix of distilled and rice wine vinegar); more as needed

½ teaspoon kosher salt; more as needed

Freshly ground black pepper

1 teaspoon granulated sugar (optional); more as needed

2 medium cucumbers

2 tablespoons snipped fresh dill (optional)

Put the vinegar, ¼ cup water, the salt, pepper to taste, and sugar (if using) in a medium bowl and stir to mix.

Peel the cucumbers, unless the skins are very thin and tender. Slice them very thinly and add to the bowl. Mix in the dill, if using. Chill in the fridge for at least 2 hours so the cucumbers can marinate.

Taste and add more water if they're too sharp or more vinegar if too flat, and adjust the salt, pepper, and sugar to taste. Serve using a slotted spoon so the salad isn't too wet.

Prep School

Seeds or no seeds? That's a decision based on personal preference, as cucumber seeds are generally tender and inoffensive. However, the seed pocket is often watery, which can detract from the crisp texture of the flesh, so removing the seeds before slicing the cukes is sometimes a good idea.

Split the cucumber lengthwise, then either scrape out the seeds using a small, slightly pointed spoon or else run the tip of a paring knife along each side of the seeds, angled in a V shape, and cut out the channel of seeds.

CSA Snapshot

Field Day Farms
Bozeman, Montana
www.fielddayfarms.com

THE FARMER: Mariann Van Den Elzen

THE CSA LIFE: This certified organic farm was founded on a 1-acre piece of land that Van Den Elzen leased in exchange for supplying the landowner with food. The farm has continued to grow that way, but recently consolidated its growing fields to one ranch that offers them room to expand. Field Day Farms has teamed with two nearby farms to provide a varied supply for their traditional summer and winter CSAs. They also offer an "à la carte" option, where CSA members can order what they like online.

Pickled Okra

Okra is a vegetable that appears in many CSA boxes, and many CSA members have no idea what to do with it. Southerners, of course, will have plenty of ideas, but this recipe for pickles is perfect for using the shapely little pods throughout the year. Pickled okra is fantastic on a charcuterie plate, chopped into a potato salad, or even as a garnish for a martini.

This recipe comes from Allison Adams, a member of Daniel Parson's CSA in South Carolina. She likes her okra spicy, so she uses fresh cayenne chiles, which are the source of cayenne pepper. You should match your chile variety to your heat tolerance.

MAKES ABOUT 4 PINTS

3½ pounds small okra pods
½ cup pickling salt
1 sprig fresh dill or 2 teaspoons
    dill seed

3 cups white or apple-cider vinegar
4 cloves garlic, peeled
2 small fresh hot red chiles,
    cut in half

Trim the stems of the okra, being careful not to cut into the pods. Combine the salt, dill, 3 cups water, and the vinegar in a large saucepan. Bring the brine to a boil.

Meanwhile, boil four 1-pint canning jars and lids to sterilize them. Pack the okra into the still-hot jars, leaving ¼ inch headspace. Add 1 garlic clove and 1 chile half to each jar. Pour the hot brine over the okra. Remove air bubbles by tapping the jars on the counter gently and by poking a sterile skewer or knife into the jars in a few places.

Screw on the two-piece lids and process for 15 minutes in a boiling water canner, according to the canner instructions. Check the seals once the jars have cooled. Store any jars without a tight vacuum seal in the refrigerator. Let the pickles sit for at least 2 weeks before tasting them.

CSA Snapshot

Parson Produce
Clinton, South Carolina
www.parsonproduce.com

THE FARMER: Daniel Parson

THE CSA LIFE: Parson farms on 2 acres belonging to The Farmhouse Bed and Breakfast, which is also an alpaca and Nigerian dwarf goat farm. Parson converted the pastureland into an intensive vegetable production garden using organic methods. The garden grows almost every vegetable except corn. Parson earned a master's degree with a focus on cover crops and organic methods, which he applies with great success to these lush and productive acres.

Cook's Tip

In late summer, you'll start seeing bunches of tall, rangy dill weed, heavy with starburst-shaped seed heads. This is the mature version of the fresh dill that you more frequently use as tender fronds to snip over deviled eggs. Adding a whole head to a jar of pickles not only adds the herb's flavor, but it looks pretty, too.

Jalapeño Poppers

Mike Nolan and his wife, Diem Nguyen, of Earth Spring Farm make these poppers with the jalapeños from their garden, freezing them in quart-size freezer bags. When they have company throughout the year, they simply pop them in the toaster oven for a fun and easy appetizer.

If you like the zing of fresh chiles, bake the poppers just long enough to warm and crisp them. To soften the bite of the chiles, bake the poppers longer. If jalapeños are too spicy for you altogether, try this recipe with small sweet peppers. MAKES 24 PIECES

One 8-ounce package cream cheese, softened

1 cup shredded sharp Cheddar

1 cup shredded Monterey Jack

6 slices bacon, cooked and crumbled

¼ teaspoon kosher salt

¼ teaspoon garlic powder

¼ teaspoon chili powder

1 cup dry breadcrumbs, such as panko

12 fresh jalapeños, cut in half lengthwise and seeded

Sour cream, for dipping (optional)

Guacamole, for dipping (optional)

Ranch dressing, for dipping (optional)

In a large mixing bowl, combine the cream cheese, Cheddar, Monterey Jack, bacon, salt, garlic powder, and chili powder. Mix well with a wooden spoon until everything's well blended. Put the breadcrumbs on a plate.

Spoon about 2 tablespoons filling into each pepper half, then roll the peppers in the breadcrumbs. (You may freeze them at this point if you'd like, and cook them later.)

Heat the oven to 350°F. Arrange the poppers on a greased baking pan. Bake for about 20 minutes for spicy flavor, 30 minutes for medium flavor, and 40 minutes for mild. Serve the poppers hot, either alone or with one or more of the dipping sauces.

Cook's Tip

Many hot chile plants have a mind of their own, producing fruit with heat levels that range from milquetoast to meltdown levels, all from one plant. A jalapeño, for example, can range from around 2,500 Scoville units (measure of chile heat) to 8,000. You can't taste every chile before you use it, so just be aware that you may encounter some surprises!

CSA Snapshot

Earth Spring Farm
Gardners, Pennsylvania
www.earthspringcsa.com

THE FARMER: Mike Nolan

THE CSA LIFE: This CSA farm serves the Harrisburg area in Pennsylvania and the Washington D.C., area from their land at the northern end of Michaux State Forest in Cumberland County, Pennsylvania. With the South Mountains always in view, this family works the land in an area steeped with rich agricultural history. Mike became more committed to sustainability later during study in Denmark, where he was exposed to progressive ideals of controlling urban sprawl, biking as transportation, and small-scale urban farm production. After an extensive hands-on farming education, Mike returned to the East to put this knowledge to use on his own farm.

Spicy Tomatillo Summer Salsa

Field Day's take on the classic salsa verde brings more vegetables into play, making this salsa more nutritious than traditional versions and a fresh partner for so many summer foods: grilled fish or meat, an omelet with feta and potatoes, a muffaletta-style sandwich, and, of course, tacos and quesadillas.

If you find yourself with fresh sorrel, add a few of the tangy-sour leaves along with the cilantro. MAKES ABOUT 2 CUPS

8 ounces tomatillos (8 to 12 medium)

2 or 3 cloves garlic

2 scallions or young summer leeks, roots trimmed, white and light green parts only, cut into several pieces

2 fresh jalapeños or other small hot fresh chiles, cored and seeded

1 kohlrabi bulb (optional; if not using kohlrabi, add another small cucumber), peeled and cut into large chunks

1 small cucumber, peeled, seeded, and cut into large chunks

½ cup lightly packed fresh cilantro or fresh flat-leaf parsley leaves and tender stems

Kosher salt

Remove the husks and stems from the tomatillos. Rinse off any sticky juices.

Chop the ingredients in the food processor, adding them in the following order and pulsing after each addition: garlic, scallions, jalapeños, kohlrabi, cucumber, tomatillos, and cilantro. Season to taste with salt, and serve at room temperature or chilled. The salsa will keep for up to 4 days, stored in the fridge.

Cook's Tip

Despite the similarity in name and appearance, a tomatillo is only distantly related to a tomato (same family, different genus). It is not the same thing as a green tomato and will not ripen to red. Tomatillos are more closely related to the Cape gooseberry, also called a ground cherry. If you can find a pineapple tomatillo—about the size of a cherry tomato, with a golden color—give it a try. It's fruity and fragrant.

CSA Snapshot

Field Day Farms
Bozeman, Montana
www.fielddayfarms.com

THE FARMER: Mariann Van Den Elzen

THE CSA LIFE: This certified organic farm was founded on a 1-acre piece of land that Van Den Elzen leased in exchange for supplying the landowner with food. The farm has continued to grow that way, but recently consolidated its growing fields to one ranch that offers them room to expand. Field Day Farms has teamed with two nearby farms to provide a varied supply for their traditional summer and winter CSAs. They also offer an "à la carte" option, where CSA members can order what they like online.

Fennel and Apple Slaw

For this refreshing salad, choose any type of bulbing brassica: radish, turnip, or kohlrabi. At Heart of the City CSA in Cleveland, Ohio, they first made the slaw with sweet, tender Hakurei turnips and it was delightful. You can peel the kohlrabi and large turnips or keep the skin for added nutrition, color, and flavor. The slaw is delicious alongside grilled pork chops or tenderloin. SERVES 4

Juice of ½ lemon; more as needed

1 tablespoon honey; more as needed

⅛ teaspoon kosher salt; more as needed

2 firm apples, cored, peeled, and grated on the large holes of a box grater

1 medium to large fennel bulb, leaves and tops of the stems trimmed, quartered, and sliced as thinly as possible

1 bunch radishes or turnips, or 2 small kohlrabi bulbs (about 8 ounces total), peeled if necessary and grated on the large holes of a box grater

1 tablespoon minced fresh chervil (optional)

In a medium bowl, combine the lemon juice, honey, and salt, stirring until blended well. Add the apples, fennel, and radishes, and toss to combine. Let stand for 10 minutes to let the flavors meld.

Add the chervil, if using. Taste and adjust with more lemon juice, honey, or salt before serving.

CSA Snapshot

Heart of the City
Cleveland, Ohio
www.urbangrowthfarms.com

THE FARMERS: Peter McDermott, Virginia Houston, Molly Murray, and Erin Laffay

THE CSA LIFE: This CSA is the collaboration of two small urban farms, Urban Growth and Erie's Edge. These enthusiastic young farmers got their start with this urban CSA operation on the west side of Cleveland in 2008, when they responded to the need for more fresh vegetables in the diets of their local community members. They also all have learned the value of growing food as a way to connect a diverse range of people.

Cook's Tip

When we hear the word *slaw*, we usually think of a side dish to barbecue or fried seafood, but this sweet-tangy concoction can be spectacular on sandwiches, such as a roast beef or turkey sandwich or a Vietnamese bahn mi.

Summer Bread Salad

This salad is really all about the interaction between tomato and bread, with the oil acting as the catalyst. Use a nice artisan loaf, preferably something "holey." If you don't have time for the bread to get slightly stale, you can cut it into cubes and bake them in a 300°F oven for about 20 minutes to dry them out. Feel free to play with other vegetable combinations, but don't stray too far from the classic—it's too good! SERVES 4

6 ripe tomatoes, cut in half cross-wise, seeds gently squeezed out, and cut into 1-inch chunks

6 cups 1-inch cubes of good Italian bread, such as ciabatta

1 cucumber, peeled, cut in half lengthwise, seeded, and cut crosswise into ¼-inch-thick slices

1 red bell pepper, cored, seeded, and diced

½ small red onion, thinly sliced

½ cup pitted Kalamata olives

½ cup extra-virgin olive oil; more as needed

¼ cup sherry vinegar; more as needed

Kosher salt and freshly ground black pepper

½ cup lightly packed fresh basil leaves

½ cup lightly packed fresh mint leaves

Put the tomatoes, bread, cucumbers, peppers, onions, and olives in a large bowl and toss to mix. Drizzle with the olive oil and vinegar and season well with salt and pepper. Toss again.

Let marinate for at least 30 minutes and ideally 1 hour, tossing occasionally to distribute the juices. Right before serving, toss in the basil and mint and then taste and adjust with more salt and pepper, oil, or vinegar. Serve at room temperature.

Cook's Tip

Sherry vinegar shows up frequently in good cooks' pantries because of its rich and mellow flavor. Unlike balsamic vinegar, sherry vinegar isn't actually sweet, but it has been aged in various woods so it has developed vanilla undertones that give an illusion of sweetness or softness. If you can't find sherry vinegar, you can get a similar result with a half-and-half blend of balsamic and red-wine vinegar.

CSA Snapshot

Snow's Bend Farm
Coker, Alabama
www.snowsbendfarm.com

THE FARMERS: Margaret Ann Toohey and David Snow

THE CSA LIFE: The farm is located near Tuscaloosa, Alabama, and boasts an ecological mix of wooded hills, coves, ridges, forested swamp, and bottomland pasture. The name of their soil type is as picturesque as the scenery: "Tuscaloosa Choccolocco," made up of fine silt and organic matter deposited over thousands of years of flooding. The farmers began their organic operation in 2004, after years of learning and farming around the world. They began with just a quarter-acre, which has grown to more than 10 acres with over 250 varieties of vegetables, herbs, fruits, and flowers, plus more acreage in which they raise hogs. The couple has plans for adding a perennial fruit orchard and an heirloom seed-saving garden.

Roasted Beet and Carrot Salad with Basil-Cilantro Purée

Root vegetables and roasting are a match made in vegetable heaven. The high oven temperature caramelizes the natural sugars in the roots and makes the texture tender on the inside, slightly chewy on the outside. But because root vegetables are naturally high in sugar, take care not to let them burn—check frequently during cooking and stir them around on the baking sheet.

You can make the purée, which is a vibrant green, fragrant counterpoint to the sweet roots, using herbs other than basil and cilantro, as well. All basil is nice, or substitute some fresh mint or parsley for either of the herbs listed. SERVES 4

For the Basil-Cilantro Purée

1 cup lightly packed fresh basil leaves

1 cup lightly packed fresh cilantro

1 or 2 cloves garlic

½ cup extra-virgin olive oil

½ teaspoon kosher salt; more as needed

Freshly ground black pepper

For the vegetables

4 medium beets, peeled or scrubbed and cut into ½-inch dice

¼ cup olive oil

1 teaspoon kosher salt

½ teaspoon freshly ground black pepper

4 large carrots, peeled or scrubbed and sliced into ½-inch rounds

MAKE THE BASIL-CILANTRO PURÉE

Put the basil, cilantro, and garlic in a food processor and pulse a few times. With the motor running, pour in the oil and process until you have a nice purée, like a loose pesto. Add the salt and a few twists of pepper, pulse twice to blend, then taste and adjust the seasoning. Transfer to a small bowl, cover, and chill while you roast the vegetables.

continued on p. 44

CSA Snapshot

Urban Roots
Austin, Texas
www.urbanrootsatx.org

THE FARMERS: Max Elliott and Mike Evans

THE CSA LIFE: Covering more than 3 acres within Austin's city limits, this farm sits 5 miles east of downtown along the banks of Boggy Creek. Urban Roots offers paid internships to local teens; during the summer term, the young people participate in a rich program of job training, community involvement, and leadership development. Elliott and Evans proudly state that they are an "inefficient operation" because they complete all their farm tasks by hand. The farmers donate 40 percent of their harvest to local soup kitchens and food pantries.

ROAST THE VEGETABLES

Heat the oven to 400°F. Toss the beets with half of the olive oil, ½ teaspoon of the salt, and ¼ teaspoon of the pepper and spread onto a baking sheet so that there is one even layer of beets. Do the same with the carrots on a separate baking sheet so that you can control cooking time for each vegetable. Roast the vegetables until tender and slightly browned, 15 to 20 minutes, stirring and shaking the pan once or twice as they cook so that they brown evenly. Let cool.

Toss the roasted beets and carrots together and arrange on a serving platter. Drizzle with the Basil-Cilantro Purée. Serve at room temperature or slightly chilled.

Cook's Tip

Beets and carrots are definitely coloring outside the lines these days, with white, magenta, and purple carrots showing up alongside their orange kin and with beets ranging in colors from yellow to pink-and-white striped. When you make this salad, have fun with the color selection.

German-Style Potato Salad

Potato salad is one of those dishes that invokes passionate debate. The key issue: vinegar or mayo? This version, from Whitton Farms in Arkansas, straddles the two, with enough apple-cider vinegar to provide true tang but with a touch of creaminess from mayonnaise as well. And forget about adding celery or hard-cooked egg—this salad is all about highlighting the potatoes. If the potato skins are very thin, there's no need to peel them.

SERVES 8 TO 10

⅔ cup mayonnaise

½ cup apple-cider vinegar; more as needed

¼ cup vegetable or extra-virgin olive oil

¼ cup finely chopped fresh flat-leaf parsley

2 tablespoons granulated sugar

2 teaspoons kosher salt; more as needed

Freshly ground black pepper

3 pounds waxy potatoes, such as Bintje, Carola, German Butterball, or Red Bliss, peeled and cut into ¼-inch slices

¼ cup finely chopped onions

In a large bowl, whisk together the mayonnaise, vinegar, oil, parsley, sugar, salt, and a large pinch of pepper.

Bring a large pot of salted water to a boil. Add the potatoes, and cook until tender but still firm, about 15 minutes. Drain thoroughly and then gently pour the warm potatoes into the bowl containing the dressing. Add the onions.

Gently fold everything together and let stand for at least 1 hour before serving, to let the flavors blend and penetrate the potatoes.

Just before serving, taste and adjust the vinegar, salt, and pepper.

Cook's Tip

Potatoes vary in starch content, with high-starch potatoes having a more floury, fluffy texture when cooked, making them great for mashed potatoes; lower-starch varieties have a denser, "waxier" texture. Waxy potatoes hold their shape better when sliced or diced and so are preferable for salads. Most fingerlings are waxy, as are some red potatoes such as Red Bliss. A good in-between choice is a yellow potato such as Yukon Gold.

CSA Snapshot

Whitton Farms
Tyronza, Arkansas
www.whittonfarms.com

THE FARMERS: Keith and Jill Forrester

THE CSA LIFE: Whitton Farms is a small, organically inspired farm in the Arkansas Delta. Both Keith and Jill are former public school teachers who became farmers after moving to Keith's family's cotton farm, which had been in the family for close to 100 years. Gradually the Forresters are transforming former pastureland into rich plots for heirloom vegetables and flowers, which they share with their CSA members and customers at the Memphis Farmers Market.

Bacon, Beet, and Apple Salad

This is a beautiful fall or winter salad that is hearty enough to be a main dish. There's a lot of room for improvisation, depending on what's in your CSA box or at the market. A mix of red and gold beets would be stunning; you could swap the arugula for another spicy or hearty green such as mizuna or even frisée. If you prefer to go meatless, just leave out the bacon and cook the shallots in a couple tablespoons of fruity olive oil. SERVES 6

2 bunches small beets (about 1½ pounds), tops and roots trimmed, roots scrubbed or peeled

2 to 3 tablespoons extra-virgin olive oil; more as needed

Kosher salt and freshly ground black pepper

4 slices thick-cut bacon, cut crosswise into ½-inch strips

2 medium shallots, thinly sliced crosswise

2 teaspoons fresh thyme leaves

¼ cup apple-cider vinegar

½ teaspoon granulated sugar (optional)

3 tablespoons pumpkin seeds

6 cups tightly packed arugula

2 sweet-tart apples, such as Braeburn or Fuji, peeled and cut into ½-inch cubes

2 ounces goat cheese

CSA Snapshot

LadyBird Farms
Pocatello, Idaho
www.ladybirdfarms.com

THE FARMERS: Jessica McAleese and Jeremy Shreve

THE CSA LIFE: This small farm, located 8 miles south of Pocatello, Idaho, is nestled in the heart of the high mountain desert. On just 1 acre of land (for now!), LadyBird grows more than 50 varieties of vegetables, herbs, and flowers, most of which is shared with CSA members. The team at LadyBird believes they grow more than just good food. The CSA has built, empowered, and supported the region's community food system and created a lasting partnership between local farmers and consumers who strive for ecological, economical, and socially just ways to grow and eat their food.

Heat the oven to 375°F. Cut the beets into wedges about 1 inch thick at the widest point. Toss them with the olive oil, season generously with salt and pepper, and put them in a shallow baking dish. Roast the beets until they're tender and slightly wrinkly, 30 to 45 minutes.

In a small sauté pan, cook the bacon on medium-high heat until the fat is rendered. Remove the bacon from the pan with a slotted spoon, leaving the fat in the pan, and drain on paper towels. Add the shallots and thyme to the bacon fat and cook until the shallots have softened, 3 to 4 minutes. Pour the shallots into a small bowl and add the vinegar and sugar, if using. (Don't wash the pan yet.)

Taste the vinaigrette and add 1 to 2 tablespoons of olive oil (this will depend on how fatty your bacon is); add pepper to taste.

Place the pumpkin seeds in the sauté pan you used to cook the bacon. Cook on medium heat, swirling the pan to prevent the seeds from burning, until they are toasted and have golden brown spots, 3 to 4 minutes. Transfer the seeds to a small plate to cool.

continued on p. 48

In a large bowl, combine the arugula with about 1 tablespoon of the vinaigrette and toss to coat. Arrange the arugula on a serving platter or in a wide serving bowl. Toss the roasted beets with another couple of tablespoons of vinaigrette and mound them on the greens. Do the same with the apples; arrange on the salad. Distribute the bacon over the ingredients, crumble the goat cheese on top, and sprinkle on the toasted pumpkin seeds. Drizzle with any remaining vinaigrette. Serve right away.

Prep School

There are two schools of thought when it comes to roasting beets. Some people like to roast them whole or halved, wrapped in foil or arranged in a baking dish with a bit of liquid and a cover. Even though they are cooked in the oven, the beets are essentially steaming, not roasting. This is a good method when you just want a hands-off way to get them tender.

The second method actually cooks the beets via the hot air of the oven, a true roast. The beets are cut into whatever size you want for your final dish, tossed in some olive oil, seasoned with salt and pepper and perhaps some herbs, and then spread in a baking dish and roasted until tender. The surface will shrivel slightly and caramelize around the edges, deepening the beets' already earthy-sweet flavor.

Curly Endive Salad with Goat Cheese, Bacon, and Honey-Mustard Dressing

Curly endive, similar to frisée, is a favorite in France but not as well known in the United States. Its bittersweet flavor and sturdy but frilly texture make it a wonderful base for hearty salads, especially when bacon is involved. The best heads of curly endive will have a generous white and light yellow "heart" of center leaves that are sweetest and most tender.

For a variation of this salad, use walnuts and blue cheese in place of the pine nuts and goat cheese. SERVES 6

⅓ cup pine nuts

1 heaping tablespoon Dijon mustard

1 teaspoon fresh lemon juice

1 teaspoon honey

¼ teaspoon kosher salt

⅛ teaspoon freshly ground black pepper

¼ cup olive oil

1 medium head curly endive, tough outer leaves removed and bottom trimmed

⅓ pound sliced bacon, diced and cooked until crisp

3 ounces fresh goat cheese, crumbled

Put the pine nuts in a large, dry frying pan over low heat and toast, stirring frequently, until golden, about 5 minutes; set aside.

Whisk the mustard, lemon juice, honey, salt, and pepper in a large bowl, and then whisk in the oil. Tear the endive into small (2-inch) pieces and add to the bowl along with the bacon. Toss to dress the endive thoroughly.

Arrange mounds of salad on each serving plate, distribute the goat cheese on top, and sprinkle with the pine nuts. Serve right away.

Cook's Tip

Members of the chicory family—curly endive, radicchio, Treviso, and escarole, for example—can be quite bitter. The bitterness is part of their charm, but it needs to be balanced with other ingredients to keep it in check. A generous dose of fat and salt will help soften any sharp edges; in this salad, the bacon and goat cheese play that role deliciously.

CSA Snapshot

Mud Lake Farm
Hudsonville, Michigan
www.mudlakefarm.com

THE FARMERS: Steve and Kris Van Haitsma

THE CSA LIFE: Located on 36 largely uncultivated acres, this west Michigan farm shares space with deer, rabbits, muskrats, turkeys, and a huge variety of birds. The Van Haitsmas specialize in greens, which they grow in geo-thermally biomass-heated hydroponic greenhouses (with no pesticides), and their CSA is a "salad CSA," which includes favorite varieties such as a small green bibb lettuce called Dancine, a green Batavia lettuce called Loma, and a miniature red romaine known as Breen lettuce.

Smoked Trout and Kohlrabi Canapés

This elegant canapé recipe calls for kohlrabi, but green apple works nicely also. The smoked trout spread is best when you make it with Harvest Moon's homemade horseradish mayonnaise, but crème fraîche is excellent, too. Hot-smoked salmon is a nice substitute for the smoked trout, or you could even use both and serve pink and white canapés. MAKES 36 CANAPÉS

4 large or 6 medium kohlrabi

8 ounces flaked smoked trout

½ cup Harvest Moon Farms Mayonnaise (recipe on the facing page) or crème fraîche

1 tablespoon freshly grated horseradish, or 1 tablespoon prepared horseradish, drained

1 tablespoon chopped fresh tarragon

2 tablespoons fresh lemon juice

Kosher salt and freshly ground black pepper

2 tablespoons chopped fennel fronds

Peel the kohlrabi and then cut them into ⅛-inch-thick slices (so they're like crackers). You should get about 8 slices per kohlrabi. If you want perfectly shaped slices, use a cookie cutter to stamp the slices into circles.

Put the trout, mayonnaise, horseradish, tarragon, and lemon juice in a food processor or blender and blend until smooth. Season lightly with salt and pepper. (Most smoked trout is salty, so taste before seasoning.)

Spread the trout mixture evenly on the kohlrabi slices and top with fennel fronds. Serve on a chilled platter (place the platter in the freezer for 30 minutes before serving).

CSA Snapshot

Harvest Moon Farms
Viroqua, Wisconsin
www.harvestmoon-farms.com

THE FARMERS: Jennifer and Bob Borchardt

THE CSA LIFE: These homesteaders have a large certified organic farm located in southwest Wisconsin's Driftless Region near Viroqua. Harvest Moon participates in a unique farm-to-school program: Farmers visit the school to give an introduction to farming, the kids cook produce from the farm for lunch, and later they visit the farm. Visitors to this idyllic farm enjoy a range of events, including concerts, fundraisers, dinner parties, beer tastings, and a large customer appreciation farm dinner.

Harvest Moon Farms Mayonnaise

Farm-fresh eggs make a gorgeous mayo, so if you belong to an egg CSA, this is the recipe for you. MAKES ABOUT 2½ CUPS

2 large eggs, at room temperature
2 tablespoons white vinegar
1½ teaspoons fresh lemon juice
½ teaspoon Dijon mustard
1 teaspoon kosher salt

Scant ⅛ teaspoon freshly ground
  white pepper
1 cup vegetable oil
1 cup olive oil

Put the eggs, vinegar, lemon juice, mustard, salt, and pepper in a blender or food processor and blend until mixed. Add the vegetable oil and then the olive oil in a slow, steady stream until emulsified. Taste and adjust the seasoning.

"Our members often comment on how the [CSA] has literally changed their lives. They experience vegetables they would not have ventured to buy at the store because they were unfamiliar with them and not sure how to prepare them. Their palates have become discerning about freshness and purity, which has made eating out much less attractive."

—Nanette Ardoin, Acadian Family Farms

Kale "Seviche" Two Ways

North Carolina farmer George O'Neal makes this super-nutritious salad with Red Russian kale, but any variety will work. Tuscan kale, also called black kale or cavolo nero, is also a good choice—it's quite tender and its non-ruffled leaves are easy to cut. O'Neal likes to dress his salad with Asian flavors, but the nutty-sweet flavor of kale is adaptable to all types of ingredients. SERVES 4

For the "seviche"

1 bunch kale (about 8 ounces; any variety will do)

1 large carrot, peeled and grated on the large holes of a box grater

¼ cup apple-cider vinegar

¼ cup extra-virgin olive oil

Kosher salt and freshly ground black pepper

For an Asian variation

Hot sauce, such as Sriracha

1 tablespoon rice vinegar

1 teaspoon soy sauce or tamari sauce

1 teaspoon toasted sesame oil

2 tablespoons white or black sesame seeds

For an Italian variation

2 anchovy fillets, minced

1 small orange or ½ medium grapefruit, peeled, segmented, and cut into ¼-inch pieces

¼ cup pine nuts, lightly toasted

MAKE THE "SEVICHE"

Cut the stems off the kale, then wash the leaves and dry them thoroughly. If the kale has thick ribs, cut them out by slicing along each side so that you're just left with the tender leaf.

Stack 3 or 4 leaves and roll them up tightly lengthwise. Using a very sharp knife, cut across the roll into very thin strips about ⅛ inch thick—this is called cutting a chiffonade. Put the kale chiffonade and the grated carrot into a large bowl.

Drizzle in the vinegar and olive oil, season generously with salt and pepper, and toss to distribute completely. Let sit for at least 30 minutes or up to 2 hours—the kale will wilt slightly and become more tender and sweet.

MAKE AN ASIAN VARIATION

Just before serving, season the "seviche" with a few drops of the hot sauce, the rice vinegar, soy sauce, and sesame oil. Taste and adjust the seasoning. Sprinkle with the sesame seeds and serve.

MAKE AN ITALIAN VARIATION

Just before serving, toss the "seviche" with the minced anchovies and citrus pieces. Taste and adjust the seasoning. Sprinkle with the pine nuts and serve.

CSA Snapshot
Lil' Farm
Hillsborough, North Carolina
www.lilfarmnc.com

THE FARMER: George O'Neal

THE CSA LIFE: Lil' Farm's fun tag line, "never whack," means no herbicides or pesticides in the gardens, nor antibiotics for his 300 chickens. This beginning farmer believes in farm transparency—if you want to see how your food is being grown, come out to these few acres north of Durham for a visit. You will see happy, socializing chickens and a mobile tractor that allows them a natural diet and fresh pasture. With help from a grant, George started an equipment co-op that allows him and ten other farms to have access to trucks, tractors, and tools.

Pear Salad with Dried Cherry Vinaigrette

Mudlake Farms grows lettuces and microgreens, which are the first tiny sprouting leaves of vegetables, herbs, and lettuces—super delicate yet intensely flavorful. If you can't get microgreens, you could use a mix of fresh tender herbs. The dressing would also be delicious with dried cranberries instead of cherries, but look for something minimally sweetened. If you're lucky enough to get Asian pears in your CSA box, their juicy crunch would be a nice addition to this salad.

The recipe makes more dressing than you'll need for one meal, so use the rest on roasted beets or even with sliced roast pork. SERVES 4

For the dressing

½ cup dried Michigan cherries

Small chunk of onion (about the size of a wine cork)

¼ cup apple-cider vinegar; more as needed

2 tablespoons honey

½ teaspoon dry mustard

½ teaspoon kosher salt; more as needed

Tiny pinch of cayenne; more as needed

½ cup extra-virgin olive oil

For the salad

1 to 2 heads lettuce, such as Bibb and/or red oak leaf, torn into bite-size pieces

1 cup cut microgreens or sprigs of tender fresh herbs (flat-leaf parsley, dill, chervil)

1 or 2 firm but ripe Bosc pears, cored and cut into slices or chunks

1 cup shredded sharp Cheddar, aged Gouda, or cave-aged Gruyère (cut into julienne strips)

MAKE THE DRESSING

Put about half the cherries in a food processor along with the onion, vinegar, honey, mustard, salt, and cayenne. Pulse until well blended, and then with the motor running, drizzle in the oil. Taste and adjust with more vinegar, salt, or cayenne.

MAKE THE SALAD

Put the lettuce and microgreens in a large bowl, add 3 to 4 tablespoons of the dressing (depending on how much lettuce you have), and toss to lightly but thoroughly coat the leaves. Put a mound of lettuce on each plate. Arrange a few pieces of pear on the greens and drizzle a little more dressing over them. Finally, sprinkle the salads with the cheese and the remaining dried cherries, and serve right away. Pass the extra dressing at the table, if you like.

CSA Snapshot

Mud Lake Farm
Hudsonville, Michigan
www.mudlakefarm.com

THE FARMERS: Steve and Kris Van Haitsma

THE CSA LIFE: Located on 36 largely uncultivated acres, this west Michigan farm shares space with deer, rabbits, muskrats, turkeys, and a huge variety of birds. The Van Haitsmas specialize in greens, which they grow in geothermally biomass-heated hydroponic green-houses (with no pesticides), and their CSA is a "salad CSA," which includes favorite varieties such as a small green bibb lettuce called Dancine, a green Batavia lettuce called Loma, and a miniature red romaine known as Breen lettuce.

Cook's Tip

Picking a ripe Bosc can pose a challenge. Boscs are almost crisp even when ripe, so you need to look for subtle clues. Check the neck by applying gentle pressure with your thumb. As long as you sense a little "give," the Bosc should be ripe enough to eat.

Cabbage and Fennel Salad with Meyer Lemon and Tangerines

This fresh and delicious salad really shows off the lighter side of cabbage, which can be sweet and sophisticated when paired with other delicate flavors. Fennel can be fibrous, so be sure to slice it as thin as you can for the best texture. Meyer lemons have a beautiful perfume and are less acidic than a regular lemon. If you can't find Meyers, use half lemon and half tangerine juice.   SERVES 6

1 pound green or Savoy cabbage
  (1 small head or ½ large head)
1 fennel bulb (about 8 ounces), very
  thinly sliced
¼ cup extra-virgin olive oil
3 tablespoons toasted sesame oil
1 teaspoon apple-cider vinegar

Juice of 1 Meyer lemon
1 teaspoon kosher salt
2 large tangerines, peeled, seeded,
  and cut into chunks
¼ cup chopped scallions
2 tablespoons black sesame seeds

With a short, stiff knife, cut the core from the cabbage. If using a whole cabbage, cut it in half; lay the flat side on a cutting board, and then using a chef's knife cut into ⅛-inch slices. Put the cabbage into a large bowl with the sliced fennel.

Whisk together the olive oil, toasted sesame oil, vinegar, lemon juice, and salt; pour the dressing over the cabbage and fennel, and toss to coat thoroughly. Let sit for about 15 minutes, then gently mix in the tangerines, scallions, and sesame seeds; toss again.

Serve cold or at room temperature. For a slightly dressier presentation, arrange a bed of the cabbage mixture on a platter, top with a pile of tangerine chunks, and then sprinkle with the scallions and sesame seeds.

CSA Snapshot
Worden Farm
Punta Gorda, Florida
www.wordenfarm.com

THE FARMERS: Chris and Eva Worden

THE CSA LIFE: Worden Farm is a certified organic, 85-acre farm in southwestern Florida, where the hot summers mean that the growing season is fall, winter, and spring. Both Wordens have doctoral degrees in agriculture, just one of the many ways they've dedicated their lives to organic farming and food. The farm engages its members through workshops, farm feasts, and other special events.

Cook's Tip
Meyer lemons are highly seasonal, appearing in winter and lasting only through early spring. They are perishable, too, and aren't often shipped out of their region. Meyers are a cross between a lemon and a common orange or mandarin orange, and their juice is sweeter and less biting than a regular lemon. If you can't find a Meyer lemon, you can approximate the flavor by using half regular lemon and half orange or tangerine juice.

Swiss Chard and Feta Phyllo Pastries

This is a twist on the classic Greek dish spanakopita, spinach pie. Here, Swiss chard stands in for the spinach, adding great flavor and a slightly more substantial texture. If you find yourself with a few random handfuls of other greens, such as arugula, mizuna, or baby kale, add them to the chard. MAKES 15 TRIANGLES

1 pound Swiss chard
¼ cup plus 2 tablespoons olive oil
1 medium onion, finely chopped
Kosher salt and freshly ground
    black pepper
3 cloves garlic, minced

1 tablespoon sherry vinegar
8 ounces feta, crumbled
2 tablespoons finely snipped
    fresh dill
Grated zest of 1 lemon
Few scrapes of freshly grated
    nutmeg

1 large egg, lightly beaten
½ package phyllo dough, thawed
4 tablespoons unsalted butter,
    melted

Trim off any dry ends from the chard stems, and then cut the stems from the leaves by running a sharp knife along either side. Stack the leaves, roll them into a cylinder, and cut into thin ribbons, then chop the ribbons a few times to make smaller pieces.

Chop the stems into small pieces (about the same size as the onions). Heat a large frying pan with 2 tablespoons of the olive oil. Add the onions and chard stems, season with salt and pepper, and cook over medium heat for about 7 minutes, or until very soft, stirring frequently. Add the garlic and cook for 1 minute or until fragrant. Add the vinegar to deglaze the pan, scraping up any browned bits from the bottom. Add the chard leaves to the pan and cook, tossing frequently, until they're completely wilted and tender, 5 to 6 minutes (add a few spoonfuls of water if the pan is looking dry). Transfer to a bowl and let cool. Then add the feta, dill, lemon zest, and nutmeg, and season with salt and pepper. Taste and adjust the seasoning. Stir in the egg.

Heat the oven to 350°F. Make sure the phyllo is completely thawed and pliable. Unroll it onto a large cutting board or work surface, cut lengthwise into 3 long pieces, and cover with a piece of plastic wrap and then a damp cloth.

CSA Snapshot

Millsap Farms
Springfield, Missouri
www.millsapfarms.com

THE FARMER: Curtis Millsap

THE CSA LIFE: The farm consists of 3 acres of vegetables, a beginning orchard, pigs, chickens, turkeys, forest, and ponds on 20 acres, plus 10 acres of leased land. The Millsaps are committed to education about food and agriculture and often host school visits to the farm. On a larger scale, they run an internship and apprenticeship program that gives aspiring farmers the chance to start a small enterprise on the Millsaps' land, as a way to launch themselves into the farming life.

Combine the remaining ¼ cup olive oil with the melted butter. To assemble the triangles, brush a strip of phyllo with the oil mixture and lay a second strip on top. Scoop about 2 tablespoons chard mixture and mound it at one end of the strip. Fold the short end over to line up with the long end, creating a triangle. Keep folding the triangle down the strip—the way you fold a flag—to form a neat triangular packet. Arrange the triangle on a baking sheet, brush the top lightly with the oil-butter mixture, and repeat with the rest of the phyllo and chard.

Bake until the triangles are brown and crisp, 20 to 25 minutes. Let cool for at least 10 minutes before serving hot or at room temperature.

Prep School

Phyllo dough has a semi-deserved reputation for being tricky to work with, but don't let that scare you. There are two enemies when dealing with phyllo dough: moisture and not enough moisture. Don't get phyllo wet and don't let it dry out (keep the stack of phyllo leaves covered with a piece of plastic wrap and a damp towel).

Cook's Tip

These pastries freeze beautifully, so make a double batch and freeze half, unbaked, on a baking sheet until firm, then transfer to a zip-top freezer bag; push out all the air before sealing. There's no need to thaw before baking—just increase the cooking time by about 10 minutes.

Roasted Squash Appetizers

Chef Jonathan Miller created these earthy crostini for Mariquita Farm. They're really almost tiny sandwiches—delicate but substantial enough to keep your guests on track during cocktail hour. They are best when served slightly warm, but you can still do most of the work ahead: Cook and mash the squash the day before and then just warm it in a saucepan or microwave. Roast the mushrooms the day before as well, but don't cut into wedges. Reheat in a 400°F oven for 5 minutes, and then cut and assemble the hors d'oeuvres.

Feel free to embellish a bit: A thin slice of smoked duck breast, finely chopped pickled vegetables, or a dollop of walnut-parsley pesto would be delicious on top.

MAKES 16 HORS D'OEUVRES

1 small or half a large acorn squash (about 1½ pounds)
Kosher salt and freshly ground black pepper
½ cup mascarpone
4 to 6 fresh sage leaves, chopped
2 medium portobello mushrooms

Olive oil, for the mushrooms
2 cloves garlic, minced
½ of a sourdough baguette, sliced into 16 rounds and lightly toasted or grilled
¼ cup sliced fresh chives

CSA Snapshot

Mariquita Farm
Watsonville, California
www.mariquita.com

THE FARMER: Andrew Griffin

THE CSA LIFE: This organic farm has members in California's Silicon Valley, the Peninsula, and San Francisco, including many restaurants. They like to say they take their members on a "food tour of the world," as they specialize in unusual varieties of vegetables and herbs, such as French fingerling potato varieties, Asian cooking greens, and Native American squash and beans.

Heat the oven to 400°F. Line a baking sheet with parchment or foil. Cut the squash in half lengthwise and put it cut side down on the baking sheet. Roast until very soft and caramelized, 45 to 60 minutes. Let cool until you can handle it, and scoop out the seeds and strings. Then scoop out the flesh and mash it in a small bowl. Stir in a little salt and pepper, the mascarpone, and the sage. Taste for seasoning and add more salt or pepper as needed.

While the squash roasts, roast the portobellos. Cut off and discard the stems (or use for something else, like broth), and season the gill side of each portobello cap with some olive oil, salt, and the garlic. Arrange gill side up on another baking sheet and roast in the oven with the squash until very soft and starting to brown and shrivel a bit, 15 to 20 minutes.

When the mushroom caps are cool, cut them into small dice. Spread a little roasted squash on a piece of bread, top it with some mushrooms, and finish with a sprinkle of chives. Serve slightly warm.

Every-Season Brown Rice Salad

The beauty of this salad is that you can make it with whatever combination of vegetables comes in your CSA box or looks good at the market. The foundation—grains, nuts, chicken, and a lemony dressing—stays the same, but you can mix and match the other ingredients to suit the season.

Brown rice is chewy and delicious (and healthful), but quinoa, wheat berries, or even wild rice would be equally wonderful. SERVES 4

For the basic salad

3 cups cooked and slightly cooled brown rice or other grain

1 cup cooked diced chicken (chickpeas or baked tofu would be a nice alternative)

½ cup walnuts, pecans, or almonds, lightly toasted and coarsely chopped

3 tablespoons chopped fresh flat-leaf parsley

In spring

1 cup fresh peas, quickly blanched in boiling water (or raw, if you like)

1 large or several baby carrots, peeled and either diced or thinly sliced

4 to 6 large asparagus spears, lightly steamed and cut into ½-inch pieces

1 small bunch fresh chives, sliced into ½-inch pieces

In summer

1 red bell pepper, cored, seeded, and diced

Kernels from 1 to 2 ears corn, quickly blanched in boiling water (or raw, if you like)

1 pint cherry tomatoes, cut in half

1 small cucumber, peeled, seeded, and diced

½ bunch scallions, white and light green parts only, chopped

In fall

2 apples, firm pears, or Asian pears, peeled and diced

2 celery stalks, finely chopped

1 mild fresh chile, such as Anaheim or poblano, cored, seeded, and finely diced

1 shallot, minced

In winter

2 cups diced butternut squash, tossed in olive oil and roasted until tender at 375°F (about 25 minutes)

1 apple, peeled and diced

1 large leek, white and light green parts only, cleaned well and very thinly sliced

For the dressing

2 tablespoons fresh lemon juice; more as needed

1 tablespoon apple-cider vinegar

1 teaspoon grainy mustard

½ teaspoon granulated sugar

½ teaspoon kosher salt

Freshly ground black pepper

Few dashes of hot sauce; more as needed

3 tablespoons olive oil; more as needed

CSA Snapshot

Crooked Sky Farms
Phoenix, Arizona
www.crookedskyfarms.com

THE FARMER: Frank Martin

THE CSA LIFE: Farmer Frank has always thought of seeds as magical and of himself as a farmer. The intensive chemical use in farming in Arizona during the 1950s literally made him ill, so his parents started to practice organic methods out of necessity. After losing his father to what was assumed to be pesticide exposure, Frank committed himself to being a different kind of farmer and a committed steward of the land. Today, the certified organic Crooked Sky Farms is a large operation that employs a team of healthy workers that supplies rural Arizona with amazing produce and a great community resource.

Put the brown rice, chicken, nuts, and parsley in a large serving bowl. Add your seasonal ingredients and toss to mix well.

Whisk together the lemon juice, vinegar, mustard, sugar, salt, a few twists of pepper, some hot sauce, and the olive oil. Pour the dressing over the salad and toss again. Taste and adjust the seasoning. Let the salad rest for at least 15 minutes before serving, and adjust the seasoning, lemon juice, hot sauce, or olive oil at the last minute.

Cook's Tip

The flavor and texture of toasted nuts is so much nicer than raw, so it's worth the extra effort to toast them. Heat the oven to 350°F, spread the nuts evenly on a baking sheet or in a heatproof frying pan, and bake for 5 to 8 minutes, depending on the nut. They should smell fragrant and look slightly darker but not too dark. The texture will become crisp once they're cool.

Roasted Garlic Purée

Plan B Organics' 50-acre farm in Ontario, Canada, grows 5 acres of certified organic garlic each season. That means they're frequently making and using roasted garlic. The process is mostly hands-off, and the roasted garlic purée will keep in the fridge for up to a week, so it's handy to have a stash available for spreading on sandwiches, stirring into soups, mixing into hamburgers, or using it any other way you can think of. MAKES ABOUT ½ CUP

5 large heads garlic
Kosher salt
¼ cup olive oil

Heat the oven to 400°F. With a sharp knife, cut ¼ to ½ inch off the pointed end of the garlic heads, so the individual cloves are visible.

Put the garlic in a small baking dish, cut side up. Sprinkle with salt, and then drizzle with the olive oil, making sure it drips in between the cloves.

Cover the dish with foil and bake for about 20 minutes; remove the foil and continue cooking until the garlic is very soft and caramelized, about another 15 to 20 minutes. Let the garlic cool, and then squeeze the soft roasted garlic into a small bowl.

Mash the garlic to form a paste, adding in a bit of the roasting oil from the pan, if you like.

CSA Snapshot

Plan B Organics
Branchton, Ont., Canada
www.planborganicfarms.ca

THE FARMERS: Rodrigo Venturelli, Alvaro Venturelli, and Melanie Golba

THE CSA LIFE: Plan B has been farming on 50 acres of sandy loam, set upon a bed of limestone, for more than 15 years. The farm, located about an hour southwest of Toronto, Ontario, Canada, backs onto 100 acres of natural bush and wetland that filters their water. The farmers are further developing their land through naturalizing the farm's buffers by planting native trees and plants.

"Garlic is the warrior of the winter and requires a little extra attention for harvesting and curing. Tomatoes are a quintessential farm crop and customer favorite that take lots of love and work and provide ample rewards. And for a good fall crop, there's nothing like radishes. They germinate in about 3 days and are ready to harvest just 20 days later. How's that for instant gratification!"

—Paige Witherington, Serenbe Farms

Cook's Tip

Use the garlic as a condiment on anything you like, including the following:

SPICED ROASTED GARLIC HUMMUS

Add 1 tablespoon roasted garlic purée to 8 ounces hummus; stir to blend well. Stir in ¼ teaspoon ground cumin, ¼ teaspoon paprika, a tiny pinch ground cloves, 1 teaspoon fresh lemon juice, and ¼ cup chopped fresh cilantro.

ROASTED GARLIC CROSTINI

Spread a teaspoon of roasted garlic purée on a small slice of toasted or grilled baguette. Top with a layer of soft fresh cheese, such as goat cheese or quark, and chopped fresh chives. Or top the roasted-garlic baguette slice with a thin slice of fresh mozzarella and an anchovy fillet.

ROASTED GARLIC CREAM SAUCE

Simmer 1 cup heavy cream until it's slightly reduced and thickened, 5 to 10 minutes. Whisk in 1 to 2 tablespoons roasted garlic purée and ⅓ cup freshly grated Parmesan, and season well with salt and freshly ground black pepper. Serve with cheese and spinach tortellini.

SOUPS

Chard

Creamy Broccoli Soup with Grated Cheese

Broccoli and cheese soup is one of those traditional recipes that is so wonderful when done well, but more often than not it turns out Army green and gloppy. Not so with this version, however, which is lovely and light and fulfills the promise of a soup that actually tastes like broccoli. The trick is to just barely cook the broccoli—until it's tender but not beyond—and to thicken the soup with just a small amount of flour. The choice of cheese you add is up to you: Crumbly aged Cheddar, creamy Fontina, or tangy fresh goat cheese would all be delicious. SERVES 4

1½ pounds broccoli

4 cups low-sodium chicken broth or water

Kosher salt

4 tablespoons unsalted butter

1 cup chopped onions

1 tablespoon unbleached all-purpose flour

½ cup heavy cream

½ teaspoon freshly ground white pepper; more as needed

½ cup grated cheese, such as Cheddar or Fontina

Trim away any dry ends of the broccoli stems. Cut or break the broccoli into large florets. With a sharp paring knife or vegetable peeler, peel away the fibrous outer layer of the stems, and then cut them into ½-inch slices.

Put all of the broccoli into a soup pot, add the broth and ½ teaspoon salt, and simmer just until tender, about 10 minutes. Do not overcook. Scoop out the broccoli and reserve it in a bowl. Reserve the broth in the pot.

In another large pot, heat the butter over medium-high heat, add the onions and a pinch of salt, and cook, stirring frequently, until the onions are very soft and fragrant, 5 to 6 minutes. Don't let the onions brown. Add the flour and stir to blend.

Pour the reserved broth into the onion-flour mixture, whisking to avoid lumps. Bring to a gentle boil and cook for a minute or two, until slightly thickened. Add the cooked broccoli and the cream and simmer for another couple of minutes. Let cool slightly and then purée in a blender (you might need to do this in more than one batch). Return the soup to the pot, add the pepper, and taste; adjust the seasoning with more salt or pepper as needed.

Ladle into soup bowls, top with the cheese, and serve right away.

CSA Snapshot

Delta Sol Farm
Proctor, Arkansas
www.deltasolfarm.com

THE FARMER: Brandon Pugh

THE CSA LIFE: Located along the Mississippi River about 30 minutes from Memphis, Tennessee, this certified organic farm sits in flat and humid Delta country. The farm's slogan is "Good Farmin' From Real Nearby," a neighborly spirit that's evident as CSA members chitchat with Pugh's mother, Shelley, when they pick up their boxes at her house. Pugh, who calls his members "super-rad friends" and says his farm is the "coolest" organic farm, interacts with members through a newsletter that helps members feel more connected with what's happening in the field.

Cook's Tip

For a special accompaniment to this soup, make some crisp cheese wafers: Line a baking sheet with parchment or a silicone baking mat. For each wafer, sprinkle about 2 tablespoons shredded or grated Parmesan, aged Cheddar, or Manchego to form a flat 4-inch circle. Bake at 375°F until the cheese has melted and turned light golden brown, 6 to 8 minutes. Let cool until crisp.

Roasted Red Pepper Bisque with Seafood Garnish

Potato adds a subtle thickening element to this already lush soup, but the amount is small enough that you just feel its effects rather than taste it. You may also use yellow peppers for the soup or any mix of sweet pepper variety you find in your CSA box or at the market. Thick-walled Lipstick or pimiento peppers are lovely choices. If you have an abundance of sweet peppers, go ahead and roast more than you need; once you've peeled and seeded them, you can store the extras in a freezer bag in the freezer for up to 2 months.

The soup is delicious on its own, with just a sprinkling of herbs, but the addition of the seafood transforms it into something special. SERVES 4 TO 6 AS A FIRST COURSE

4 or 5 large red bell peppers

3 tablespoons unsalted butter

1 medium leek, ends trimmed, sliced thinly crosswise, and thoroughly rinsed to remove any grit

1 medium potato, peeled and cubed

4 cups chicken or vegetable broth or water; more as needed

½ to 1 cup heavy cream or crème fraîche

1 teaspoon fresh lemon juice; more as needed

¼ teaspoon hot sauce, such as sriracha; more as needed

Kosher salt and freshly ground black pepper

For the seafood garnish

1 tablespoon vegetable oil

8 ounces scallops, rinsed

8 ounces large shrimp, peeled and deveined

4 ounces cooked crabmeat (optional)

2 tablespoons chopped fresh flat-leaf parsley, basil, mint, or a combination (optional)

CSA Snapshot

Quiet Creek Farm
Kutztown, Pennsylvania
www.quietcreekfarmcsa.com

THE FARMERS: John and Aimee Good

THE CSA LIFE: This 8-acre certified organic farm is part of the 300-acre Rodale Institute property in the Pennsylvania Dutch community of Berks County. Rodale's organic apple orchard and grain fields and a neighboring organic dairy farm's grazing cows border the farm, and farm visitors are invited to enjoy some peaceful time by the namesake creek behind the harvest barn. The Goods focus on the most flavorful and nutritious varieties, and grow close to 20 types of tomato alone. They enjoy showing members how the weather and environment relate to the triumphs and failures of each year's harvest and the ways the farm operates within nature, not independently of it.

Heat the oven to 400°F. Arrange the peppers on a baking sheet (lined with parchment for easier cleanup), and roast until very soft, slightly collapsed, and browned all over. This may take up to an hour; turn them occasionally so they get browned all over.

Take the peppers from the oven and cover them with a clean dish towel or piece of foil; leave to steam until cool enough to handle. Once the peppers are cool, gently pull out the stem and core, along with most of the seeds. Peel off the skin, pull open the peppers, and scoop out any remaining seeds. Set aside.

Melt the butter in a large soup pot. Add the leeks and cook over medium heat until soft and fragrant, 5 to 8 minutes. Add the potatoes and broth; cover and cook over medium heat until the potatoes are tender, about 6 minutes.

Add the roasted peppers and cook for about 5 minutes more, until both the peppers and potatoes are very tender. Add ½ cup of the cream; remove from the heat and let cool slightly.

Purée the soup in a blender and then return it to the pot over low heat. Add the lemon juice and hot sauce. Taste, add salt, pepper, more lemon juice or hot sauce, and a touch more cream if you like. Keep the soup warm while you cook the seafood.

MAKE THE SEAFOOD GARNISH

Heat the oil in a frying pan over medium-high heat. Pat the scallops and shrimp dry and sauté until no longer translucent in the center, 2 to 5 minutes depending on their size. The scallops should be lightly golden brown. If using crabmeat, just warm gently in a frying pan, but don't let it actually cook.

To serve, divide the hot soup among shallow soup bowls, and arrange a mound of shrimp, scallops, and crab (if using) in the center. Sprinkle with the chopped herbs (if using).

Cook's Tip

Scallops usually have a small tab of muscle attached to one side; it's especially noticeable on sea scallops, but even tiny bay scallops can have it. Before you rinse the scallops, sort through them and simply peel or pull off the tab. It's perfectly edible but a bit chewy.

Summertime Corn Soup

This soup uses the wonderful summertime trio of corn, peppers, and tomatoes, so think of making a double or triple batch and freezing it. Come winter, you'll have a delicious and welcome reminder of summer. Simmering the corncobs in the soup intensifies the sweet corn flavor, so don't skip that step. SERVES 4

4 ears of corn, husks and
  silks removed
3 tablespoons olive oil
1 medium onion, chopped
Kosher salt
1 teaspoon ground cumin
1 teaspoon ground coriander
1 teaspoon chili powder
1 fresh jalapeño, seeded and minced
1 clove garlic, minced

5 medium tomatoes, peeled,
  seeded, and chopped
  (about 2½ cups)
3 medium waxy potatoes, such as
  Carola, German Butterball, or Red
  Bliss, scrubbed and diced with
  skins on (about 1½ cups)
1 green or red bell pepper, cored,
  seeded, and finely diced
½ cup half-and-half or heavy cream
½ cup grated mild Cheddar

Hold each ear of corn with the flat end in a large bowl and use a sharp knife to cut down the cob, removing the kernels. You should have about 2 cups of kernels. Reserve the cobs.

In a heavy-based stockpot, heat the olive oil, then add the onions and ½ teaspoon salt. Cook over low heat until the onions are soft, about 10 minutes.

Add the cumin, coriander, chili powder, jalapeños, and garlic to the pot and sauté until the jalapeños are slightly softened, 2 to 3 minutes.

Add the tomatoes and cook them until they release their juices and soften, about 10 minutes. Add the potatoes, bell pepper, reserved corn-cobs, and 3 cups water. Cover and simmer until the potatoes are tender but still firm, 8 to 10 minutes. Add the corn kernels and cook for 1 minute more, until the kernels are heated through.

Remove the stockpot from the stove. Remove the corncobs. Using an immersion blender, blend the soup until about half of it is puréed, or put half the soup in a blender and purée it, and then combine.

Add the half-and-half and cheese and return the soup to the stove. Heat over low heat until the cheese is melted; do not boil. Taste and season with more salt as needed. Ladle into soup bowls and serve right away.

Prep School

A few silk strands left on an ear of corn that's destined for the grill is no big deal, as they'll be quickly singed off. When you're cutting kernels for a soup, though, you want to eliminate as much silk as possible.

Once you've pulled off the husks and accessible silk, dampen a paper towel and wipe the ear from tip to stem to capture any clinging strands. If you want to get compulsive about it, you can use a soft clean vegetable brush (or unused toothbrush) to gently brush silk strands from the crevices.

Chilled No-Cook Tomato Soup with Fresh Basil Oil

This gorgeous summer soup comes from Peter O'Grady, a personal chef and supporter of Borden Farms CSA in Colorado, which specializes in tomatoes. When it's full-on tomato season, this soup is a lovely way to use tomatoes beyond a sliced tomato salad. Like a delicate and refreshing gazpacho, this soup is delicious on its own and is also a perfect base for the addition of chopped peppers, cucumbers, or a tumble of colorful cherry tomato halves. SERVES 4

4 pounds very ripe tomatoes, preferably some interesting heirloom varieties

1 teaspoon sherry vinegar or red-wine vinegar

Pinch of granulated sugar

Kosher salt and freshly ground black pepper

Basil Oil (recipe on the facing page)

Crème fraîche, for serving

Rinse the tomatoes, cut out the cores, and cut away any surface blemishes. Cut the tomatoes into large chunks. Fit a food mill with a disk that's small enough to capture the seeds, and pass the tomatoes through the mill into a bowl. You should have about 1 quart. (You can use a food processor or blender for this, but it will make the soup slightly frothy and a lighter shade of pink, so a better alternative to a food mill is to peel and seed the tomatoes first, put the seeds through a fine-mesh sieve to capture the juices, and then chop the tomato flesh finely by hand.)

Add the vinegar and a pinch of sugar (the amount will depend on the ripeness of your tomatoes), and season generously with salt and pepper. Chill the soup for at least 1 hour and up to overnight. Taste again right before serving and adjust the seasoning.

Divide the soup among serving bowls or cups and drizzle some basil oil over the surface. Stir the crème fraîche to loosen it and drizzle a few drops onto each serving of soup (don't use too much or you'll lose the fresh flavor of the tomatoes).

CSA Snapshot
Borden Farms
Delta, Colorado
www.bordenfarms.com

THE FARMERS: Guy and Lynn Borden and crew

THE CSA LIFE: Sitting at an elevation of 5,200 feet in the historic farming and ranching community of Pea Green, this 14-acre USDA certified organic family farm benefits from the high desert valley's fertile soil and snowmelt from the surrounding Rocky Mountains. Guy Borden is known as "The Tomato Guy," and he loves to share his enthusiasm for heirloom tomato varieties, such as Dr. Wyche's Yellow, Pruden's Purple, and Sungold.

Basil Oil

MAKES ABOUT 1 CUP

1 bunch fresh and fragrant basil,
  thick stems removed

1 cup mild extra-virgin olive oil

Process the basil and oil in a blender or food processor and then transfer to a jar. Let the oil infuse in the refrigerator for a few hours or overnight.

Strain the oil through a fine-mesh sieve. Be sure to store the oil in the refrigerator, where it will keep for up to 1 week.

Cook's Tip

To get perfectly clear herb oils, strain first through a fine-mesh sieve to remove most of the solids and then strain again through a coffee filter. This can take some time, so keep your filtering setup in the fridge during the process to keep the oil perfectly fresh and safe.

"It's hard to choose from some 200 varieties of fruits and vegetables, but family favorites are lemon cucumbers, Truck Buster watermelons, and Golden Peach heirloom tomatoes, which are actually a little fuzzy!"
—Harmony Dillaway, 47 Daisies

Harvest Vegetable Soup with Red Lentils and Curry

This soup will take on the character of whatever vegetables you add to the base—sweet and mellow with lots of roots; bright and summery with bell peppers, corn, and green beans; spicy-sweet with winter squash and chiles. You may use other types of lentils, but the red ones soften nicely to give the soup body. SERVES 6

5 tablespoons olive oil

2 tablespoons black mustard seeds

1 tablespoon cumin seeds

3 cloves garlic, chopped

1 medium onion, finely diced

2 celery ribs, chopped

3 tablespoons curry paste or curry powder

2 cups red lentils

1½ cups puréed or finely chopped tomatoes (one 14.5-ounce can)

2 cups diced or chopped vegetables: options include roots such as carrots, turnips, potatoes; leafy greens such as Swiss chard, lacinato kale, spinach; and fruiting vegetables such as zucchini, eggplant, green beans

One 14-ounce can coconut milk (light is fine)

Kosher salt

½ cup chopped fresh cilantro or flat-leaf parsley

Put the oil in a large soup pot or Dutch oven; add the mustard seeds, cumin seeds, garlic, onions, and celery and sauté until the mustard seeds pop and the celery and onions are fragrant and translucent, 3 to 4 minutes.

Add the curry paste and cook, stirring, for another 30 seconds or so. Add the lentils, tomatoes, 6 cups water, and the longer-cooking vegetables, like the roots. (Add any fruiting vegetables in the middle of cooking time and any tender leafy greens toward the end of cooking time.)

Cook, uncovered, over medium heat until the lentils are soft and all vegetables are tender, about 40 minutes, stirring occasionally and adding more water as needed.

Stir in the coconut milk and season generously with salt. Simmer gently for a few more minutes to blend the flavors. Divide among soup bowls and sprinkle with the cilantro.

CSA Snapshot

Worden Farm
Punta Gorda, Florida
www.wordenfarm.com

THE FARMERS: Chris and Eva Worden

THE CSA LIFE: Worden Farm is a certified organic, 85-acre farm in southwestern Florida, where the hot summers mean that the growing season is fall, winter, and spring. Both Wordens have doctoral degrees in agriculture, just one of the many ways they've dedicated their lives to organic farming and food. The farm engages its members through workshops, farm feasts, and other special events.

Cook's Tip

Frying the spices before adding other ingredients to the dish develops flavor in two ways: The spices themselves cook, which ups their intensity, and the spice flavors permeate the cooking oil, which helps to distribute the flavors throughout the dish.

Roasted Potato and Corn Chowder

During the summer, Indiana farmer Tamera Mark puts up her corn kernels in 4-cup bags and stocks the freezer so that it's easy for her to have a taste of summer in the winter by making this chowder. Freshly shucked corn is, of course, delicious in this recipe, too. Her special touch of roasting the potatoes gives the soup deeper flavor, but you can skip it if need be. SERVES 4

4 medium potatoes (any type), peeled if skins are thick and cut into 1-inch dice

¼ cup plus 1 tablespoon olive oil

Kosher salt

2 cups chopped leeks, white and light green parts only, washed well

2 tablespoons unsalted butter

2 tablespoons unbleached all-purpose flour

4 cups milk or half-and-half; more as needed

4 cups sweet corn kernels

Freshly ground black pepper

Dash of hot sauce

Heat the oven to 400°F.

Spread the potatoes on a rimmed baking sheet, drizzle with ¼ cup of the olive oil, season generously with salt, and then toss to coat evenly. Roast until the potatoes are tender and golden brown, about 20 minutes.

Meanwhile, add the remaining 1 tablespoon olive oil to a heavy-based frying pan and sauté the leeks over medium heat until very soft, sweet, and translucent, about 15 minutes.

Melt the butter in a large soup pot, add the flour, and whisk to form a smooth roux. Add the milk slowly, whisking constantly until smooth; simmer for another couple of minutes to cook off any raw flour flavor.

Add the leeks, corn, and roasted potatoes. If the soup seems too thick, add a bit more milk or water. Season to taste with salt, pepper, and hot sauce.

CSA Snapshot

Iron Creek Farm
LaPorte, Indiana
www.ironcreekfarm.com

THE FARMERS: Tamera and Pat Mark

THE CSA LIFE: Iron Creek is located just a few miles south of Michigan on the beautiful rich black soils of northern Indiana. The Mark family has been on the land for more than 100 years, and their pride of land is evident through the environmental stewardship and commitment to their certified organic standards. Just as they want to protect their three daughters from harmful chemicals, they protect their local wildlife and improve the soil and water quality.

Cook's Tip

The texture and flavor of frozen corn is best if you blanch the corn quickly before freezing (this prevents enzymes from affecting the corn). Boil the kernels for about 1 minute, then drain well. Spread out on a tray and freeze until the kernels are firm. Pile into a freezer container or bag, press out all the air, and freeze completely.

Chicken, Summer Vegetable, and Tortilla Soup

Think of this soup as sort of a Southwestern minestrone—loads of fresh vegetables and herbs in a savory broth—but in this case, crisp corn tortillas are used instead of pasta. Try any combination of vegetables that you like—though be sure to include the tomatoes, which help flavor the broth. Feel free to leave out the chicken and use vegetable broth or water to make the soup vegetarian. SERVES 4 TO 6

1 tablespoon vegetable or olive oil

½ cup finely chopped onions

Kosher salt

4 to 6 cloves garlic, chopped

1 tablespoon chili powder, mild or hot

1 tablespoon tomato paste

2 quarts homemade or low-salt canned chicken broth

6 cups mixed fresh vegetables: options include julienned or diced zucchini or yellow squash, chopped tomatoes, chopped tomatillos, corn kernels, fresh mild chiles

½ cup chopped fresh cilantro leaves

3 cups chopped or shredded cooked chicken

For the topping

3 handfuls plain tortilla chips, crushed

1 cup shredded Colby or Monterey Jack or crumbled queso fresco, feta, or ricotta salata

½ cup sour cream

Lime wedges, for serving

Put the oil in a large soup pot or Dutch oven, add the onions and a pinch of salt, and cook over medium-high heat until the onions are soft and translucent, 5 to 6 minutes. Add the garlic and chili powder and cook for another minute or so. Stir in the tomato paste, add the broth, and bring to a simmer.

Add the vegetables to the broth, starting with the longer-cooking ones first, such as chiles and tomatillos. Simmer for a few minutes and then add the squash, tomatoes, and/or corn, along with about half of the cilantro. Simmer the soup until all the vegetables are tender, 15 to 35 minutes, depending on what you're adding and how small you've cut things. Add the chicken and simmer for another few minutes to heat through. Taste and adjust with more salt as needed.

To serve, divide the soup among wide soup bowls and top with the rest of the cilantro, some crushed tortilla chips, shredded or crumbled cheese, and a drizzle of sour cream. Let each diner squeeze lime juice over the soup at the table.

CSA Snapshot

Acadian Family Farm
Fort Cobb, Oklahoma
www.acadianfamilyfarm.word-press.com

THE FARMERS: Rod and Nanette Ardoin

THE CSA LIFE: This farm sits on the plains of southwest Oklahoma in Tornado Alley. The Ardoins named their certified organic farm after the descendants of the 17th-century French colonists who settled in Acadia, Canada, and who later resettled in a region of Louisiana now referred to as Acadiana. The Acadians were known for their small, self-sufficient farms. Both Rod and Nanette are originally from southwest Louisiana and are both of French descent. Their CSA takes the form of a "Veggie Club," in which members pay a deposit at the beginning of the season, then pay for weekly shares, and get the deposit refunded through free vegetables at the end of the season.

Cook's Tip

You can make your own tortilla chips by cutting corn tortillas into strips, frying a few at a time in hot oil until deep golden, and draining on paper towels. The tortillas will crisp as they cool, so don't be tempted to overcook them.

Siberian Borscht with Seasonal Vegetables and Sauerkraut

This recipe was contributed by 47 Daisies CSA member Dondie Martynov, who learned to make it while actually living in Siberia. Beets, potatoes, carrots, and onions are the basics, but you can add other vegetables that you have on hand, according to the season: in late summer, green beans, bell peppers, and yellow squash; in fall or winter, parsnips, turnips, celery root, or leeks. Mushrooms would also be delicious, but you should sauté them in a little oil or butter before adding them to the soup.

This is definitely one of those soups that's even better the second day, so if you can, make it a day ahead, but don't add the final amount of dill or the sour cream until you're ready to serve. SERVES 6

2 pounds beef short ribs or stew meat (the soup is better with a little of both)
1 bay leaf
2 teaspoons kosher salt
¼ teaspoon freshly ground black pepper
2 tablespoons olive oil
1 large onion, chopped
1 large carrot, grated or chopped
¼ cup tomato paste

½ cup chopped fresh flat-leaf parsley
½ cup snipped fresh dill
1 cup sauerkraut, drained
2 large beets, peeled and grated
2 large potatoes (any variety), cut into ½-inch dice
2 teaspoons fresh lemon juice; more as needed
¼ teaspoon hot sauce; more as needed
½ cup sour cream or plain yogurt

CSA Snapshot

47 Daisies
Ruston, Louisiana
www.47daisies.com

THE FARMERS: Dylan and Harmony Dillaway

THE CSA LIFE: In an area dominated by majestic pine forest, this southern farm sits in the Piney Hills region of north-central Louisiana. The Dillaways grow their crops using certified naturally grown methods and call farming "a passion, a calling, and a blur of life, love, and aching muscles!" Dylan has farmed from childhood, starting his first CSA at age 17. The Saturday pick-ups bring people to the farm and allow members to be involved in selecting their produce. Several members bring compost each week to share and are learning the farm way of life simply by visiting on a regular basis.

Put the short ribs into a large pot. Add 8 cups water, the bay leaf, salt, and pepper. Bring to a boil, then reduce the heat to a simmer and cook, partially covered, until the meat is tender and falling off the bones, 1 to 1½ hours.

While the meat is simmering, heat the oil in a frying pan over medium-high heat, add the onions and carrots, and sauté until tender. Add the tomato paste, parsley, and half the dill. Cook for 1 to 2 minutes, stirring, to slightly toast the tomato paste. Remove from the heat.

Remove the bay leaf and the short ribs from the pot. When they're cool enough to handle, pull or cut away all the meat and add it back to the pot.

Add the mixture from the frying pan and simmer everything for about 10 minutes. Add the sauerkraut, beets, and potatoes, and continue to simmer until the vegetables are very tender, another 20 to 30 minutes. Add the lemon juice, hot sauce, and all of the remaining dill except for about a tablespoon and simmer for a final 5 minutes.

Taste and adjust the seasoning with more salt and pepper, lemon juice, or hot sauce. Ladle the borscht into bowls and top each serving with a dollop of sour cream and a few sprinkles of dill.

Cook's Tip

To make a vegetarian version of this dish, eliminate the beef, use a vegetable broth instead of the beef cooking liquid, and add a heaping tablespoon of smoked paprika to the onions as you sauté them. The paprika adds complexity, and its smokiness evokes a meaty flavor.

Escarole and White Bean Soup with Garlic-Parmesan Crostini

This soup, contributed by Ginny Bucciaglia, is simple, hearty, and extraordinarily delicious. It's a perfect example of what the Italians call *cucina povera*—peasant cooking—in which the most basic ingredients are transformed into soul-satisfying dishes. You could substitute any variety of kale for the escarole, though the slightly bitter note of escarole works well. And if you have a CSA that includes bread, this is the perfect destination for some slices of a slightly stale artisan loaf. SERVES 4 TO 6

½ cup extra-virgin olive oil

½ medium onion, finely chopped

2 teaspoons fresh thyme leaves or chopped fresh rosemary

Kosher salt and freshly ground black pepper

2 tablespoons minced garlic

½ cup dry white wine, such as Sauvignon Blanc (optional)

1 head escarole, coarsely chopped

4 cups low-sodium or homemade chicken or vegetable broth

Two 15-ounce cans cannellini beans, drained

Fresh lemon juice

Six ½-inch slices rustic bread, such as ciabatta or pain au levain

1 clove garlic

¾ cup freshly grated Parmigiano-Reggiano

CSA Snapshot
Fort Hill Farm
New Milford, Connecticut
www.forthillfarm.com

THE FARMERS: Paul Bucciaglia and Rebecca Batchie

THE CSA LIFE: Fort Hill Farm, located in southwestern Connecticut, grows certified organic vegetables for 300 CSA shareholders and customers at the Westport Farmers' Market. The farm is situated on a terrace above the Housatonic River, operating on land leased from Sunny Valley Preserve, a project of The Nature Conservancy. The farm focuses heavily on soil nutrition through the growth of cover crops and the application of compost and rock powders. It offers a full-season apprenticeship program for individuals interested in learning how to farm.

Heat the oil in a large soup pot over medium heat. Add the onions and thyme and season lightly with salt and pepper. Cook, stirring frequently, until the onions are translucent and fragrant, 4 to 6 minutes. Add the garlic and cook for another 30 seconds.

Add the wine (if using) and simmer for about 5 minutes. Add the escarole, cover the pot, and steam until the escarole starts to soften, about 10 minutes. Add the broth and 1 cup water, and then gently stir in the beans.

Bring to a boil, then reduce the heat and simmer for about 30 minutes, partially covered, until the ingredients have married nicely and the soup looks slightly thickened. Add up to another cup of water if the beans start to pop through during cooking or if the soup is too thick. Season with salt, pepper, and lemon juice to taste. Keep warm while you make the garlic toasts.

continued on p. 84

Position an oven rack about 5 inches below the element and heat the broiler. Arrange the bread slices on a baking sheet and toast on one side until golden brown and crisp. Remove the slices and rub the toasted side with the garlic clove. Flip the slices over, sprinkle the untoasted side with about half the cheese, return to the broiler, and toast until the cheese is browned and bubbly.

To serve, put a crostini in each bowl or soup plate. Ladle the soup over the bread. Serve with the remaining cheese at the table.

"I'd like to be a farmer's-market-all-the-time person, but I just don't always have time. A CSA guarantees that I'll have farm-direct, fresh vegetables all the time, and that I don't get desperate and eat frozen food in the middle of summer. Plus, I love supporting the land-scape and community by investing in local food."

—Jessica B., Crow, OR

Golden Roots and Greens Soup

Soups like this are a boon to the seasonal cook. Once you have the basic architecture of the soup, you can vary the actual ingredients to suit what you have on hand. The base of this soup is puréed root vegetables, accented with some onions and garlic, and the other component is chopped or sliced leafy greens. Whether you use turnips or parsnips, kale or collards, you'll end up with a hearty and delicious dinner. SERVES 6

3 tablespoons unsalted butter or olive oil

1 medium onion, chopped, or 1 large leek, white and light green parts only, washed well and chopped

Kosher salt and freshly ground black pepper

1 clove garlic, chopped

2 large or 4 medium potatoes (any type), peeled if skins are thick and cut into chunks

1 medium celeriac, peeled and cut into chunks

2 large carrots, peeled and cut into chunks

6 to 7 cups homemade or low-sodium chicken broth, vegetable broth, or water

1 bunch kale, Swiss chard, baby bok choy, spinach, escarole, or other hearty greens, chopped

Plain yogurt, sour cream, or crème fraîche, for serving

Melt the butter in a large soup pot or Dutch oven over medium-high heat, add the onions and a bit of salt and pepper, and sauté until the onions are soft and fragrant, about 8 minutes. Add the garlic and sauté for another minute.

Add the potatoes, celeriac, carrots, and broth. Adjust the heat to a nice simmer and cook, covered, until all the roots are tender, about 30 minutes.

Purée the soup in a blender or with an immersion blender. Return the soup to the pot, add the greens, and cook until the greens are tender and bright green. Taste and adjust the seasoning. Serve with a dollop of yogurt.

CSA Snapshot

Quiet Creek Farm
Kutztown, Pennsylvania
www.quietcreekfarmcsa.com

THE FARMERS: John and Aimee Good

THE CSA LIFE: This 8-acre certified organic farm is part of the 300-acre Rodale Institute property in the Pennsylvania Dutch community of Berks County. Rodale's organic apple orchard and grain fields and a neighboring organic dairy farm's grazing cows border the farm, and farm visitors are invited to enjoy some peaceful time by the namesake creek behind the harvest barn. The Goods focus on the most flavorful and nutritious varieties, and grow close to 20 types of tomato alone. They enjoy showing members how the weather and environment relate to the triumphs and failures of each year's harvest and the ways the farm operates within nature, not independently of it.

Cook's Tip

An immersion blender is a handy tool for the soup-maker. While it won't purée to the satiny-smooth levels that a blender will, an immersion blender will turn chunky vegetables into smooth soups with no fuss. You can make this recipe with literally one pot—and if it's a pretty pot, you can bring your soup right to the table.

Roasted Onion and Parsnip Bisque

This is a soup made from humble ingredients that has a luxurious personality. The roasted roots and onions are sweet and rich, and the cream adds texture. It's a lovely way to start a dinner party or a good soup to serve alongside a small salad of bitter and spicy greens. SERVES 6

2 pounds parsnips, ends trimmed and cut into 1-inch rounds

1¼ pounds onions, peeled and cut into large wedges

1 medium carrot, ends trimmed

¼ cup olive oil

Kosher salt and freshly ground black pepper

6 cups homemade or low-sodium chicken broth, vegetable broth, or water; more as needed

1 cup crème fraîche or heavy cream

1 teaspoon fresh lemon juice; more as needed

¼ cup sliced fresh chives

Heat the oven to 375°F. Put the parsnips, onions, and carrot in a large bowl, drizzle with the olive oil, and season lightly with salt and pepper. Spread evenly on two rimmed baking sheets and roast until soft and slightly browned but not dark brown. The onions should be very soft, collapsed, and slightly browned around the edges. This should take 35 to 45 minutes.

Scrape about one-third of the vegetables into a blender, add 1 cup of broth, and process until puréed. Pour the purée into a large soup pot and repeat with another 1 cup broth and the remaining vegetables.

Pour the remaining 4 cups broth into the soup pot, add the crème fraîche and lemon juice, and bring to a simmer. Simmer for about 10 minutes to blend all the flavors; if the soup is thick, thin with a bit more broth. Taste and season generously with salt and pepper; add more lemon juice if the soup tastes too sweet. Divide among serving bowls or cups and sprinkle with the chives.

Prep School

Crème fraîche has a delicious nuttiness and slight tang that make it a fantastic ingredient for enriching soups and sauces. You can make your own, with some good cream and a little time.

Stir together 2 cups cream (not ultra-pasteurized) and 2 tablespoons cultured buttermilk in a saucepan; heat just to about 85°F. Transfer to a clean jar or bowl, cover with cheesecloth, and leave at room temperature for 8 to 24 hours, until thickened. Stir and then refrigerate before using.

CSA Snapshot

Garen's Greens at Riverside Farm
North Berwick, Maine

THE FARMER: Garen Heller

THE CSA LIFE: Heller is farming on land contributed by Riverside Farm, located along the Great Works River. One of the state's oldest farms, Riverside has been in owner "Farmer Dave's" family since 1743. Heller specializes in salad greens, heirloom tomatoes, and root crops, currently selling them at farmer's markets and to restaurants. Before opening Garen's Greens, Heller farmed at Back River Farm, where he ran a CSA. Heller helps other people become growers, too, offering home garden consultations and raised bed construction services.

Caldo Verde with Kale and Chorizo

This classic peasant soup from Spain and Portugal is one of those dishes where the whole is about a million times more than the sum of its parts. The correct sausage is key, however; don't get the raw sausage called chorizo; you need the dry-cured style. If you can't find chorizo or linguiça, then substitute with a good-quality dried salami.

Cutting the greens into very fine shreds is also critical for this soup because their angel hair–like fineness will give the soup a distinct and wonderful texture. SERVES 4

2 tablespoons olive oil

8 ounces Spanish dry-cured chorizo or linguiça sausage, cut into ⅛-inch slices

1 medium onion, diced

2 cloves garlic, minced

¼ teaspoon kosher salt; more as needed

¼ teaspoon freshly ground black pepper; more as needed

1 pound russet potatoes, peeled and cut into 1-inch cubes

4 cups homemade or low-sodium canned chicken broth

1 pound lacinato kale (also called Tuscan kale or cavolo nero) or collards, ribs cut out, leaves rolled, and sliced across into very thin chiffonade

Heat 1 tablespoon of the oil in a soup pot or Dutch oven over medium-high heat until it shimmers. Add the chorizo to the oil and sauté until it has released some of its red oil into the olive oil and become fragrant, 2 to 3 minutes. Remove the chorizo with a slotted spoon and set aside.

Add the remaining 1 tablespoon olive oil to the pot and sauté the onions and garlic until fragrant and translucent. Add the salt and pepper.

Add the potatoes to the onions and garlic, and stir to coat. Add the chicken broth and bring to a boil. Reduce the heat and simmer until the potatoes are fork-tender, 15 to 20 minutes.

Using a potato masher or a wooden spoon, crush about half the potatoes in the pot, creating a creamy look to the soup; leave half of the potatoes as cubes.

Add the kale to the pot, and stir to coat. You'll need to do this in two or three batches because the kale has so much volume; add some kale, stir it in until it wilts, then add some more.

Add 4 cups water and the chorizo to the pot (reserving a few slices to top each serving), and bring to a boil. Reduce the heat, cover, and simmer until the kale is tender, 8 to 15 minutes, depending on the kale. Taste and adjust the seasoning. Ladle into bowls and top with the reserved chorizo.

CSA Snapshot
Half Pint Farm
Burlington, Vermont
www.halfpintfarm.com

THE FARMERS: Mara and Spencer Walton

THE CSA LIFE: Half Pint Farm, as the name suggests, is small, just 2 acres. The half-pint size is exactly what these experienced farmers wanted. In researching farms around the world, they found this to be the most abundantly productive size that was manageable for two people. They get a boost from the milder microclimate of the Vermont Intervale region; the farm resides in the Winooski watershed, a region that floods frequently, which creates their beautiful soil—a sandy silt loam.

PASTA & GRAINS

Radish Leaf Pesto with Linguine

This emerald green pesto has an exceptional liveliness that comes from the character of the radishes. Serve the radishes with some sweet butter and coarse salt as an hors d'oeuvre and then follow with a bowl of pasta dressed with the pesto. Linguine and trenette are great pasta shapes for pesto, but this would also be fantastic on winter squash gnocchi (see p. 112). SERVES 4 AS A FIRST COURSE

2 cups lightly packed radish leaves

2 cloves garlic

3½ tablespoons fresh oregano, chopped

3 to 4 tablespoons fresh lemon juice

1 cup blanched whole almonds

¾ teaspoon kosher salt

½ teaspoon freshly ground black pepper

Pinch of crushed red pepper flakes

¾ cup extra-virgin olive oil

½ cup freshly grated Parmigiano-Reggiano

8 ounces dried linguine, trenette, or penne

Put the radish leaves, garlic, oregano, lemon juice, almonds, salt, pepper, and red pepper flakes in a food processor and pulse to form a coarse purée. With the motor running, pour in the olive oil and process until smooth. Add half the cheese and pulse a few more times. Taste (be careful of the processor blade!) and add more salt or pepper if you like. Set aside until ready to dress the pasta.

Bring a large pot of generously salted water to a boil, add the pasta, and cook until properly done (check the package for cooking time). Scoop out and reserve about 1 cup of the cooking water, then drain the pasta thoroughly.

Put the pasta back into the pot, add the pesto, and gently fold together. Add a little reserved pasta water as needed to keep the consistency creamy rather than sticky. Serve in shallow pasta bowls right away, with the remaining cheese on the side.

CSA Snapshot

Dog Mountain Farm
Carnation, Washington
www.dogmtnfarm.com

THE FARMERS: David and Cindy Krepky

THE CSA LIFE: A sweeping landscape surrounds Dog Mountain Farm—rolling hills of thick Northwest forests and the long snow-capped Cascade Mountain range. The farmers concentrate on making sure their soil is healthy in order to create the most nutrient-dense food. On-farm programs teach a wide range of skills, such as sheep shearing, chicken processing, teamster training, soap making, animal husbandry, food production, and culinary traditions including food preservation and bread and cheese making.

Cook's Tip

You can improvise when making this recipe, using different nuts and herbs. Hazelnuts and walnuts make delicious pestos, and, of course, the more traditional pine nuts would work well, too. For herbs, any of the more tender herbs—basil, flat-leaf parsley, dill, cilantro, mint, chervil—would be delicious, alone or in combination.

PASTA & GRAINS   91

Spring Pasta with Fava Beans and Green Garlic

Fava beans are such an icon of spring—tender, impossibly green, and fleeting . . . which is a good thing, because they're a pain in the neck to prepare. Shelling, blanching, and peeling off the interior skin can be fiddly, yet it's worth it for special occasions, such as finding a few pounds of fava beans in your CSA box!

This delicate pasta dish showcases favas properly, pairing them simply with other early spring vegetables and saucing them lightly with just a splash of cream and a shower of Parmesan. SERVES 4

3 pounds fava beans, in their pods
1 pound dried rigatoni
¼ cup olive oil
5 stalks green garlic, thinly sliced
1 spring onion, white and light green parts only, sliced

¼ cup dry white wine
½ cup crème fraîche
1 cup freshly grated Parmesan
Kosher salt and freshly ground black pepper

Prepare the fava beans according to the instructions in the sidebar on the facing page.

Bring a large pot of salted water to a boil, add the pasta, and cook until al dente, following the package directions. Meanwhile, in a large sauté pan, heat the oil over medium heat. Add the green garlic and spring onions and cook until the vegetables are softened, about 5 minutes. Add the fava beans and the wine, and cook until the wine is slightly reduced, about 3 minutes longer.

When the pasta is ready, scoop out about 1 cup of the cooking water and reserve. Drain the pasta thoroughly, return to the pot, and add the fava bean mixture. Turn off the heat, and stir in the crème fraîche and Parmesan; add a few spoonfuls of cooking water as desired to create a creamy consistency. Season generously with salt and pepper.

CSA Snapshot

**Freewheelin' Farm
Santa Cruz, California
www.freewheelinfarm.com**

THE FARMERS: Darryl Wong, Amy Courtney, and Kirstin Yogg

THE CSA LIFE: At Freewheelin' Farm, a 180-degree view of the ocean surrounds the growers in their fields. The beauty of the ocean is contrasted by harsh winds that whip across the vegetable fields, earning these 8 acres the nickname "the tundra" and making it impossible to grow some hot-weather crops such as tomatoes and peppers. Since 2002, this team of farmers has been going beyond strictly organic methods, delivering some of their CSA shares by bicycle to decrease their petroleum consumption and always taking special care to conserve natural resources.

Prep School

Fava beans have a slightly Dr. Seussian character to them—they grow in large cushiony pods with a fuzzy interior. Favas can be deceiving in that it takes a large amount of pods to yield a modest amount of edible beans, so plan accordingly: You'll need about 1½ pounds of pods to produce 1 scant cup of peeled beans.

1. Break open the pods, either by pulling them apart or by slipping your finger into the seam and sliding it up like a zipper. Lift out the beans.

2. Bring a pot of water to a boil, and boil the beans for about 1 minute. Drain and then chill the beans under cool running water or in an ice bath.

3. Favas have one end that's slightly flatter and slightly wider than the other, with a scar where the bean was attached to the pod. Grasp the fava between your fingers with the scar facing up, and with the thumbnail or your other hand, tear into the scar end and peel the whitish membrane back. Pinch gently, and the emerald green bean within will slide right out. Very small beans are ready to eat as is, having been cooked enough by the blanching. Larger beans need a touch more cooking.

Baked Winter Squash Roll-Ups

Indiana farmer Beth Eccles loves the shapely squash called Rugosa Violina, which translates from Italian as "wrinkled violin." It's similar to butternut in shape and size with all the beauty and flavor of an heirloom variety. When she cooks for her family, she makes this baked pasta dish with gluten-free noodles made from rice flour (she suggests Tinkyada® brand), which behave just like wheat flour noodles. Paired with a simple green salad, this makes a simple but special winter meal. SERVES 6

1 medium winter squash, about 2 pounds, cut in half and seeds removed

1 tablespoon extra-virgin olive oil

Kosher salt and freshly ground black pepper

One 9-ounce package rice flour or no-boil lasagna noodles (Barilla® is a good brand)

½ cup heavy cream or crème fraîche

1 cup freshly grated Parmigiano-Reggiano

A few scrapes of freshly grated nutmeg

¼ cup chopped fresh flat-leaf parsley (optional)

Heat the oven to 400°F. Put the squash halves on a baking sheet and roast until very tender when pricked with a fork, 45 to 55 minutes. Set aside to cool. (You may cook the squash ahead of time and refrigerate or freeze it.) When cool enough to handle, scoop the squash flesh away from the peel and place in a bowl. Drizzle with the olive oil, add a sprinkle of salt and pepper, and mash to make a soft purée. Taste and adjust the seasoning. Measure out about 2 cups; freeze any excess for next time or another use.

Turn the oven down to 375°F. Bring a large pot of salted water to a boil, add the lasagna, and cook just until soft. (No-boil noodles will only take a couple of minutes; start testing soon. For rice noodles, follow the package instructions.) Drain the pasta well and arrange the noodles on parchment paper.

Grease a 9 x 13-inch baking dish with a little olive oil or butter. Spread approximately 2 tablespoons of the squash mixture on a noodle, leaving free 1 inch on each end and ½ inch on each side (2 tablespoons for each noodle should fill about 16 noodles; if your box contains fewer, larger

noodles, use more filling). Carefully roll up the noodle loosely, to keep the squash filling from oozing out the sides. Continue the process until you have used up all of your noodles.

Arrange the rolls side by side in the baking dish, seam side down. Pour the cream over the rolls and sprinkle the cheese over the top. Dust with salt, pepper, nutmeg, and the chopped parsley (if using). Cover with foil and bake for 30 minutes, then remove the foil and bake for another 5 to 10 minutes, until the top is nicely browned.

"We like to create a dining room table centerpiece out of several colors and varieties of winter squash. When the mood strikes, we'll just grab one that looks interesting and head into the kitchen."

—Freida Lansing, Windermere Farms & Apiaries

Best-Ever Roasted Tomato Sauce

Colorado farmer Guy Borden grows loads of heirloom tomatoes from which he makes this easy and flavorful sauce, which is a wonderful way for anyone to showcase end-of-summer tomatoes. Make a triple batch and freeze the extra. At Borden Farms, they use big beefsteak-type tomatoes, but you could use small slicers or plum tomatoes instead. The sauce makes a great base for tomato soup, too. Just thin it out with some vegetable or chicken broth and add a touch of cream. MAKES ABOUT 3 CUPS

4 pounds ripe tomatoes, cored and cut in half

½ sweet onion (such as Walla Walla or Vidalia), chopped

2 cloves garlic, coarsely chopped

1 tablespoon granulated sugar; more as needed

1 teaspoon kosher salt; more as needed

2 tablespoons chopped fresh herbs (basil, oregano, rosemary, or a combination)

¼ cup extra-virgin olive oil

Heat the oven to 375°F. Arrange the tomatoes cut side down in a large glass baking dish in a single layer (you may need to use two). Scatter the onions, garlic, sugar, salt, and herbs on top of the tomatoes and drizzle with the olive oil.

Roast until the tomatoes shrivel and collapse and their juices start pooling in the bottom of the baking dish, about 2 hours, though the time can vary greatly depending on the size and consistency of the tomatoes.

Let the roasted tomatoes cool slightly, and then scrape everything into a blender or food processor and process until smooth. If you want to remove the skins and seeds (which is unnecessary, though it makes for a prettier, smoother sauce), run the sauce through a food mill. Taste and adjust the seasoning with more salt or sugar.

CSA Snapshot

Borden Farms
Delta, Colorado
www.bordenfarms.com

THE FARMERS: Guy and Lynn Borden and crew

THE CSA LIFE: Sitting at an elevation of 5,200 feet in the historic farming and ranching community of Pea Green, this 14-acre USDA certified organic family farm benefits from the high desert valley's fertile soil and snowmelt from the surrounding Rocky Mountains. Guy Borden is known as "The Tomato Guy," and he loves to share his enthusiasm for heirloom tomato varieties, such as Dr. Wyche's Yellow, Pruden's Purple, and Sungold.

Cook's Tip

Roasted tomato halves freeze beautifully, so roast a few extra pounds when you make this sauce. Put them in a freezer container or bag, press out the air, and freeze to use later in other styles of sauce or in stews, soups, or braises.

Ricotta Risotto with Dandelion Greens and Orange

Dandelion greens are much appreciated in other countries, especially France and Italy, but here in North America, we don't have much of a relationship with them. Their chief attribute—aside from their nutritiousness—is the bold bitter flavor. When moderated with some olive oil and cheese, that bitterness becomes an exciting accent, but you need to be sure you don't let it overwhelm the dish. Taste a bit of the dandelion greens first to get a sense of their bitterness, and taste again once they've been tempered by the heat of cooking. You may substitute another tender bitter green, such as lacinato kale, tatsoi, mizuna, or curly endive, if dandelions aren't available. SERVES 2 OR 3

4 cups low-sodium canned chicken broth

2 tablespoons extra-virgin olive oil

1½ teaspoons minced garlic

1 large bunch tender dandelion greens, trimmed to 2-inch lengths to yield 3 loosely packed cups

⅓ cup sliced cleaned baby leeks, white and tender green parts only (you may substitute spring onions or scallions)

1 cup carnaroli or other risotto rice

⅓ cup white vermouth

½ cup whole-milk ricotta

½ teaspoon finely grated orange zest

1 cup freshly grated pecorino romano

Freshly ground black pepper

In a small saucepan, warm the chicken broth over medium heat; cover the pan and reduce the heat to keep the broth warm.

In a Dutch oven, heat 1½ tablespoons of the olive oil over medium heat; add the garlic and cook, stirring with a wooden spoon, until fragrant, about 1 minute. Add the dandelion greens and cook, stirring, until the leaves are bright green and beginning to wilt, about 5 more minutes. Taste again; the greens should be considerably less bitter. Transfer the mixture to a bowl and set aside.

Add the remaining 1½ teaspoons olive oil to the Dutch oven and then add the leeks. Cook for 1 minute, stirring to make sure the leeks don't burn. Add the rice and stir to coat until opaque, about 1 minute. Add the vermouth and cook until almost all of it has evaporated.

Ladle about 1 cup of the warmed broth into the rice mixture, constantly stirring until almost all the liquid is absorbed by the rice. Continue adding the remaining broth, 1 cup at a time, stirring and allowing the rice to absorb the liquid each time before adding more. The rice mixture should be barely simmering throughout the additions of broth. After

20 minutes, taste the rice. You want the finished rice to be slightly firm and creamy, not mushy, with a bit of liquid remaining. If the rice is tender, remove the pot from the heat. If the rice needs a little more cooking, start with a minute or two, adding a bit more broth if necessary.

Remove the pot from the heat and briskly stir in the ricotta. Any remaining liquid in the rice should come together with the cheese to create the creamy finished consistency. Stir in the dandelion greens. Fold in the orange zest and about ½ cup of the cheese; season generously with black pepper.

Divide the rice among warm bowls or shallow plates, and serve right away with the remaining cheese at the table.

CSA Snapshot
MA'O Organic Farms Wai'anae, Hawaii
www.maoorganicfarms.org

THE FARMERS: Kukui Maunakea-Forth, Gary Maunakea-Forth, and the young workers in the program

THE CSA LIFE: This 24-acre certified organic farm is located on the west side of the island of O'ahu and consists of six major *ahupua'a* (ancient land divisions).

MA'O is the acronym for *mala 'ai 'opio*, which means "the youth food garden," and at MA'O, it's not just food that's cultivated, but the young people themselves. The farm has workshops, school programs, and college classes in nutrition, agriculture, business, and Hawaiian culture, all in service of building leadership and improving the health and vitality of the community. The crops include many familiar to mainland farms but also island specialties such as bananas, taro, curry leaves, and mango.

Orzo Salad with Cherry Tomatoes, Arugula, and Gorgonzola

Pasta is always a suitable partner for seasonal vegetables, especially in a salad to serve at room temperature for a light lunch or as part of an antipasti spread. Orzo is a tiny shape that keeps a nice firm texture and yet soaks up the flavors of the dressing and tomatoes in the salad, which keeps the dish from feeling stodgy the way some pasta salads do. The ingredients here are just a start; feel free to add corn kernels, blanched green beans, diced roasted red peppers, or anything else that looks bright and tasty. Some crumbled crisp bacon would be a fine addition, too. SERVES 4 TO 6

1½ cups orzo (or other tiny pasta)

3 tablespoons extra-virgin olive oil

Grated zest of 1 lemon

2 tablespoons fresh lemon juice; more as needed

1 teaspoon balsamic vinegar; more as needed

½ teaspoon kosher salt; more as needed

Freshly ground black pepper

2 cups cherry tomatoes, cut in half (use a mix of colors and shapes, if possible)

1 cup coarsely chopped arugula

¼ cup very thinly sliced shallots

Handful of coarsely chopped fresh basil

¼ cup crumbled Gorgonzola

Bring a medium pan of generously salted water to a boil. Add the orzo, cover, and cook for 9 to 11 minutes, or until the orzo is tender but still firm to the bite (check the package for cooking time). Drain well, and toss the warm orzo with the olive oil, lemon zest, lemon juice, balsamic vinegar, salt, and a few twists of black pepper. Let the orzo cool, tossing occasionally. Taste and adjust with more salt, pepper, lemon juice, or vinegar.

Put the cooled orzo in a large bowl and gently fold in the tomatoes, arugula, shallots, and basil. Sprinkle the cheese over the top of the salad. Season to taste with more salt and pepper.

CSA Snapshot

Bay Branch Farm
Lakewood, Ohio
www.baybranchfarm.com

THE FARMERS: Annabel Khouri and Eric Stoffer

THE CSA LIFE: Creating a farm out of a vacant lot required intensely dedicated restoration of the soil health. Using mainly a hoe and their hands, Annabel and Eric utilize SPIN farming (small plot intensive) methods to create enough produce to supply their à la farm carte buying club. They don't use any chemicals, herbicides, or pesticides. Annabel and Eric continue to build their soil food web by minimizing tilling, adding compost teas, and even counting beneficial microbes under a microscope.

"The anticipation of getting our CSA box was half the fun, and everything was ultra fresh. The tomatoes and strawberries were especially succulent. Our farmer always included a sheet with recipes for some of the produce as well as a bit of homespun philosophy, so we felt an extra connection to him."

—Patsy K., Woodside, CA

Winter Squash and Kale Risotto with Manchego

At LadyBird Farms, kale and winter squash both make frequent appearances in the CSA boxes. LadyBird grows several varieties of winter squash, including Red Kuri and a local heirloom variety called Lower Salmon River, but any firm yellow winter squash will work in this recipe. A delicious way to use a lot of squash and kale, this gorgeous golden risotto can be served as a vegetarian entrée, but it is a particularly delicious accompaniment to braised lamb shanks or grilled rack of lamb. SERVES 6

3 cups ½-inch-dice Red Kuri or other winter squash

3 tablespoons olive oil

Kosher salt and freshly ground black pepper

1 tablespoon minced garlic

1 bunch kale (any variety), stems removed and torn into 2-inch pieces

6 cups low-sodium vegetable stock

4 tablespoons unsalted butter

1 medium onion, finely diced

1½ cups arborio or carnaroli rice

½ cup dry white wine (such as Sauvignon Blanc or Pinot Grigio)

4 ounces Manchego or other aged sheep's milk cheese or Parmigiano-Reggiano

Heat the oven to 400°F. Toss the diced squash with 2 tablespoons of the oil, season lightly with salt and pepper, and spread into an even layer on a rimmed baking sheet. Roast until tender and slightly browned around the edges, 20 to 30 minutes. Set aside but keep warm.

In a large saucepan, heat the remaining 1 tablespoon oil and the garlic over medium heat until the garlic softens slightly, 1 minute. Add about half of the kale, stirring to coat it with oil and allowing it to wilt and make room in the pan, then add the rest. When all the kale is wilted and coated with oil, add the vegetable stock and a pinch of salt and bring to a gentle simmer. Allow the kale to cook until it is tender, 10 to 20 minutes, depending on the variety. Remove the kale from the stock with a slotted spoon and transfer it to a bowl, setting it aside. Keep the stock on medium-low heat while you make the risotto.

Melt the butter in a large saucepan on medium-low heat. Add the onions and cook until they are very soft and translucent, 10 to 15 minutes. Add the rice and stir to coat it with butter. Cook the rice, stirring frequently, until it looks shiny and starts to smell toasty, about 5 minutes. Add the wine and bring the rice to a very gentle simmer, stirring constantly, until the rice has absorbed most of the liquid.

continued on p. 104

CSA Snapshot

LadyBird Farms
Pocatello, Idaho
www.ladybirdfarms.com

THE FARMERS: Jessica McAleese and Jeremy Shreve

THE CSA LIFE: This small farm, located 8 miles south of Pocatello, Idaho, is nestled in the heart of the high mountain desert. On just 1 acre of land (for now!), LadyBird grows more than 50 varieties of vegetables, herbs, and flowers, most of which is shared with CSA members. The team at LadyBird believes they grow more than just good food. The CSA has built, empowered, and supported the region's community food system and created a lasting partnership between local farmers and consumers who strive for ecological, economical, and socially just ways to grow and eat their food.

Add about 1 cup of the hot vegetable stock to the rice, and continue simmering, stirring occasionally until the rice has absorbed it. Repeat this process until all the stock has been added and the rice is tender but still firm, stirring frequently and keeping the mixture at a very low simmer. When all the stock has been added, fold in the cooked kale and any remaining liquid. Add the cheese and fold gently until it is melted. Season with pepper, then taste the risotto and adjust the seasoning.

Spoon the risotto into bowls, then pile the roasted squash on top. Serve immediately.

"This CSA arrangement has worked so well for us, and we are enjoying your box so much! I'm like a kid . . . waiting to dive into that wonderful box of edible delights. Can't wait to see what new deliciousness is headed our way as the weather cools."

—E.S., Asheville, North Carolina

Angel Hair Pasta with Cherry Tomato Sauce

Here is an example of the beauty of simplicity—a combination of so few ingredients gives you so much in the way of flavor, plus the dish takes literally only the time needed to cook the pasta. Use a mix of tomato varieties, if you can, and try to include some deep orange Sun Golds—they are sweet and fruity, and their moist flesh collapses nicely into a sauce. SERVES 2 OR 3

¼ cup extra-virgin olive oil

2 cloves garlic, minced

1 pound cherry tomatoes, cut in half if large

Kosher salt and freshly ground black pepper

8 ounces dried angel hair pasta

½ cup torn fresh basil leaves

Freshly grated Parmesan, for serving

Bring a large pot of salted water to a boil. As the water is heating, heat the olive oil in a large, deep frying pan over medium heat. Add the garlic, taking care not to let it burn. Add the tomatoes, pressing lightly as they cook so that they split open and release their juices. Season generously with salt and pepper. Once the tomatoes have started to collapse and get juicy, turn the heat to low and cook until they're nicely saucy and quite hot, another 2 to 4 minutes.

Cook the pasta in the boiling water according to the package directions. Drain.

Add the drained pasta to the sauce in the frying pan and toss well. Add the basil and toss once more, then divide among pasta bowls and serve right away, with grated cheese and more ground pepper to pass at the table.

Cook's Tip

If you feel the urge to tinker with the basic recipe, you can always add some minced hot chiles, a few chopped olives or capers, or even a can of good-quality, oil-packed tuna.

CSA Snapshot

**Delta Sol Farm
Proctor, Arkansas
www.deltasolfarm.com**

THE FARMER: Brandon Pugh

THE CSA LIFE: Located along the Mississippi River about 30 minutes from Memphis, Tennessee, this certified organic farm sits in flat and humid Delta country. The farm's slogan is "Good Farmin' From Real Nearby," a neighborly spirit that's evident as CSA members chitchat with Pugh's mother, Shelley, when they pick up their boxes at her house. Pugh, who calls his members "super-rad friends" and says his farm is the "coolest" organic farm, interacts with members through a newsletter that helps members feel more connected with what's happening in the field.

"Turnips Two Ways" Pasta

This light and fresh pasta dish is an excellent demonstration of two important things: 1) turnips are delicious! and 2) the leafy green tops of root vegetables are as tasty as their underground bulbs. These delicate Japanese turnips are much more tender and less biting than their larger cousins, with none of the sulfur notes you may have tasted in big turnips. As for the greens, when the turnips are very fresh, the greens will be in pristine condition. Simply cut them off and treat them as you would any other cooking green. SERVES 4

2 bunches Hakurei (or other sweet Japanese) turnips (about 1 pound total), washed and greens separated from roots

¼ cup olive oil

Kosher salt and freshly ground black pepper

1 stalk green garlic, finely chopped

8 ounces dried delicate pasta, such as capellini or fettuccine

1 to 2 tablespoons fresh lemon juice

½ to 1 cup freshly grated Parmigiano-Reggiano

Put a large pot of water on to boil for the pasta.

Wash the turnip greens thoroughly in several changes of cool water to remove any grit (or bugs!). Coarsely chop and set aside; it's fine if the greens are still slightly wet. Rinse the turnip roots, pat dry, and cut into ⅛-inch slices.

Heat 2 tablespoons of the olive oil in a large frying pan over medium-high heat, and sauté the turnip slices, stirring and flipping frequently so they brown nicely as they soften. Season with salt and pepper, add the garlic, and continue cooking for a few more minutes, until the turnips are tender and browned (but don't let the garlic get brown). Scrape the turnips out of the pan and set aside, keeping them warm.

Return the pan to the heat, add the remaining 2 tablespoons oil, and then add the slightly wet turnip greens. Reduce the heat to medium low, and let the greens steam and wilt until collapsed and tender but still bright green, tossing frequently with tongs. Season lightly with salt and pepper.

Meanwhile, cook the pasta according to the package directions. Right before draining, scoop out about 1 cup of the cooking water and reserve. Drain the pasta well and then add it to the frying pan with the turnip greens. Toss in the turnip rounds and any oil that was on them. Add 1 tablespoon of the lemon juice and toss. Add about two-thirds of the cheese and toss again, adding a few spoonfuls of the reserved cooking water as needed to give the dish a nice consistency. Taste again and add more of the lemon juice, salt, or pepper as needed. Serve the remaining cheese at the table.

CSA Snapshot

Serenbe Farms
Chattahoochee Hills, Georgia
www.serenbefarms.com

THE FARMERS: Paige Witherington and Justin Dansby

THE CSA LIFE: Just 45 minutes southwest of Atlanta, this farm is nestled in a sustainable New Urbanist community called Serenbe. A pine and hardwood forest borders one side of the farm while, on the other, a row of cottages houses green-thumbed neighbors who support farming endeavors. The 4 acres under cultivation are farmed organically, and more acreage is being developed. Serenbe has created a successful community composting system, using waste from residents and local restaurants, which provides a portion of the nutrition needed on the farm.

Bok Choy and Soba Noodles in Sesame Dressing

If you have a CSA, you are very likely to see a lot of bok choy and other cabbages such as Napa. This dish is a perfect destination for that type of hearty green. The bok choy will sweeten as it cooks, with the leaves becoming meltingly tender while the succulent ribs keep a bit of crunch. This dish is delicious at any temperature and makes for amazing cold leftovers. SERVES 3 OR 4

9 ounces buckwheat soba noodles

2 tablespoons sunflower or canola oil

1 medium onion and/or 1 stalk green garlic, coarsely chopped

1 large head bok choy or other greens, coarsely chopped

2 teaspoons rice vinegar, apple-cider vinegar, or white-wine vinegar

4 teaspoons soy sauce or tamari

2 teaspoons honey

2 teaspoons toasted sesame oil

4 scallions, finely chopped

About ¼ cup sesame seeds

2 cups pea shoots or sugar snap peas, coarsely chopped

Cook the soba noodles in boiling water according to the package directions. Drain and set aside.

Heat the oil in a large frying pan. Add the onions and/or green garlic, and sauté over medium-high heat until they begin to soften. Add the bok choy and continue to sauté over medium heat, tossing occasionally, until the bok choy is just cooked and no longer crunchy, about 8 minutes.

In a large bowl, combine the vinegar, soy sauce, honey, and sesame oil. Whisk to combine. Add the noodles to the bowl and toss to coat. Add the bok choy mixture, scallions, sesame seeds, and pea shoots, and then mix it all together.

Cook's Tip

Dried soba noodles are easy to find in most grocery stores; they look like dusky brown spaghetti and are sold in packets. You can sometimes find fresh soba noodles, as well, which have a lovely chewy texture. Many soba noodles do contain wheat flour as well as buckwheat, so if you're looking for a gluten-free noodle, read the package carefully.

CSA Snapshot

Stout Oak Farm
Brentwood, New Hampshire
www.stoutoakfarm.com

THE FARMERS: Kate and Jeff Donald

THE CSA LIFE: Stout Oak Farm is a 58-acre farm in Brentwood, New Hampshire, located on the historic farm property known as Creamery Brook Farm. The Donalds grow 4 acres of vegetables for their CSA members, as well as farmer's markets and restaurants. Though Kate has been a farmer for more than a dozen years, she and Jeff just recently began the New Hampshire farm and are hard at work building out the infrastructure, such as hoop houses, cold-storage rooms, and a new farm store. Their CSA members help, through their support and also through volunteer work such as a potato-digging party.

Polenta with Sautéed Greens and Crispy Sage

This dish is the epitome of wholesome comfort food. The creamy polenta is satisfying like pasta but more nutritious, and the sautéed greens are packed with goodness, no matter which greens you use. The fried sage leaves will be a revelation, too—light and crunchy, they make a surprising garnish for all sorts of Italian-inspired dishes. Try them on herb-rubbed roasted pork loin or wild mushroom risotto. SERVES 3 OR 4

4 cups low-sodium canned chicken broth or water
1½ teaspoons kosher salt
1 cup stone-ground cornmeal
3 tablespoons unsalted butter, cut into pieces
Freshly ground black pepper

¾ cup freshly grated Parmesan; more for serving
¼ cup extra-virgin olive oil
20 to 40 fresh sage leaves
Sautéed Greens (recipe on the facing page)

Bring the broth and salt to a boil in a heavy-based pot. Add the cornmeal in a steady stream while stirring with a whisk or wooden spoon. Reduce the heat to low and cover the pot. The polenta should steam but not bubble busily. Stir every 5 minutes or so, being sure to scrape the sides and bottom of the pot with a wooden spoon each time. Cook until the polenta is smooth and creamy, 30 to 40 minutes, or even longer if you are using coarsely ground meal.

Add the butter, a few twists of freshly ground pepper, and the cheese.

Heat the olive oil over medium-high heat in a frying pan. When the oil starts to shimmer, add enough sage to cover the bottom of the pan. Gently flip the sage leaves with a fork or small spatula so that all sides get coated with oil. Cook for just a couple of minutes, until the sage leaves are curled, dark in color, and crispy. Drain on a paper towel–lined plate. Cook the rest of the sage leaves in the same oil if you couldn't fit them all in the first batch. (If you like, reserve the sage oil for another use.)

Spoon the polenta into shallow bowls or pasta plates. Arrange a mound of greens next to the polenta and then finish with a scattering of crispy sage leaves and more freshly grated Parmesan over everything.

CSA Snapshot
Village Farm
Freedom, Maine
www.villagefarmfreedom.com

THE FARMERS: Polly Shyka and Prentice Grassi

THE CSA LIFE: Nestled in the rolling hills of western Waldo County, Maine, this certified organic farm's diverse acres of crops are a welcome change from the surrounding rows of corn and green pastures that cover the majority of the region's farming landscape. The farmers practice extensive rotational grazing and other soil conservation techniques. Gratitude is a daily harvest on this Maine farm. The farmers feel fortunate to work with aspiring apprentices, provide food for local families, grow seedlings, tend the plants and animals, and be stewards of the soil and water each day.

Sautéed Greens

SERVES 3 OR 4

2 bunches (about 2 pounds total)
   beet greens, chard, spinach, or
   other leafy greens
¼ cup extra-virgin olive oil
3 cloves garlic, chopped
1 tablespoon fresh lemon juice

A few dashes of hot sauce
Kosher salt and freshly ground
   black pepper

Trim off and discard any toughs stem ends from the greens. Wash the
greens well in several changes of cool water to remove any grit or bugs.
Drain in a colander.

Remove any thick stems (especially if you're using chard) by slicing
along both sides. Chop the stems finely. Stack the leaves, roll into a loose
cylinder, and then cut across into wide ribbons. It's fine if the greens are
still slightly wet.

Heat the oil in a large frying pan or Dutch oven over medium high
and add the chopped stems. Cook, stirring constantly, until they begin
to soften, 2 to 3 minutes. Add the chopped garlic and cook for another
few seconds, until fragrant, taking care not to let the garlic burn. Add the
greens, cover the pan, and cook until the greens have wilted down, about
3 minutes. Remove the lid and continue cooking, tossing frequently, until
the moisture in the bottom of the pan has cooked off. Add the lemon
juice and hot sauce, and then season generously with salt and pepper.

Winter Squash Gnocchi with Pesto

Homemade gnocchi are always a treat, and when made with winter squash, they are also full of nutrition and flavor. The sticky, wet batter takes some getting used to, but ultimately it's easy to work with. Contributor Tracy Noel also makes a gluten-free version: In place of the 1 cup flour, use ½ cup potato starch and ¼ cup brown rice flour.

Sauce the gnocchi with a fresh pesto for an herbal contrast, or sauté in butter, simmer for a minute in a splash of cream, and toss with Parmesan and lots of black pepper. SERVES 2

2 cups cooked and mashed winter squash (see the sidebar on the facing page)

2 large eggs, lightly beaten

1 cup unbleached all-purpose flour; more as needed

¾ cup cornmeal; more for rolling the gnocchi

Kosher salt

½ cup homemade pesto (see the recipes on p. 43, 91, and 203)

Put the squash, eggs, flour, cornmeal, and 1 teaspoon salt in a bowl. Using a fork, mix everything together to form a thick, moist batter.

Sprinkle a cutting board generously with more cornmeal. Spoon about one-quarter of the batter onto the board. Pat and roll the batter into a 1-inch-diameter log; the batter will be very soft and sticky, so don't aim for uniformity or tidiness, and use cornmeal liberally. If the batter is impossible to roll, add some flour to the board and roll to incorporate.

Cut the log into 1-inch pieces, setting each piece aside on a corner of the cutting board. Repeat until you've used all the batter.

Bring a large pot of water to a boil, and add 1 tablespoon salt. Carefully add about one-quarter of the gnocchi to the boiling water. Stir gently to prevent them from clumping together.

When all of the pieces float to the top (in about 5 minutes), boil for 1 minute more, and then lift out the gnocchi with a slotted spoon. Drain well, and pile onto a warmed serving dish. Repeat until all the gnocchi are cooked. Drizzle with the pesto and serve immediately.

CSA Snapshot

**Growing Home's
Les Brown Memorial Farm
Marseilles, Illinois
www.growinghomeinc.org**

THE FARMERS: Tracy Noel, Joe Avon, Stephanie Douglass, and Yoram Shanan

THE CSA LIFE: This 10-acre certified organic farm sits on a stretch of nice glacial deposit soil in LaSalle County, an area known for its deep canyons and majestic views. Running a CSA requires these Illinois farmers to be experts at growing every one of the 190 different varieties of vegetables and herbs found on the farm. They are helped in their efforts by workers from Growing Home's job training program, which uses organic agriculture as a vehicle for career and community development.

Prep School

Some squashes can be watery, which would make these gnocchi heavy. The trick is to cook off excess moisture once you've puréed the squash. Start with about 1 pound of peeled and seeded winter squash. Butternut, delicata, acorn, and Red Kuri are nice varieties for this.

1. Cut the squash into chunks, season lightly with salt, wrap tightly in a foil packet, and bake in a 375°F oven for 30 to 40 minutes, until the squash is very tender. Let cool slightly, then mash with a potato masher or large fork.

2. Transfer to a saucepan or frying pan and cook over medium heat, stirring constantly, to evaporate excess moisture. This will make the texture denser and nicer and will concentrate the flavor.

MAINS

Crustless Quiche with Spinach, Cheese, and Bacon

Iron Creek farmer Tamera Mark serves this baked egg dish for Christmas morning because she can prepare everything the night before and just add the eggs in the morning. That same easy prep makes it a natural for weeknight meals, too, and it's a flexible recipient for all types of vegetables. Just be sure that what you add is very tender and quick cooking, like spinach, fresh corn, or thinly sliced summer squash, or else precook the vegetables before you add them to the quiche batter.

This is a rich dish, so a small piece goes a long way. Leftovers are superb tucked between two slices of ciabatta or baguette with some spicy greens for a next-day sandwich.

SERVES 8 TO 10

8 ounces bacon, diced

8 cups lightly packed spinach leaves (tough stems removed before measuring)

Kosher salt and freshly ground black pepper

12 large eggs

4 tablespoons unsalted butter, melted and cooled

½ cup unbleached all-purpose flour

1½ teaspoons baking powder

3 cups cottage cheese (4% or 2% fat)

2 cups shredded sharp Cheddar

CSA Snapshot

Iron Creek Farm
LaPorte, Indiana
www.ironcreekfarm.com

THE FARMERS: Tamera and Pat Mark

THE CSA LIFE: Iron Creek is located just a few miles south of Michigan on the beautiful rich black soils of northern Indiana. The Mark family has been on the land for more than 100 years, and their pride of land is evident through the environmental stewardship and commitment to their certified organic standards. Just as they want to protect their three daughters from harmful chemicals, they protect their local wildlife and improve the soil and water quality.

Heat the oven to 350°F. Butter a 9 x 13-inch glass baking dish.

Cook the bacon over medium heat in a large frying pan until crisp. Scoop out the bacon and drain it on paper towels; pour off the excess fat and save for another use.

Add the spinach to the bacon pan and cook over medium heat until wilted and tender, 3 to 5 minutes. If the spinach is rendering a lot of water, pour it off, pressing the spinach with a large spoon to get rid of as much as possible. Season lightly with salt and pepper.

Crack the eggs into a large bowl and whip them until light and fluffy. Add the cooled butter, the flour, baking powder, cottage cheese, Cheddar, spinach, and bacon. Season with pepper. Pour into the prepared baking dish. Bake until slightly puffed, nicely golden brown, and no longer liquidy in the center, 45 to 55 minutes. Let cool for at least 15 minutes before cutting into squares and serving.

Leek, Spinach, and Feta Torta

This elaborate but spectacular layered savory pie takes a bit of time to make, but it's delicious and gorgeous as part of an antipasti spread, perfect for Sunday brunch. It's sort of an omelet and a quiche combined, so now's the time to use those lovely local eggs that you were lucky enough to get in your most recent CSA box. **SERVES 10 TO 12**

For the crust

2½ cups unbleached
   all-purpose flour

1½ teaspoons kosher salt

1 cup (2 sticks) cold unsalted butter,
   cut into a few chunks

For the filling

2 tablespoons olive oil

3 large leeks, white parts only, split
   in half and sliced crosswise

One 3-inch sprig fresh rosemary

1 medium sprig fresh thyme

Kosher salt and freshly ground
   black pepper

2 pounds fresh spinach or orach,
   tough stems removed (do not dry
   after rinsing)

1 tablespoon grated lemon zest

18 large eggs

2 tablespoons unsalted butter

1 pound feta

1 cup half-and-half

Freshly grated nutmeg

Grease the bottom and sides of a 10-inch springform pan.

MAKE THE CRUST

Put the flour and salt in a food processor and pulse to mix. Add the butter and pulse until the dough looks like coarse sand. Drizzle in a bit of cold water and pulse quickly to blend, adding only enough so that the dough holds together when you pinch it (start with ¼ cup and go up to ½ cup if needed). Do not overmix at this point or your dough will be tough.

   Wrap the dough in plastic and let it chill for about 20 minutes. Divide the dough into a chunk that's about one-third and another that's two-thirds. Lightly flour the work surface and roll out the larger chunk to a 16-inch circle (keep the smaller chunk wrapped). Carefully roll the circle of dough around the rolling pin, lift it, and position it over the springform pan. Gently ease the dough into the pan so that it comes up the sides; you'll need to carefully pleat the dough in a few places to make it fit. Gently press the dough into the corners of the pan, taking care not to tear any holes. If you do get a hole, just pinch and press to patch it. Chill the crust and remaining dough while you make the filling.

CSA Snapshot

Fish Hawk Acres
Rock Cave, West Virginia
http:wvfishhawkacres.com

THE FARMER: Dale Hawkins

THE CSA LIFE: This group of growers has united to better market their product by creating a huge range of value-added products. They have adopted the "community supported kitchen" model to offer customers not just raw ingredients, but also products that have been created from the crops that they grow. Customers can order food, à la carte, and choose from products such as salad dressings and mixes, breads, side dishes, meat, crab cakes, and desserts.

COOK THE LEEKS

Put the oil, leeks, rosemary, and thyme in a large frying pan, season lightly with salt and pepper, and cook over medium heat until the leeks become very soft, sweet, and almost compote-like, 20 to 30 minutes. Stir frequently during cooking, and as the leeks cook down, be sure to scrape the pan to dislodge the cooked-on juices. Taste and season with more salt and pepper as needed; the leeks should be very savory. Set aside to cool.

COOK THE SPINACH

Heat a large frying pan or Dutch oven and add the spinach, a few handfuls at a time, tossing with tongs to encourage it to wilt. Cook the spinach until it has all wilted and is tender. If there is a lot of liquid, pour it off, squeezing the spinach to get it as dry as possible. Add the lemon zest, season generously with salt and pepper, and toss to distribute. Set aside to cool.

MAKE THE OMELETS

Whisk together 6 eggs along with 1 teaspoon kosher salt and ¼ teaspoon black pepper. Heat 1 tablespoon of the butter in a 10-inch nonstick pan over medium heat. Pour in the eggs and don't disturb them until the bottom sets, 30 seconds to 1 minute. Start lifting the edges of the eggs with a spatula and tilting the pan so that the liquidy egg runs underneath. Continue lifting, tilting, and shaking the pan until the eggs are mostly cooked, but not browned. Slide the omelet onto a plate and then invert the plate to plop the omelet back into the pan. Cook for another minute or so to set the second side, and then slide onto a cooling rack. Repeat the process with another 6 eggs and the remaining 1 tablespoon butter, so that you have two 10-inch flat omelets.

ASSEMBLE THE TORTA

Crumble half the feta into the crust and spread it to make an even layer. Lay one of the omelets on top of the feta, trimming to fit as needed.

Spread the leeks into an even layer on the omelet and top with the second omelet. Spread the layer of spinach and finish with the rest of the feta.

Heat the oven to 350°F. Whisk together the remaining 6 eggs and the half-and-half. Season with 1 teaspoon salt, several twists of black pepper, and a few scrapes of fresh nutmeg and whisk to blend. Pour the custard into the torta a little bit at a time, waiting for the liquid to settle before you add more.

continued on p. 120

> "What are my favorites on the farm? It's a toss-up between verdant parsley and Japanese turnips. I like the parsley raw and fresh from the ground and the turnips roasted."
>
> —Brandon Pugh, Delta Sol

Roll out the second chunk of dough into an 11-inch circle. Position it on the top of the torta, pinching the edges to seal the top and bottom crust. If you like, crimp the edges decoratively. With a sharp paring knife, cut slits in the top crust to let steam escape during cooking.

Put the torta on a baking sheet and bake until the crust is deep golden brown and the filling has set, about 1 hour. Let cool on a rack for about 20 minutes, then carefully loosen the springform and remove the sides. Continue cooling for another 30 minutes or so until the torta is mostly cooled, then slice and serve warm, at room temperature, or cold.

Cook's Tip

Farm-fresh eggs aren't usually standard sizes, so if you're unsure about whether you're using enough, weigh them. This recipe calls for 18 large eggs, which should weigh 2½ pounds (40 ounces) in the shell.

Crêpes with Grilled Asparagus in Mornay Sauce

This is a wonderfully retro dish that will remind you of how delicious a classic cheese sauce can be, not to mention how fun it is to cook crêpes. The recipe looks long, but you can make the sauce and the crêpes a day ahead, and then just grill the asparagus right before you assemble the dish. If you take this do-ahead approach, be sure to reheat the Mornay sauce (on the stove over low heat) and reheat the crêpes, either with a quick zap in the microwave or by wrapping them in foil and popping them in a 350°F oven for 10 minutes. MAKES 12 CRÊPES; SERVES 6

For the Mornay sauce

2 tablespoons unsalted butter

2 tablespoons unbleached all-purpose flour

1¾ cups whole milk

¼ teaspoon kosher salt

Freshly ground black pepper

½ to ¾ cup grated cheese (such as Touvelle from Rogue Creamery, a good farmhouse Cheddar, or Fontina)

For the crêpes

3 eggs

2 cups milk

1 cup unbleached all-purpose flour

2 tablespoons unsalted butter, melted; more for the pan

1½ teaspoons kosher salt

½ teaspoon freshly ground white pepper

For the asparagus

4 dozen medium asparagus spears, fibrous ends trimmed and discarded

2 tablespoons olive oil

Kosher salt and freshly ground black pepper

MAKE THE MORNAY SAUCE

In a medium saucepan, combine the butter and flour over medium-high heat and whisk to blend. Cook, whisking constantly, for about 1 minute. Let the mixture (called a roux) cool off the heat.

Whisk in the milk, return the pan to medium-high heat, and bring to a simmer, whisking frequently to avoid lumps. Simmer until smooth and glossy and no taste of flour remains, 5 to 7 minutes. Reduce the heat to low. Add the salt, several grinds of pepper, and then the cheese, stirring until melted. Taste and adjust the seasoning. Keep warm until ready to assemble the crêpes.

MAKE THE CRÊPES

Put the eggs and milk in a blender and blend for about 5 seconds to mix well. Add the flour, butter, salt, and white pepper, and blend for another 20 seconds to make a smooth batter. Let the batter rest for at least 1 hour at room temperature, or ideally overnight in the fridge.

continued on p. 122

CSA Snapshot

Sweet Water Farm
Hugo, Oregon
www.sweetwaterfarmhugo.com

THE FARMERS: Sam and Denise Smith Rowe

THE CSA LIFE: Sweet Water Farm is a small family-owned and operated farm located in an 18-acre mini-watershed in Hugo, Oregon, near the base of Mt. Sexton in the northern part of the Rogue River Valley. Sam and Denise work the fields, with their young children, Ari and Ivory, overseeing the operation. Inspired by the principles of permaculture and biodynamics, Sweet Water's mission is to provide healthy food to the community while taking care of the place they call home.

COOK THE CRÊPES

Heat a nonstick or well-seasoned frying pan or crêpe pan with a bottom diameter of about 8 inches over medium-high heat. Brush with a thin coat of melted butter (you can use a folded paper towel for this). Pour ¼ cup of batter into the pan and immediately start to tilt and turn the pan so the batter spreads into an even circle. If there are a few empty spots, you can just spoon a few more drops of batter into them. Cook until the underside is nicely browned, about 2 minutes, then flip with your fingers or a small spatula or table knife. Cook the second side until done, another minute or so. The first side will always be prettier, so that's your presentation side. Transfer to a plate and continue with the rest of the batter, allowing the pan to heat up if it has cooled.

GRILL THE ASPARAGUS

Heat the grill (or a stovetop grill pan) to high. Toss the asparagus in the olive oil and season generously with salt and black pepper. Grill the asparagus until tender and slightly charred on the edges, turning once or twice, about 8 minutes, depending on their thickness.

ASSEMBLE THE DISH

Place 4 asparagus spears in a crêpe and roll it up. Make another crêpe roll and cut it in half crosswise on a sharp bias. Spoon about 2 tablespoons of warm Mornay sauce onto the center of the plate, then place the whole rolled crêpe on top. Arrange the cut halves on the first crêpe so that you can see the asparagus inside. Drizzle the top of the crêpes with a bit more Mornay sauce; repeat with the rest of the crêpes, and serve right away.

Grilled Flank Steak with Asian Green Sauce

It seems like every cuisine has some sort of herb-based sauce—to use on meat or rice or just for dipping your bread. This vivacious sauce, intended for a juicy flank steak off the grill, is like a French *sauce verte* but uses the Asian herb shiso, along with miso, daikon radish, and sesame oil, to nudge the character of the sauce a lot farther east than Europe. The recipe comes from a CSA in Hawaii, where everyday cooking draws from many Asian traditions as well as native island cuisine. If you don't have access to Meyer lemons, use a regular lemon or a blend of lemon and orange juice.   SERVES 2 TO 4

For the steak
One 1¼- to 1½-pound flank steak
Kosher salt

For the Asian green sauce
4 or 5 large fresh basil leaves, cut into chiffonade (to make ¼ cup)
6 to 7 green shiso leaves, cut into chiffonade (to make ⅓ cup; you may substitute fresh mint leaves)
1½ teaspoons Meyer lemon zest

2 teaspoons fresh Meyer lemon juice; more as needed
1 medium clove garlic, minced
2 teaspoons white miso
1 tablespoon grated peeled daikon radish
5 tablespoons extra-virgin olive oil
½ teaspoon sesame oil
2 tablespoons minced Asian pear or ripe but firm Bosc pear

Hot steamed rice, for serving

CSA Snapshot
MA'O Organic Farms
Wai'anae, Hawaii
www.maoorganicfarms.org

THE FARMERS: Kukui Maunakea-Forth, Gary Maunakea-Forth, and the young workers in the program

THE CSA LIFE: This 24-acre certified organic farm is located on the west side of the island of O'ahu and consists of six major *ahupua'a* (ancient land divisions).

MA'O is the acronym for *mala 'ai 'opio*, which means "the youth food garden," and at MA'O, it's not just food that's cultivated, but the young people themselves. The farm has workshops, school programs, and college classes in nutrition, agriculture, business, and Hawaiian culture, all in service of building leadership and improving the health and vitality of the community. The crops include many familiar to mainland farms but also island specialties such as bananas, taro, curry leaves, and mango.

Season both sides of the steak generously with salt. Roll the meat to make it more compact, put it in a bowl, cover with plastic wrap, and refrigerate overnight.

The next day, prepare the Asian green sauce by combining the basil, shiso, lemon zest, lemon juice, garlic, miso, daikon, olive oil, sesame oil, and minced pear in a bowl. Gently stir to mix thoroughly. Taste and add more lemon juice if you like. Set aside until ready to eat.

Heat the grill to medium high. Pat both sides of the steak dry with a paper towel. Grill the steak until well seared with a nice crust on one side, 4 to 6 minutes. Flip the steak using tongs and continue grilling on the other side until it's cooked to your liking, another 4 to 5 minutes (give or take a few minutes depending on the heat of the fire and thickness of your steak).

Transfer the steak to a cutting board and let it rest for 10 minutes. Slice the steak against the grain at a slight angle to the desired thickness. Serve with the Asian green sauce and steamed rice.

Artichoke and Herb Frittata with Parmesan

A frittata is a delicious destination for all types of vegetables and herbs, so once you get the basic method for making a frittata, you'll never again wonder what to do with your produce. Frittatas often aren't served piping hot, so they are excellent make-ahead dishes for company. And any leftovers make beautiful sandwiches. This combination of artichokes and herbs is especially lovely and is a great way to use up those cute but somewhat perplexing baby artichokes. SERVES 4 TO 6

½ cup freshly grated Parmesan

¼ cup torn or sliced fresh basil leaves

¼ teaspoon kosher salt

¼ teaspoon freshly ground black pepper

6 large eggs, lightly beaten

2 tablespoons olive oil

1 shallot, minced

1 tablespoon minced fresh thyme leaves

10 baby artichokes, trimmed and steamed until tender

Heat the oven to 350°F. Add half the cheese, the basil, salt, and pepper to the eggs in a bowl and whisk to mix.

Heat the oil in a 10-inch, ovenproof nonstick frying pan over medium heat. Add the shallots and sauté until they're soft and fragrant, 3 to 4 minutes. Add the thyme and artichokes; toss to coat with the oil, and spread them out evenly in the pan.

Pour the egg mixture into the frying pan; stir the eggs lightly with a fork but don't scrape the bottom surface. Once the bottom has set, after 30 seconds or so, lift the edges of the frittata with a thin spatula or table knife and tilt the frying pan to let the uncooked eggs run underneath. Continue cooking, lifting the edges and tilting the frying pan until the eggs on top are no longer liquidy.

Sprinkle the remaining Parmesan over the frittata and then transfer the frying pan to the oven; bake until the surface is set and golden brown, 3 to 5 minutes.

Run a spatula around the edge of the frying pan to loosen the frittata and invert it onto a cooling rack. Once it's just barely warm, transfer it to a cutting board or serving plate and cut into wedges. Serve warm, at room temperature, or chilled.

CSA Snapshot

Mariquita Farm
Watsonville, California
www.mariquita.com

THE FARMER: Andrew Griffin

THE CSA LIFE: This organic farm has members in California's Silicon Valley, the Peninsula, and San Francisco, including many restaurants. They like to say they take their members on a "food tour of the world," as they specialize in unusual varieties of vegetables and herbs, such as French fingerling potato varieties, Asian cooking greens, and Native American squash and beans.

Baby artichokes may be tiny versions of the large spiny globes, but they still are quite fibrous and tough on the outside, so they need a careful trimming before cooking.

1. Start by snapping off the outer leaves until you get to the pale green interior cone of leaves.

2. Next, trim the stem so it's just an inch or so long. Pare off the fibrous exterior of the stem and pare away the base of the leaves to make a smooth surface.

3. Cut about an inch off the tip of the leaf cone (the tips are the most fibrous part).

4. Split the artichokes lengthwise. Truly young artichokes won't have developed a hairy "choke" yet, so no need to remove it. Rub the artichokes with some lemon juice or float them in a bowl of lemon water to prevent browning until you're ready to use.

5. To cook baby artichokes, steam or boil them until tender, and then use in recipes or eat as part of a vegetable platter. You can also grill them, but it's best to parboil first, and then brush with olive oil and grill to finish.

"Gratitude is a daily harvest on this farm. We feel so fortunate to work with aspiring farmers, provide food for local families, serve wholesale customers, grow seedlings for hearty gardeners, tend the plants and animals well, and be stewards of soil and water health."

—Polly Shyka, Village Farm

Rustic Leek Tart

Leeks often play only a supporting role in dishes, so this tart is a chance to bring them center stage. Long, gentle cooking brings out their natural sweetness and develops a silky, almost "melted" texture. An herbal note is all you need as a complement, but you can up the ante a touch with the addition of 4 ounces of cooked pancetta and ⅓ cup grated Gruyère or Parmigiano-Reggiano, making this more like an Alsatian leek tart. Here, frozen puff pastry is used (get an all-butter kind, if you can), but you could use your favorite pastry dough and roll out a circle, spread the leeks on top, and fold up the edges to make a rustic galette. SERVES 6 AS A FIRST COURSE, 2 OR 3 AS A MAIN COURSE

3 pounds leeks (about 6), roots trimmed, white and light green parts only

4 tablespoons unsalted butter

Few sprigs of fresh thyme or rosemary, leaves removed from stems

Kosher salt and freshly ground black pepper

Unbleached all-purpose flour, for rolling the pastry

1 sheet frozen puff pastry, thawed

Slice the leeks in half lengthwise and then cut them crosswise into thin slices. Put the leeks in a strainer or colander and rinse well, but leave a few drops of water clinging to them.

Heat a large sauté pan over medium heat and add the butter. Once the butter has melted, add the leeks and thyme and season generously with salt and pepper. Stir to coat the leeks in the butter, cover the pan, and cook over medium heat until the leeks start to get quite soft and moist, about 10 minutes.

Uncover the pan and continue cooking, stirring and scraping the bottom of the pan frequently, until the leeks are very "melted," sweet, and fragrant and any excess liquid has cooked off, another 5 to 10 minutes. Let the leeks cool.

Heat the oven to 400°F. Dust your counter or work surface with flour, lay out the pastry dough, and roll to an 11 x 15-inch rectangle; slide it

continued on p. 128

CSA Snapshot

Woodland Gardens
Winterville, Georgia
**www.woodlandgardensorganic.
com**

THE FARMERS: Celia Barss and John Cooper

THE CSA LIFE: Woodland Gardens is a small certified organic farm just outside of Athens, Georgia. Celia Barss grew up in Papua, New Guinea, and lived around the globe before starting to farm. Cooper has a strong background in agricultural business management. They farm on land provided by private owners who have chosen to preserve it through this sustainable farming operation. The farmers are constantly experimenting with new varieties, looking for vegetables and fruit that delight their members, such as red-veined sorrel and the local muscadine grapes.

onto a baking sheet (it's easier if the sheet is rimless) and prick the dough all over with a fork. Moisten the edges with a little water, then fold them up to make a ½-inch border.

Spread the cooled leeks over the pastry and bake until the pastry is puffed around the edges and nicely browned on the underside, 20 to 25 minutes.

Slide the tart onto a rack to cool. Cut into squares and serve warm.

Prep School

Farm-fresh leeks are delicious, but they are often quite dirty because of the way they grow. This recipe describes one way to clean them. Here's another method that allows you to clean the leeks without slicing them first.

1. Trim off the tough green tops and the hairy root end. Split the leek lengthwise about two-thirds of the way down toward the root.

2. Run the leeks under cold water, riffling through the layers of leaves to separate them, and let the water flush out the dirt. Squeeze out excess water and either use whole or cut as you like.

Potato, Leek, and Rosemary Pizza

Potatoes and leeks are wonderful companions in soup, and here the duo is a subtle pizza topping. When you cook leeks slowly, they take on a satiny texture, so that when spread on the pizza dough they act almost like a sauce. Jill Forrester of Whitton Farms sometimes adds a tomato-based sauce to her leek and potato pizza, but this recipe offers a simpler "white" version. Fresh rosemary and goat cheese accent the vegetables. You can opt out of making your own pizza dough by buying it from a local pizza parlor or good grocery store. MAKES ONE 12-INCH PIZZA

For the pizza dough

2¼ cups white bread flour; more for dusting

1 teaspoon instant yeast

1½ teaspoons kosher salt

¾ cup lukewarm water

1 tablespoon olive oil; more for kneading

1 cup cornmeal, for dusting and the crust

For the topping

3 tablespoons extra-virgin olive oil

2 leeks, white and light green parts only, rinsed well and thinly sliced

Kosher salt and freshly ground black pepper

2 cloves garlic, chopped

1 tablespoon chopped fresh rosemary

2 medium potatoes (preferably low starch, such as most fingerlings or Red Bliss), peeled (unless the skins are thin) and thinly sliced

½ red onion, thinly sliced

4 ounces soft goat cheese, crumbled

MAKE THE DOUGH

Sift the flour into a large bowl and add the yeast and salt. Stir the water and oil together and pour into the bowl. Mix all contents together with a wooden spoon to make a sticky dough.

Dust some flour over the work surface and your hands and knead the dough until it's smooth and elastic, about 8 minutes.

Cover the dough with a damp dish towel and let it rise for an hour in a warm place. It should double in size.

MAKE THE TOPPING

Heat 2 tablespoons of the oil in a frying pan over medium heat, add the leeks, and season lightly with salt and pepper. Cook, stirring frequently, until the leeks are very soft and sweet and beginning to turn golden brown, 15 to 20 minutes. Add the garlic and rosemary and cook for another minute, then set aside to cool.

continued on p. 130

CSA Snapshot

Whitton Farms
Tyronza, Arkansas
www.whittonfarms.com

THE FARMERS: Keith and Jill Forrester

THE CSA LIFE: Whitton Farms is a small, organically inspired farm in the Arkansas Delta. Both Keith and Jill are former public school teachers who became farmers after moving to Keith's family's cotton farm, which had been in the family for close to 100 years. Gradually the Forresters are transforming former pastureland into rich plots for heirloom vegetables and flowers, which they share with their CSA members and customers at the Memphis Farmers Market.

Put the potato slices in a medium saucepan, cover with water, salt the water generously, and bring to a boil. Cook until tender but not falling apart, 2 to 5 minutes, depending on the thickness of the slices and type of potato. Drain well and blot dry on paper towels.

FINISH THE PIZZA

Heat the oven to 450°F. Dust the work surface with the cornmeal and shape the pizza dough by pressing with your fingers until the dough forms an even circle (it doesn't have to be perfect!) about 12 inches in diameter. Slide your hands under the dough and transfer it to a heavy baking sheet.

Spread the leeks over the dough, arrange the potato slices on the leeks, scatter the onion slices over the potatoes, and top with the goat cheese. Drizzle the remaining 1 tablespoon olive oil over everything and season with salt and pepper.

Bake until the cheese is softening and browning slightly and the crust is golden brown around the edges and underneath, 10 to 13 minutes. Transfer to a cutting board and cut into wedges.

Cook's Tip

If you find yourself with an abundance of leeks, go ahead and cook them all up as described in this recipe, taking as much time as needed so they soften and "melt" and become sweet. Keep the extra in the fridge to add to omelets, use on sandwiches, or stir into soups, pastas, and risottos. They are an instant flavor boost and will keep for up to a week in the fridge.

swiss chard

cucumbe

peppers

Cele

sweet corn

goat
horn pepp

summer squash

Carr

Grilled Tuna Niçoise Salad with Tahini Dressing

Serving a big platter of composed salad is a fantastic way to entertain in the summer. Here, the focal point is grilled tuna, but the real stars of the show are the farm-fresh vegetables that surround it. The classic components for a Niçoise salad are potatoes, green beans, and tomatoes, but zucchini is always abundant through the summer; feel free to add anything else that looks good.

The dressing recipe makes a lot and it's not very French—more like something you'd find at an American natural-foods store. But it is absolutely delicious on this salad and on plenty more of what you'll be eating during the week, so any leftover dressing will be welcome. SERVES 4 TO 6

For the tahini dressing
½ cup tahini

3 tablespoons red-wine vinegar

¼ cup soy sauce or tamari

2 tablespoons fresh lemon juice

2 teaspoons ground ginger

1 clove garlic, minced

Freshly ground black pepper

½ cup olive oil

For the salad
1 pound new potatoes, cut in half if large

Kosher salt

8 ounces green beans, ends trimmed

1 pound fresh tuna

8 ounces small zucchini or other summer squash, cut into ½-inch slices on the diagonal

Olive oil, for grilling

Freshly ground black pepper

2 large ripe tomatoes, cored and cut into wedges, or 1 pint cherry tomatoes

4 hard-cooked eggs, peeled and cut into eighths

12 to 16 black olives

½ cup chopped fresh cilantro, flat-leaf parsley, mint, or a mix

MAKE THE DRESSING
In a small bowl or a food processor, combine the tahini, ½ cup water, the vinegar, soy sauce, lemon juice, ginger, and garlic. Season to taste with black pepper and then add the olive oil, whisking or processing to blend it in. Taste and adjust the seasonings.

COOK THE TUNA AND ASSEMBLE THE SALAD
Heat a grill or grill pan to medium high.

Put the potatoes into a medium pan of water, bring to a boil, add 1 tablespoon of salt, and boil until the potatoes are very tender when poked with a knife, about 20 minutes. Scoop them out with a slotted spoon or tongs (keep the water on the heat) and put them in a bowl. Add 2 tablespoons dressing, toss to coat, and let cool.

Add the beans to the boiling water and cook until tender, 3 to 7 minutes, depending on the thickness. Drain thoroughly and let cool.

CSA Snapshot
North Country Farms
Kilauea, Kauai, Hawaii
www.northcountryfarms.com

THE FARMERS: Lee Roversi and her grown children

THE CSA LIFE: Perched 200 feet above the Pacific Ocean, this organic farm sits in the rolling open land of the Garden Island of Kauai. The family farmers practice activism by producing fresh food with integrity for their community. The farm produces year-round, and in addition to greens and vegetables, there are orchard trees bearing avocados, limes, grapefruit, oranges, mangos, lychee, and papaya.

Brush the tuna and the zucchini with olive oil and season generously with salt and pepper. Grill the tuna over medium heat until medium rare inside, 3 to 5 minutes per side, depending on the thickness. Transfer to a plate and keep warm. Grill the zucchini over high heat until nicely browned and tender, about 3 minutes per side.

Arrange all the salad components in an attractive way on a large platter or on individual plates: tomato and egg wedges, slightly warm potatoes, grilled zucchini slices, and green beans. Cut the tuna into chunks and add to the salad. Drizzle the tahini dressing generously over all the ingredients. Scatter the black olives on top and sprinkle the herbs over everything.

Prep School

To hard-cook an egg so that the white is tender and supple and the yolk is fluffy but not dry and green ringed, you just need to watch the clock.

Put the eggs in a saucepan and add enough cold water to cover them by about 1 inch. Set the pan over medium-high heat, and as soon as the water reaches a brisk simmer, start timing. As the eggs cook, adjust the heat as needed to maintain a brisk simmer. Simmer the eggs for 8 minutes, and then drain and cool under running water. The yolk will be completely solid, light yellow, and crumbly, but with no sign of the telltale green or gray ring around the yolk that's caused by overcooking.

Grilled Ono with Green Papaya Slaw

MAʻO Organic Farms in Hawaii takes advantage of Waiʻanae's fertile soil to produce a huge vibrant array of organic produce, which they sell through their CSA boxes and at farmer's markets across Oahu.

This recipe combines fresh produce from MAʻO with another local item: the fish called ono (you might also see it sold as wahoo), which has a firm texture and mild flavor. You can substitute any sturdy grill-friendly fish, such as halibut or tuna or even a rich fish such as mackerel.

Green papaya is simply unripe papaya, which is used in many southeast Asian dishes. It has a lovely crunch when shredded and loves to soak up dressings; you can use grated cucumber or jícama in a pinch. SERVES 4

Vegetable oil, for the grill

Four 6- to 8-ounce ono (wahoo) steaks, 1 inch thick

1½ cups shredded green papaya

½ cup shredded French Breakfast radishes

½ cup shredded carrots

¼ cup thinly sliced scallions, white and light green parts only

¼ cup chopped fresh cilantro

3 tablespoons fresh lime juice

1 tablespoon honey

1 tablespoon fish sauce

1 tablespoon macadamia oil (or other neutral oil)

½ fresh Thai bird chile or other hot fresh chile, minced

Kosher salt

½ cup chopped, toasted macadamia nuts

Prepare a medium-hot gas or charcoal grill. When hot, brush the grill surface with a paper towel dipped in oil. Set the fish on a plate to come to room temperature.

In a medium bowl, combine the papaya, radishes, carrots, scallions, and cilantro. In a small bowl, whisk together the lime juice, honey, fish sauce, oil, and chile peppers. Set aside.

Season the fish well with salt. Grill for 3 to 4 minutes per side, until just barely opaque in the center. Transfer to serving plates.

Pour the dressing over the papaya mixture and toss well to combine. Add the macadamia nuts and mix. Place a generous mound of the slaw over each fish steak, allowing excess dressing to drain over the bowl before transferring to the plate. Serve right away.

CSA Snapshot
MAʻO Organic Farms
Waiʻanae, Hawaii
www.maoorganicfarms.org

THE FARMERS: Kukui Maunakea-Forth, Gary Maunakea-Forth, and the young workers in the program

THE CSA LIFE: This 24-acre certified organic farm is located on the west side of the island of Oʻahu and consists of six major *ahupuaʻa* (ancient land divisions).

MAʻO is the acronym for mala ʻai ʻopio, which means "the youth food garden," and at MAʻO, it's not just food that's cultivated, but the young people themselves. The farm has workshops, school programs, and college classes in nutrition, agriculture, business, and Hawaiian culture, all in service of building leadership and improving the health and vitality of the community. The crops include many familiar to mainland farms, but also island specialties such as bananas, taro, curry leaves, and mango.

Grilled Shrimp and Scallions on Barley with Cucumbers, Tomatoes, and Feta

This summery main dish gets its inspiration from a traditional Greek salad, but with the addition of nutritious and chewy barley as well as plump grilled shrimp and smoky-sweet grilled scallions. Most often used raw, scallions are lovely grilled; the key is to cook them slowly enough so that the interior softens before the outside gets too browned. SERVES 3 OR 4

3 tablespoons fresh lime juice

1 clove garlic, minced

Few dashes of hot sauce

Kosher salt and freshly ground black pepper

½ cup extra-virgin olive oil; more for grilling

1 cup barley

2 cups water or homemade or low-sodium chicken broth

1 pound large or jumbo shrimp, peeled and deveined

2 bunches scallions, white and light green parts only

1 large or 2 small cucumbers, peeled, seeded, and cut into small chunks

2 large ripe tomatoes, cut into chunks

½ cup crumbled feta

½ cup chopped fresh flat-leaf parsley, mint, cilantro, or a mix

Whisk together the lime juice, garlic, hot sauce, ½ teaspoon salt, a few twists of black pepper, and the olive oil; set aside.

Put the barley, water, and 1 teaspoon salt in a medium saucepan, cover, bring to a boil, and then adjust the heat to a gentle simmer. Cook the barley until tender and most of the water has been absorbed, about 45 minutes. Drain well (if there's still some liquid left). Toss the barley with about half of the dressing and set aside to cool.

Heat the grill to medium. Toss the shrimp with a little olive oil and season generously with salt and pepper. Do the same with the scallions. Grill the shrimp until they're no longer translucent in the center, about 2 minutes per side. Transfer to a platter and keep warm. Grill the scallions (don't let them slide through the grill grates!), turning frequently, until they are limp and tender and just starting to char on the outside, about 10 minutes total. Chop into 1-inch pieces.

Toss the barley with the grilled scallions, the cucumbers, and tomatoes. Add a bit more dressing, toss again, and taste, adjusting with more dressing or seasoning as needed. Pile a mound of barley salad on each plate, top with a few grilled shrimp, and sprinkle with the feta and parsley. Serve slightly warm.

CSA Snapshot

Bay Branch Farm
Lakewood, Ohio
www.baybranchfarm.com

THE FARMERS: Annabel Khouri and Eric Stoffer

THE CSA LIFE: Creating a farm out of a vacant lot required intensely dedicated restoration of the soil health. Using mainly a hoe and their hands, Annabel and Eric utilize SPIN farming (small plot intensive) methods to create enough produce to supply their *à la farm carte* buying club. They don't use chemicals, herbicides, or pesticides. Annabel and Eric continue to build their soil food web by minimizing tilling, adding compost teas, and even counting beneficial microbes under a microscope.

Cook's Tip

Many high-quality fetas are available at good grocery stores and specialty stores, so make a point of sampling them to find a favorite. One delicious French variety called Valbreso is made from 100 percent sheep's milk. It is slightly creamier and sweeter than many fetas.

Grilled Peach and Chicken Salad with Fresh Mint Vinaigrette

Stone fruits are excellent candidates for the grill because they keep their shape even as their sugars caramelize in the heat. Nectarines would be just as nice as peaches, so use what's looking best; a handful of sugar snap peas would add even more color and some crunch. It's your choice whether to peel your peaches or leave the skins on; they will soften slightly on the grill. SERVES 4

For the salad

Two 8-ounce boneless, skinless chicken breasts

4 teaspoons olive oil; more for the grill

Kosher salt and freshly ground black pepper

3 medium peaches (about 1 pound total), cut in half and pits removed

1 small English cucumber, cut in half and thinly sliced

3 tablespoons finely chopped red onions (about ¼ onion)

For the vinaigrette

¼ cup finely chopped fresh mint

¼ cup white-wine vinegar

1 to 2 tablespoons granulated sugar (depending on the sweetness of the peaches)

1 tablespoon fresh lemon juice

1 tablespoon extra-virgin olive oil

¼ teaspoon kosher salt

⅛ teaspoon freshly ground black pepper

¼ cup fresh mint leaves, torn into small pieces

4 handfuls salad greens (optional)

CSA Snapshot

Whitton Farms
Tyronza, Arkansas
www.whittonfarms.com

THE FARMERS: Keith and Jill Forrester

THE CSA LIFE: Whitton Farms is a small, organically inspired farm in the Arkansas Delta. Both Keith and Jill are former public school teachers who became farmers after moving to Keith's family's cotton farm, which had been in the family for close to 100 years. Gradually the Forresters are transforming former pastureland into rich plots for heirloom vegetables and flowers, which they share with their CSA members and customers at the Memphis Farmers Market.

MAKE THE SALAD

Place the chicken breasts between two pieces of wax paper or parchment and pound until they are about ½ inch thick. Rub all over with 2 teaspoons of the olive oil and season both sides generously with salt and pepper. Heat the grill to medium, brush with oil, and grill the chicken until it's just cooked through but still juicy, 6 to 9 minutes total (check by cutting into a corner). Transfer to a cutting board and let rest for 10 minutes.

Toss the peach halves in the remaining 2 teaspoons olive oil. Place them cut side down on the grill and cook until slightly softened and nice grill marks form, 2 to 3 minutes; turn over and cook for another

continued on p. 138

2 minutes. Transfer to a cutting board. When the chicken and peaches are cool enough to handle, cut the chicken on an angle into ¼-inch slices and cut the peaches into ¼-inch wedges or chunks. Place in a bowl with the cucumbers and onions.

MAKE THE VINAIGRETTE

Put the mint, vinegar, sugar, lemon juice, olive oil, salt, and pepper in a food processor and process until smooth.

Drizzle the vinaigrette over the chicken mixture and toss gently to coat. Cover and refrigerate the salad until chilled and the flavors have married, at least 30 minutes. Just before serving, toss with the torn mint leaves and serve alone or on a bed of fresh greens.

Prep School

Peaches come in two varieties—freestone and cling. Getting the pit from a cling peach can be tricky.

1. Start by making a clean cut around the peach, from pole to pole, cutting all the way through to the pit. Twist gently to release one of the halves, without the pit.

2. To remove the pit from the other half, insert the tip of a paring knife, a vegetable peeler, or your finger and just pry it out. If it's stubborn, cut around it first with the knife.

Baked Cauliflower and Cheddar Casserole

This dish has all the rich creaminess of traditional mac and cheese, but cauliflower takes the place of pasta, making the dish immensely more nutritious. This dish is a good opportunity to cook with lime green Romanesco cauliflower or the already cheddary-looking orange cauliflower. Serve this as a meatless main dish or a hearty side to something beefy, such as a pot roast or pan-fried steaks. SERVES 6

1 large head cauliflower, cut into small florets

1 cup heavy cream

1 teaspoon dry mustard

½ teaspoon Worcestershire sauce

2 cups shredded extra-sharp Cheddar

Kosher salt

¼ teaspoon freshly ground black pepper

Heat the oven to 375°F. Grease an 8-inch-square baking dish. Bring a large pot of salted water to a boil, add the cauliflower, and cook until crisp-tender, about 5 minutes. Drain well and spread out on paper towels to dry completely. Transfer the cauliflower to the baking dish and set aside.

In a small saucepan, bring the cream to a simmer over medium-high heat, and cook until it's reduced by about one-quarter. Remove the pan from the heat and whisk in the mustard and Worcestershire, and then add 1½ cups of cheese, stirring slowly until it's totally melted. Season generously with salt and add the black pepper; taste and adjust the seasonings as needed.

Pour the sauce on top of the cauliflower, nudging the florets around to coat them with sauce. Sprinkle the remaining ½ cup cheese over the top and bake until browned and bubbling around the edges, 20 to 25 minutes. Let cool for 10 minutes before serving.

CSA Snapshot

John Givens Farm/Something Good Organics
Goleta, California
www.johngivensfarm.com

THE FARMERS: John and Carolyn Givens

THE CSA LIFE: Carolyn Givens knew she wanted to join the agricultural community after a farmer brought a CSA box into the office where she worked. Years later, with 180 acres in 12 locations stretching over 30 miles, John and Carolyn provide fresh, local organic produce of excellent quality all year long to the locals in Santa Barbara and surrounding areas. These farmers focus on agricultural diversity to provide a healthier diet and ecosystem. The coastal community has a unique environment that allows this farm to operate successfully year-round.

Sautéed Sweet Peppers and Onions with Italian Sausage

The familiar pepper-and-onion combo becomes sublime when you use some of the wonderful pepper and onion varieties that are available from local farms (or your own garden). Becky Watson, a family member of the Bordens, loves Marconi peppers and Walla Walla sweet onions. You can add complexity by using a few hot chiles as well.

On their own, the vegetables and sausages make a satisfying main dish, but they are also terrific on a crusty roll or with some polenta mixed with Fontina cheese—either loose and creamy or set firm and cut into squares.   SERVES 2

¼ cup olive oil

1 pound sweet peppers (such as bell, Jimmy Nardone, Lipstick, pimiento, or Marconi), cored, seeded, and cut into ¼-inch strips

1 large sweet onion, sliced (a yellow onion would be fine, too)

¼ teaspoon fennel seeds

Kosher salt and freshly ground black pepper

2 to 3 cloves garlic, sliced

¼ cup chopped fresh flat-leaf parsley

2 Italian (or your favorite) sausages (6 to 8 ounces total)

Ciabatta rolls or cooked polenta, for serving (optional)

In a large frying pan or Dutch oven, heat the olive oil over medium-high heat and add the peppers, onions, and fennel seeds. Season lightly with salt and pepper and cook, tossing frequently, until the vegetables start to sizzle lightly.

Turn the heat to medium low, add the sliced garlic, and continue cooking, stirring occasionally, until all the vegetables are very tender, fragrant, and sweet, 20 to 30 minutes. They should be lightly browned but not dark. Taste and adjust with more salt and pepper as needed, and then add the parsley.

Meanwhile, cook the sausages: Put the sausages in a small frying pan with about ½ cup water over medium-high heat. Cover and simmer, turning occasionally, for about 10 minutes, then uncover and continue cooking until all the water has evaporated and the sausages are nicely browned, another 10 to 12 minutes. (If you like, you can split the sausages lengthwise before this second step of cooking, in order to get more browned surface. If you are using "fully cooked" sausages, simply brown them in a frying pan with a bit of oil until heated through.)

Serve the peppers and onions with the sausages on their own, piled onto ciabatta rolls, or with polenta.

CSA Snapshot

Borden Farms
Delta, Colorado
www.bordenfarms.com

THE FARMERS: Guy and Lynn Borden and crew

THE CSA LIFE: Sitting at an elevation of 5,200 feet in the historic farming and ranching community of Pea Green, this 14-acre USDA certified organic family farm benefits from the high desert valley's fertile soil and snowmelt from the surrounding Rocky Mountains. Guy Borden is known as "The Tomato Guy," and he loves to share his enthusiasm for heirloom tomato varieties, such as Dr. Wyche's Yellow, Pruden's Purple, and Sungold.

Quick Curry of Eggplant, Peppers, and Shiitakes

This Thai-inflected curry is meatless but feels meaty due to the chewy texture of the eggplant chunks and the savory umami flavors of the mushrooms. If you don't have shiitakes available, use creminis, which are really just baby portabellas. Asian eggplants are usually long and slender, though you'll find roly-poly round ones as well. Asian varieties are generally firmer and less seedy than the large globe eggplants, which is a plus. But if you need to use a globe or other Italian variety in this recipe, go right ahead. SERVES 3 OR 4

5 tablespoons olive or vegetable oil

2 bell peppers (any color), cored, seeded, and cut into ½-inch strips

1 medium onion, thinly sliced

Kosher salt

1½ pounds Asian eggplant, peeled and cut into 1-inch chunks

8 to 10 shiitake mushrooms, stems trimmed, sliced

4 cloves garlic; 3 smashed, 1 minced

1 tablespoon red or green Thai curry paste (Thai Kitchen® brand is easy to find); more as needed

2 tablespoons smooth peanut butter

One 14-ounce can coconut milk

1 tablespoon fish sauce; more as needed

1 tablespoon fresh lime juice; more as needed

2 cups warm cooked brown rice

1 lime, quartered

Heat 2 tablespoons of the oil in a large frying pan over medium-high heat. Add the peppers and onions, season lightly with salt, and cook, stirring frequently, until soft and fragrant, 10 to 12 minutes. Scrape into a bowl and set aside. Add the remaining 3 tablespoons oil, the eggplant, mushrooms, and smashed garlic and continue cooking, stirring and tossing, until the eggplant is starting to soften and brown, another 10 to 12 minutes. Add the minced garlic and cook for about 30 seconds longer, and then take the pan off the heat, cover it, and let the eggplant steam for 5 minutes or so.

Whisk together the curry paste, peanut butter, and coconut milk and add the mixture to the frying pan. Add back the onions and peppers, bring to a simmer, and simmer until all the vegetables are thoroughly tender, the flavors are blended, and the sauce has reduced and thickened a bit. Add the fish sauce and lime juice and taste for seasoning, adding more fish sauce (for saltiness), curry paste, or lime juice to taste.

Serve over warm rice with a lime quarter for each diner to squeeze over the curry.

CSA Snapshot

Parson Produce
Clinton, South Carolina
www.parsonproduce.com

THE FARMER: Daniel Parson

THE CSA LIFE: Parson farms on 2 acres belonging to The Farmhouse Bed and Breakfast, which is also an alpaca and Nigerian dwarf goat farm. Parson converted the pastureland into an intensive vegetable production garden using organic methods. The garden grows almost every vegetable except corn. Parson earned a master's degree with a focus on cover crops and organic methods, which he applies with great success to these lush and productive acres.

Cook's Tip

Eggplant can be deceptive: It looks fairly soft and spongy, and yet it can stubbornly resist softening during cooking. Pulling it off the heat and letting it steam for a few minutes is a great trick. In this recipe, it steams in the covered frying pan. When grilling, once the eggplant is nicely browned and mostly cooked, pull it off the grill, cover with foil, and let it steam and soften to the final desired creaminess.

Moroccan Chicken with Potatoes and Chiles

This easy-to-make stew is based on a classic Moroccan tagine, cooked in a conical clay pot and fragrant with spices and tangy preserved lemon. This version adds a few more goodies from the garden: mild fresh chiles and potatoes, though you could also use bell peppers, zucchini, or even cherry tomatoes. SERVES 4 TO 6

6 to 8 skinless chicken thighs

8 ounces mild fresh chiles, cored, seeded, and thinly sliced crosswise

One 2-inch piece fresh ginger, peeled and chopped

6 cloves garlic, chopped

4 tablespoons olive or canola oil

2 teaspoons turmeric

¼ teaspoon crumbled saffron

Kosher salt

1 medium onion, chopped

2 bay leaves

1 tablespoon minced preserved lemon peel

½ cup green olives

1 pound low-starch potatoes, such as fingerlings or Yukon Gold, peeled and cut into disks or chunks

Put the chicken, chiles, ginger, garlic, olive oil, turmeric, and saffron in a large, heavy pot, such as a Dutch oven. Season lightly with salt, bring to a simmer over medium heat, and cook, uncovered, for about 15 minutes. Stir often to prevent sticking, and resist the temptation to add water or other liquid; the chicken will stew in its own juices.

Add the chopped onions, bay leaves, preserved lemon, and olives. Cover the pot and cook for about 10 minutes, then add the potatoes and ½ cup water. Continue to simmer over low heat until the chicken is cooked through and the potatoes are very tender, another 20 to 30 minutes. If the stew looks too liquidy, simmer, uncovered, for a few more minutes. Taste and adjust seasonings.

CSA Snapshot

47th Avenue Farm
Portland, Oregon
www.47thavefarm.com

THE FARMER: Laura Masterson

THE CSA LIFE: This city farm began on an oversized double lot located on 47th Avenue in the Woodstock neighborhood of southeast Portland. Over the last dozen years or so, it has expanded to include land on historic property in the town of Lake Oswego and 38 acres in the heart of the Willamette Valley on Grand Island. Farmer Masterson gets some of the work done using a pair of handsome honey-maned draft horses named Bonnie and Patty. She also is an active mentor and trainer for aspiring young farmers.

Cook's Tip

Preserved lemons are whole lemons preserved in salt, sold in jars in imported food stores and specialty grocers. The rind is the part you eat; the salt curing makes it tender and briny with a lemony flavor that's unique.

Herbed Pork Tenderloin with Citrus au Jus and Broccoli Raab

Along with growing vegetables, Hudson Ranch in Napa Valley raises a variety of pigs, from Berkshires to Hampshires. They have a heavenly life dining on fruits and vegetables from the large garden, whey from a nearby dairy, and tortillas from a local producer. They graze on open, grassy pastures and wallow in the mud at the shore of the farm's lake. If you can make this dish with pork from locally raised, happy pigs, you'll definitely taste the difference. SERVES 4

⅓ cup coarsely chopped fresh rosemary

2 teaspoons kosher salt

1 teaspoon freshly ground black pepper

½ teaspoon marash or Aleppo pepper (or other crushed dried red pepper)

4 cloves garlic

One 1½-pound pork tenderloin (or 2, if small)

2 tablespoons olive oil

1 cup fresh orange or tangerine juice

1 large bunch broccoli raab, tough ends trimmed

½ cup French black oil-cured olives, pitted and coarsely chopped

Heat the oven to 350°F. With a mortar and pestle, coarsely crush the rosemary, salt, black pepper, marash pepper, and garlic to make a wet rub. Pat the pork dry and liberally apply the rub on all sides.

Heat the olive oil in a large, heavy, ovenproof skillet, such as cast iron, over medium-high heat, and brown the tenderloin on all sides. Take care not to let the herb paste burn.

Add the citrus juice to the pan and place in the oven. Cook until an instant-read thermometer reads 145° to 150°F, about 20 minutes. Remove the meat from the pan, tent with foil, and let rest on a cutting board for about 10 minutes. Reserve the cooking juices in the pan. Bring a pot of generously salted water to a boil.

While the pork is resting, cook the broccoli raab in the boiling salted water until the stalks are tender, about 5 minutes. Drain thoroughly, and when cool enough to handle, chop coarsely. Keep warm.

Add the olives to the pan with the cooking juices, and cook over high heat until the juices are slightly reduced and beginning to thicken; taste and adjust the seasonings.

When you're ready to serve, pour any accumulated pork juices into the pan of orange sauce. Slice the pork. Arrange a portion of broccoli raab on each plate, lay a slice or two of pork on top, and spoon over some pan sauce.

CSA Snapshot

Hudson Farm
Napa, California
www.hudsonranch.com

THE FARMER: Robert Lee Hudson

THE CSA LIFE: Owner Robert Lee Hudson grew up in Houston, Texas, but learned all about wine in Burgundy, France. He brought the knowledge back to the gently rolling hills of the beautiful Napa Valley to create Hudson Farm, a large estate that includes vineyards, a ranch, and a large vegetable garden that supplies their CSA program. This 2,000-acre farm produces a stunning array of products, including heirloom pork and poultry.

"Deconstructed" Eggplant Parmesan

This summery dish takes the basic elements of eggplant Parmesan and gives them a lighter, prettier treatment. The recipe is designed for an Italian or globe eggplant, but you can certainly use one of the more slender Asian varieties—you'll just have more slices and might need a touch more crumbs and cheese. Don't top the eggplant with the tomato salad until just before you serve it, in order to keep the nice crunch.

SERVES 4 AS A FIRST COURSE, 2 AS A MAIN COURSE

2 large ripe tomatoes, cut into small chunks (or use 2 cups cherry tomatoes cut in half)

¼ cup chopped red onion

1 small clove garlic, minced

8 ounces fresh mozzarella bocconcini (the small balls), cut in half

2 tablespoons extra-virgin olive oil

Kosher salt and freshly ground black pepper

1 medium globe eggplant (about 1½ pounds), stem trimmed

2 cups coarse fresh breadcrumbs or panko

½ cup freshly grated Parmigiano-Reggiano

2 large eggs, beaten with a fork

4 to 6 leaves fresh basil, cut into fine chiffonade

CSA Snapshot

**Cherry Grove Organic Farm
Princeton, New Jersey
www.cherrygroveorganic.com**

THE FARMERS: Matthew Conver and Mary Stuehler

THE CSA LIFE: This certified organic Garden State farm encompasses 19 beautiful acres surrounded by woods and a creek in central New Jersey. The farm crew and members alike are excited by the unfolding of the seasons at the farm—the peas that arrive in June and the watermelons that ripen just in time for their Labor Day Watermelon Celebration. After the last tomatoes disappear, everyone is consoled by out-of-this-world carrots all fall and winter! The CSA also includes a u-pick option for some of the produce, giving the members a mini-retreat from daily life.

Make the tomato salad by tossing the tomatoes, onions, garlic, mozzarella, and olive oil in a bowl. Season with salt and pepper. Set aside while you cook the eggplant.

Heat the oven to 400°F. Oil a 9 x 13-inch baking dish.

With a vegetable peeler, peel the eggplant skin in alternating strips so it's striped, and then cut the eggplant into ½-inch slices.

Mix the breadcrumbs with the cheese and spread on a plate. Put the eggs in a shallow bowl.

Dip each eggplant slice into the egg and then into the crumb mixture, patting to secure the coating. Arrange the slices in the baking dish in a single layer (you may need to use more than one dish).

Bake the eggplant until it's very tender on the inside and nicely browned and crisp on the outside. Remove the dish from the oven and let the eggplant rest for about 10 minutes, to further soften it. Arrange a few slices on each plate and nestle some tomato salad next to them. Sprinkle the basil over the top.

Cook's Tip

Panko breadcrumbs originated in Japan, though some domestic companies produce them now. They are dried breadcrumbs with a neutral flavor and a coarser, crunchier texture than regular dried breadcrumbs from a box, making them a nice substitute for fresh crumbs.

Baked Omelet with Garden Vegetables, Pancetta, and Gruyère

This is a terrific dish for summer brunch while sitting on the patio with a pitcher of mimosas. Pancetta, an unsmoked Italian bacon, adds terrific flavor, but if you'd prefer to make this vegetarian, leave it out and increase the amount of butter by 1 tablespoon. And feel free to improvise with your vegetable selection, though potatoes and onions of some kind are a must. SERVES 4 TO 6

6 large eggs

2 tablespoons heavy cream

¼ teaspoon kosher salt;
  more as needed

⅛ teaspoon freshly ground
  black pepper; more as needed

1 tablespoon unsalted butter

¼ cup finely diced pancetta

1 cup chopped Walla Walla or other
  sweet onions

1 cup thinly sliced bell peppers or
  mild fresh chiles (any color)

1 cup ½-inch-dice new potatoes,
  boiled until just tender

1 cup cherry tomatoes, cut in half

1 teaspoon minced garlic

2 tablespoons chopped fresh
  flat-leaf parsley

½ cup grated Gruyère

¼ cup chopped scallions, white and
  light green parts only

Heat the oven to 350°F. In a large bowl, whisk together the eggs, cream, salt, and pepper. Set aside.

In a 10-inch, ovenproof frying pan, melt the butter over medium-high heat. Add the pancetta and cook, stirring, until it has rendered its fat and is brown and slightly crisp. If there's a lot of fat, pour off all but a couple of tablespoons, then add the onions, peppers, and potatoes. Season lightly with salt and pepper, and cook, stirring, until the vegetables are soft and lightly browned, 4 to 5 minutes.

Add the cherry tomatoes, garlic, and 1 tablespoon of parsley, and cook until the garlic is fragrant, another 30 seconds.

Scrape the vegetables into a bowl and set aside; don't wash out the frying pan. Reheat the frying pan over medium-high heat for a few seconds and then pour in the egg mixture; cook for 30 to 60 seconds, just to get the bottom set. Add the pancetta-vegetable mixture, spreading it evenly in the frying pan.

Transfer the frying pan to the oven and bake until the eggs are firm, 20 to 25 minutes (don't let them get too brown, however). Sprinkle the cheese over the top and cook for another minute or so, until it starts to melt. Remove the pan from the oven and slide the omelet onto a large serving platter. Let cool for at least 10 minutes before serving. Garnish with the remaining 1 tablespoon parsley and the chopped scallions.

CSA Snapshot

**Borden Farms
Delta, Colorado
www.bordenfarms.com**

THE FARMERS: Guy and Lynn Borden and crew

THE CSA LIFE: Sitting at an elevation of 5,200 feet in the historic farming and ranching community of Pea Green, this 14-acre USDA certified organic family farm benefits from the high desert valley's fertile soil and snowmelt from the surrounding Rocky Mountains. Guy Borden is known as "The Tomato Guy," and he loves to share his enthusiasm for heirloom tomato varieties, such as Dr. Wyche's Yellow, Pruden's Purple, and Sungold.

Roast Leg of Lamb with Wilted Escarole

A leg of lamb is a luxurious cut of meat. Its size makes it impressive, and the flavor of the lamb is rich, sweet, and fragrant with herbs and garlic from the marinade. The lamb is topped with a warm salad of slightly bitter escarole (you could also use its cousin Batavian endive or even frisée), mellowed from being wilted in oil and laced with vinegar. It's an unexpected pairing and yet the perfect foil for the richness of the meat. SERVES 8

2 medium onions, sliced
8 cloves garlic, lightly crushed
8 fresh thyme sprigs
8 fresh oregano or marjoram sprigs

One 750-milliliter bottle
  dry white wine
1 cup olive oil
One 5- to 6-pound whole leg of lamb,
  most of the fat trimmed

Kosher salt and freshly ground
  black pepper
Wilted Escarole Vinaigrette
  (recipe on the facing page)

In a shallow dish large enough to hold the lamb, mix the onions, garlic, thyme, oregano, wine, and olive oil and then add the lamb. Rub the marinade all over the lamb. Cover, refrigerate, and let the lamb marinate overnight (or for at least 8 hours). Turn the lamb frequently if you can.

Heat the oven to 450°F. Remove the lamb from the marinade about 30 minutes before cooking. Dry it by blotting with some paper towels. Pick out the thyme, oregano, and garlic from the marinade and then chop the ingredients finely to make a stiff paste. Season with salt and pepper. Rub the paste all over the lamb.

Put the lamb on a rack over a shallow baking pan and put into the oven. Roast for 15 minutes, and then reduce the heat to 350°F. Roast for 30 minutes longer, then turn the lamb over and roast for another 30 minutes. Turn again and roast for 15 minutes longer (total roasting time is 1½ hours). Remove the lamb from the oven and let it rest for 15 minutes before carving.

To serve, carve the lamb and lay it out on one side of a warm platter. Drizzle with the carving juice, pile the wilted escarole on the other side of the platter, and pour any vinaigrette remaining in the pan over the lamb and the escarole.

CSA Snapshot

Mariquita Farm
Watsonville, California
www.mariquita.com

THE FARMER: Andrew Griffin

THE CSA LIFE: This organic farm has members in California's Silicon Valley, the Peninsula, and San Francisco, including many restaurants. They like to say they take their members on a "food tour of the world," as they specialize in unusual varieties of vegetables and herbs, such as French fingerling potato varieties, Asian cooking greens, and Native American squash and beans.

Wilted Escarole Vinaigrette

SERVES 8

1½ to 2 pounds escarole
½ cup extra-virgin olive oil

2 tablespoons red-wine vinegar;
    more as needed
Kosher salt and freshly ground
    black pepper

Trim the base of the escarole and wash the leaves; cut into about ¾-inch strips. Just before you carve the lamb, heat the olive oil in a sauté pan over low heat until it's very warm but not hot. Add the escarole to the pan all at once and cover so it steams and sautés at the same time (it will sizzle, so be careful). Stir in the vinegar. Season generously with salt and pepper; taste and add more seasoning or vinegar to taste.

"The young farmers at Serenbe Farms have learned that farming is hard, relentless work but that it pays off for people who love the land and accept the appreciation from happy customers. Connecting to the community and watching babies grow into young, fearless kids (who love their veggies) also make the job more rewarding—and more real."

—Paige Witherington, Serenbe Farms

Stuffed Poblano Casserole with Black Beans, Corn, and Rice

This Southwest-inspired casserole is definitely rib-sticking, perfect for a potluck with hungry college kids or an après-ski dinner. Farmer Beth Eccles of Indiana's Green Acres farm freezes organic poblanos, so she can make this dish year-round. You can experiment with different types of rice; each adds its own character to the dish. If you want to make this vegetarian, omit the sausage and add another ½ cup each of the beans and corn.

SERVES 4 OR 5

1 teaspoon kosher salt

1 teaspoon turmeric (optional)

2 cups rice (use any type of rice you like other than quick cooking)

¼ cup finely chopped fresh cilantro

¼ cup olive oil

1 pound bulk pork sausage

½ cup diced onions

½ cup corn kernels (frozen is okay)

½ cup finely diced celery root

1 clove garlic, minced

½ cup cooked black beans (drained canned is fine)

1 pound queso fresco (or other good melting cheese), cubed, shredded, or grated

8 to 10 fresh poblano chiles, cored and seeded (open up the entire top so that the pepper can be easily stuffed)

Bring 4 cups water, the salt, and turmeric (if using) to a boil in a medium saucepan; add the rice, turn down the heat, and cover the pan. Cook at a gentle simmer until the water is absorbed and the rice is tender (follow the package directions). Fluff with a fork and let cool. Stir in the cilantro and set aside.

Heat the oven to 375°F. Put 1 tablespoon of the olive oil in a large frying pan, then add the sausage, onions, corn, celery root, and garlic and sauté until the sausage is no longer pink, about 10 minutes. Stir in the beans and half of the cheese. Set aside about a cup of this topping for the casserole.

Divide the sausage mixture among the chiles, spooning it into the bottom half of each chile. Fill the remaining half of each chile with some of the cooked rice.

Drizzle a large, heavy baking dish with 2 more tablespoons of the olive oil. (An enameled cast-iron gratin pan is nice or a 9 x 13-inch glass baking dish. You may need to use two dishes, depending on the size and shape of your chiles.)

continued on p. 152

CSA Snapshot

**Green Acres
North Judson, Indiana
www.greenacresindiana.com**

THE FARMERS: Beth and Brent Eccles

THE CSA LIFE: Beth's grandparents, Morizo and Namie Sakaguchi, moved from Japan and began farming this land in 1933. The farmers were well known among Chicago's restaurants for growing the best Napa cabbage, daikon radish, bitter melon, and Japanese eggplant. Today, two generations later, the Eccles family continues this tradition in the heartland of the United States. They do their absolute best to take care of the land and are proud members of the Certified Naturally Grown family.

Arrange the stuffed peppers in the dish. Distribute the reserved sausage mixture and remaining rice over the top of the peppers. Sprinkle the remaining cheese all over the top. Drizzle the remaining 1 tablespoon olive oil over the casserole.

Cover the dish with foil, and bake until the chiles are soft when pricked with a fork, about 1 hour. Remove the cover and bake for an additional 5 minutes, or until the cheese is nicely bubbly. Let rest for at least 10 minutes before serving.

Cook's Tip

Celery root, also called celeriac, is a softball-size, hairy root vegetable. It can look off-putting, but it's worth getting to know. Once you pare away the tough skin (carefully, with a sharp knife), you'll find creamy colored, firm flesh with a very delicate, sweet celery flavor. Cook it as you would other root vegetables—diced and roasted or boiled and mashed. To eat it raw, shred or julienne finely and toss with vinaigrette or homemade mayonnaise.

Roasted Green Chile Cheeseburgers

A quick relish made from chopped chiles adds zest to this burger. This is a perfect dish to make if you're lucky enough to also be a member of a local meat CSA; in any case, choose good meat from humanely raised animals. If the meat is grass fed, it's likely to be quite lean, so take care not to overcook or you'll have dry burgers. If you're grinding the meat yourself, you can always grind in a bit of fatty pork—or even bacon—for added moisture and richness. SERVES 4

1 to 1½ pounds ground beef (depending on the size burgers you want)
1 cup chopped roasted, peeled, and seeded fresh green chiles
1 clove garlic, minced

2 tablespoons apple-cider vinegar
2 tablespoons olive oil
1½ teaspoons dried oregano or 2 teaspoons chopped fresh oregano
Pinch of kosher salt

4 English muffins, split
4 slices Monterey Jack or Cheddar
4 thick slices ripe tomato

Take the ground beef out of the refrigerator to take the chill off. Heat a grill or grill pan to medium high. Stir together the chopped chiles, garlic, vinegar, oil, oregano, and salt.

Divide the beef into quarters and gently shape into ½-inch-thick patties that are slightly thinner in the center. Don't squeeze or compress the meat.

Grill the burgers to the degree of doneness that you like; medium rare will probably take 3 to 4 minutes per side. Remember that the burgers will continue to cook a bit once they're off the heat, so stop a touch short of your final doneness goal.

As the burgers are cooking, lightly grill the interiors of the English muffins and keep them warm.

A few seconds before you remove the burgers from the grill, lay the cheese on each one so it starts to melt. Transfer the burgers to the bottoms of the English muffins, top with the chiles, tomato slices, and the muffin tops, and serve right away.

Cook's Tip

Roast extra chiles and freeze them for later use. Contributor Jennifer Woods uses this trick to preserve the texture: Add just enough water to cover the chiles in the freezer container so that they are encased in water, which provides a protective barrier that can also prevent freezer burn.

CSA Snapshot

Crooked Sky Farms
Phoenix, Arizona
www.crookedskyfarms.com

THE FARMER: Frank Martin

THE CSA LIFE: Farmer Frank has always thought of seeds as magical and of himself as a farmer. The intensive chemical use in farming in Arizona during the 1950s literally made him ill, so his parents started to practice organic methods out of necessity. After losing his father to what was assumed to be pesticide exposure, Frank committed himself to being a different kind of farmer and a committed steward of the land. Today, the certified organic Crooked Sky Farms is a large operation that employs a team of healthy workers that supplies rural Arizona with amazing produce and a great community resource.

Potato and Vegetable Enchiladas with Green Salsa and Melted Cheese

This homey casserole is a dish that combines the comfort-food quality of cheesy enchiladas with some real nutrition from the greens and other vegetables, so feel free to indulge. The key ingredients are the potatoes, which hold everything together, and the greens, which are delicious with the green salsa and cheese. You can experiment with the other vegetables if you like, substituting parsnips for the carrots, adding corn or peppers, or using a different type of summer squash. SERVES 4 TO 6

1 pound potatoes, scrubbed and quartered (medium-starch potatoes, such as Yukon Golds, work well)

One 16-ounce jar tomatillo salsa

Kosher salt

2 tablespoons olive oil

1 bunch scallions, white and light green parts only, chopped

1 medium zucchini, cut into ¼-inch dice

2 cups finely chopped greens such as kale, collards, or Swiss chard

2 medium carrots, grated on the large holes of a box grater

Hot sauce, such as Sriracha

12 corn tortillas

2 cups shredded or crumbled cheese (Monterey Jack or mild Cheddar are nice when mixed with some cotija or feta)

½ cup coarsely chopped fresh cilantro

CSA Snapshot

Growing Home's
Les Brown Memorial Farm
Marseilles, Illinois
www.growinghomeinc.org

THE FARMERS: Tracy Noel, Joe Avon, Stephanie Douglass, and Yoram Shanan

THE CSA LIFE: This 10-acre certified organic farm sits on a stretch of nice glacial deposit soil in LaSalle County, an area known for its deep canyons and majestic views. Running a CSA requires these Illinois farmers to be experts at growing every one of the 190 different varieties of vegetables and herbs found on the farm. They are helped in their efforts by workers from Growing Home's job training program, which uses organic agriculture as a vehicle for career and community development.

Put the potatoes in a medium pan of generously salted water and bring to a boil. Cook until they're very tender, about 20 minutes. Scoop out about ½ cup of cooking water and reserve, then drain. Put the potatoes back in the pot, add about 2 tablespoons of salsa, and mash with a potato masher, fork, or wooden spoon, adding a little of the cooking water to make them creamy. Taste and season with salt if needed.

Put the olive oil in a large frying pan over medium-high heat, add the scallions and zucchini, season with a little salt, and sauté until the vegetables are softened and starting to turn golden, 4 to 5 minutes. Add the chopped greens and about 2 tablespoons water, cover the pan, lower the heat to medium, and continue cooking until the greens have wilted and softened, another 7 to 9 minutes.

Add the grated carrots and a few drops of hot sauce; taste the vegetables for seasoning, and add more salt or hot sauce if you like. Gently fold the sautéed vegetables into the mashed potatoes.

Heat the oven to 350°F. Spoon and spread ¼ cup of the salsa over the bottom of a 9 x 13-inch glass baking dish. Heat a heavy frying pan, and toast a tortilla, flipping it frequently, until it's warm and pliable. Spoon some potato filling onto the tortilla and roll it up gently. Place the rolled tortillas in the baking dish, seam side down. Continue with the rest of the tortillas and filling, nestling them tightly together in the dish.

Pour the remaining salsa over the enchiladas and distribute the cheese evenly over the top. Bake until the cheese is bubbling and the filling is hot, 20 to 30 minutes. Let cool for a few minutes, then sprinkle the cilantro over the enchiladas and serve.

Cook's Tip

Mashing potatoes with cooking water in place of some or all of the usual milk or cream is a clever way to moisten the purée without adding too much richness. The cooking water will be lightly salted and contain some potato starch, so it adds more flavor and body than just plain water. Scoop it from the pot just before you drain the potatoes.

Apple and Brussels Sprouts Hash with Fried Eggs

The world is finally realizing how versatile Brussels sprouts are and using their nutty-sweet flavor and subtle crunch in so many delicious ways. In this dish developed by Chef Eric Ottensmeyer of Leon's Full Service in Decatur, Georgia, the sprouts team up with apples and bacon—so autumnal!—in a savory and nutritious hash. Serve it as a side dish or top it with a gently fried egg for a main dish. It does take a few minutes to slice the sprouts, but the final texture of the dish makes it worth the slight effort. SERVES 4

1 pound Brussels sprouts, ends trimmed

4 ounces bacon (4 or 5 slices), diced

3 tablespoons unsalted butter

1 sweet or yellow onion, thinly sliced

Kosher salt

1 tart firm apple, such as Braeburn, peeled and diced

2 tablespoons apple-cider vinegar

1 cup low-sodium vegetable or chicken stock

2 teaspoons fresh lemon juice

Freshly ground black pepper

4 large eggs

Trim any dried ends of the sprouts and pull off any yellowed leaves. Cut each sprout in half, lay the flat side on the cutting board, and cut into 1/8-inch slices. Set aside.

In a large frying pan, cook the bacon over medium heat until just crisp, about 10 minutes. Scoop out the bacon and set it aside. Pour off the fat from the frying pan and save it for another use.

Put the frying pan back over medium heat, and add 2 tablespoons of the butter. When the butter stops foaming, add the onions and a pinch of salt and cook, stirring frequently, until the onions are soft, fragrant, and beginning to brown, 10 to 12 minutes.

Add the sliced sprouts to the frying pan, add a bit more salt, and toss to combine the onions and sprouts. Continue cooking until the sprouts begin to brown, then add the apples. Stir in the vinegar and scrape up any browned bits from the bottom of the frying pan. Add the stock and cook at a lively simmer until the liquid is almost completely evaporated, about 5 minutes. Add the reserved bacon and the lemon juice. Season with pepper; taste and adjust the seasoning. Keep warm as you cook the eggs.

Heat the remaining 1 tablespoon butter in a large nonstick pan. When the butter stops foaming, gently break the eggs into the pan; use a spatula to keep the whites from spreading too much, and let each egg set slightly before you add the next so they don't run into each other. Season with salt and pepper. Fry the eggs as the diners request (sunny side up, over easy, and so forth). Divide the hash among dinner plates and slide an egg on top of the hash. Serve right away.

CSA Snapshot
Riverview Farms
Ranger, Georgia
www.grassfedcow.com

THE FARMERS: Three generations of the Swancy family—parents Carter and Beverly, current farmers Wes and Charlotte, Brad and Julia, and Drew and Beth, and their children

THE CSA LIFE: Now one of the largest certified organic farms in Georgia, the farm almost shut down after 25 years of farming by Carter and Beverly, when the changing economics of farming sapped the profitability from Carter's row crop cultivation plus pork production model. But rather than relinquish the farm, the children stepped in and built a thriving organic CSA operation with over 30 varieties of vegetables and fruit, plus corn to produce polenta and grits, along with grass-fed beef and Berkshire pork.

Whole Roasted Chicken with Root Vegetables and Apples

This is one of those rare but wonderful dishes that are truly one-dish meals. Once you've prepared your vegetables and chicken, you slide them in the oven and when you come back, your whole dinner is ready. Root vegetables are ideal for roasting—they'll take about the same amount of time as the chicken, and they hold their shape even as they soak up the delicious cooking juices. The apples will break down and get slightly mushy, making a sort of tangy sauce that holds everything together. **SERVES 4**

1 medium celery root
(about 8 ounces)

4 spring onions (red or white,
or both)

1 bunch carrots (about 8 ounces)

1 bunch small Japanese turnips
(about 8 ounces; Tokyo and Scarlet
Queen are favorites)

4 medium potatoes

2 apples (Pink Lady is a nice choice)

1 large beet

Kosher salt and freshly ground
black pepper

8 cloves garlic

One 3- to 4-pound whole chicken

2 lemons

½ cup olive oil

CSA Snapshot

Riverdog Farm
Guinda, California
www.riverdogfarm.com

THE FARMERS: Tim Mueller, Trini Campbell, their daughter, and 50 full-time employees

THE CSA LIFE: This certified organic farm is located in the beautiful Capay Valley of northern California. Hot summers and winter frost encourage fruits and vegetables grown in their rich creek-bottom soil to be exceptionally tasty, prompting many Bay Area restaurants including Chez Panisse and Oliveto to become customers. Riverdog also raises hogs and hens in open pasture and cultivates 100 acres of grain, including barley, triticale, cowpeas, and permanent alfalfa pasture for animal feed. Mueller and Campbell, who met in college in Iowa, where they started a sustainable agriculture course, began farming 2 acres; their farm is now close to 300.

Heat the oven to 400°F. Peel the celery root using a sharp and sturdy paring knife, and cut it into 1-inch cubes. Peel and halve or quarter the onions, depending on their size. Cut the carrots, turnips, potatoes, apples, and the beet into 1-inch cubes or halves that are about 1 inch square.

Put all the vegetables in a very large Dutch oven or rimmed baking pan, and season well with salt and pepper.

Tuck the garlic cloves under the skin of the chicken. Cut the lemons in half and squeeze the juice over it, and then stuff the cavity with the rinds. Season the chicken generously with salt and pepper.

Put the chicken on top of the vegetables, and drizzle everything with the olive oil. Roast, occasionally basting the chicken with the cooking juices. Stir the vegetables occasionally to keep them from drying out. Continue cooking until the leg bones feel loose and the juices run clear, about 1½ hours. Let the chicken rest for 15 minutes before carving, and then transfer everything to a serving platter and serve warm.

"Before we started farming, we hadn't even eaten an Asian turnip; now we grow a stunning red variety called Scarlet Queen and a white one called White Doll. We like to caramelize the turnips in butter and thyme, or just eat them raw in a salad or with hummus."

—Jenny Jackson, Jenny Jack Sun Farm

Beet and Kale Pizza

Not your typical pizza Margherita, this vegetable pizza is rustic, exciting, and delicious. You can buy pizza dough in most grocery stores, so take advantage of the convenience, which allows you to whip up this pizza without much planning. You do need to cook the vegetables before assembly, but the method is simple. The farmers at Heritage Prairie CSA in Illinois like to use goat cheese (they also cook the greens in Old Style® or Pabst Blue Ribbon® beer, with a dash of soy sauce—we're keeping it simpler here), but lots of cheeses would be good, even a blue cheese. MAKES ONE 11-INCH PIZZA

¼ cup olive oil

2 cloves garlic

1 bunch kale (8 ounces; any kind), stems trimmed and leaves coarsely chopped

Kosher salt and freshly ground black pepper

3 beets (about 12 ounces total), scrubbed or peeled and sliced into ¼-inch rounds

1 large onion, thinly sliced

1 teaspoon fresh thyme leaves

Unbleached all-purpose flour, for rolling the dough

Raw pizza dough (for 1 pizza)

Cheese of your choice: 4 ounces fresh goat cheese, ½ cup shredded mozzarella mixed with ½ cup freshly grated Parmigiano-Reggiano, or 1 cup shredded Fontina

In a large frying pan, place 1 tablespoon of the olive oil and the garlic, and sauté over medium heat until the garlic is fragrant, about 30 seconds (don't let it brown). Add the kale, with any water still clinging to it from washing. Season generously with salt and pepper, and increase the heat to medium high. Cook, tossing frequently, until the kale is wilted and tender, 12 to 20 minutes, depending on the variety (add a bit more water if the pan starts to look dry).

Meanwhile, heat the oven to 400°F. Toss the beets with another 1 tablespoon of the olive oil, season with salt and pepper, spread on a baking sheet, and roast until tender and starting to brown slightly, about 20 minutes.

While the beets are cooking, put the remaining 2 tablespoons olive oil in a large frying pan over medium high, add the onions and thyme, season with some salt, and cook, stirring frequently, until the onions are soft, sweet, and fragrant and starting to caramelize slightly, 25 to 35 minutes.

continued on p. 162

CSA Snapshot
Heritage Prairie Farm
Elburn, Illinois
www.heritageprairiefarm.com

THE FARMERS: Bob Archibald and Bronwyn Weaver

THE CSA LIFE: On some summer nights, a greenhouse glows bright against the dark, flat plains of Illinois, when Heritage Prairie Farm transforms its working greenhouse into a spectacular fine dining experience for weddings and special events. By day, the farming couple employs a combination of high-production, low-acreage, four-season methods based on techniques developed by Eliot Coleman. They've been able to greatly extend the season to offer some of the first tomatoes and last spinach, carrots, and radishes in their area.

Once the beets are out of the oven, increase the heat to 475°F and line a baking sheet with parchment. Dust your counter or work surface with flour and roll out the pizza dough to an 11-inch round. Transfer to the baking sheet. Distribute the kale, beets, and onions over the surface of the pizza and top with the cheese.

Bake until the crust is golden brown, the underside looks crisp and brown, and the cheese is bubbling, 18 to 25 minutes. Cut into wedges and serve right away.

Cook's Tip

Caramelized onions are a delicious and versatile ingredient, and one that's useful to have on hand for spontaneous meals. Make a triple batch with this recipe, and use one-third for the pizza and keep the other two-thirds in the fridge to use throughout the week. Use on sandwiches or bruschetta, stir into vegetable soups, fill an omelet, or toss with other vegetables and pasta.

"Despite my enormous garden, I joined a CSA this year to help out a friend who is starting a new farm and also to challenge myself as a cook. I figured getting vegetables and herbs from someone else, without me picking them out, would be a great opportunity. I have learned to adore Swiss chard and kale (which is crazy abundant this year) and made some new favorites because of the CSA basket and not my own whims. Supporting local agriculture is so important to me, so joining this CSA was a no-brainer."

—Kathy G., South Berwick, ME

Baked Acorn Squash Stuffed with Apples, Pork, and Spicy Couscous

Acorn squash is so conveniently shaped and sized for stuffing, and its sweet and nutty flesh pairs nicely with many flavors, so it's the perfect "vessel" for improvisation. Canadian farmer Brenda Hsueh likes to make savory stuffing with the leftover goodies in her fridge, which often include Chinese meats such as roasted duck or barbecued pork, but you can use any type of sausage, ham, or bacon you like. And, of course, you can go meatless, adding perhaps a handful of nuts and dried fruit to the mix. The recipe here calls for couscous because it's quick and tasty, but you could use rice or another grain as well. SERVES 2

1 medium acorn squash
  (about 1 pound)

1 tablespoon olive oil

Kosher salt and freshly ground
  black pepper

1 cup couscous (or 2 cups leftover
  cooked rice)

1 tart apple, such as Braeburn,
  peeled, cored, and finely diced

½ cup chopped cooked pork, duck,
  sausage, bacon, or pancetta

Hot sauce, such as Sriracha,
  to taste

2 teaspoons pure maple syrup

CSA Snapshot
Black Sheep Farm
Ontario, Canada
www.justblacksheep.com

THE FARMER: Brenda Hsueh

THE CSA LIFE: Brenda learned that fulfilling her dream of owning a small-scale, organic farm was more work than she ever imagined while she was working for ten years in the financial industry. This second-generation Chinese Canadian manages to raise sheep, vegetables, and chickens near Owen Sound in rural Ontario while fighting pests, drought, and weeds. She single-handedly started this journey to create a socially responsible and ecologically sound farm in 2009, and now works with committed intern Jeremy Stojan.

Heat the oven to 375°F. Cut the squash in half lengthwise and remove the seeds from the cavity by scraping them out with a spoon. Cut a small slice off the curved side of each half, so it can sit flat without wobbling.

Using a fork or sharp paring knife, poke holes in the flesh of the cut faces and cavities of the squash halves, and then brush with the olive oil. Season generously with salt and pepper.

Bring 1½ cups of water to a boil, add ½ teaspoon salt, and then add the couscous. Cover the pan tightly and remove it from the heat. Leave to absorb for 5 to 6 minutes, and then uncover and fluff with a fork. Stir in the apples, chopped meat, and a few drops of hot sauce. Taste and adjust the seasonings so that the stuffing is nicely savory.

Fill each cavity with the stuffing, mounding and tamping down as needed. Drizzle with the maple syrup. Arrange the squash in a baking dish, add about ½ inch of water, and bake until the squash is completely tender, 45 minutes to 1 hour, depending on the size of the squash.

Chicken and Kohlrabi Curry

Kohlrabi isn't a traditional Thai ingredient, but its crisp texture and mild, sweet turnip flavor is a lovely foil for the flavors in Thai red curry paste, which you can find in most grocery stores and in any Asian market. CSA farmer Mariann Van Den Elzen suggests Mae Ploy® brand; they also make coconut milk. Fresh tomatoes and a splash of white wine add the bright notes to this gently spicy curry. SERVES 4

3 or 4 small kohlrabi (leaves and bulbs, about 1 pound total)

1 pound boneless, skinless chicken breasts or thighs

Kosher salt

2 tablespoons grapeseed or vegetable oil

2 tablespoons unsalted butter

1 small onion, thinly sliced

5 garlic scapes, cut into 1-inch pieces; 1 head green garlic, white and pale green parts only, minced; or 3 large cloves garlic, minced (use what's available according to the season)

2 shallots, minced

¼ cup dry white wine

8 ounces medium tomatoes, quartered

One 14-ounce can coconut milk

2 tablespoons red curry paste; more as needed

1 tablespoon brown sugar

Cooked hot white rice, for serving

Cut off the leaves from the kohlrabi; rinse well to remove any grit, then dry in a salad spinner or on clean dishtowels. Cut away any tough ribs and cut the leaves into 1-inch strips. Rinse the bulbs, and then peel, quarter, and cut the quarters into thin slices. (If your kohlrabi don't have leaves, just skip that step, using only the bulbs.)

Cut the chicken into small chunks and season lightly with salt. In a large, deep frying pan or Dutch oven, heat 1 tablespoon of the oil over medium-high heat. Add the chicken and sauté quickly until just barely done, 3 to 5 minutes. Transfer the chicken to a plate and set aside.

Add the remaining 1 tablespoon oil and the butter to the saucepan; when it's hot, add the onions and cook, stirring occasionally, until tender and golden, 5 to 6 minutes. Stir in the kohlrabi leaves, the garlic, and shallots and cook, stirring, for a couple of minutes. Add the white wine, cover the pan, and cook until the leaves are mostly wilted, about 5 minutes, stirring occasionally. Mix in the tomatoes and reduce the heat.

In a small bowl, stir together the coconut milk, curry paste, and brown sugar. Pour the coconut mixture into the frying pan. Simmer until the curry has thickened slightly, about 5 minutes. Add the chicken and juices and simmer for another minute or so to heat through. Taste and adjust the seasonings with more salt or curry paste. Serve in shallow bowls next to a mound of hot rice.

CSA Snapshot
Field Day Farms
Bozeman, Montana
www.fielddayfarms.com

THE FARMER: Mariann Van Den Elzen

THE CSA LIFE: This certified organic farm was founded on a 1-acre piece of land that Van Den Elzen leased in exchange for supplying the landowner with food. The farm has continued to grow that way, but recently consolidated its growing fields to one ranch that offers them room to expand. Field Day Farms has teamed with two nearby farms to provide a varied supply for their traditional summer and winter CSAs. They also offer an "à la carte" option, where CSA members can order what they like online.

Cook's Tip

Long before garlic forms the familiar papery heads tight with individual cloves, it goes through two deliciously edible stages:

GARLIC SCAPE This is the curly green stalk that grows out of a garlic plant in very early spring. Most farmers remove them, thinking the head will grow bigger with no scape to divert energy. Crunchy, with a mild garlic flavor, the scapes are easy to cook with, though slightly fibrous on the outside. Cut into short pieces and sauté, roast, or add to soups, stews, risottos, or stir-fries. Or purée them raw with olive oil, pine nuts, and aged grating cheese to make a garlicky pesto.

GREEN GARLIC Before the garlic plant actually forms heads divided into cloves, it looks like a scallion or other slender spring onion. The flavor is sweet and mild, and so it can be used generously in dishes. Green garlic makes a beautiful puréed soup, finished with a touch of crème fraîche.

Swiss Chard, White Beans, and Turkey Sausage on Cornbread Cakes

In certain parts of the American South, these rustic little cornbread cakes are a frequent part of a meal, but they may not be familiar to the rest of Americans. Quick to whip up and a tasty companion to any sort of saucy dish, they're likely to become part of your regular family suppers. Farmer Freida Lansing doesn't use an egg in her cornbread cakes, but the addition makes the batter a touch easier to use. SERVES 2 OR 3

1 bunch Swiss chard, ends trimmed, thick ribs cut out and reserved

2 tablespoons olive oil

1 medium onion, chopped

Kosher salt and freshly ground black pepper

4 ounces turkey kielbasa, diced

3 cloves garlic, chopped

4 medium tomatoes, chopped, or one 14-ounce can whole peeled tomatoes

One 14-ounce can white beans, such as Great Northern or cannellini, rinsed and drained

1 teaspoon fresh lemon juice; more as needed

Few drops of hot sauce

¼ cup freshly grated Parmesan (optional)

6 Cornbread Cakes (recipe on the facing page)

Finely chop the chard ribs. Cut the leaves into ½-inch chiffonade.

In a large frying pan, heat the oil over medium-high heat, add the onions and chopped chard stems, season lightly with salt and pepper, and sauté until soft and fragrant, about 4 minutes. Add the kielbasa and garlic and cook for another minute or two, stirring.

Add the chard leaves, handfuls at a time, tossing until they wilt to allow room for the next handful. Add the tomatoes, season with more salt and pepper, adjust the heat to a lively simmer, and cook until the chard is tender and the liquid from all the vegetables has reduced and thickened slightly.

Add the white beans and cook a bit more to heat through and blend the flavors. Add the lemon juice, hot sauce, and Parmesan, if using; taste and adjust the seasonings with more salt, pepper, lemon juice, or hot sauce. Serve with the warm Cornbread Cakes.

CSA Snapshot

**Windermere Farms & Apiaries
Memphis, Tennessee
www.winfarms.com**

THE FARMERS: Ken and Freida Lansing

THE CSA LIFE: Located on a beautiful oasis within the Memphis city limits, this certified organic 17-acre property sits on old family land in a meadow between two wooded hills. In just a few short years, the Lansings have learned that CSA members become friends. The members they've served pray for their crops and family needs, suffer with them when a flood comes, and rejoice with them when they have perfect strawberry weather.

Cornbread Cakes

MAKES SIX 3-INCH CAKES

1 cup cornmeal
¼ cup unbleached all-purpose flour
1 teaspoon baking powder

¼ teaspoon kosher salt
1 large egg
Olive oil and unsalted butter,
    for frying

In a medium bowl, whisk together the cornmeal, flour, baking powder, and salt. Crack the egg into the measuring cup with ½ cup water and beat with a fork to blend. Pour the egg and water into the dry ingredients and mix together with a few strokes of a wooden spoon or spatula, just until the ingredients are combined. It's okay if there are a few small lumps.

Heat 1 tablespoon oil and 1 tablespoon butter in a frying pan over medium-high heat. When the fat is hot, pour in about ¼ cup batter to make a small cake, about 3 inches across. Pour in a few more cakes, but don't crowd the pan or it will be too hard to flip the cakes.

When the edges of the cakes start to brown and you see small holes on the top, after 2 to 3 minutes, carefully flip with a spatula and cook the second side for another minute or so until cooked through and lightly browned. Continue cooking the cakes, adding more oil and butter as needed, until all the batter is used up.

Serve the cornbread cakes warm, topped with the Swiss chard and beans.

Prep School

Leafy greens can be hard to wrangle when raw, but chopping them once they're cooked can be messy. The best approach is to slice them into ribbons, called chiffonade, before you cook them. You can make chiffonade as wide or as skinny as you like. The technique is the same whether you're talking tennis racquet–size collard greens or delicate basil leaves:

1. Trim off tough stem ends and discard. Cut out tough ribs by slicing along either side with a sharp knife. (Reserve the ribs to slice or chop and use in the recipe.)

2. Stack a few leaves on top of each other and carefully roll them into a cylinder. Slice crosswise to make ribbons. If you want to actually chop your greens, you can turn the coils of sliced greens and cut them crosswise again to chop into pieces.

Pioneer Beef Stew

While beef plays the lead role in a beef stew, it's really the vegetables that create the character. As they cook together, their juices mingle and contribute to the broth that will unite all the ingredients into a bowl of nutritious comfort. The combination of onions and root vegetables can be pretty sweet, so be sure to balance that earthy sweetness with enough garlic, salt and pepper, and red pepper flakes. The wine will also provide some welcome acidity to the mix. SERVES 8

2 to 3 tablespoons olive oil

2 pounds beef stew meat, such as chuck, cut into 1-inch chunks

Kosher salt and freshly ground black pepper

2 pounds potatoes, peeled and cubed

1 pound onions or leeks, chopped

1 to 2 bunches turnips (about 12 ounces), scrubbed and diced

1 bunch carrots (8 ounces), scrubbed and diced

2 or 3 parsnips, scrubbed and diced

3 cloves garlic

1 cup red or white wine

1 cup beef or chicken broth or water; more as needed

Pinch of crushed red pepper flakes

½ cup chopped fresh flat-leaf parsley

Heat the oil in a large Dutch oven over medium-high heat. Add enough beef chunks to make a single layer, season well with salt and pepper, and cook, turning frequently, until nicely browned on all sides. This should take 8 to 10 minutes. Transfer the beef to a bowl, and repeat with the rest of the meat.

Put all the meat back into the Dutch oven, add the potatoes, onions, turnips, carrots, parsnips, garlic, wine, and broth. Season again lightly with salt and pepper and a pinch of red pepper flakes.

Cover the pot, adjust the heat to a lazy simmer, and cook, stirring occasionally, until the meat is completely tender, 2 to 2½ hours (though you should start testing before that). If it looks like the pot is getting dry, add a bit more broth or water. Toward the end of the cooking, remove the lid so the liquid can reduce a bit. Right before serving, taste and adjust the seasonings. Add the parsley and serve hot or warm.

CSA Snapshot

Mariquita Farm
Watsonville, California
www.mariquita.com

THE FARMER: Andrew Griffin

THE CSA LIFE: This organic farm has members in California's Silicon Valley, the Peninsula, and San Francisco, including many restaurants. They like to say they take their members on a "food tour of the world," as they specialize in unusual varieties of vegetables and herbs, such as French fingerling potato varieties, Asian cooking greens, and Native American squash and beans.

Cook's Tip

This makes a fairly brothy stew. If you'd like a slightly thicker gravy, sprinkle 3 tablespoons flour over the meat as you brown it.

You can also make this stew in a large slow cooker. Brown the meat and then combine everything but the parsley. Cook on low for 8 hours. Add the parsley before serving.

Corned Beef with Cabbage and Root Vegetables

This traditional dish is not only hearty and warming, but it's also infinitely adaptable, happily accepting a variety of cabbages, root vegetables, even onions and leeks. The more vegetables you include, the more complex the broth, which is key to the dish. The broth is completely unthickened, but it should have plenty of intense flavor to enliven the meat and vegetables and pull the dish together. The flavors and textures of this perfect cold-weather supper are even better the next day.   SERVES 4 TO 6

One 3½-pound corned beef
  (bottom round or brisket)
2 medium yellow onions, quartered
2 bay leaves
8 black peppercorns
6 whole cloves
6 large carrots, peeled and cut
  into chunks
1 large or 3 small rutabagas, peeled
  and cut into chunks

6 medium potatoes (preferably low
  or medium starch, such as Yukon
  Gold), peeled and cut in half
1 medium head green or Savoy
  cabbage, washed, cored, and cut
  into 6 wedges
Kosher salt and freshly ground
  black pepper

CSA Snapshot

Pete's Greens
Craftsbury, Vermont
www.petesgreens.com

THE FARMER: Pete Johnson

THE CSA LIFE: This farm is a certified organic, four-season vegetable farm located on the edge of Vermont's Northeast Kingdom. Johnson has been farming since his childhood, starting a pumpkin farm when he was nine. He grows many of his crops in greenhouses that are heated with bio-grease from restaurants. The farm also has a huge root cellar in the barn, with different climatic zones, to ensure a supply of fresh vegetables throughout the winter.

Rinse the corned beef to wash off the brine, and then put it in a large soup pot or Dutch oven. Add the onions, bay leaves, peppercorns, and cloves; add enough water to cover.

Bring to a boil over high heat, cover, and adjust the heat to a gentle simmer. Simmer the corned beef for about 2 hours, occasionally skimming off the froth that forms on the surface.

Add the carrots, rutabagas, and potatoes (and any other vegetables you may be using). Return to a simmer and continue cooking, covered, for another 15 minutes. Add the cabbage wedges and simmer until all the vegetables are quite tender, another 15 to 25 minutes.

Let the beef sit in the broth for a few minutes to cool slightly, and then transfer to a cutting board and keep warm under some foil. Strain the broth into a large saucepan, reserving the vegetables but discarding the bay leaves, peppercorns, and cloves. Cook the broth over medium-high

heat to reduce it by about a third, concentrating the flavor, about 25 minutes. Season to taste with salt and pepper.

Put the vegetables in the broth and heat through for about 5 minutes. Sliced the corned beef across the grain into ¼-inch slices. Arrange the beef and vegetables on a large platter (slightly bowl shaped, to catch the broth). Moisten with the broth and serve hot, with more broth on the side for people to pass at the table.

Cook's Tip

Savoy cabbage looks like a head of green cabbage wearing a party dress. The leaves are tightly puckered and ruched, and the head is slightly more loosely formed than regular cabbage, though it's still round. The flavor is sweet and nutty, and the leaves are flexible, making it an excellent cabbage for stuffing. Turn the leftover corned beef and vegetables into a filling and make stuffed cabbage leaves!

SIDES

Hudson Ranch
Potatoes
Banana Fingerling
7-10-12- 30. Lbs

Grilled Radicchio Wedges with Creamy Anchovy-Caper Dressing

Grilling may seem a surprising treatment for what's normally seen as a salad green, but the slight char from the grill is lovely with the bitterness of the radicchio and its cousins. The wedges soften and wilt in the heat, taking on a bit of smoke. Use the grilled radicchio as the base of a simple salad with the Creamy Anchovy-Caper Dressing, as a partner for some creamy polenta, or to top a big juicy cheeseburger. SERVES 4 AS A SALAD

2 heads Chioggia or Treviso-type radicchio (you may also use escarole or puntarelle)

Extra-virgin olive oil

Kosher salt

Creamy Anchovy-Caper Dressing (recipe on p. 176)

Heat a grill to medium-high.

Quarter each radicchio head. Cut first in half, starting at the base and slicing down through the top of the head, and then cut each half in half. Each quarter should have a piece of the stem at its base to hold it together.

Brush each wedge generously with olive oil and sprinkle with salt. Arrange the wedges on the grill and cook until the bottom side starts to brown and crisp, 3 to 5 minutes. Using tongs, flip and cook the second side like the first, flipping one more time until all three sides have been seared and crisped by the grill. (You may also do this in a heavy frying pan or grill pan. Coat the pan with a bit of olive oil and set the heat to high. Set the wedges in the pan and cover with a heavy lid that's smaller that the diameter of the pan, so that it presses directly on the radicchio. Cook until the bottoms are crisp and starting to brown, 3 to 5 minutes, and the tops of the wedges are wilted and tender.)

Serve warm, with the dressing drizzled over the top.

continued on p. 176

CSA Snapshot

Village Farm
Freedom, Maine
www.villagefarmfreedom.com

THE FARMERS: Polly Shyka and Prentice Grassi

THE CSA LIFE: Nestled in the rolling hills of western Waldo County, Maine, this certified organic farm's diverse acres of crops are a welcome change from the surrounding rows of corn and green pastures that cover the majority of the region's farming landscape. The farmers practice extensive rotational grazing and other soil conservation techniques. Gratitude is a daily harvest on this Maine farm. The farmers feel fortunate to work with aspiring apprentices, provide food for local families, grow seedlings, tend the plants and animals, and be stewards of the soil and water each day.

Creamy Anchovy-Caper Dressing

The Italian flavors in this easy dressing are a nice match to the grilled radicchio.

MAKES ABOUT ½ CUP

10 anchovy fillets, drained
1 small clove garlic
2 tablespoons fresh lemon juice
1 tablespoon drained capers

1 tablespoon extra-virgin olive oil
3 tablespoons heavy cream
Freshly ground black pepper
Kosher salt (optional)

Put the anchovies, garlic, lemon juice, and capers in a food processor and process until blended; you'll probably have to stop and scrape down the sides of the bowl with a rubber spatula a couple of times.

With the motor running, slowly pour in the olive oil and then the cream and process for about 10 seconds, until the mixture is well blended and the cream has started to thicken slightly; the dressing won't be completely smooth. Season to taste with pepper. You probably won't need salt because of the anchovies and capers, but taste and add some if you do.

Cook's Tip

Once you get the hang of grilling greens, you'll see a world of possibilities. Here are a few ideas to get you launched. Split a head of romaine, brush with oil, and grill until slightly wilted and charred around the edges. At the same time, grill some olive oil–brushed bread, to cube and use for croutons in a grilled Caesar salad. Or fold radicchio leaves around squares of meltable cheese topped with a few capers and hot chiles in oil. Brush with olive oil and grill until the radicchio is wilted and the cheese has started to melt. Serve with a drizzle of vinaigrette.

"Better than Christmas morning! A weekly treasure box of seasonal veggies, flowers, and fruit to inspire meals and connect me with a farm and green growing things. I learned to make tomatillo salsa because of receiving a zillion tomatillos one summer. Now that's a ritual."

—Judith D., Seattle, WA

Sautéed Asparagus with Lime and Tahini

Tahini—the creamy sesame paste that you've probably tasted as part of hummus—is a wonderful ingredient to use in vegetable cookery because it brings a lush flavor and texture without actually adding any butter, cream, or cheese. You can find tahini in most grocery stores, usually in a can, which will need to be refrigerated after opening but which will last quite a while. Also try this recipe using green beans later in the summer.   SERVES 4

3 tablespoons olive oil
3 tablespoons fresh lime juice
2 tablespoons tahini
½ teaspoon minced garlic

Kosher salt
1 pound asparagus, ends trimmed or snapped off, cut into 1½-inch pieces

Whisk together 2 tablespoons of the oil, the lime juice, tahini, garlic, and a pinch of salt in a small bowl. Taste and adjust the flavoring so the balance of nutty, tangy, and salty is to your liking.

Heat the remaining 1 tablespoon olive oil in a large wok or cast-iron skillet over medium-high heat. When the oil is hot, add the asparagus and sauté until it begins to soften and get slightly browned, about 4 to 6 minutes. Season with more salt to taste.

Transfer to a serving bowl or platter and quickly drizzle the tahini mixture on top. Serve right away.

Cook's Tip

In order to trim an asparagus spear properly, you need to know where it changes from tender to stringy. One trick is to hold the spear in two hands and gently bend it, moving from the end toward the tip. It should snap at the point where it's tender.

CSA Snapshot

**Growing Home's
Les Brown Memorial Farm
Marseilles, Illinois
www.growinghomeinc.org**

THE FARMERS: Tracy Noel, Joe Avon, Stephanie Douglass, and Yoram Shanan

THE CSA LIFE: This 10-acre certified organic farm sits on a stretch of nice glacial deposit soil in LaSalle County, an area known for its deep canyons and majestic views. Running a CSA requires these Illinois farmers to be experts at growing every one of the 190 different varieties of vegetables and herbs found on the farm. They are helped in their efforts by workers from Growing Home's job training program, which uses organic agriculture as a vehicle for career and community development.

Asian Greens with Tangy Sauce

"Fresh greens" doesn't always mean salad. Elsewhere Farm's Clare Hintz turns to this zesty preparation when she's busy with farm work but wants a delicious and nutrition-packed meal. Serve it as a first course, as you would a salad, or as a side to whatever else is on the menu. You can mix and match the greens according to what's on hand or in your CSA box. The salty-spicy-nutty flavors in the sauce help to balance the bite of strong greens such as mizuna and other Asian mustards. You can use any cooking green, though, including milder varieties such as Swiss chard, spinach, or collards. Just check the doneness by tasting, since each type of green cooks at a different rate.   SERVES 2 OR 3

2 tablespoons soy sauce

1 tablespoon toasted sesame oil

1 tablespoon honey

¼ teaspoon dried red pepper flakes or ⅛ teaspoon cayenne or other ground chile powder

1 pound mixed Asian salad greens (tatsoi, Tokyo Bekana, and mustards)

1 tablespoon canola or other vegetable oil

1½ teaspoons grated fresh ginger

3 garlic cloves, finely chopped

Stir together ¼ cup water with the soy sauce, sesame oil, honey, and red pepper flakes. Set aside.

Rinse the greens and blot or spin them dry. Heat the canola oil in a large frying pan over medium heat. Add the ginger and garlic, cook for just a few seconds (do not let the garlic brown), and then add the greens slowly, tossing until they're wilted and starting to soften, about 1 minute.

Pour in the sauce, toss to coat everything, and continue cooking until the greens are tender (but not mushy), another minute or so. If the greens need to wilt further, turn off the heat and cover the pan to let them steam down for a few more minutes. Serve hot or at room temperature.

Cook's Tip

When you're cooking with greens that have thick center ribs, it's hard to get the rib parts tender before the leaves get mushy. The trick to even cooking is to first cut out the ribs, and then chop them. Add them to the pan first and cook for a few minutes to give them a head start before you add the leaves.

CSA Snapshot

Elsewhere Farm
Herbster, Wisconsin
www.facebook.com/ ElsewhereFarm

THE FARMER: Clare Hintz

THE CSA LIFE: With a doctorate in sustainability education and regenerative agriculture, farmer Clare Hintz is more than qualified to lead the permaculture classes she teaches. Friends of the farm come out to this land in northern Wisconsin, near Lake Superior, for events such as a cider-pressing party and Fruit Diversity Field Day. One fruit she grows on her farm is a perfect example of how the principles of biodiversity can ensure the survival of our food supplies. The saskatoon berry is a native prairie plant that tastes and looks very similar to blueberries. When drought hit the land, this berry was strong enough to withstand the weather and outperformed the more popular varieties.

Lemon and Dill Green Beans

In this easy dish, the fresh grassy flavor of green beans is amplified by the fresh dill and lemon. Other tender herbs would be delicious, too, including tarragon, chervil, parsley, mint, and cilantro—just mix and match according to what's in your CSA box or garden.

SERVES 4

1 tablespoon plus 1 teaspoon kosher salt

1½ pounds green beans or other fresh snap or string bean

2 tablespoons unsalted butter or olive oil

⅛ teaspoon freshly ground black pepper

1 teaspoon chopped garlic

1 tablespoon chopped fresh dill

1 tablespoon fresh lemon juice

½ cup chopped or slivered almonds, lightly toasted

Bring a large pot of water to a boil, add about 1 tablespoon of the salt, and cook the beans until just tender, about 8 minutes. Drain well.

In a large frying pan, heat the butter over medium-high heat. When it stops foaming, add the beans, the remaining ½ teaspoon salt, and the pepper, and sauté, tossing frequently, for 2 to 3 minutes, until glossy. Add the garlic and cook for another 30 seconds or so (don't let the garlic brown), and then finish by adding the dill and lemon juice.

Pile the beans into a serving dish and top with the chopped almonds. Serve right away.

CSA Snapshot

Windermere Farms & Apiaries
Memphis, Tennessee
www.winfarms.com

THE FARMERS: Ken and Freida Lansing

THE CSA LIFE: Located on a beautiful oasis within the Memphis city limits, this certified organic 17-acre property sits on old family land in a meadow between two wooded hills. In just a few short years, the Lansings have learned that CSA members become friends. The members they've served pray for their crops and family needs, suffer with them when a flood comes, and rejoice with them when they have perfect strawberry weather.

Stuffed and Baked Pattypan Squash with Prosciutto and Parmesan Filling

Pattypan squash are mild, slightly nutty, and generally firmer than a longer summer squash such as zucchini. Their pretty colors, ranging from celadon green to vivid yellow, and scalloped edges make them a fun choice for serving at dinner parties. This is a good do-ahead dish; cook the squash on the first side according to the recipe. Stuff them and then refrigerate until your dinner. Finish cooking them following the recipe, but add a few minutes additional roasting time. SERVES 4

4 ounces prosciutto, very finely chopped

½ cup freshly grated Parmigiano-Reggiano

½ cup lightly packed coarse fresh breadcrumbs

2 tablespoons chopped pitted Kalamata olives

1 tablespoon olive oil

Kosher salt and freshly ground black pepper

4 medium pattypan or other summer squash (about 5 ounces each)

Toss together the prosciutto, cheese, breadcrumbs, olives, and olive oil. Season with salt and pepper, and then taste and adjust the seasoning. (You may not need to add much salt because of the other salty ingredients.) Set aside.

Heat the oven to 400°F. Line a baking sheet with parchment or foil. Cut the squash in half horizontally to make two disks. Cut a small slice off the underside of each disk so it sits flat. Scoop out some of the center to make space for the filling.

Arrange the pattypans on the baking sheet, cut side down. Roast the squash until tender, about 10 minutes. Turn the squash over and spoon the filling into the center, mounding it a bit. Continue roasting for another 8 to 10 minutes, until the filling is hot and the cheese has started to melt. Serve warm or at room temperature.

Cook's Tip

To make thin meats, such as prosciutto, pancetta, and bacon, easy to chop into fine pieces, pop them into the freezer for 10 to 20 minutes to firm up slightly before chopping.

Summer Vegetable Frito

Frito is a Spanish dish that's similar to ratatouille, but the cooking method makes it much more intensely flavorful. It's super versatile, too, making a lovely side dish, a topping for pasta or polenta, a bruschetta topping, a filling for an omelet, or an awesome sandwich filling. Brian Bondy of Rio Arriba Farms just serves it in a bowl with crusty bread for dipping. The quantities are approximate—take a Mediterranean attitude and just use whatever looks delicious. SERVES 4

¾ cup extra-virgin olive oil

1 tablespoon chopped garlic

1 large eggplant, peeled and cut into ¼-inch slices

Kosher salt and freshly ground black pepper

2 summer squash (such as zucchini or yellow squash), cut into ¼-inch slices

2 yellow, orange, or red bell peppers, cored, seeded, and cut into ½-inch strips

1 large onion, thinly sliced

2 cups canned crushed tomatoes or finely chopped ripe fresh tomatoes

1 tablespoon balsamic vinegar (optional)

Heat a large, heavy frying pan over medium-high heat and add just enough of the olive oil to cover the bottom of the pan. Add about 1 teaspoon of the garlic; don't let it burn. Quickly arrange some eggplant slices in the frying pan without overlapping. Drizzle a little more oil over the top of the eggplant and season generously with salt and pepper. Cook until the undersides are lightly browned, about 4 minutes. Flip the slices, then continue cooking until the eggplant is tender all the way through, another 5 to 6 minutes. Repeat with the remaining eggplant and set aside on a plate.

Cook the squash, peppers, and onions in the same manner, one vegetable at a time: First add some oil to the pan, then a bit of garlic, and then layer the vegetables in the pan. Season with salt and pepper, cook until nicely browned, flip, and cook until very tender. As each vegetable finishes cooking, transfer to the plate with the eggplant.

When you've finished cooking all the vegetables, add the remaining oil and garlic (if there is any) to the pan, and then add the crushed tomatoes. Adjust the heat to a simmer and cook until the tomatoes are slightly thickened and glistening with oil, about 10 minutes. If you like, add the balsamic vinegar. Add back all the cooked vegetables and simmer to blend and reheat. Taste and adjust the salt and pepper. Serve warm or at room temperature.

CSA Snapshot

Rio Arriba Farms
Abiquiu, New Mexico
www.rioarribafarms.com

THE FARMER: Jeff Nitz

THE CSA LIFE: This CSA gets its produce from Red Mountain Farms in Abiquiu, as well as from surrounding farms. Their offerings are farmed organically. They've created their CSA particularly for members who live some 40 miles outside of Santa Fe, bringing local, organically grown produce to a community that typically lacks access to good fresh food.

Cook's Tip

You can make this flavorful dish even more savory by including capers, chopped olives, raisins, and minced hot chiles in oil. Stir these ingredients into the frito when you add back the vegetables in the final step.

Barbecued Green Beans

Who says only dried beans should get the delicious baked-bean treatment? This dish, in which you can use any type of string bean—green, wax, purple, romano, and more—has all the sweet-smoky flavors of the classic picnic fare, but with the nutritious boost from fresh vegetables. SERVES 6 TO 8

4 slices bacon, chopped
½ cup chopped onions
½ cup ketchup
¼ cup packed dark or light brown sugar

1 tablespoon Worcestershire sauce
2 pounds green beans, ends trimmed and strings removed if needed

Put the bacon and onions into a small frying pan over medium heat, and cook until the bacon has rendered its fat and is starting to brown and the onions are soft, fragrant, and starting to caramelize, about 10 minutes. Drain off excess fat. Add the ketchup, brown sugar, and Worcestershire sauce. Simmer for 2 minutes, until slightly thickened.

Heat the oven to 350°F. Put the green beans in a 9 x 13-inch baking dish. Pour the bacon mixture over the beans, and toss gently to coat. Bake until the beans are completely tender and the barbecue sauce is bubbling slightly, 20 to 30 minutes. Let cool for about 5 minutes before serving.

CSA Snapshot

**Earth Spring Farm
Gardners, Pennsylvania
www.earthspringcsa.com**

THE FARMER: Mike Nolan

THE CSA LIFE: This CSA farm serves both the Harrisburg area in Pennsylvania and the Washington, D.C., area from their land at the northern end of Michaux State forest in Cumberland County, Pennsylvania. With the South Mountains always in view, this family works the land in an area steeped with rich agricultural history. Growing up as a 4-H member, Mike was surrounded by this culture. He became more committed to sustainability later during study in Denmark, where he was exposed to progressive ideals of controlling urban sprawl, biking as transportation, and small-scale urban farm production. After an extensive hands-on farming education, Mike returned to the East to put this knowledge to use on his own farm.

Cook's Tip

Make this dish vegetarian by leaving out the bacon and Worcestershire and adding about 2 teaspoons of smoked paprika (pimentón de la Vera) when you cook the onions.

Green Beans with Tomatoes, Oregano, and Feta

Long-cooked green beans develop a chewy texture and rich flavor that beats crisp-tender every time. Here, they are slowly simmered with tomatoes and herbs and finished with some salty feta. This dish is loosely based on the Greek dish called *fashoulakia*, but with nice, meaty green beans and the addition of slivered fennel. Chef/farmer Lori Greene, from Downing Hollow Farm, in Tennessee, prefers a fatter, heartier bean such as Italian romano beans or French Merveille de Piemonte.

The dish is extra pretty if you use all colors of heirloom tomatoes including the oranges, pinks, yellows, whites, and greens. This is a wonderful dish for summer entertaining because the flavors are even more developed when served at room temperature. Make the dish ahead and sprinkle with feta and fresh herbs at the last minute. Lori also likes to serve this warm over orzo. SERVES 4 TO 6

3 tablespoons olive oil

1 cup finely chopped onions

2 cloves garlic, minced

1 medium fennel bulb, thinly sliced, some fronds reserved

Kosher salt and freshly ground black pepper

3 to 4 cups medium-diced, seeded, skinned tomatoes, or two 14½-ounce cans stewed tomatoes, with their juices

2 pounds green beans, strings removed if necessary, stem ends trimmed, and cut into 2-inch pieces

⅓ cup finely chopped fresh flat-leaf parsley

2 tablespoons finely chopped fresh mint

½ cup crumbled feta

CSA Snapshot

Downing Hollow Farm
Olive Hill, Tennessee
www.downinghollowfarm.com

THE FARMERS: Alex Greene, Lori Godwin-Greene, and children Henry and Hattie

THE CSA LIFE: This food-producing duo shares a rich history working in professional kitchens, growing up on farms, and performing live music. Following four-season farming pioneer Eliot Coleman's principles, they only use organic pesticides as a last resort on their farm, which is nestled in the hill country between Memphis and Nashville. Experience has shown them that very healthy plants growing in healthy soil, teeming with biotic activity, can often stand up to pests all on their own.

Heat the olive oil in a deep frying pan or wide saucepan over medium heat. Add the onions and garlic; sauté until soft and fragrant, about 3 minutes. Add the fennel, season lightly with salt and pepper, and sauté for another 3 minutes. Add the tomatoes and then bring everything to a gentle simmer. Reduce the heat, cover the pan, and stew for about 30 minutes, until the mixture becomes nicely saucy.

Add the beans and simmer until they are tender, 15 to 30 minutes, depending on the variety of bean. Add the parsley and mint, taste and adjust the seasonings, and simmer for another 5 minutes.

Spoon into a serving bowl or platter and top with the crumbled feta and a fennel frond or two.

Smoky Spiced Grilled Okra

Many CSA members are challenged by deliveries of okra in their weekly boxes. Once you've made gumbo a few times, what's next? Try this dish, which is super quick to make and zippy with spices and mustard. Serve these with cocktails, as finger food or on small bamboo skewers; or pile them onto a platter as a side dish to a vegetable frittata, grilled fish, or fried chicken. You can play with the spice combinations, adding more chili powder and cayenne to increase the heat quotient. The recipe makes more spice than you'll need for one recipe; keep the extra in a small jar or zip-top bag. SERVES 4

1 teaspoon kosher salt

1 teaspoon chili powder

½ teaspoon pimentón (sweet smoked paprika)

½ teaspoon ground coriander

½ teaspoon ground cumin

½ teaspoon freshly ground white pepper

½ teaspoon cayenne

¼ teaspoon garlic powder

1 pound okra, rinsed and dried

2 tablespoons olive oil

1 tablespoon Dijon mustard

Heat a grill to high. Put the salt, chili powder, pimentón, coriander, cumin, white pepper, cayenne, and garlic powder in a small bowl and stir to mix.

Trim the tips of the okra stems but don't cut into the pods. Whisk the oil and mustard together in a large bowl, add the okra, and toss to coat. Add 2 teaspoons of the spice mixture and toss again to distribute thoroughly.

Grill the okra, turning frequently, until they are slightly softened and nicely browned, 2 to 4 minutes. (Make sure you position the okra so they don't slip between the grill grates. Use a grill basket if you have one.) Arrange on plates or a platter and serve right away.

CSA Snapshot
Jenny Jack Sun Farm
Pine Mountain, Georgia
www.jennyjackfarm.com

THE FARMERS: Jenny and Chris Jackson

THE CSA LIFE: In small and quaint Pine Mountain, this chemical-free farm lies at the foothills of the Appalachian Mountains in west-central Georgia, an hour southwest of Atlanta. The Jacksons' local community has given them the chance to grow and provide food for their neighbors rather than having to truck it to the closest quality farmer's markets in Atlanta.

Sautéed Eggplant with Chard and Cilantro

Julia Wiley of Mariquita Farm near Watsonville, California, lived in China and learned to make this dish from several friends there. It's a lovely way to showcase delicate Asian-type eggplants and to combine them with fresh greens, which is an unusual pairing. If you can't find Erbette chard—which is a delicate, slightly ruffly green-and-white chard—use whatever chard you have. SERVES 6 TO 8

2 cloves garlic, chopped

2 tablespoons rice vinegar

1 tablespoon soy sauce

1 tablespoon toasted sesame oil

1 tablespoon black bean sauce

2 teaspoons granulated sugar

2 pounds small white or purple eggplants

3 tablespoons peanut or safflower oil

2 to 4 cloves garlic, chopped

1 bunch Erbette chard, washed and coarsely chopped (don't dry the leaves after rinsing)

1 bunch fresh cilantro, chopped

Hot cooked rice, for serving

Make the sauce by whisking together the garlic, vinegar, soy sauce, sesame oil, black bean sauce, and sugar with a few drops of water to make a pourable sauce. Set aside.

Cut the eggplants into large bite-size pieces. Heat the oil in a frying pan or wok over high heat. Add the eggplants and cook for about 2 minutes. Reduce the heat to medium-high, add the garlic, and continue cooking, stirring often, until the eggplants are mostly cooked through, another 5 minutes or so; take care not to burn the garlic.

Add the chard and continue cooking, tossing the chard with tongs until it's wilted, 1 or 2 more minutes. Add the sauce to the vegetable mixture. Remove from the heat, and fold in the cilantro. Serve with rice.

CSA Snapshot
**Mariquita Farm
Watsonville, California
www.mariquita.com**

THE FARMER: Andrew Griffin

THE CSA LIFE: This organic farm has members in California's Silicon Valley, the Peninsula, and San Francisco, including many restaurants. They like to say they take their members on a "food tour of the world," as they specialize in unusual varieties of vegetables and herbs, such as French fingerling potato varieties, Asian cooking greens, and Native American squash and beans.

"Sunchokes have become one of my favorite vegetables to grow and eat. They're super drought-tolerant and pest- and disease-resistant, and their sweet, crunchy flavor is so delicious. My favorite way to prepare them is to roast them with oil and lemon juice until they become soft."

—Jenny Jackson, Jenny Jack Sun Farm

Summer Squash and Cheesy Custard Casserole

Keep this casserole "pure" with summer squash only, or add fresh herbs, spinach, sweet peppers, mild chiles, or any other vegetables that you like (though North Carolina farmer George O'Neal cautions against turnips, which "have no place here"). SERVES 4 TO 6

2 pounds summer squash (yellow, pattypan, or zucchini)

½ cup (1 stick) unsalted butter

1 sweet onion, such as Vidalia or Walla Walla, very thinly sliced

Kosher salt and freshly ground black pepper

½ cup milk

½ cup heavy cream

5 large eggs

2 cups shredded cheese (Cheddar, Parmesan, Fontina, or other melting cheese)

2 cups coarse fresh breadcrumbs (you may also use crushed crackers)

CSA Snapshot
Lil' Farm
Hillsborough, North Carolina
www.lilfarmnc.com

THE FARMER: George O'Neal

THE CSA LIFE: Lil' Farm's fun tag line, "never whack," means no herbicides or pesticides in the gardens, nor antibiotics for the 300 chickens. This beginning farmer believes in farm transparency—if you want to see how your food is being grown, come out to these few acres north of Durham for a visit. You will see happy, socializing chickens and a mobile tractor that allows them a natural diet and fresh pasture. With help from a grant, George started an equipment co-op that allows him and ten other farms to have access to trucks, tractors, and tools.

Heat the oven to 400°F. Butter a 9 x 13-inch baking dish.

Trim the ends of the squash and then slice them into ⅛-inch rounds. Heat 4 tablespoons of the butter over medium heat in a large frying pan, add the onions, and cook until very soft, sweet, and beginning to brown, about 15 minutes. Transfer to a bowl. Add another 1 tablespoon butter and add about half of the squash, season with salt and pepper, and sauté until the squash has softened and is slightly golden brown, about 5 minutes. Repeat with another tablespoon of butter and the remaining squash.

Whisk the milk, cream, and eggs together in a large bowl, and then add the cheese and season with salt and pepper. Fold in the squash and onions and pour into the baking dish.

Melt the remaining 2 tablespoons butter and toss it with the breadcrumbs to coat them evenly. Sprinkle over the top of the casserole, and cover with foil. Bake for 30 minutes, then remove the foil and continue to bake until the top is nicely browned, the filling is firm, and a knife inserted in the center comes out clean, another 10 to 15 minutes.

Let the casserole cool for at least 15 minutes before you serve it, for the best flavor and texture.

Roasted Ratatouille

This is one of those "throw together" dishes that you'll find yourself making again and again. It truly takes only minutes to prepare and you can use whatever Mediterranean vegetables you have on hand—the proportions really don't matter (though don't skip the tomatoes). What does matter is that you cook the vegetables long enough so they become soft and their juices can mingle.   SERVES 4

About 8 cups summer vegetables cut into chunks, such as eggplant, zucchini, red bell peppers, and tomatoes
⅓ cup extra-virgin olive oil
Kosher salt and freshly ground black pepper

2 or 3 sprigs fresh rosemary
5 or 6 sprigs fresh thyme
2 or 3 cloves garlic, chopped
1 teaspoon balsamic vinegar (optional)

Heat the oven to 375°F. Toss the vegetables with the olive oil and season generously with salt and pepper. Spread the vegetables, rosemary, and thyme in a single layer in a large ovenproof baking dish and roast the vegetables for about 25 minutes.

Sprinkle the garlic over the vegetables, stir to mix a bit, and continue roasting until the vegetables are thoroughly soft and collapsed and browning around the edges, another 15 to 20 minutes. Transfer the vegetables to a serving bowl. Cover and let the vegetables steam for another few minutes. Taste and adjust the seasoning, folding in the vinegar (if using). Serve warm or at room temperature.

CSA Snapshot
Breezy Willow Farm
West Friendship, Maryland
www.breezywillowfarm.com

THE FARMERS: The Caulder family: RJ, Ken, Jason, and Casey Caulder-Todd

THE CSA LIFE: This organic farm has been using sustainable and responsible growing methods for the past 28 years. Breezy Willow Farm includes a farm store on site, stocked with the best elements of an old-time general store, making this farm a treasured resource in eastern Maryland. Along with local partners, they create products such as grains, noodles, bread, jam, honey, canned vegetables and fruit, pickles, sauces, mustard, soaps, and scarves. All this is sold along with their vegetables and meat. Their heritage breed animals are raised on pasture, the way nature intended.

Cook's Tip

It can be hard to decide whether or not to peel eggplant. On the one hand, the skin can be tough, so it's nice to remove it. But on the other hand, eggplant skin is attractive and helps to hold the flesh together as it cooks. A good compromise is to peel the eggplant in alternating strips, using a sharp vegetable peeler.

Grilled Zucchini with Feta and Olives

This dish is a lesson in why zucchini should be picked young. When slender and firm, the squash has a sweet, nutty flavor and moist but dense texture, making it a perfect vehicle for the more intense flavors of olives, pesto, and feta. These pretty "boats," contributed by Borden Farms supporter and personal chef Peter O'Grady, look great as part of an antipasti spread, and they are also nice as a side dish to simple grilled meat or fish.

SERVES 4

4 medium green or yellow zucchini
(about 1 pound total)

Olive oil

Kosher salt and freshly ground
black pepper

4 teaspoons basil pesto

3 ounces pitted Kalamata olives,
sliced

3 ounces feta, crumbled

Cut a small slice off both long sides of a zucchini to create two flat spots, which will allow the zucchini to sit flat. Halve the zucchini lengthwise, and using a small sharp spoon or the tip of a paring knife, cut along each side of the seeds. Scoop out the seeds, leaving a pocket down the length. Repeat with the remainder of the squash.

Heat a grill pan or cast-iron skillet over medium-high heat; also heat the oven to 450°F.

Brush the flat side of the squash with some olive oil and place flat side down on the hot pan. Cook until the flat side is nicely browned and the squash is starting to soften, 3 to 4 minutes. Transfer the squash to a shallow baking dish.

Season the squash lightly with salt and pepper and spread with the pesto in a thin, even layer. Lay the sliced olives down the length of the cavity and dot with the cheese. Roast in the oven until the squash is just getting tender and the cheese is starting to color, 8 to 12 minutes. Serve warm or at room temperature.

CSA Snapshot

Borden Farms
Delta, Colorado
www.bordenfarms.com

THE FARMERS: Guy and Lynn Borden and crew

THE CSA LIFE: Sitting at an elevation of 5,200 feet in the historic farming and ranching community of Pea Green, this 14-acre USDA certified organic family farm benefits from the high desert valley's fertile soil and snowmelt from the surrounding Rocky Mountains. Guy Borden is known as "The Tomato Guy," and he loves to share his enthusiasm for heirloom tomato varieties, such as Dr. Wyche's Yellow, Pruden's Purple, and Sungold.

Spicy Caramelized Sweet Corn

A 10-inch cast-iron skillet is perfect for this dish because it heats up so nicely—and the sunny yellow corn just looks so pretty in it!—but any heavy frying pan will do. Serve this as a side dish for barbecued chicken, pork chops, or sliced skirt or flank steak. It also makes a fantastic bed for a piece of grilled halibut. SERVES 4

3 tablespoons unsalted butter

2 cups corn kernels (from 3 to 4 ears corn)

2 scallions, thinly sliced, white and light green parts only

1 fresh jalapeño, cored, seeded, and minced

Kosher salt

1 tablespoon fresh lime juice

4 lime wedges

Heat the butter in a large, heavy frying pan over medium-high heat until bubbling. Add the corn, scallions, and jalapeños, stirring to coat with the butter. Cook, stirring occasionally, until the corn begins to brown and stick to the bottom of the pan, about 10 minutes. (You might hear some kernels popping toward the end.) Add 2 tablespoons water and stir, scraping the bottom of the pan to deglaze any extremely delicious brown bits. When the water has boiled off, season with salt to taste. Remove from the heat and stir in the lime juice. Serve immediately, with lime wedges.

CSA Snapshot

Millsap Farms
Springfield, Missouri
www.millsapfarms.com

THE FARMER: Curtis Millsap

THE CSA LIFE: The farm consists of 3 acres of vegetables, a beginning orchard, pigs, chickens, turkeys, forest, and ponds on their 20 acres, plus 10 acres of leased land. The Millsaps are committed to education about food and agriculture and often host school visits to the farm. On a larger scale, they run an internship and apprenticeship program that gives aspiring farmers the chance to start a small enterprise on the Millsaps' land, as a way to launch themselves into the farming life.

Beet and Kohlrabi Latkes

This twist on potato pancakes is colorful and much more nutritious . . . but still plenty delicious, crispy, and savory. Earth Spring's Jamie Flickinger likes this recipe when her CSA box (or refrigerator vegetable drawer) contains just a couple of the vegetables. The latkes are delicious straight from the frying pan, but the trio of sauces for dipping at the table is nice, too. SERVES 2 TO 4

For the horseradish sauce

½ cup sour cream

2 tablespoons prepared horseradish (or grated fresh, if you have it)

1 teaspoon fresh lemon juice

Kosher salt and freshly ground black pepper

For the dill-caper sauce

½ cup sour cream

1 tablespoon chopped capers

1 tablespoon chopped fresh dill

1 teaspoon fresh lemon juice

Kosher salt and freshly ground black pepper

For the chipotle sauce

½ cup sour cream

1 teaspoon adobo sauce from a can of chipotle chiles

1 teaspoon fresh lime or lemon juice

Kosher salt

Pinch of ground cumin

For the latkes

1 small to medium kohlrabi

1 large or 2 small beets

1 small onion

1 large egg, beaten

2 to 3 tablespoons unbleached all-purpose flour

Kosher salt and freshly ground black pepper

Vegetable oil, for frying

MAKE THE SAUCE OF YOUR CHOICE

For any of the sauces, stir all the ingredients together in a small bowl, taste and adjust the seasonings, and set aside.

MAKE THE LATKES

Peel the kohlrabi, beets, and onion. Coarsely grate the vegetables on the large holes of a box grater. Put the vegetables in a strainer and press out as much liquid as possible. Transfer the grated vegetables to a medium bowl and mix them with the egg and the flour (adding just enough to soak up the free juice), and season generously with salt and pepper. The mixture should cling together loosely.

CSA Snapshot

Earth Spring Farm
Gardners, Pennsylvania
www.earthspringcsa.com

THE FARMER: Mike Nolan

THE CSA LIFE: This CSA farm serves both the Harrisburg area in Pennsylvania and the Washington, D.C., area from their land at the northern end of Michaux State Forest in Cumberland County, Pennsylvania. With the South Mountains always in view, this family works the land in an area steeped with rich agricultural history. Growing up as a 4-H member, Mike was surrounded by this culture. He became more committed to sustainability later during study in Denmark, where he was exposed to progressive ideals of controlling urban sprawl, biking as transportation, and small-scale urban farm production. After an extensive hands-on farming education, Mike returned to the East to put this knowledge to use on his own farm.

Heat a large, heavy frying pan over medium heat for a few minutes. (Skip this initial heating if using a nonstick frying pan.) Add a ⅛-inch layer of oil and let it heat until hot but not smoking. Spoon ⅓ cup of the mixture into the frying pan and gently press it out flat. Add as many latkes as will fit easily in the pan (you need room to get a spatula in to flip). Fry the latkes until cooked through and nicely browned, 5 to 7 minutes per side. (Don't rush the cooking, because you need the vegetables to cook through and get tender.) Serve immediately with the sauce.

Cook's Tip

Freshly grated horseradish is delicious but can be potent! To grate it, use a rasp-style grater, and keep your face away from the root as you're working. And only take a gentle sniff at first, unless you want to wake up your sinuses.

Rustic Sweet Potato Cornbread with Crunchy Pecans

This deep golden quick bread tastes like a hybrid between cornbread and a moist snack cake, though it is dense and hearty. You can make it with sweet potatoes, pumpkins, or any kind of winter squash. Serve it with a spicy chili or hearty bean soup, and store leftovers (if there are any) in the fridge. The next morning, heat a slice in the toaster oven and top with a pat of butter and a drizzle of molasses. Because of the nutrient-rich sweet potatoes, it's a sweet treat with benefits! MAKES ONE 9-INCH BREAD

1 cup unbleached all-purpose flour, or a mix of whole-grain, pastry, or spelt and all-purpose

¾ cup stone-ground cornmeal or polenta

1 teaspoon baking powder

½ teaspoon baking soda

1 teaspoon kosher salt

¾ cup chopped pecans

2 large eggs, beaten

⅓ cup dark brown sugar

¼ cup canola or olive oil

2 cups cooked and mashed sweet potatoes (from 3 large sweet potatoes)

2 tablespoons unsalted butter

Heat the oven to 350°F. In a medium bowl, whisk together the flour, cornmeal, baking powder, baking soda, salt, and about half of the pecans. In a large bowl, mix together the eggs, brown sugar, and oil. Add the cooked sweet potatoes to the egg-sugar mixture and stir to blend well (it's okay to leave a few small lumps intact).

Add the dry ingredients to the sweet potato mixture and stir just until blended.

Heat a 9-inch cast-iron skillet or heavy frying pan until quite hot, and then add the butter. Once it stops foaming, scrape in the batter, smoothing the top slightly. Sprinkle the remaining pecans over the top and put the pan in the oven.

Bake the cornbread until it pulls away from the edges of the pan and a toothpick inserted in the center comes out with only a few moist crumbs clinging to it, 35 to 45 minutes.

Let cool for a few minutes, and then invert the cornbread onto a rack to finish cooling. Serve slightly warm, with lots of butter.

CSA Snapshot
Fort Hill Farm
New Milford, Connecticut
www.forthillfarm.com

THE FARMERS: Paul Bucciaglia and Rebecca Batchie

THE CSA LIFE: Fort Hill Farm, located in southwestern Connecticut, grows certified organic vegetables for 300 CSA shareholders and customers at the Westport Farmers' Market. The farm is situated on a terrace above the Housatonic River, operating on land leased from Sunny Valley Preserve, a project of The Nature Conservancy. The farm focuses heavily on soil nutrition through the growth of cover crops and the application of compost and rock powders. It offers a full-season apprenticeship program for individuals interested in learning how to farm.

Southern-Style Collard Greens

A pot of Southern-style greens is a delicious anchor to any meal. Collards are the classic ingredient to use, and once you've tasted them, you'll see why. They have a nutty-sweet flavor with none of the mustardy bite that some greens can have, and their texture becomes satiny and tender yet never mushy. But any lovely leafy greens can be cooked in this same way, or you can mix collards with other varieties. Some diced bacon or ham is traditional, but K. Rashid Nuri of Truly Living Well farm in Georgia likes to keep the greens vegetarian, relying on good olive oil and a touch of garlic and heat to provide the accents. SERVES 3 OR 4

1 pound collard greens, tough
   ends trimmed
¼ cup extra-virgin olive oil
1 small onion, finely chopped
1 teaspoon kosher salt

2 cloves garlic
⅛ teaspoon crushed red pepper
   flakes or a pinch of cayenne
1 teaspoon fresh lemon juice
   (optional)

Rinse each collard leaf thoroughly, to remove any grit or bugs (do not dry them). Stack several leaves on top of each other and roll together into a cylinder. With a large knife, slice across to cut the collards into thin strips (called chiffonade). Set aside.

Put the olive oil in a large pot or deep frying pan and heat over medium-high heat. Add the onions and salt and cook, stirring frequently, until the onions start to sizzle lightly (don't let them brown). Turn the heat to medium low and continue cooking, stirring and scraping frequently, until the onions are very soft, fragrant, and lightly caramelized, 20 to 25 minutes.

Add the garlic and red pepper flakes, stir for a few seconds, and then add the collards. Toss with tongs until they collapse, and then add about ½ cup water. Cover the pot and simmer over medium-low heat until the greens are nicely tender, stirring occasionally. This could take from 20 minutes to 45 minutes, depending on the size and toughness of the collards.

If there is still a lot of liquid in the pot once the greens are tender, turn up the heat and boil for a minute or two to evaporate most of it, but leave plenty to keep the greens moist and juicy (this is called "pot liquor," and it's full of flavor and nutrition). If you like, stir in the lemon juice, then taste and adjust the salt and pepper.

CSA Snapshot
**Truly Living Well Center for Natural Urban Agriculture
Atlanta, Georgia
www.trulylivingwell.com**

THE FARMER: Eugene Cooke

THE CSA LIFE: This urban farm and educational campus is located in the heart of downtown Atlanta, Georgia, on several plots around the city. The newest location is on the site of a former low-income housing project. The farm engages the local community through classes, internships, markets, and summer camps to raise awareness about the value of local food systems, to increase horticultural literacy, and to produce delicious healthy food. The center's farm operations include fruit trees, community gardens, wheelchair-accessible raised beds, and honeybees.

Cook's Tip
If you want to add bacon to this dish, dice it finely and add it to the onions in step 2, so that it can cook slowly and render much of its fat, which will flavor the greens as they cook.

Creamed Parmesan Swiss Chard

Eating farm-fresh, nutritious vegetables doesn't mean you can't indulge in a little richness now and then; in fact, quite the opposite. This dish is a take on the classic steakhouse creamed spinach, made all the more delicious by using Swiss chard instead. If you want to serve this as part of a dinner party menu, you can make the cream sauce the day ahead and steam the chard ahead, too. Right before serving, just gently reheat the sauce, add the chard, and cook over low heat until hot. SERVES 4 TO 6

2 bunches Swiss chard, tough
   ends trimmed
2 tablespoons unsalted butter
2 tablespoons unbleached
   all-purpose flour
1½ cups milk

½ cup heavy cream
¼ cup freshly grated Parmesan
⅛ teaspoon freshly grated nutmeg
Kosher salt and freshly ground
   black pepper

With a sharp paring knife, cut out the thick ribs from the chard and cut the ribs crosswise into very thin slices. Stack the leaves in a pile, roll up into a loose cylinder, and cut across into ½-inch strips. Steam the ribs and leaves in an inch or so of boiling water in a covered pot (or a steamer basket) until tender, 3 to 5 minutes, depending on maturity of the chard. Drain well in a colander. When cool enough to handle, squeeze out as much moisture as you can. Set the chard aside.

In a large frying pan, melt the butter over medium heat. Add the flour and whisk to blend; cook for about 2 minutes, whisking constantly. Add the milk and then the cream in a steady stream, continuing to whisk constantly. Cook the sauce until it begins to simmer and has thickened quite a bit, whisking and scraping around the edges of the pan to avoid lumps (if you get a few lumps, don't worry—just take the pan off the heat and whisk like crazy to blend them in). Whisk in the Parmesan and nutmeg, and season generously with salt and pepper.

Fold in the cooked chard and cook until heated through. Taste and adjust the seasonings. Serve hot.

CSA Snapshot

North Country Farms
Kilauea, Kauai, Hawaii
www.northcountryfarms.com

THE FARMERS: Lee Roversi and her grown children

THE CSA LIFE: Perched 200 feet above the Pacific Ocean, this organic farm sits in the rolling open land of the Garden Island of Kauai. The family farmers practice activism by producing fresh food with integrity for their community. The farm produces year-round, and in addition to greens and vegetables, there are orchard trees bearing avocados, limes, grapefruit, oranges, mangos, lychee, and papaya, plus a pineapple field and banana groves.

Cook's Tip

Turn this dish into a baked gratin by piling the creamed greens into a gratin or baking dish and topping with another ¼ cup grated Parmesan mixed with ½ cup breadcrumbs (you can use panko) and 1 tablespoon olive oil or melted butter. Sprinkle over the top of the greens and bake in a 450°F oven for a few minutes, until the topping is browned and bubbling.

Grilled Carrots with Carrot Top Pesto

Sharon Pixley, a member of 47 Daisies' CSA, makes the pesto for these carrots using the carrot tops themselves, which are, of course, fresh and healthy when they're straight from the farm—a bonus! You can make a more traditional pesto as well, using whatever tender herb looks good, or use a combination, as in this recipe. Blanching the carrots before grilling yields the best texture—still firm but not crunchy. SERVES 4

For the pesto

Carrot tops from a 1-pound bunch carrots

1 cup loosely packed fresh basil

1 clove garlic

½ teaspoon kosher salt; more as needed

¼ cup pine nuts

½ cup olive oil

For the grilled carrots

1 large bunch thin carrots (about 1 pound), peeled or just scrubbed if the skins are delicate (if the carrots are thick, split them lengthwise)

2 tablespoons extra-virgin olive oil

Kosher salt and freshly ground black pepper

MAKE THE PESTO

Bring a large pot of lightly salted water to a boil. Trim the thick stems and any wilted greens from the carrot tops, and plunge the trimmed greens into the water. Blanch for about 1 minute, then scoop them out and spin dry in a salad spinner (keep your water hot, as you'll use it again). Chop coarsely and measure out about 2 cups.

Put the blanched greens in a food processor along with the basil, garlic, salt, and pine nuts. Pulse until you have a coarse purée, then with the motor running, pour in the olive oil and process until smooth. Taste (be careful of the processor blade!) and add more salt if you like. Set aside.

GRILL THE CARROTS

Bring the carrot top water to a boil again and blanch the carrots just until tender, 5 to 6 minutes. Drain well, and when cool enough to handle, slice in half lengthwise. Toss with the olive oil to coat and season with salt and pepper. Heat a grill to medium-high heat (you may also use a cast-iron grill pan) and place the carrots cut side down on the grill. Let cook until charred marks form on the underside, 2 to 3 minutes, then flip and grill for another 3 to 4 minutes. Arrange the carrots on a serving platter and serve with a bowl of the pesto on the side.

CSA Snapshot

47 Daisies
Ruston, Louisiana
www.47daisies.com

THE FARMERS: Dylan and Harmony Dillaway

THE CSA LIFE: In an area dominated by majestic pine forest, this southern farm sits in the Piney Hills region of north-central Louisiana. The Dillaways grow their crops using certified naturally grown methods, and call farming "a passion, a calling, and a blur of life, love, and aching muscles!" Dylan has farmed from childhood, starting his first CSA at age 17. The Saturday pickups bring people to the farm and allow members to be involved in selecting their produce. Several members bring compost each week to share and are learning the farm way of life simply by visiting every week.

Cook's Tip

Grilling root vegetables can be tricky because most are quite dense and dry, so it can be difficult to get them fully tender solely from the heat of the grill. Precooking them by steaming or boiling allows the root to get mostly tender, and then they can finish cooking on the grill, developing a lovely caramelized surface.

Mashed Potato and Vegetable Pancakes

Infinitely adaptable and so easy to make, these vegetable-studded potato pancakes are a wonderful midweek meal on their own or as an accompaniment to roast meat or poultry. The mashed potatoes hold everything together and give you a starchy surface that browns nicely. You can vary the "add-ins" depending on what you have available, making them a clever destination for leftovers. Here, the onions and peppers are left raw for some crunch, but you could gently sauté them before adding to the potatoes, if you like. Corn kernels and minced hot chiles would be a delicious addition; feel free to use other tender herbs as well. MAKES 6 PANCAKES

2 large or 4 medium potatoes (Yukon Gold or Carola would be nice)

Kosher salt

1 large bunch scallions, white and most of the green parts, finely chopped

1 small sweet red pepper, such as Jimmy Nardello, or ½ red bell pepper, cored, seeded, and finely chopped

¾ cup finely chopped cooked chard or kale

1 tablespoon minced fresh flat-leaf parsley

1 tablespoon potato starch or unbleached all-purpose flour

Freshly ground black pepper

2 large eggs, beaten

Oil, for frying (sunflower or safflower is best)

Sour cream, for serving (optional)

Peel the potatoes, cut them into chunks, and put them in a medium pot with water to cover by 1 inch. Add 2 teaspoons salt and boil until very tender, about 20 minutes. Drain and then mash them with fork or a potato masher; a few lumps are okay. (You may also use cold leftover mashed potatoes.)

Add the scallions, red peppers, kale, parsley, and potato starch to the potatoes and fold together until well blended. Season generously with salt and pepper, tasting to adjust the seasonings, and then stir in the eggs.

Heat a skillet, preferably cast iron, over medium-high heat. Add about 3 tablespoons oil and wait for 30 seconds or so, until the oil is very hot. Spoon about ½ cup batter into the pan to form a small thick cake (the pancakes are easier to flip when they're not too wide). Add as many as will comfortably fit in the pan. Fry until nicely browned, 3 to 4 minutes. Flip and fry the other side until browned and the pancakes are heated through. Keep cooked pancakes warm in a low oven while you cook the rest of the batter. Serve hot, with sour cream, if you like.

CSA Snapshot

**Growing Home's
Les Brown Memorial Farm
Marseilles, Illinois
www.growinghomeinc.org**

THE FARMERS: Tracy Noel, Joe Avon, Stephanie Douglass, and Yoram Shanan

THE CSA LIFE: This 10-acre certified organic farm sits on a stretch of nice glacial deposit soil in LaSalle County, an area known for its deep canyons and majestic views. Running a CSA requires these Illinois farmers to be experts at growing every one of the 190 different varieties of vegetables and herbs found on the farm. They are helped in their efforts by workers from Growing Home's job training program, which uses organic agriculture as a vehicle for career and community development.

"Carmen peppers and Cherokee green tomatoes are adored among farmers and members. But the items that show up at almost every summer farm table meal are grilled lettuce, radicchio, and bok choy."

—Polly Shyka, Village Farm

Roasted Roots with Golden Onions

The beauty of this dish is that you can use whatever mix of root vegetables you have. They all are superstars in the oven, getting tender and creamy on the inside, delicately crusty and brown on the outside. They have a high sugar content, however, so do watch out that they don't burn. Use a heavy rimmed baking sheet, and give the vegetables a stir a few times during cooking. Cooking the onions and garlic on the side turns them silky and sweet; their moisture helps to hold the dish together. You can use these roasted roots as a side dish on their own, dress them in a simple vinaigrette for a salad, or add them to a soup or chili for even more depth of flavor. SERVES 4

5 small or medium new potatoes, scrubbed

3 medium carrots, scrubbed or peeled

1 rutabaga, peeled

1 large turnip, peeled, or 1 bunch small Japanese turnips, scrubbed

1/3 cup chopped fresh hearty herbs (rosemary, thyme, oregano, sage, or a mix)

1/4 cup sunflower or olive oil

Kosher salt

2 large onions, sliced

3 cloves garlic, chopped

1 cup roasted sunflower seeds

Heat the oven to 425°F. Cut the potatoes, carrots, rutabaga, and turnip into chunks about 1 inch wide. Put the cut vegetables, herbs, 2 tablespoons of the oil, and 1 teaspoon salt into a large bowl and toss to coat well.

Pour the oiled, salted vegetables onto a large rimmed baking sheet or baking dish and spread in an even layer; use more than one if necessary. Roast, stirring occasionally, until the vegetables are very tender when poked with a fork and the edges are starting to brown, 45 to 60 minutes.

While the roots are roasting, heat a large frying pan, add the remaining 2 tablespoons oil, add the onions and a small pinch of salt, and sauté the onions until very soft, sweet, and fragrant and just turning golden brown, about 25 minutes. Add the garlic and cook for another minute or two. Set aside until the roots are cooked, then fold the onions and garlic into the roots. Pile into a serving bowl, sprinkle with the roasted sunflower seeds, and serve warm.

Cook's Tip

Garlic and onions are often cooked together, but they don't behave the same in the frying pan. Garlic is delicate and usually finely chopped, so it will burn and become bitter quickly. Onions are full of moisture and can withstand more heat. It's a good idea to add garlic later in the cooking process so it can cook but not overcook.

CSA Snapshot

Calypso Farm and Ecology Center
Fairbanks, Alaska
www.calypsofarm.org

THE FARMERS: Susan Willsrud, Tom Zimmer, and Christie Shell

THE CSA LIFE: Education is the number one priority on this non-profit farm. Calypso has been putting vegetables on plates through their CSA since 2002. They also run various educational programs including a network of school gardens, a farmer training program, farm field trips, and gardening workshops. They have 3 cultivated acres near Fairbanks, Alaska, surrounded by 27 acres of natural boreal forest; the farm hosts over 2,000 visitors a year through field trips and events.

Balsamic-Braised Red Cabbage with Apples and Red Currant Jelly

This is one of those magical dishes that gets better as it sits, so begin a day or two before you plan to serve it. The flavors in the dish are sweet and tangy, making it a wonderful partner for anything pork: pan-fried pork chops, slow-roasted pork shoulder, spicy sausages, or even as a bed for grilled pork belly. Fresh Fork's Trevor Clatterbuck uses red cabbage, but white or Savoy would be fine if you don't have red.

The recipe makes a lot, but leftovers can be added to a soup or a hash or folded into mashed potatoes for a kind of Eastern European colcannon. SERVES 8 TO 10

4 tablespoons unsalted butter or lard

1 cup diced onions

3 sweet-tart apples, such as Braeburn or Cox's Orange Pippin, peeled, cored, and chopped

¼ cup packed dark or light brown sugar

½ cup balsamic vinegar; more as needed

Kosher salt and freshly ground black pepper

1 medium head red cabbage, shredded

1 teaspoon fresh thyme leaves or ½ teaspoon dried thyme

1 bay leaf

½ cup red currant jelly or jam

Melt the butter in a heavy-based pan over medium heat and add the onions. (Make sure the pan has a lid that fits tightly.) Cook the onions over medium heat for about 5 minutes. Add the apples, brown sugar, and vinegar, and season lightly with salt and pepper. Cook, stirring frequently, for about 5 minutes or until the ingredients are nicely softened, and then add the cabbage, thyme, and bay leaf. Continue cooking and stirring for about 10 minutes.

Add 1 cup water and the currant jelly. Adjust the heat to low and cover the pot. Let the cabbage cook very slowly for about 2 hours; stir from time to time to keep anything from sticking or burning, and add a little more water if the pan looks dry. Make sure the heat is kept very low.

Remove the pot from the heat and let it cool. Refrigerate overnight.

The next day, return the pot to low heat and let the cabbage rewarm very slowly. Cook until the cabbage is very soft. Taste and adjust the seasonings with salt and pepper and a few more drops of balsamic vinegar, if needed.

CSA Snapshot

Fresh Fork Market
Cleveland, Ohio
www.freshforkmarket.com

THE FARMER: Trevor Clatterbuck, founder

THE CSA LIFE: Fresh Fork Market is a weekly subscription service that delivers fresh, local foods, not by one farm but by a collective. The new twist on a CSA model was started in 2008 by four Case Western Reserve University students. The market is sourced by 36 different farmers providing food to 55 restaurants, caterers, schools, and hospitals, as well as thousands of individual families. They also host cooking demos, food preservation parties, wine and beer pairing classes, and pig roasts.

Cook's Tip

Red currants, and the jellies and jams made from them, are more common in European cooking than in American cooking, but they are deliciously versatile and worth getting to know. The berries come from a plant in the gooseberry family (they are not related to dried currants, which are a grape). Sweet and tart, they pair nicely with meats, especially pork and lamb.

Roasted Red Potatoes with Melted Cheese

This dish couldn't be easier—you make it with only one pan—and it's comforting and delicious. It's also endlessly variable. Crooked Sky Farms marketer Jennifer Woods likes to use Cheddar cheese, but Monterey Jack, Fontina, or any other meltable cheese would be just fine, as would a mix of other root vegetables instead of or in addition to the potatoes. SERVES 2 TO 4

1 pound small red-skinned potatoes or other nice small potato

1 tablespoon olive oil

Kosher salt and freshly ground black pepper

About 3 ounces meltable cheese, cut into thick slices

Heat the oven to 425°F. Cut the potatoes into 1-inch cubes and pile onto a rimmed baking sheet. Add the olive oil and season generously with salt and pepper. Toss the potatoes with your hands to coat them evenly and then spread them in an even layer on the baking sheet.

Roast until tender, turning with a spatula once or twice during cooking, 20 to 25 minutes. When they're cooked, scooch them together in the center of the baking sheet and lay the sliced cheese over the potatoes in one layer.

Put the baking sheet back in the oven and continue cooking until the cheese is just melted, 4 to 6 minutes. Slide everything onto a serving platter and serve right away.

CSA Snapshot

Crooked Sky Farms
Phoenix, Arizona
www.crookedskyfarms.com

THE FARMER: Frank Martin

THE CSA LIFE: Farmer Frank has always thought of seeds as magical and of himself as a farmer. The intensive chemical use in farming in Arizona during the 1950s literally made him ill, so his parents started to practice organic methods out of necessity. After losing his father to what was assumed to be pesticide exposure, Frank committed himself to being a different kind of farmer and a committed steward of the land. Today, the certified organic Crooked Sky Farms is a large operation that employs a team of healthy workers that supplies rural Arizona with amazing produce and a great community resource.

Cook's Tip

This dish is reminiscent of the Swiss dish called raclette, which is melted cheese served with bread or potatoes and condiments such as capers and tangy pickles called cornichons. To get the same cheesy-tangy appeal, chop some cornichons or other sour pickle, and sprinkle them and some capers over the cheese just before serving.

DESSERTS

Rhubarb Custard Pie

Rhubarb is a remarkable fruit (well, vegetable, really). On its own, it's unpalatably sour, but mixed with enough sugar, it becomes juicy, sweet-tart, and intriguing. This old-timey pie, with a dense custard filling, is a nice showcase for spring's abundance of rhubarb. The recipe comes from Mary Bird, the grandmother of Bryn Bird of Bird's Haven Farms CSA in Ohio. MAKES ONE 9-INCH PIE

For the crust
1½ cups unbleached
  all-purpose flour
1 teaspoon kosher salt
½ cup cold shortening or
  unsalted butter
About 2 tablespoons ice water

For the filling
2 cups ½-inch pieces rhubarb
1½ cups granulated sugar
3 large eggs
½ cup heavy cream
3 tablespoons unbleached
  all-purpose flour
2 tablespoons unsalted butter,
  melted
½ teaspoon kosher salt

Heat the oven to 400°F.

MAKE THE CRUST
Put the flour and salt in a food processor and pulse to blend. Add the shortening and pulse again until the mixture forms small crumbs. Pulse in 1 tablespoon of ice water, and then test the consistency of the dough by pinching it together. If it feels dry and crumbly, pulse in another tablespoon of ice water.

Dump the crust into a 9-inch pie pan and press it into an even layer over the bottom and up the sides. Pinch and flute the edges; chill the crust in the freezer as you prepare the filling.

MAKE THE FILLING
Toss the rhubarb with 1 cup of the sugar, then pile it into a strainer or colander set over a bowl to catch the juice. Let it sit for at least 1 hour.

Spread the macerated rhubarb over the pastry in the pie pan. Mix the eggs, the remaining ½ cup sugar, the cream, flour, butter, salt, and the collected rhubarb juices and pour the mixture over the fruit in the pastry.

Bake the pie for 10 minutes, then reduce the heat to 300°F. Continue baking until the custard is set and the crust is golden brown, another 25 to 35 minutes. Let the pie cool before slicing and serving.

CSA Snapshot
Bird's Haven Farms
Granville, Ohio
www.birdshavenfarms.com

THE FARMERS: Owned by Tom and Ann Bird, farmed by youngest son Lee Bird, and managed by youngest daughter Bryn Bird

THE CSA LIFE: Located in central Ohio, this large, multigenerational family of farmers has discovered growing methods that allow them to produce high-quality produce without the use of herbicides, such as planting under plastic and using tunnels and greenhouses. Bird's Haven Farms returns yearly with customer favorites, but also loves to try new varieties, along with u-pick strawberry fields, seasonal décor, and vegetable starts.

Prep School
One more reason to love rhubarb is that it's very easy to prepare.

1. Start by trimming off any remaining leaves or leaf bits—rhubarb leaves are toxic, so don't be tempted to include them.
2. Trim each end of the stalk, especially the thicker end, which can sometimes be tough or discolored.
3. Cut the rhubarb according to your recipe, usually into slices or small chunks. There's no need to peel it, as the skin softens considerably during cooking.

Grandmothers' Rhubarb Bars

Every spring in farmyards across the country (including North Dakota, where this recipe comes from), backyards, farmyards, and CSA bins fill up with bright red and green stalks of rhubarb. The roots that were planted in the prairie by countless grandmothers are the source of delicious family traditions now. Riverbound CSA serves a version of these sweet and tangy bar cookies at their spring open house; the easy, do-ahead nature of the recipe makes them perfect for any gathering or potluck.   MAKES 24 BARS

For the crust and topping
1½ cups quick-cooking oats

1½ cups unbleached
   all-purpose flour

½ teaspoon baking soda

½ teaspoon kosher salt

1¼ cups packed dark or light brown
   sugar

1 cup plus 2 tablespoons
   (2¼ sticks) unsalted butter,
   cut into chunks

1 cup chopped walnuts

For the filling
3 cups chopped rhubarb

1 to 1½ cups granulated sugar
   (depending on the tartness of
   your rhubarb)

2 tablespoons cornstarch

1 teaspoon pure vanilla extract

MAKE THE CRUST AND TOPPING

Put the oats, flour, baking soda, salt, and brown sugar in a food processor and pulse a few times to blend. Add the butter and about half the nuts and process until the mixture starts to clump together.

Put half of the mixture into a 9 x 13-inch baking dish. Add the remaining nuts to the rest of the oatmeal mixture, pulse once just to blend, and reserve in the refrigerator for the crumb topping.

Press the crust mixture into the baking dish to form an even layer over the bottom. Chill while you make the rhubarb filling.

CSA Snapshot

Riverbound Farm
Mandan, North Dakota
www.riverboundfarm.com

THE FARMERS: Brian and Angie McGinness

THE CSA LIFE: Riverbound Farm is located in Mandan, North Dakota, on the edge of the Missouri River. Pastureland, fields, cottonwood forest, and the river all merge together to form the farm, which was homesteaded by Angie's great-grandparents. The farmers each have years of experience, which they put to use daily as they address the challenges provided by the North Dakota weather and the occasional flood from the river. A recent "modernization" effort consisted of adding a team of draft horses to the farm. The McGinnesses invite their members to the farm for educational activities such as picnics, discussion groups, hiking, bird-watching, gardening, and nature education classes.

MAKE THE FILLING

Heat the oven to 375°F. Put the chopped rhubarb, sugar, cornstarch, vanilla, and ¼ cup water into a medium saucepan over medium-high heat; bring to a boil, stirring constantly, and then reduce the heat to a simmer. Continue cooking and stirring until the filling is thick and jam-like, 15 to 25 minutes. Let the filling cool, and then pour it over the bottom crust. Crumble the remaining topping mixture over the top as evenly as possible; it's okay if some rhubarb peeks through.

Bake until the bottom crust and topping are nicely golden and the filling is bubbling just a bit around the edges, 25 to 35 minutes. Cool completely before cutting into approximately 2-inch squares.

Cook's Tip

If the ends of your rhubarb stalks look tough and fibrous, simply peel them lightly with a vegetable peeler to remove some of the stringy outer layer.

Cardamom Carrot Cake

Carrots are regular visitors in most CSA boxes, so it's nice to have both savory and sweet dishes to use them in. Oil makes this cake super moist; be sure your oil is absolutely fresh. If you've had it for more than a couple of weeks, give it a taste before you add it to the batter, just in case it has gotten rancid.

This type of snack cake is nice served simply, with perhaps a dusting of confectioners' sugar or a spoonful of whipped cream, but if you want to serve it frosted, a cream cheese frosting is the classic choice. Adding a teaspoonful of grated orange or lime zest to the frosting would be a nice complement to the cardamom. SERVES 12

4 large eggs
1½ cups granulated sugar
½ cup packed light or dark brown sugar
1½ cups vegetable or mild olive oil
2 cups unbleached all-purpose flour
2 teaspoons baking soda
2 teaspoons ground cardamom
1 teaspoon kosher salt
½ teaspoon ground cinnamon
3 cups grated carrots
Confectioners' sugar, for dusting (optional)

Heat the oven to 350°F. Grease the inside of a 9 x 12-inch cake pan, dust with flour, and tap to remove any excess. Set aside.

With an electric mixer, beat together the eggs, granulated sugar, brown sugar, and oil until nicely blended. Sift together the flour, baking soda, cardamom, salt, and cinnamon. Add to the wet ingredients in one pour, and beat on low speed until just blended. Add the carrots and fold in with a spatula.

Pour the batter into the pan, and bake until the cake shrinks slightly from the sides and a toothpick inserted in the center doesn't have wet batter on it anymore, about 45 minutes. Let cool in the pan.

Sift confectioners' sugar over the top (if using), and serve slightly warm or at room temperature.

CSA Snapshot

Barking Moon Farm
Applegate, Oregon
www.barkingmoonfarm.com

THE FARMERS: Josh Cohen, Melissa Matthewson, and their children, Everett and Ava

THE CSA LIFE: With a combined educational background in restoration ecology and agriculture, this farming couple embarked on a farming internship that would eventually lead them to start their own 10-acre farm in Applegate Valley, at the foot of the Siskiyou Mountains, in 2007. In the main season, they grow for a cooperative CSA. In the winter, they have a specialty CSA for about 80 members, through which they offer dry beans, popcorn, flour corn, and other alternative crops.

"I think that lychee are perhaps my most treasured fruit on the farm. The season is short and the fruit delectable. People are unfamiliar with fresh lychee, having mostly had canned lychee in syrup—a very poor substitute for the real thing!"

—Lee Roversi, North Country Farm

Fresh Strawberry Cake with Strawberry Compote Drizzle

This light and pretty cake is a nice destination for summer berries. Some recipes call for puréeing the berries that go into the batter, but that can turn the cake a funny shade of mauve, so here they're simply diced. Do take the time to dice them finely, so that they're nicely distributed throughout the cake. Serve the cake with the Strawberry Compote Drizzle and, if you like, a dollop of freshly whipped cream. SERVES 8

2¼ cups cake flour
¼ teaspoon kosher salt
2½ teaspoons baking powder
½ cup (1 stick) unsalted butter
1½ cups granulated sugar
2 large eggs, at room temperature

1 teaspoon pure vanilla extract
1 cup buttermilk
8 ounces strawberries, trimmed and finely diced (about 1 cup)
Strawberry Compote Drizzle (recipe on p. 220)

Heat the oven to 350°F. Grease and flour a 12-cup bundt or tube pan.

Put the flour, salt, and baking powder in a bowl and whisk to blend and lighten.

With an electric mixer on medium speed, cream the butter and sugar together, beating until the mixture is quite light and fluffy, about 4 minutes. Add the eggs one at a time, scraping down the mixing bowl and beating well between each addition. Beat in the vanilla.

With the mixer on low, beat in about one-third of the flour mixture. As soon as the flour is almost blended, add about half the buttermilk and beat until blended. Repeat with the next portion of flour and continue until you've added all the flour and buttermilk. Stop beating as soon as that happens; overbeating will cause the cake to be tough.

Beat in the strawberries until just combined.

Pour the batter into the prepared pan, spreading the surface so it's even. Bake until a toothpick inserted into the center comes out clean, 40 to 50 minutes.

Cool the cake in the pan on a wire rack; when it's cool, gently invert it onto a cake stand or platter. Serve with the Strawberry Compote Drizzle.

continued on p. 220

CSA Snapshot

Snow's Bend Farm
Coker, Alabama
www.snowsbendfarm.com

THE FARMERS: Margaret Ann Toohey and David Snow

THE CSA LIFE: The farm is located near Tuscaloosa, Alabama, and boasts an ecological mix of wooded hills, coves, ridges, forested swamp, and bottom-land pasture. The name of their soil type is as picturesque as the scenery: "Tuscaloosa Choccolocco," made up of fine silt and organic matter deposited over thousands of years of flooding. The farmers began their organic operation in 2004, after years of learning and farming around the world. They began with just ¼ acre, which has grown to more than 10 acres with over 250 varieties of vegetables, herbs, fruits, and flowers, plus more acreage in which they raise hogs. The couple has plans for adding a perennial fruit orchard and an heirloom seed-saving garden.

Strawberry Compote Drizzle

MAKES ABOUT 1 CUP

8 ounces strawberries, trimmed
and quartered

½ cup confectioners' sugar; more
as needed

1 tablespoon unsalted butter

Squeeze of fresh lemon juice; more
as needed

Pinch of salt; more as needed

Cook's Tip

If you don't have buttermilk for the cake, you can get perfectly fine results from a one-to-one mixture of low-fat milk and plain yogurt, preferably low fat. The acid in the yogurt will give you the same tender crumb that the buttermilk does.

In a small saucepan, combine the strawberries, sugar, and ¼ cup water. Cook over medium heat until the strawberries are very soft and the mixture becomes compote-like and thick, stirring occasionally. Stir in the butter, lemon juice, and salt. Taste and add more sugar, lemon juice, or salt as needed. Serve chunky, or transfer to a blender and purée until smooth. Serve either warm or cold.

Cocoa Custard with Roasted Strawberries and Rosemary Cream

Pastry chef Nicole Krasinski, co-owner of the San Francisco Bay–area restaurant State Bird, gets produce, including fresh fragrant rosemary, from Mariquita Farm. She contributes this recipe on their behalf, suggesting it as a wonderful base for all types of seasonal fruit. In winter, instead of using strawberries, Nicole candies thin slices of Meyer lemon, chops them, and incorporates them into the rosemary whipped cream. SERVES 6

For the toppings
1 cup heavy cream
¼ cup fresh rosemary leaves, slightly chopped
2 pints strawberries, hulled
⅓ cup plus 3 tablespoons granulated sugar

For the custard
6 tablespoons unsalted butter
½ cup granulated sugar
2 tablespoons light or dark brown sugar
½ cup unsweetened Dutch-processed cocoa powder
2 cups heavy cream
2 large eggs

CSA Snapshot
**Mariquita Farm
Watsonville, California
www.mariquita.com**

THE FARMER: Andrew Griffin

THE CSA LIFE: This organic farm has members in California's Silicon Valley, the Peninsula, and San Francisco, including many restaurants. They like to say they take their members on a "food tour of the world," as they specialize in unusual varieties of vegetables and herbs, such as French fingerling potato varieties, Asian cooking greens, and Native American squash and beans.

MAKE THE TOPPINGS
Combine the cream and rosemary and refrigerate overnight. The next day, strain the cream through a fine-mesh strainer, discard the rosemary, and keep the cream cold until ready to whip.

Heat the oven to 300°F. Toss the strawberries with 3 tablespoons sugar and spread on a baking sheet in a single layer. Roast until the juices have thickened and the berries are quite soft and beginning to shrivel, 25 to 35 minutes. Remove from the oven and let cool to room temperature.

MAKE THE CUSTARD
Reduce the oven temperature to 250°F. In a medium, heavy-bottomed saucepan, combine the butter, granulated sugar, brown sugar, cocoa, and cream. Stir constantly with a whisk over medium heat until the mixture begins to simmer around the edges and all the ingredients are dissolved. Immediately remove it from the heat.

Put the eggs in a bowl and whisk in ½ cup of the hot cocoa, then whisk the egg and cocoa mixture back into the pot; continue whisking until smooth. Pour the mixture into a loaf pan. (The custard should be at

continued on p. 222

least ¼ inch deep for whatever size you choose; if the pan is too big and the custard layer is thin, it will overbake.)

Put the pan in the oven and bake for 6 minutes, then rotate the pan 180 degrees and continue baking. Keep checking every few minutes until the custard is just set; the center will still jiggle a little if you tap the pan.

Fill a bowl with ice and set a metal bowl inside it. Strain the custard into the metal bowl and whisk for about 30 seconds. Keep the custard on the ice until it is completely cooled, and then transfer to an airtight container. The custard will keep in the refrigerator for up to for 4 days.

TO SERVE

When ready to serve, combine the rosemary cream and remaining ⅓ cup granulated sugar and whip to soft peaks. Place a spoonful of the custard in a small bowl, top with the whipped cream, and garnish with the roasted strawberries.

Plum Cake with Walnut Topping

This cake has a super-moist crumb, thanks to brown sugar and yogurt; the acid in the yogurt tenderizes the gluten in flour. The batter is quick to make, and the cake adapts readily to many types of fruit, so it's a lovely recipe to have in your repertoire for spur-of-the-moment entertaining. In different times of the year, try it with rhubarb, raspberries, or pears.　SERVES 6 TO 8

For the cake
2 cups unbleached all-purpose flour
1 teaspoon baking soda
½ teaspoon kosher salt
4 tablespoons unsalted butter
1½ cups packed light or dark
　brown sugar
1 large egg
1 cup whole-milk or low-fat yogurt
1½ cups sliced Italian prune plums
　or another small variety that's not
　too juicy

For the topping
½ cup granulated sugar
1 tablespoon ground cinnamon
½ cup chopped walnuts
2 tablespoons unsalted butter,
　melted

MAKE THE CAKE

Heat the oven to 350°F. Butter the bottom and sides of a 9 x 12-inch cake pan. Line the pan with parchment paper and butter the paper. Dust the pan with flour and tap out the excess.

In a bowl, whisk together the flour, baking soda, and salt. In the bowl of a stand mixer fitted with the paddle attachment or with a handheld mixer, beat the butter and sugar on medium speed until light, about 5 minutes. Reduce the speed to low and add the egg. Mix in the yogurt. Add the flour mixture and mix just until combined. With a spatula, gently fold in the plums. Spread the batter in the prepared pan.

MAKE THE TOPPING AND BAKE THE CAKE

Mix the sugar, cinnamon, walnuts, and melted butter together in a bowl, and then sprinkle over the top of the cake.

Bake until a toothpick inserted in the center of the cake comes out clean, 35 to 40 minutes. Let cool on a rack for 20 minutes before serving.

CSA Snapshot

Stoneledge Farm LLC
South Cairo, New York
www.stoneledgefarmny.com

THE FARMERS: Pete Kavakos Sr., Deborah Kavakos, and their son, Peter Kavakos Jr.

THE CSA LIFE: This certified organic farm is nestled in the foothills of the northern Catskill Mountains; the homestead is supported by a stone ledge that runs below the surface of the soil, giving the farm its name, with much of the farm located along the Catskill Creek on prime agricultural soils. The family began farming over 20 years ago, starting with a small amount of land. Through the support of their CSA members, they've grown; the farm is now over 200 acres with a thriving membership of more than 1,400. Stoneledge Farm offers CSA memberships at sites throughout the Hudson Valley, metropolitan New York, and Connecticut.

Berry Crisp

Berries are, of course, wonderful when you eat them fresh, but they take on a spicy, complex character when you cook them. This easy dessert captures that character beautifully. With a pecan-laden streusel topping, the crisp cooks until the berry juices thicken and intensify. It's important to let the crisp cool enough so the ice cream doesn't melt immediately, but rather melts and mingles slowly with the berry juices, making its own delicious sauce. If you happen to have any crisp left over, it is delicious layered with plain yogurt for a slightly indulgent breakfast parfait.

You can make the dessert with berries that you've frozen, too, for a taste of summer in the winter. Just let them thaw in a colander first before proceeding with the recipe.

SERVES 4

6 cups mixed berries (strawberries, cut into pieces if large, blueberries, raspberries, and blackberries)
¼ cup turbinado (raw) sugar
1 tablespoon cornstarch
1 teaspoon grated lemon zest
1 tablespoon fresh lemon juice
1 cup quick-cooking oats
⅔ cup chopped pecans

¼ cup unbleached all-purpose flour
½ cup packed light brown sugar
½ teaspoon kosher salt
½ cup (1 stick) unsalted butter, slightly softened at room temperature, cut into ½-inch pieces
Vanilla, ginger, or lemon ice cream (or your favorite flavor), for serving

Heat the oven to 375°F. Toss the berries with the turbinado sugar, cornstarch, lemon zest, and juice. Add to a large dish or divide among individual shallow baking dishes (like you'd use for crème brûlée) or ramekins.

In a bowl, combine the oats, pecans, flour, brown sugar, and salt. Add the butter and rub and squeeze with your fingertips until the mixture comes together in small clumps. Distribute the topping evenly over the berries.

If using small dishes, arrange them on a large rimmed baking sheet to catch any drips, or put the large dish in the oven. Bake until the fruit is bubbling and the topping is golden brown, about 50 minutes. Let cool until just barely warm, and then top with a scoop of ice cream and serve right away.

CSA Snapshot

**Windermere Farms & Apiaries
Memphis, Tennessee
www.winfarms.com**

THE FARMERS: Ken and Freida Lansing

THE CSA LIFE: Located on a beautiful oasis within the Memphis city limits, this certified organic 17-acre property sits on old family land in a meadow between two wooded hills. In just a few short years, the Lansings have learned that CSA members become friends. The members they've served pray for their crops and family needs, suffer with them when a flood comes, and rejoice with them when they have perfect strawberry weather.

Whole-Wheat Shortcakes with Fresh Berries

Whole-wheat baked goods can sometimes feel stodgy—more virtuous than delicious—but these tender shortcakes, from Grand Central Baking Co.'s Piper Davis, are exceptions. She makes these with whole-wheat pastry flour, which is finely milled and adds a lightly nutty flavor. Use whatever fruit looks most inviting, and feel free to mix stone fruit such as nectarines and plums with the berries.   MAKES 6 SHORTCAKES

For the shortcakes

2 cups whole-wheat pastry flour

1 tablespoon baking powder

½ teaspoon kosher salt

¼ cup granulated sugar; more as needed (optional)

½ cup (1 stick) cold unsalted butter, cut into ½-inch cubes

¾ to 1 cup cold heavy cream; more as needed (optional)

For the fruit

2 pints (2½ to 3 cups) berries or chunks of other ripe fruit

¼ cup granulated sugar, depending on the sweetness of the fruit

2 tablespoons fresh lemon juice

For the cream

1 cup whipping cream

2 tablespoons confectioners' sugar

1 teaspoon pure vanilla extract

MAKE THE SHORTCAKES

Combine the whole-wheat flour, baking powder, salt, and sugar in the bowl of a stand mixer or mixing bowl with high sides and pulse or whisk to mix. Add the butter cubes all at once and blend using the paddle attachment of the mixer on low speed, 1 to 2 minutes; you can also mix by hand, using a pastry cutter, two knives, or simply by pinching with your fingers. The mixture will resemble coarse meal with small butter pieces sprinkled throughout.

While the mixer is running, add ¾ cup of the cream in one quick addition. Mix only until the dry ingredients are moistened and the dough begins to come together in large clumps. If it remains dry and crumbly, add a bit more cream. This will take only a few rotations of the paddle. If you are mixing the dough by hand, make a well, pour the liquid in the middle, and combine with a fork.

Turn the dough out onto a lightly floured surface and knead gently several times, until you have a cohesive mass. Roll or pat the dough into a rectangle about 6 x 9 inches and 1 inch thick. Cut six 3-inch squares using a cutter dipped in flour or a sharp knife. Place the shortcakes on a baking sheet lined with parchment paper and refrigerate for about 20 minutes.

CSA Snapshot

Creative Growers
Noti, Oregon
www.creativegrowers.com

THE FARMERS: David and Lori Hoyle

THE CSA LIFE: These agriculturists who specialize in heirloom and European varieties feel that their land and crops are extensions of themselves. They have been tending the land at the foothills of the Coast Range, west of Eugene, Oregon, for the past 11 years. The success of each crop is a very important and deeply personal matter, and the hope is that their customers can taste the difference. This urgency and attention to detail is appreciated by the many award-winning chefs from both Portland and Eugene who use the specialty produce in their restaurants.

Set a rack in the middle of the oven and heat the oven to 350°F. Gently brush any excess flour from the shortcakes. For crisp tops, brush them lightly with cream and sprinkle with sugar. Bake the shortcakes for 30 to 35 minutes, or until golden brown on top and toasty brown on the bottom. Set aside to cool.

PREPARE THE FRUIT

Slice or mash the fruit, sprinkle with the sugar and lemon juice, and allow to sit for at least 1 hour at room temperature or up to 6 hours refrigerated.

WHIP THE CREAM AND ASSEMBLE THE SHORTCAKES

Right before serving, whip the cream with a whisk or mixer until it holds soft peaks. Add the sugar and vanilla and whip for a few more strokes to combine. Take care not to overwhip the cream.

Use a serrated knife or a fork to split the shortcakes. Spoon about ¼ cup fruit and some of the juices on the bottom half of the shortcake. Put a nice dollop of whipped cream on the fruit and cover it with a shortcake top. Repeat with more fruit and whipped cream.

Cook's Tip

Try adding a splash of liqueur to complement the fruit—Grand Marnier with strawberries, framboise or cassis with raspberries and blackberries, and bourbon with peaches.

Old-Fashioned Peach Ice Cream

Such a timeless pleasure of summer, this recipe doesn't use an egg-based custard but relies only on the flavor of the peaches and cream. If you can make this with cream from your local dairy, all the better. MAKES ABOUT 2 QUARTS

5 medium peaches, peeled, pitted, and cut into chunks (about 1½ pounds)

1½ cups heavy whipping cream

¾ cup granulated sugar; more as needed

1 tablespoon fresh lemon juice

1 teaspoon pure vanilla extract

Raspberries or blackberries, for serving (optional)

Shortbread Cookies with Fresh Herbs (recipe on p. 230), for serving (optional)

Put the peaches, cream, sugar, lemon juice, and vanilla in a blender and purée until very smooth. Taste and add a touch more sugar if you need to.

Pour into an ice cream maker and churn following the manufacturer's instructions. Transfer the soft ice cream to a metal bowl and freeze for another hour or so to firm up.

Scoop into bowls and serve with fresh berries and/or a couple of cookies on the side (if using).

CSA Snapshot

Whitton Farms
Tyronza, Arkansas
www.whittonfarms.com

THE FARMERS: Keith and Jill Forrester

THE CSA LIFE: Whitton Farms is a small, organically inspired farm in the Arkansas Delta. Both Keith and Jill are former public school teachers who became farmers after moving to Keith's family's cotton farm, which had been in the family for close to 100 years. Gradually the Forresters are transforming former pastureland into rich plots for heirloom vegetables and flowers, which they share with their CSA members and customers at the Memphis Farmers Market.

Shortbread Cookies with Fresh Herbs

Besides the ice cream on p. 229, pair these simple-to-make, buttery cookies with fruit compote or even just a bowl of fresh berries for a satisfying seasonal dessert. You can experiment with the herbs you use and add a few drops of almond extract or ½ teaspoon ground ginger for a variation. **MAKES ABOUT 32 COOKIES**

½ cup whole-wheat pastry flour

1½ cups unbleached all-purpose flour

1 cup (2 sticks) unsalted butter, softened at room temperature

⅔ cup confectioners' sugar

⅓ cup finely chopped fresh herbs (rosemary, lemon thyme, and anise hyssop are lovely options)

2 teaspoons pure vanilla extract

½ teaspoon kosher salt

Heat the oven to 350°F. Line a baking sheet with parchment.

Put the whole-wheat flour and the all-purpose flour in a medium bowl and whisk to blend. Put the butter and sugar in a large bowl, and with an electric mixer or a sturdy wooden spoon, mix until well blended and creamy. Add the herbs, vanilla, and salt and beat for a few more seconds to blend well.

Add the flour mixture to the butter-sugar mixture and mix just until the flour is incorporated; don't overbeat or the cookies will be tough.

Roll about 1 tablespoon of dough into a ball and flatten it to about ¼ inch thick as you arrange on the baking sheet, leaving 1 inch of space between each cookie. (You can also divide the dough in half and shape two logs. Slice each log into 16 cookies.) Bake until the cookies are firm and beginning to brown on the bottom, 15 to 20 minutes. Transfer the cookies to a rack and cool completely before serving. Store in an airtight container for up to 3 days.

CSA Snapshot

**Calypso Farm and Ecology Center
Fairbanks, Alaska
www.calypsofarm.org**

THE FARMERS: Susan Willsrud, Tom Zimmer, and Christie Shell

THE CSA LIFE: Education is the number one priority on this non-profit farm. Calypso has been putting vegetables on plates through their CSA since 2002. They also run various educational programs including a network of school gardens, a farmer training program, farm field trips, and gardening workshops. They have 3 cultivated acres near Fairbanks, Alaska, surrounded by 27 acres of natural boreal forest; the farm hosts over 2,000 visitors a year through field trips and events.

Buckwheat Corn Cakes with Fresh Fruit

Growing Home's Tracy Noel makes these cakes for breakfast year-round with applesauce she makes from organic apples along with other fruit that she freezes in the summer. The only ingredients you're not likely to find in your CSA box are the flours and leavening, but with the new interest in locally grown grains, that may change soon. You could serve these with freshly whipped cream instead of the ice cream. Or serve these fruit-studded cakes for breakfast with a touch of butter and maple syrup (or jam). MAKES FOUR 5-INCH CAKES

1 large egg

¼ cup applesauce

½ cup whole milk, rice milk, or almond milk

¼ cup cornmeal

¼ cup buckwheat flour

¼ cup potato flour (whole-wheat pastry flour also works)

1 teaspoon baking powder

¾ teaspoon baking soda

Oil, for frying (sunflower or safflower is best)

1½ cups fruit; choose from blackberries, blueberries, raspberries, halved strawberries, chopped apples, or sliced bananas

Unsalted butter, for serving (optional)

Maple syrup, for serving (optional)

Fresh fruit, for serving (optional)

Ice cream, for serving (optional)

In a medium bowl, whisk the egg and applesauce together until well blended, and then whisk in the milk. In a separate bowl or on a plate, mix the cornmeal, buckwheat flour, potato flour, baking powder, and baking soda together, and then add all at once to the wet ingredients.

Stir the batter briskly with a wooden spoon, just enough to mix all the ingredients, and then let it sit; the batter should be very thick.

Heat a large frying pan or pancake griddle over medium heat. Add about 1 tablespoon oil (to form a nice layer). When the oil is hot, spoon enough batter into the pan to form a 5-inch-round cake about ½ inch thick (if batter is sticky, spread it quickly with a spoon).

As the cake cooks, gently press the fruit onto the surface, leaving at least ¼ inch of space between fruit chunks. When the first side is nicely browned, after about 3 minutes, carefully flip the cake and brown the second side for 2 to 3 minutes, making sure the interior is fully cooked. Keep the cakes warm in a low oven as you repeat with the rest of the batter.

Serve hot, with the accompaniments of your choice.

CSA Snapshot

Growing Home's Les Brown Memorial Farm Marseilles, Illinois www.growinghomeinc.org

THE FARMERS: Tracy Noel, Joe Avon, Stephanie Douglass, and Yoram Shanan

THE CSA LIFE: This 10-acre certified organic farm sits on a stretch of nice glacial deposit soil in LaSalle County, an area known for its deep canyons and majestic views. Running a CSA requires these Illinois farmers to be experts at growing every one of the 190 different varieties of vegetables and herbs on the farm. They are helped in their efforts by workers from Growing Home's job training program, which uses organic agriculture as a vehicle for career and community development.

Cook's Tip

Potato flour is exactly what it sounds like—flour ground from dried potatoes. It brings moistness to baked goods, and it is often used in rolls and sandwich breads. Bob's Red Mill® and King Arthur® both sell potato flour.

Chocolate-Beet Snack Cake with Cream Cheese Frosting

This moist, old-fashioned cake is the contribution of Bird's Haven Farms' CSA member Kitty Leatham, who likes the fact that the cake offers more nutrition than a typical dessert. You'll find many versions of a beet-cocoa cake in traditional cookbooks; some clever cook long ago discovered how nicely earthy, sweet beets meld into chocolate cake. Be sure to use red beets rather than golden, to keep the color rich and deep.

To make this a layer cake, divide the batter among three 8-inch-round cake pans lined with parchment paper. Reduce the baking time to about 25 minutes. SERVES 8 TO 12

For the cake

4 medium beets, scrubbed

1 cup plus 2 tablespoons canola oil; more for the beets

2 cups unbleached all-purpose flour

1½ teaspoons baking soda

1 teaspoon kosher salt

½ cup unsweetened natural cocoa powder

3 large eggs

1½ cups granulated sugar

2 teaspoons pure vanilla extract

For the cream cheese frosting

1 pound cream cheese, softened at room temperature

½ cup (1 stick) unsalted butter, softened at room temperature

3 cups confectioners' sugar

2 teaspoons fresh lemon juice

1 teaspoon pure vanilla extract

Pinch of kosher salt

MAKE THE CAKE

Heat the oven to 375°F. Cut the greens and root end off the beets, leaving about 1 inch of the stems attached. This will keep the beets from bleeding while being cooked. (Save the greens for a salad.) Lightly rub canola oil over each beet and put them in a roasting pan with a tight-fitting lid or cover with foil. Roast until completely tender when poked with a fork, 45 to 60 minutes. Let cool, and then rub or peel off the skins. Run the beets through the medium disk of a food processor to shred them, or grate them on the large holes of a box grater. Measure out 1½ cups.

Reduce the oven to 350°F; butter and flour a 9 x 13-inch baking pan.

Combine the flour, baking soda, salt, and cocoa in a medium bowl and whisk to blend thoroughly. Put the eggs, sugar, canola oil, and vanilla in a large bowl, and beat at medium speed with an electric mixer until well

continued on p. 234

blended, 2 to 3 minutes. Slowly beat in the dry ingredients, mixing only until just blended. Fold in the grated beets by hand.

Scrape the batter into the prepared pan and smooth the top. Bake until the cake bounces back when you press lightly with your finger, 30 to 40 minutes. Set the pan on a rack to cool.

MAKE THE FROSTING
Beat the cream cheese and butter together with the mixer until smooth, about 1 minute. With the mixer on low, slowly add the sugar. Once all the sugar is incorporated, increase the mixer speed to high and beat until light and fluffy and no lumps remain. Beat in the lemon juice, vanilla, and salt.

FINISH THE CAKE
Spread the cooled cake with the frosting and cut into squares.

Spiced Cantaloupe Tea Loaf

A fresh-from-the-farm melon is a beautiful thing in summer, but melons aren't the greatest keepers, nor do they freeze well, so this lovely tea bread is the perfect destination for any abundance you may have. This recipe uses cantaloupe, a specialty from Lattin Farms in Nevada, but any dense-fleshed sweet melon will work, as long as it's not too watery.

MAKES TWO 8-INCH LOAVES

3 cups unbleached all-purpose flour
1¾ teaspoons ground cinnamon
1½ teaspoons kosher salt
1 teaspoon ground ginger
1 teaspoon baking soda
1 teaspoon baking powder

2 cups granulated sugar
3 large eggs
1 cup neutral oil, such as vegetable or canola
2 teaspoons pure vanilla extract
1¾ cups grated ripe cantaloupe

Heat the oven to 350°F. Grease and flour two 5 x 8-inch loaf pans.

Put the flour, cinnamon, salt, ginger, baking soda, and baking powder in a medium bowl and whisk to blend.

With an electric mixer or a wooden spoon, beat the sugar, eggs, oil, and vanilla together in a bowl until well blended and slightly frothy, about 2 minutes. Fold in the grated cantaloupe. Add the dry ingredients to the wet mixture and fold until just blended; don't overmix or your tea cakes will be tough.

Divide the batter between the loaf pans and bake until a toothpick inserted into the center comes out dry, about 1 hour. Let cool on a rack, then invert. Serve just slightly warm or at room temperature.

CSA Snapshot
Lattin Farms
Fallon, Nevada
www.lattinfarms.com

THE FARMERS: Rick Lattin and B. Ann Lattin

THE CSA LIFE: One of the largest corn mazes in the United States can be found on Lattin Farms, and when viewed from above, it loudly proclaims, "Know your farmer, know your food." Rick and B. Ann have been mixing fun with a passion for agriculture and reconnecting with the earth for the past 35 growing seasons, following in the footsteps of their ancestors—Rick's great-grandparents began farming in the region in the very early 1900s. The Lattins' CSA is the largest in northern Nevada.

"We like Atlantis and Aphrodite melons and pick them only after they slip easily off the vine. The fully ripened melons are sweet and juicy and vastly different from the orange mush found in inferior melons."

—Aimee Good, Quiet Creek Farm

Buttery Brown Sugar–Apple Crisp

So simple and yet so delicious, this classic apple crisp is a wonderful way to enjoy seasonal apples. The dessert is better when it's not piping hot, so plan to take it out of the oven right before dinner and serve it warm afterward. It's perfect all on its own, but a scoop of ice cream or a dollop of fresh whipped cream can only make perfection more perfect. SERVES 4

2 pounds apples (about 4 large), peeled and cut into ⅛-inch-thick slices
1 teaspoon ground cinnamon
½ teaspoon kosher salt

¾ cup unbleached all-purpose flour
½ cup granulated sugar
½ cup packed dark brown sugar
½ cup (1 stick) cold unsalted butter, cut into ½-inch pieces

Heat the oven to 350°F. Butter a 10-inch pie dish.

Toss the apple slices with the cinnamon and ¼ teaspoon of the salt. Pile into the pie dish.

In a large bowl, whisk together the flour, granulated and brown sugars, and the remaining ¼ teaspoon salt. Mix in the butter pieces with your fingers or a pastry cutter to make little clumpy crumbs that hold together when you squeeze them. Crumble the topping over the apples. Bake until the apples are tender and bubbling around the edges and the topping is brown and crisp, about 40 minutes. Let cool for at least 15 minutes before serving.

CSA Snapshot

Dog Mountain Farm
Carnation, Washington
www.dogmtnfarm.com

THE FARMERS: David and Cindy Krepky

THE CSA LIFE: A sweeping landscape surrounds Dog Mountain Farm—rolling hills of thick Northwestern forests and the long snow-capped Cascade Mountain range. The farmers concentrate on making sure their soil is healthy in order to create the most nutrient-dense food. On-farm programs teach a wide range of skills, such as sheep shearing, chicken processing, teamster training, soap making, animal husbandry, food production, and culinary traditions including food preservation and bread and cheese making.

Cook's Tip

Make this dessert using a mix of apples, which will give you more complex flavor and also textural complexity, because some apples will soften more quickly than others. A great combination is Braeburn for tartness, Golden Delicious for sweet apple flavor, and an heirloom such as Ashmead's Kernel for some spice.

Classic Sweet Potato Pie

It's a delightful—and fortunate—irony that sweet potatoes, which are nutritional powerhouses, are also fantastic dessert ingredients. Their natural toffee-sweet flavor and soft, moist consistency make them perfect for pies, cakes, breads, and puddings.

This pie is a nice alternative to pumpkin for winter holidays, but it would be welcome any time of year as a dessert or afternoon snack. Nanette Ardoin and her husband specialize in growing sweet potatoes, so naturally she is a pro at sweet potato pie.

MAKES ONE 9-INCH PIE

¾ cup granulated sugar
1 teaspoon ground cinnamon
½ teaspoon kosher salt
½ teaspoon ground ginger
¼ teaspoon ground cloves

2 large eggs
2 cups cooked and mashed sweet potatoes
One 12-ounce can evaporated milk
1 uncooked 9-inch deep-dish pie shell

Heat the oven to 425°F. Mix the sugar, cinnamon, salt, ginger, and cloves in a small bowl. In a large bowl, beat the eggs with a fork or whisk until well blended and slightly frothy. Stir in the sweet potatoes and the sugar mixture. Gradually stir in the evaporated milk until well blended. Pour the custard into the pie shell.

Bake the pie for 15 minutes, then lower the temperature to 350°F. Bake for another 40 to 50 minutes, or until a knife comes out clean when inserted near the center. Let cool on a rack.

Cook's Tip

Make a flavored whipped cream to serve with this classic pie: Whip 1 cup heavy cream until it holds firm peaks, and then whip in 3 tablespoons maple syrup and ¼ teaspoon pure vanilla extract.

CSA Snapshot

Acadian Family Farm
Fort Cobb, Oklahoma
www.acadianfamilyfarm.
wordpress.com

THE FARMERS: Rod and Nanette Ardoin

THE CSA LIFE: This farm sits on the plains of southwest Oklahoma in Tornado Alley. The Ardoins named their certified organic farm after the descendants of the 17th-century French colonists who settled in Acadia, Canada, and who later resettled in a region of Louisiana now referred to as Acadiana. The Acadians were known for their small, self-sufficient farms. Both Rod and Nanette are originally from southwest Louisiana and are both of French descent. Their CSA takes the form of a "Veggie Club," in which members pay a deposit at the beginning of the season, then pay for weekly shares, and get the deposit refunded through free vegetables at the end of the season.

Sweet Potato Fritters

Cooks don't make fritters as often as they used to, which is a shame because they're quick to make and a wonderful way to elevate simple ingredients. These sweet potato fritters can be enjoyed as breakfast, as a side dish to a Southern-style meal, or as dessert, with a scoop of vanilla ice cream and a drizzle of honey. SERVES 4

2 cups cooked and mashed sweet potatoes

½ cup granulated sugar; more as needed

⅓ cup unbleached all-purpose flour; more as needed

½ teaspoon ground cinnamon

Pinch of salt

Vegetable oil, for frying

Vanilla ice cream, for serving (optional)

Confectioners' sugar, for serving (optional)

Fresh lemon juice, for serving (optional)

Honey, for serving (optional)

With a fork or a wooden spoon, stir together the mashed sweet potatoes, sugar, flour, cinnamon, and salt to make a smooth, soft batter. (Only stir until the ingredients come together—too much mixing may make the fritters tough.)

In a medium frying pan, heat about ¼ inch oil over medium-high heat. Drop 1 tablespoon of batter into the hot oil, adding as many spoonfuls as will fit easily in the pan without crowding. Fry until nicely browned on one side, about 3 minutes, and then turn and brown on the other side. If the fritters are browning too fast, lower the heat a bit. Continue with the rest of the batter, adding more oil as needed. Drain on paper towels.

Serve warm, either plain, with a scoop of vanilla ice cream, or sprinkled with confectioners' sugar and a squeeze of lemon juice or a drizzle of honey.

CSA Snapshot

Acadian Family Farm
Fort Cobb, Oklahoma
www.acadianfamilyfarm.
wordpress.com

THE FARMERS: Rod and Nanette Ardoin

THE CSA LIFE: This farm sits on the plains of southwest Oklahoma in Tornado Alley. The Ardoins named their certified organic farm after the descendants of the 17th-century French colonists who settled in Acadia, Canada, and who later resettled in a region of Louisiana now referred to as Acadiana. The Acadians were known for their small, self-sufficient farms. Both Rod and Nanette are originally from southwest Louisiana and are both of French descent. Their CSA takes the form of a "Veggie Club," in which members pay a deposit at the beginning of the season, then pay for weekly shares, and get the deposit refunded through free vegetables at the end of the season.

Liquid/Dry Measures

U.S.	Metric
¼ teaspoon	1.25 milliliters
½ teaspoon	2.5 milliliters
1 teaspoon	5 milliliters
1 tablespoon (3 teaspoons)	15 milliliters
1 fluid ounce (2 tablespoons)	30 milliliters
¼ cup	60 milliliters
⅓ cup	80 milliliters
½ cup	120 milliliters
1 cup	240 milliliters
1 pint (2 cups)	480 milliliters
1 quart (4 cups; 32 ounces)	960 milliliters
1 gallon (4 quarts)	3.84 liters
1 ounce (by weight)	28 grams
1 pound	454 grams
2.2 pounds	1 kilogram

Oven Temperatures

°F	Gas Mark	°C
250	½	120
275	1	140
300	2	150
325	3	165
350	4	180
375	5	190
400	6	200
425	7	220
450	8	230
475	9	240
500	10	260
550	Broil	290

Contributing Farms

47 DAISIES
Ruston, LA
www.47daisies.com
Dylan and Harmony Dillaway

47TH AVENUE FARM
Portland, OR
www.47thavefarm.com
Laura Masterson

ACADIAN FAMILY FARM
Fort Cobb, OK
www.acadianfamilyfarm.wordpress.com
Rod and Nanette Ardoin

BARKING MOON FARM
Applegate, OR
www.barkingmoonfarm.com
Josh Cohen, Melissa Matthewson, and their children, Everett and Ava

BAY BRANCH FARM
Lakewood, OH
www.baybranchfarm.com
Annabel Khouri and Eric Stoffer

BIRD'S HAVEN FARMS
Granville, OH
www.birdshavenfarms.com
Owned by Tom and Ann Bird, farmed by youngest son Lee Bird, and managed by youngest daughter Bryn Bird

BLACK SHEEP FARM
Ontario, Canada
www.justblacksheep.com
Brenda Hsueh

BLUEBIRD MEADOWS
Hurdle Mills, NC
www.bluebirdmeadowsnc.com
Stuart and Alice White and their baby girl, Ruth

BORDEN FARMS
Delta, CO
www.bordenfarms.com
Guy and Lynn Borden and crew

BREEZY WILLOW FARM
West Friendship, MD
www.breezywillowfarm.com
The Caulder family: RJ, Ken, Jason, and Casey Caulder-Todd

CALYPSO FARM AND ECOLOGY CENTER
Fairbanks, AK
www.calypsofarm.org
Susan Willsrud, Tom Zimmer, and Christie Shell

CHARLESTOWN FARM
Phoenixville, PA
www.charlestownfarm.org
The Anderson family: Marvin, Kathy, Bill and Liz, Charlie, Katy, Ellie, and Arne

CHERRY GROVE ORGANIC FARM
Princeton, NJ
www.cherrygroveorganic.com
Matthew Conver and Mary Stuehler

CREATIVE GROWERS
Noti, OR
www.creativegrowers.com
David and Lori Hoyle

CROOKED SKY FARMS
Phoenix, AZ
www.crookedskyfarms.com
Frank Martin

DELTA SOL FARM
Proctor, AR
www.deltasolfarm.com
Brandon Pugh

DOG MOUNTAIN FARM
Carnation, WA
www.dogmtnfarm.com
David and Cindy Krepky

DOWNING HOLLOW FARM
Olive Hill, TN
www.downinghollowfarm.com
Alex Greene, Lori Godwin-Greene, and children Henry and Hattie

EARTH SPRING FARM
Gardners, PA
www.earthspringcsa.com
Mike Nolan

ELSEWHERE FARM
Herbster, WI
www.facebook.com/ElsewhereFarm
Clare Hintz

FIELD DAY FARMS
Bozeman, MT
www.fielddayfarms.com
Mariann Van Den Elzen

FISH HAWK ACRES
Rock Cave, WV
http:wvfishhawkacres.com
Dale Hawkins

FORT HILL FARM
New Milford, CT
www.forthillfarm.com
Paul Bucciaglia and Rebecca Batchie

FREEWHEELIN' FARM
Santa Cruz, CA
www.freewheelinfarm.com
Darryl Wong, Amy Courtney, and Kirstin Yogg

FRESH CITY FARMS
Toronto, Canada
www.freshcityfarms.com
Ran Goel

FRESH FORK MARKET
Cleveland, OH
www.freshforkmarket.com
Trevor Clatterbuck, founder

GAREN'S GREENS AT RIVERSIDE FARM
North Berwick, ME
Garen Heller

THE GOOD EARTH
Lennox, SD
www.thegoodearth.us
Nancy and Jeff Kirstein

GREEN ACRES
North Judson, IN
www.greenacresindiana.com
Beth and Brent Eccles

**GROWING HOME'S
LES BROWN MEMORIAL FARM**
Marseilles, IL
www.growinghomeinc.org
Tracy Noel, Joe Avon, Stephanie Douglass, and Yoram Shanan

HALF PINT FARM
Burlington, VT
www.halfpintfarm.com
Mara and Spencer Walton

HARVEST MOON FARMS
Viroqua, WI
www.harvestmoon-farms.com
Jennifer and Bob Borchardt

HEART OF THE CITY
Cleveland, OH
www.urbangrowthfarms.com
Peter McDermott, Virginia Houston, Molly Murray, and Erin Laffay

HERITAGE PRAIRIE FARM
Elburn, IL
www.heritageprairiefarm.com
Bob Archibald and Bronwyn Weaver

HUDSON FARM
Napa, CA
www.hudsonranch.com
Robert Lee Hudson

IRON CREEK FARM
LaPorte, IN
www.ironcreekfarm.com
Tamera and Pat Mark

JENNY JACK SUN FARM
Pine Mountain, GA
www.jennyjackfarm.com
Jenny and Chris Jackson

JOHN GIVENS FARM/SOMETHING GOOD ORGANICS
Goleta, CA
www.johngivensfarm.com
John and Carolyn Givens

KITCHAWAN FARM
Ossining, NY
www.kitchawanfarm.com
Nicole Porto, Linsay Cochran, and Alexander Cochran

LADYBIRD FARMS
Pocatello, ID
www.ladybirdfarms.com
Jessica McAleese and Jeremy Shreve

LATTIN FARMS
Fallon, NV
www.lattinfarms.com
Rick Lattin and B. Ann Lattin

LIL' FARM
Hillsborough, NC
www.lilfarmnc.com
George O'Neal

MA'O ORGANIC FARMS
Wai'anae, HI
www.maoorganicfarms.org
Kukui Maunakea-Forth, Gary Maunakea-Forth, and the young workers in the program

MARIQUITA FARM
Watsonville, CA
www.mariquita.com
Andrew Griffin

MILLSAP FARMS
Springfield, MO
www.millsapfarms.com
Curtis Millsap

MUD LAKE FARM
Hudsonville, MI
www.mudlakefarm.com
Steve and Kris Van Haitsma

NORTH COUNTRY FARMS
Kilauea, Kauai, HI
www.northcountryfarms.com
Lee Roversi and her grown children

PARSON PRODUCE
Clinton, SC
www.parsonproduce.com
Daniel Parson

PETE'S GREENS
Craftsbury, VT
www.petesgreens.com
Pete Johnson

PLAN B ORGANIC
Ontario, Canada
www.planborganicfarms.ca
Rodrigo Venturelli, Alvaro Venturelli, and Melanie Golba

QUIET CREEK FARM
Kutztown, PA
www.quietcreekfarmcsa.com
John and Aimee Good

RIO ARRIBA FARMS
Abiquiu, NM
www.rioarribafarms.com
Jeff Nitz

RIVERDOG FARM
Guinda, CA
www.riverdogfarm.com
Tim Mueller, Trini Campbell, their daughter, and 50 full-time employeees

RIVERBOUND FARM
Mandan, ND
www.riverboundfarm.com
Brian and Angie McGinness

RIVERVIEW FARMS
Ranger, GA
www.grassfedcow.com
Three generations of the Swancy family— parents Carter and Beverly, current farmers Wes and Charlotte, Brad and Julia, and Drew and Beth, and their children

RUNNYMEDE FARM
Rogue River, OR
www.growfood.org
Arthur and Teri White

SCHULER FARMS
Caledonia, MI
www.schulerfarms.com
Bruce and Gerrianne Schuler

SERENBE FARMS
Chattahoochee Hills, GA
www.serenbefarms.com
Paige Witherington and Justin Dansby

SNOW'S BEND FARM
Coker, AL
www.snowsbendfarm.com
Margaret Ann Toohey and David Snow

STONELEDGE FARM LLC
South Cairo, NY
www.stoneledgefarmny.com
Pete Kavakos Sr., Deborah Kavakos, and their son, Peter Kavakos Jr.

STOUT OAK FARM
Brentwood, NH
www.stoutoakfarm.com/
Kate and Jeff Donald

SWEET WATER FARM
Hugo, OR
www.sweetwaterfarmhugo.com
Sean and Denise Smith Rowe

TRULY LIVING WELL CENTER FOR NATURAL URBAN AGRICULTURE
Atlanta, GA
www.trulylivingwell.com
Eugene Cooke

URBAN ROOTS
Austin, TX
www.urbanrootsatx.org
Max Elliott and Mike Evans

VILLAGE FARM
Freedom, ME
www.villagefarmfreedom.com
Polly Shyka and Prentice Grassi

WHITTON FARMS
Tyronza, AR
www.whittonfarms.com
Keith and Jill Forrester

WINDERMERE FARMS & APIARIES
Memphis, TN
www.winfarms.com
Ken and Freida Lansing

WOODLAND GARDENS
Winterville, GA
www.woodlandgardensorganic.com
Celia Barss and John Cooper

WORDEN FARM
Punta Gorda, FL
www.wordenfarm.com
Chris and Eva Worden

Recipe Index

Index

Numbers in **bold** indicate pages with photos